Studies in Economic Ethics and Philosophy

Series Editor
Peter Koslowski

Editorial Board
F. Neil Brady
James M. Buchanan
Richard De George
Jon Elster
Amitai Etzioni
Gérard Gäfgen
Serge-Christophe Kolm
Michael S. McPherson
Yuichi Shionoya
Philippe Van Parijs

Springer
*Berlin
Heidelberg
New York
Barcelona
Budapest
Hong Kong
London
Milan
Paris
Santa Clara
Singapore
Tokyo*

Studies in Economic Ethics and Philosophy

P. Koslowski (Ed.)
Ethics in Economics, Business, and Economic Policy
(out of print)
X, 178 pages. 1992, ISBN 3-540-55359-2

P. Koslowski and Y. Shionoya (Eds.)
The Good and the Economical
Ethical Choices in Economics and Management
(out of print)
X, 202 pages. 1993, ISBN 3-540-57339-9

H. De Geer (Ed.)
Business Ethics in Progress?
IX, 124 pages. 1994, ISBN 3-540-57758-0

P. Koslowski (Ed.)
The Theory of Ethical Economy in the Historical School
XI, 343 pages. 1995, ISBN 3-540-59070-6

A. Argandoña (Ed.)
The Ethical Dimension of Financial Institutions
and Markets
XI, 263 pages. 1995, ISBN 3-540-59209-1

G. K. Becker (Ed.)
Ethics in Business and Society.
Chinese and Western Perspectives
VIII, 233 pages. 1996, ISBN 3-540-60773-0

P. Koslowski
Ethics of Capitalism and Critique of Sociobiology.
Two Essays with a Comment by James M. Buchanan
IX, 142 pages. 1996, ISBN 3-540-61035-9

F. Neil Brady (Ed.)
Ethical Universals in International Business
X, 246 pages. 1996, ISBN 3-540-61588-1

P. Koslowski and A. Føllesdal (Eds.)
Restructuring the Welfare State
Theory and Reform of Social Policy
VIII, 402 pages. 1997, ISBN 3-540-62035-4

G. Erreygers and T. Vandevelde
Is Inheritance Legitimate?
Ethical and Economic Aspects
of Wealth Transfers
X, 236 pages. 1997, ISBN 3-540-62725-1

P. Koslowski (Ed.)
Business Ethics
in East Central Europe
XII, 151 pages. 1997, ISBN 3-540-63367-X

P. Koslowski (Ed.)
Methodology of the Social Sciences, Ethics,
and Economics in the Newer Historical School
From Max Weber and Rickert
to Sombart and Rothacker
XII, 565 pages. 1997, ISBN 3-540-63458-4

A. Føllesdal and P. Koslowski (Eds.)
Democracy and the European Union
X, 309 pages. 1998, ISBN 3-540-63457-6

Peter Koslowski (Ed.)

The Social Market Economy

Theory and Ethics
of the Economic Order

 Springer

Prof. Dr. Peter Koslowski
The Hannover Institute of Philosophical Research
Centre for Ethical Economy and Business Culture
Gerberstraße 26
D-30169 Hannover, Germany

Editorial Assistant:
Prof. Dr. Victoria Pogosian
Department of English
Herzen State Pedagogical University of Russia
Moika 48
191186 St. Petersburg, Russia

Published with the Support of
EAST | WEST | PHILOSOPHY. A PROJECT OF THE
FORSCHUNGSINSTITUT FÜR PHILOSOPHIE HANNOVER

ISBN 3-540-64043-6 Springer-Verlag Berlin Heidelberg New York

Cataloging-in-Publication Data applied for
Die Deutsche Bibliothek – CIP-Einheitsaufnahme
The **social market economy** : theory and ethics of the economic order / Peter
Koslowski. - Berlin ; Heidelberg ; New York ; Barcelona ; Budapest ; Hong Kong
; London ; Milan ; Paris ; Santa Clara ; Singapore ; Tokyo : Springer, 1998
  (Studies in economic ethics and philosophy)
  ISBN 3-540-64043-6

This work is subject to copyright. All rights are reserved, whether the whole or part of the material is concerned, specifically the rights of translation, reprinting, reuse of illustrations, recitation, broadcasting, reproduction on microfilm or in any other way, and storage in data banks. Duplication of this publication or parts thereof is permitted only under the provisions of the German Copyright Law of September 9, 1965, in its current version, and permission for use must always be obtained from Springer-Verlag. Violations are liable for prosecution under the German Copyright Law.

© Springer-Verlag Berlin · Heidelberg 1998
Printed in Germany

The use of general descriptive names, registered names, trademarks, etc. in this publication does not imply, even in the absence of a specific statement, that such names are exempt from the relevant protective laws and regulations and therefore free for general use.

Hardcover Design: Erich Kirchner, Heidelberg

SPIN 10655580   42/2202-5 4 3 2 1 0 – Printed on acid-free paper

Preface

The volume at hand publishes the proceedings of the conference "Social Market Economy. Theory and Ethics of the Economic Order in Russia and Germany", held at St. Petersburg, Russia, on February 16-18th, 1996, together with four basic texts.

The conference was organized by the Centrum für Ethische Ökonomie und Wirtschaftskultur des Forschungsinstituts für Philosophie Hannover, Hannover, Germany, in collaboration with Herzen State Pedagogical University of Russia, St. Petersburg, Russia, and with the support of EAST | WEST | PHILOSOPHY. A Project of the Forschungsinstitut für Philosophie Hannover.

Three of the four older texts have been translated from the German language for this volume. They are published here for the first time in English.

The editor wishes to thank Professor Larisa A. Gromova and Professor Victoria A. Pogosian, both of Herzen State Pedagogical University of Russia, St. Petersburg, for their assistance in organizing the conference meetings at St. Petersburg and Professor Victoria A. Pogosian and Professor Vladimir S. Avtonomov, Moscow, for their assistance in preparing the manuscript.

Hannover and Saint Petersburg, July 22, '1997

Peter Koslowski

Contents

Preface V

The Social Market Economy and the Varieties of Capitalism
Introduction
PETER KOSLOWSKI 1

Part A

Social Market Economy
Contemporary Analysis and Theory

Section I

The Theory of the Economic Order

Chapter 1

The Social Market Economy: The Main Ideas and Their Influence on Economic Policy
CHRISTIAN WATRIN 13

Discussion Summary 29

Chapter 2

The Idea of Economic Order in Contemporary Russia
KONSTANTIN S. PIGROV 32

CONTENTS

Chapter 3

Has the Market Economy Still a Chance? On the Lack of a Disciplining Challenge
MANFRED E. STREIT 50

Chapter 4

The Chances for Economic Order in Post-Soviet Russia
SERGEY A. NIKOLSKY 64

Chapter 5

The Social Market Economy: Social Equilibration of Capitalism and Consideration of the Totality of the Economic Order Notes on Alfred Müller-Armack
PETER KOSLOWSKI 73

Discussion Summary 96

Section II

The Ethics of the Economic Order

Chapter 6

The Ethics of Business in Russia
SVETLANA V. SIMONOVA 98

CONTENTS

Chapter 7

One's Own, Proper. What is Property in its Essence?
VLADIMIR V. BIBIKHIN 115

Section III

The Repersonalisation of Socialized Property

Chapter 8

Privatisation in the New Lands of the Former German Democratic Republic
WOLF-DIETER PLESSING 128

Discussion Summary 136

Chapter 9

Reprivatisation and Economic Transformation in the Countries of the Former Soviet Union
ALEXANDER I. LIAKIN 139

CONTENTS

Section IV

The Privatisation of the Agricultural Sector

Chapter 10

Independent Family Farms Versus Hierarchical Forms of Organisation Spontaneous Emergence of Property Rights Structures in Russian Agriculture
SILKE STAHL 158

Chapter 11

Russian Law and Land Privatisation
EVGENI F. SHEPELEV 184

Section V

The Economic Order in Private and in Public Law

Chapter 12

Law and Economic Order in the Structures of Russian Everyday Life
BORIS V. MARKOV 198

CONTENTS

Chapter 13

A Symbiosis with Reserve: Social Market Economy and Legal Order in Germany
KNUT WOLFGANG NÖRR 220

Discussion Summary 248

Part B

Social Market Economy. Four Basic Texts

Section I

The Theory of Economic Order

Chapter 14

The Principles of the Social Market Economy (1965)
ALFRED MÜLLER-ARMACK 255

Section II

The Ethics of the Economic Order

Chapter 15

The Ethical Content of the Social Market Economy (1988)
OTTO SCHLECHT 275

CONTENTS

Section III

Attempts to Form a Broader Basis for the Ownership of the Means of Production in the Social Market Economy

Chapter 16

The Formation of Private Property in the Hands of Workers (1956)
OSWALD VON NELL-BREUNING S. J. 291

Section IV

The Theory of Competition

Chapter 17

The Role of Competition in a Liberal Society (1979)
ERNST JOACHIM MESTMÄCKER 329

A Message of Greeting

A Message of Greeting from the Mayor of the City of Saint Petersburg
ANATOLY A. SOBCHAK 351

List of Authors and Discussants 353

Index of Names 356

The Social Market Economy and the Varieties of Capitalism
Introduction

PETER KOSLOWSKI

I. The Market and its Framework
II. Which Capitalism? Which Market Economy?
   1. Anglo-Saxon Versus Rhenish Capitalism
   2. Christian Versus Confucian Capitalism
   3. Competition Between Kinds of Capitalisms
III. Kinds of Capitalisms - Kinds of Liberalisms

The institutional setting of the market in the countries of the West varies. The differentiation of capitalisms in the West is indisputable. By the institutional setting or institutional framework of the market, the political and social institutions accompanying and supporting the market economy are described.

I. The Market and its Framework

As early as in 1955, Oswald von Nell-Breuning[1] contended that, in the theory of the market economy, the framework of the market seems to become more important and more interesting than the market itself. By the frame-

---

[1] OSWALD VON NELL-BREUNING: "Neoliberalismus und Katholische Soziallehre" (Neoliberalism and Catholic Social Teaching), in: P. M. BOARMANN (Ed.): *Der Christ und die soziale Marktwirtschaft* (The Christian and the Social Market Economy), Stuttgart (Kohlhammer) 1955, p. 117.

work of the market, he understood questions of the organization of social security, of progressive taxation and tax benefits for families and the like. What Nell-Breuning seemed to imply is that the market as the means of coordination in the economy, in the market for merchandise and for manufactured goods, is a matter of course and no matter of theoretical disagreement between liberals, neo-liberals and Catholic social thought. The disagreement between them and the differences begin when it comes to the question in which framework the market should work.

There seems to be a tendency of the market economists and of liberals in the sense of Adam Smith to shift the more interesting questions to the framework by claiming that these questions have nothing to do with the market, that the market economy must be instituted and work freely, and that all other questions as to the social and political conditions of the preservation of its working must be shifted to the "framework".

It is, however, the distinguishing feature of the theory of the social market economy in contrast to other theories of the market economy and of capitalism that it includes the institutional framework of the market in its economic theory, in its theory of the economic order. The theory of the social market economy is aware of the fact that there is not only one kind of capitalism but a variety of capitalisms.

The fact of this variety and the importance of the theory of the social market economy for its analysis and institutional understanding and design has most recently found its theoretical appraisal in Michel Albert's book *Capitalisme contre Capitalisme*[2]. His analysis of the different kinds of capitalism and his emphasis on the competition between different institutional individuations of capitalism is a reflection of the phenomenon that the political and institutional framework in which the market works becomes more interesting nowadays than the question of the market as a means of coordination itself.

---

2   MICHEL ALBERT: *Capitalisme contre Capitalisme*, Paris (Éditions du Seuil) 1991.

II. Which Capitalism? Which Market Economy?

The book at hand is an investigation into the foundations of the market economy and its institutional framework. It combines the German perspective on the market economy and capitalism with the Russian Post-Soviet perspective on the transition from a planned to a market economy. Both countries share this experience although Germany only in its Eastern part, the former DDR or German Democratic Republic. The questions of privatization in industry and agriculture are therefore given extensive treatment - not only for the analysis of the historical transitions of the years after 1989 but also as a living example for the importance and working of property rights.

The Russian Post-Soviet experience is an experience of great expectations in and disappointments with the market. The expected growth rates did not occur after the transition to a more capitalist economy. Social security and the employment guarantee for the workers did evaporate, law enforcement has been insufficient, and the structure of property rights is unsatisfactory due to the rise of a "nomenclatura capitalism" that shifted great parts of the former state monopolies to private monopolies being now in the hands of the former Soviet nomenclatura. Russian critics of this development speak of a "Byzantine form of capitalism" in today's Russia.

The necessity for developing a market economy in Russia is, however, acknowledged in general. The fundamental question, therefore, is not "Market economy or planned economy, capitalism or socialism?" but it is "Which capitalism?". In order to answer this question it is necessary to recognize that different capitalisms compete with each other in the arena of the present world and that the decision about the type of capitalism a country chooses is a question of institutional choice.[3] This book concentrates on the institutional choice of the social market economy and on the institutional choices in today's Russia.

---

3 Cf. D. SCHMIDTCHEN: "German 'Ordnungspolitik' as Institutional Choice", *Zeitschrift für die gesamte Staatswissenschaft*, 140 (1984), pp. 54-70.

PETER KOSLOWSKI

1. Anglo-Saxon Versus Rhenish Capitalism

Michel Albert has classified the present options for kinds of capitalisms in only two classes, the "Neo-American, Anglo-Saxon" and the "Rhenish" model of capitalism, the basis of which are two concepts of capitalism. Albert names the Rhenish model after the river Rhine since the economies lying at its shores, the Swiss, the German, the Belgian, and the Dutch economies, have common traits. This terminology is useful since it shifts the emphasis from the purely German perspective to a broader Central European model.

Albert does not include the different kinds of Asian capitalisms. They demonstrate, however, that his dualistic conception is not sufficient although it is of great impact for the theory of economic order in the European context. Behind his dualist classification of two capitalisms stands the far-reaching and radical thesis that the different institutional and historical individuations of capitalism are caused by completely different conceptual models of capitalism, by the "Neo-American, Anglo-Saxon" and the "Rhenish" concept of capitalism. By this radical line of his argument, he goes further than stating the empirical observation that there are different empirically distinguishable cultures of capitalism in today's world. He contends that two different theories of the economic order of capitalism compete with each other.

It is obvious that the Japanese model of capitalism is different from the American model, that the Russian Post-Soviet capitalism is different from the German social market economy, and that again the German model of the social market economy is different from the British model of Beveridgean, Keynesian or Thatcherist capitalism.

More interesting is, however, the question whether we have or shall have a deep ideological divide between the "Anglo-Saxon" and the "Rhenish" mode of capitalism and for which model of the economic order Post-Soviet Russia will opt.

Capitalism is defined by three main features: *firstly* private property, *secondly* profit and utility maximization as the motivation of the acting individuals in the economy and *thirdly* coordination by markets and the price system as the means of coordination as opposed to central planning.[4] The three main

---

4 Cf. PETER KOSLOWSKI: *Ethics of Capitalism and Critique of Sociobiology. Two Essays with a Comment by James M. Buchanan*, Heidelberg, Berlin, New York, Tokyo (Springer) 1996 (Studies in Economic Ethics and Philosophy, Vol. 10). Russian translation: *Etika kapitalisma. Evolutsia i obshchestvo*, St. Petersburg

features are private property, profit and utility maximization and coordination by markets. The American model of capitalism aims at an almost total disembedding of the market and of the three features of capitalism from distributional and political constraints.

The Rhenish model is a model of embedding the market in a social and political framework, in a framework of social policy, mainly social security policy. It puts also more emphasis on equilibration, or *Ausgleich* in German, on the equilibration of those tendencies in capitalism that lead towards monopolization and massive inequality. Equilibrating income differentials by the state in the Rhenish model of capitalism implies, for example, that the state makes sure that everyone has access to the institutions of higher education. It is significant that Germany, Austria, and Switzerland are amongst the only countries in the world where students do not have to pay at all for university education. It is striking to learn that in today's still communist China students must pay for university education.

The second equilibrating measure considered to be legitimate in the Rhenish model of capitalism is the progressive income tax which is, however, coming under pressure from the international competition for capital investment between the nations in the world. The United States have a progressive tax too, but decreased the rate of progression radically in the 1980s.

The third equilibrating measure is inheritance tax. It is interesting to note that, for most of recent history, inheritance tax has been higher in Great Britain than in Germany which demonstrates that the dualism Anglo-Saxon versus Rhenish capitalism does not work completely. Great Britain's welfare state does not fit into the scheme. Britain is neither a Neo-American nor a Rhenish model of capitalism.

The fourth equilibrating task in the Rhenish model is the task of the state to equilibrate between the regions of a country. The German constitution demands as a constitutional law that the living conditions should be equal or nearly equal in all regions of Germany. This equilibrating of living conditions is difficult to realize, especially under the conditions of reunification in the process of which some regions of the country start from a much poorer conditon than others. The economic equalization between regions is part of the idea that the state should equilibrate inequalities.

(Ekonomicheskaya Shkola) 1996 (Eticheskaya Ekonomia. Issledovanie po etike, kulture i philosophii khoziaistva, Vol. 1).

In the Rhenish model, the state is considered to be not a minimal state but first of all a social state, not a welfare state in the English tradition of the reforms introduced by Lord Beveridge,[5] the founder of the English welfare state, in the 1940s but a social state of social security in the tradition introduced by Bismarck in the 1890s.[6] The task of the social state in the Rhenish tradition is not only to secure the law as the state of the rule of law or *Rechtsstaat*, but also to provide as social state at least a minimal degree of social security. Its aim is, however, not to secure "welfare".

The European and Western perspective of the Anglo-Saxon versus Rhenish divide is, in spite of its classificatory value for Europe, not sufficient for the classification in the world scale. The world has moved with the end of communism into a new arena of debate in which more than the two mentioned traditions of capitalism compete with each other. In this debate the models of capitalism dominant outside of the Western world must be included as well.

2. Christian Versus Confucian Capitalism

In Japan, theorists claim that in today's world economy there are different types of capitalism competing with each other but they donot classify the dualism in terms of Anglo-Saxon versus Rhenish capitalism but in terms of Christian versus Confucian Capitalism. This is an important new development that is missing in Albert's analysis concentrating too much on the European-American divide. Japanese scholars contend that what causes the different traditions of capitalism are in the end different cultural-religious traditions. The East Asian capitalism and the capitalism of the New Tigers, of Korea, Thailand, Taiwan, etc. and even the new capitalism of Mainland China, are influenced by the Confucian tradition and its semi-religious origins, whereas the Western capitalist model is determined by Christianity according to the Asian thinkers.

---

5 Cf. W. H. BEVERIDGE: *Social Insurance and Allied Forces. The Beveridge Report in Brief*, London (HMSO) 1942.
6 Cf. for a comparison of the European welfare states P. KOSLOWSKI, A. FOELLESDAL (Eds.): *Restructuring the Welfare State. Theory and Reform of Social Policy*, Heidelberg, Berlin, New York, Tokyo (Springer) 1997 (= Studies in Economic Ethics and Philosophy, Vol. 12).

SOCIAL MARKET ECONOMY AND VARIETIES OF CAPITALISM

This Japanese classification of Christian versus Confucian capitalism must be mentioned since it is interesting to learn that Asians think of the Western societies as Christian societies whereas in the West there are probably only few intellectuals who will name their societies Christian societies. The European self-perception is mainly one of a secularized society that has been Christian but is now secular whereas Asians claim that even after secularization the basic belief system and the basic views on life that influence the Western economies are Christian and that religion is the thing that matters most in the differentiation of economic systems in today's world economy.

3. Competition Between Kinds of Capitalisms

Even if in the Western world the divide is between two strong traditions of the market economy, the Anglo-Saxon and the Rhenish one, a new dualism between America and Europe should be avoided. There does not exist a "clash of civilizations" between the American civilization of the pure market economy and the Rhenish capitalism of Central Europe. From Albert's analysis and the institutional comparison between the Western countries can be learnt, however, that there are alternative ways of organizing capitalist and democratic societies. There is not only one model. It is even a market argument that societies and particularly Western societies should compete by their institutional settings of the market too. They should compete with their alternative models of the market economy. These different models should be discussed in the countries in question to find out which way is the best. It will be of great importance for Russia and for its European neighbours to find out which type of a market economy and which path of economic development Russia will choose. The contributions to this book attempt to give an answer to this question.

It must be mentioned that the social market economy has come under criticism in its country of origin, in Germany. There are strong critics of the social market economy amongst economists - some also among the contributors to this volume - that contend that the tradition of the social market economy is not dynamic enough for the present globalization of economic competition, that it has developed into a corporatism not competitive enough and so on.

If one looks into the philosophical underpinnings of this criticism one can see that there are different kinds of liberalisms at stake here, different liberalisms as socio-political-economic concepts of the social and economic order. At the ground of the political debates and the debates on the economic order, there are philosophical differences. In today's world where liberalism has become more or less the dominant philosophy and socio-economic theory we find that liberalism like capitalism is not a univocal term.

III. Kinds of Capitalisms - Kinds of Liberalisms

There are different kinds of liberalism underlying the different concepts of the market economy. Three liberalisms can be distinguished: first, the empiricist tradition of liberalism coming from Adam Smith and the Scottish school with its emphasis on self-interest, second, the idealist tradition of liberalism with its emphasis on public discourse like in the work of Jürgen Habermas, and third, Christian liberalism. Christian and particularly Catholic social thought could be named "Christian liberalism" because it accepts the market as a means of coordination but demands that it should be accompanied by an institutional framework of social policy.[7] It differs from the Scottish and the Adam Smith tradition mainly by its attitude towards "self-interest". It is more critical towards self-interest than the Adam Smith tradition of liberalism and of the market economy.

Adam Smith says that it should not depend on the benevolence of the butcher whether we get our dinner and he says that this is good, that it is how it is, and that society must rely in the market on self-interest only. His well-known argument is that humankind is in need of obtaining so much from exchange that one cannot expect humans to be able to receive all they need in the exchange with others from the benevolence of the exchange partner only.

Christian liberalism is very close to Adam Smith in this question but differs from him at the same time considerably. Augustine and Thomas Aquinas

---

[7] PETER KOSLOWSKI: "Christlicher Liberalismus als europäische Philosophie der Postmoderne. Metaphysik und Politik nach der Dekonstruktion der Aufklärung" (Christian Liberalism as European Philosophy of the Postmodern. Metaphysics and Politics after the Deconstruction of Enlightenment), in: P. KOSLOWSKI (Ed.): *Europa imaginieren* (Imagining Europe), Heidelberg, Berlin, New York, Tokyo (Springer) 1992 (Studies in Economic Ethics and Philosophy, Vol. 3), pp. 75-104.

also contend that we must give space to self-interest but only as a second-best solution. We should love everybody the same as ourselves, but since this is very difficult under conditions of original sin and the scarcity of the resource of love and since our resources of love or *caritas* are rather limited we must follow the "ordo caritatis" or "ordo armoris", the order of love. That means that the economy must give space to self-interest but it does not imply that self-interest is dignified as the first-best solution. Christian liberalism looks at the market as being the second-best solution in an ideal world but as the best possible solution under conditions as they are, under the human condition as it is. In the reality of the market economy, this is almost the same position as the one of the Adam Smith tradition. There is, however, a difference in the affirmation of the role of self-interest in society that is important for the institutional framework of the market developed from these assumptions about human nature. The social market economy shares the belief that liberty is the basic principle of the economic order and that humans should be free to follow their self-interest. It does not believe, however, that liberty and the pursuit of self-interest by the invisible hand of the market lead to a social optimum all the time. Rather, they must be supported by political and economic institutions that aim at the preservation of the conditions under which human freedom can flourish.

Part A

Social Market Economy Contemporary Analysis and Theory

Section I

The Theory of the Economic Order

Chapter 1

The Social Market Economy: The Main Ideas and Their Influence on Economic Policy

CHRISTIAN WATRIN

I. The Main Ideas
   1. Competition and Individual Freedom - the Economic Order of a Free Society
   2. The Monetary Constitution
   3. Social Policy and the Market Order
II. The Influence of the Social Market Economy Programme on German Economic Policy

"The Social Market Economy cannot flourish if the spiritual attitude on which it is based - that is the readiness to assume the responsibility for one's fate and to participate in honest and free competition - is undermined by seemingly social measures in neighbouring fields."

(Ludwig Erhard 1958, p. 185)

CHRISTIAN WATRIN

One of the main outcomes of the "European Miracle"[1] is the development of a liberal social philosophy beginning in the eighteenth century and lasting until today. The Scottish School of Moral Philosophy, the liberal classical economists from Adam Smith onwards to John Stuart Mill, as well as the French (J. B. Say) and German thinkers of the late eighteenth and early nineteenth century (I. Kant, Friedrich Schiller, W. von Humboldt) laid the foundations of a free society. After the "European Catastrophe", the two World Wars (1914-18/1939-1945) and the establishment of totalitarian and authoritarian regimes in Western and Eastern Europe, an unexpected renaissance of liberal thinking began. It was lead by a small group of lawyers, economists and social philosophers in the Western World and its early origins can be traced back to the thirties and forties. It is to be hoped that this philosophy will also spread, following the annus mirabilis 1989, into Middle and Eastern Europe. Among the twentieth century scholars, who further developed the ideas of a free (or good) society, one could name Bresciani-Turroni, de Jouvenal, W. Eucken, F.A. von Hayek, Karl Popper, W. Röpke among others. Despite the fact that they were not a well-organised group and did not agree on many details of a liberal order, their common belief was that the answer to the multifarious problems of post-war Europe and the world was the rebuilding of a free society on the foundations laid in previous centuries. In this era the democratic movement gained momentum in continental Europe. After the period of Absolutism (17th and 18th centuries), political power was transferred from absolutist rule to newly founded parliaments. Under the influence of German legal philosophy, a government of law (Rechtsstaat) developed, initially in Prussia and later in various other countries. Additionally, the French revolution spurred the abolition of most economic regulations in the old society. The "idea of liberty under the law" was born. Hayek (1960, p. 205) emphasizes in his monumental "Constitution of Liberty" this development with the words: "Mankind (had) learned from long and painful experience...".

The central questions to be faced by the liberal writers in the first half of the twentieth century were: why did the young free society, which evolved in

---

1   This is the title of ERIC L. JONES' famous book *The European Miracle* in which he presents a convincing theoretical sketch why Europe became the origin of a free society and why the great Asian empires, despite their cultural achievements for the small ruling classes, never entered into the stage of a dynamic "open society" (Popper, 1992).

THE SOCIAL MARKET ECONOMY: MAIN IDEAS

the nineteenth century, enter a destructive period of warring, instead of developing into an even greater open society? And at the end of the nineteenth century, why did imperialism and aggressive nationalism, movements which were one of the causes of the First World War (Chirot 1986, p. 135), sweep Europe? And after the terrible killings, what hampered the return to a peaceful order? How could it occur that authoritarian and - in the German case - totalitarian movements took over, drawing most of Europe into a second even more devastating war, which in the end brought Stalin's troops into the centre of Europe suppressing eastern and middle European states, previously known for a history of political and economic freedom?

European scholars were faced with real problems. But, for a vast majority socialism, at least in the mild form of the British-Scandinavian model of the welfare state, was the order of the day, not personal freedom in the classical liberal sense. If there were to be a chance for a free society, convincing arguments had to be presented first as to why "historical liberalism", as Röpke used to call it, failed and why the rebuilding of a society of free people was a better solution than a socialist programme of bureaucratic management of the economy and - in the end - also of the society.

It is not surprising that the debates after the Second World War encompassed a much broader view-point in continental Europe than in the Anglo-Saxon world, where under the auspices of a long and stable tradition of democratic rule, mainly the economic aspects of the problem were discussed: the scope of the laissez-faire rule, i.e. the agenda and non-agenda of the state or - using the familiar phrase of John Stuart Mill - the limits of the laissez-faire or non-interference principle. Under the influence of Hayek, Röpke, Rüstow and others, a much broader approach was taken in German discussions. The many interdependencies between the sub-systems of a free society were discussed as, for instance, the relations between the political, the economic and the social system, the role of law, of morals and of citizens' loyalty to a state with clearly restricted powers. Economic freedom was not looked upon as being primarily an instrument to increase the efficiency of markets, but as a value in itself. As Röpke once put it, even if socialism should prove to be more efficient in producing goods than a market economy, the latter would be preferable, because of the personal freedom it conveys to citizens living under its rule. Economic freedom in a world with open borders would also be a powerful obstacle to despotic rule or a Leviathan-state, because citizens would possess an exit-option (Hirschman), which is the most efficient response for those disagreeing with the policy-performance of a country.

The end of the totalitarian age came for West Germany after its unconditional surrender in 1945. There was not much dispute that the political order should be re-established along the lines of democratic government[2]. Freedom of speech, press, information and thought were undisputed, but not the power of the state to run the economy by allocating even the simplest goods via bureaucratic directives. In an article in the first volume of Ordo (1948), the year-book of the Ordo - or Neoliberals, Müller-Armack, one of the architects of the Social Market Economy, opens a famous article on "Economic Orders - Seen from a Social Perspective" with a very pessimistic outlook. He writes: "In our time there is wide-spread consensus that central planning is the only promising way for the future". Fortunately, West Germany's currency and economic reforms occurred in the middle of that same year igniting the "German miracle" with high rates of growth for more than fifteen years. The economic policy, under which the upswing took place, was later named "Social Market Economy", and, indeed, the measures taken by the legendary German Minister of Economic Affairs at that time, Ludwig Erhard, were based on the liberal ideas expounded by the German liberals F. Böhm, von Dietze, Hensel, F.A. Lutz, Maier, F.W. Meyer, Schmitt, A. Rüstow and the previously mentioned W. Röpke and A. Müller-Armack. Not only did Müller-Armack invent the phrase "Social Market Economy", he was also the first author to publish a lengthy treatise on that topic (1946) and later became a high ranking public official shaping economic policy.

It would be a great misunderstanding to interpret the "Social Market Economy" as the brand name for a successful economic reform after a devastating war. On the contrary, the founding fathers of this conception intended a restatement of the classical liberal ideas under the prevailing historical circumstances, the end of a totalitarian regime in a country in shambles. Therefore, it must be asked, what type of liberalism the "Social Market Economy" movement represents?

---

2   It should not be overlooked, that the liberal and the socialist conceptions of democracy are incompatible in some important respects. Whereas socialists prefer the democratization of all areas of society and plead, for introducing an "economic democracy", the main concern of the liberals is to limit the powers of the collective.

THE SOCIAL MARKET ECONOMY: MAIN IDEAS

I. The Main Ideas

There are two groups to be taken into account in the German liberal movement during the forties and fifties, the Ordo-Liberals or Freiburg School as they were called with their leading figures Franz Böhm and Walter Eucken, and the proponents of the "Social Market Economy" among which Alfred Müller-Armack is the most impressive figure. Both schools agreed that a free society cannot be justified with the help of economic efficiency arguments, but that its central idea, personal liberty, is a value *per se*. Therefore, the "Social Market Economy" was not seen primarily as a programme to rebuild a war-shaken economy, but as a programme in the much broader context of liberal philosophy, a programme of how to shape the political and the economic order, culture, press, higher learning and science - to mention just a few topics where freedom is important and where institutions can be shaped according to the essence of liberalism. This has to be viewed against the historical background of the time. At least for those who believed in freedom, the Soviet Union was a shocking example of what "real socialism" and lack of personal freedom meant for political, cultural and economic life.

From this follows that the two groups had to wrestle with socialism-collectivism, on the one hand, and the previous conception of a free society, on the other. As far as collectivism is concerned, the arguments are apparent and will not be discussed further. The dispute with the older liberalism - sometimes called "Paleo-liberalism" or "laissez-faire-capitalism" - involved the question, why nineteenth century liberalism failed.

1. Competition and Individual Freedom - the Economic Order of a Free Society

The argument levelled against classical liberalism was as follows. Even though it succeeded in freeing man from the bonds of pre-industrial society, the elimination of social privileges together with the introduction of economic freedom and the renunciation of state intervention in private markets were insufficient to maintain a constitution of liberty (Böhm 1950, p. 52). The actors in the market have a strong incentive to monopolise. If they are successful in forming cartels or restraining competition they can earn higher profits and live a quieter life. This could only be inhibited, if, according to the Ordo-liberals, a strong state would enforce rules of competition which prevent cartelization.

In Germany, the opposite was the case. As Böhm (1948, p. 198) pointed out, a ruling by the Reich Supreme Court of 1897 permitted cartel agreements as fundamentally legal and fully compatible with the freedom of contract. This meant that they could be enforced by law. In the following decades Germany became the "country of cartels" (Möschel 1989, p. 144). During the Great Depression (1929-36) the cartels reacted to decreasing demand for their goods by keeping prices high and laying off workers. The high unemployment rates were one of the sources with which Hitler was able to gain power.

From this and other experiences Eucken, Böhm and others concluded that the protection of competition is one of the most important duties of a modern liberal state. According to their view the failure of the old liberals was in not recognising, that guarding private property rights and enforcing private contracts were insufficient for maintaining a liberal economic order. In their strictures against the gross misinterpretation of the freedom of contract by the Reich Supreme Court, the Ordo-liberals pointed out that it led to the creation of powerful interest groups and a new dependence of workers on their employers, of consumers on monopolists and of retailers on combines and cartels. The resulting inference for the neo-liberal programme was: unless a liberal constitutional state is prepared to see itself deteriorate into an interventionist state (e.g. the Weimar Republic) in which economic processes are manipulated to suit political opportunism, the maintenance and enforcement of a competitive system must be regarded as one of its prime objectives.

Therefore, an effective competition policy has to be one of the pillars of a Social Market Economy. This policy should not be based on discretionary decisions by politicians or bureaucrats, but instead be part of the legal system, thereby embedding competition policy into the economic order of a free society (Möschel 1989, p. 142). The protection and enforcement of workable competition was seen as a piece of "creative legislation". It was said that the decisions incumbent upon the legislators could not simply be left to a spontaneous balancing of political interests, since the stronger groups which "tyrannise the government" (Adam Smith) would otherwise pervert the law to meet their interests. Therefore, the real need was seen as gearing legislation to the common good, i.e. the rules of the competitive game of the market should be fair for everybody and should leave no room for exceptions favouring single industries or companies. Eucken, in particular, developed the idea of "vollständige Konkurrenz" - a term which should not be translated into English as "perfect competition". Instead, Eucken's notion implies that restraints on competition should not be legalised and that the real problem lies in safeguarding individual freedom in the markets, introducing fair rules of conduct and suppressing private economic power.

Because of the significance assigned by the Ordo-liberals to a well functioning system of competition as the linchpin of a new liberal economic order, they took a firm stand against the insinuation that such an order represented the "interests of capital". Their counter-argument was that the principle of universal competition should be adopted to counteract all endeavours by individuals or the state attempting to monopolise markets either at home or abroad. In their view, only this stance provided justification for considering their vision of a market economy as acceptable to everyone, from the ultimate producer or consumer, to the supplier or user of productive resources. They also believed that a systematically developed competitive market system permitted, above all, the weakest members of society to lead a life befitting a human being.

2. The Monetary Constitution

From the perspective taken by the Ordo-liberals the monetary order functions as a complement to the free economic order. Therefore, the consideration of interdependence, first, between the domestic economy and its markets and, second, between the domestic economy and the international division of labour, was one of the central topics they discussed, since the breakdown of the world economy in the early thirties. As Peter Bernholz writes in an analysis of the great debates about which monetary constitution is compatible with a free society, it is not only the case, in which the free and competitive formation of prices is a precondition for a sound and well-functioning monetary system, but, the reverse is also true: "All efforts to realise a competitive order are in vain, as long as a certain stability of money has not been secured". (Eucken quoted in Bernholz 1989, p. 194).

The awareness of sound money's importance for the smooth functioning of markets developed in the first half of the twentieth century out of the experiences of an open and of a repressed inflation. Both were the result of the two world wars, and their subsequent inadequate financing of public expenditures. Both ended in monetary reforms, in which the government debts were erased. Millions of citizens lost their savings and many experienced poverty. But, the liberal economists did not only pay attention to the social problems caused by instable money. Monetary instability was also a main concern for their scientific endeavours. They were aware of the fact that the monetary constitution greatly influences business activity and the fact that private banks can create money competitively by granting credit, which is one of the factors causing business cycles.

As far as positive proposals were concerned, their ideal was a money, which cannot be misused by governments to finance public deficits through a monetary expansion. As Hans Willgerodt stated, sound money is by definition an unpolitical money. Lutz and others backed the proposition that the gold standard is the monetary constitution, corresponding to a free market economy (cf. Bernholz 1989, p. 196). But, in the event this was not a feasible alternative, they favoured monetary constitutions, which minimized the discretionary power of those in charge of the money-machine. They proposed plans for either a hundred per cent reserve requirement in central bank money for all demand deposits (Lutz) or a commodity reserve currency with convertibility of money into a commodity bundle of fixed proportions at a fixed parity (cf. Bernholz 1989, p. 210). There was great scepticism in the workability of a third best alternative, a central-bank independent of governmental instructions, the outcome of German debates.

3. Social Policy and the Market Order

The point where the "Social Market Economy" differs most from the elder conceptions of a free society is whether social questions should be on the agenda of the state. The answer of the German neo-liberals was resoundingly affirmative. They criticized their predecessors for not taking the socialist strictures against "capitalism" seriously, as far as questions of social security were concerned. In a market economy only those offering goods or services which are demanded by others, can make a living. But, in everyone's life there are periods in which one cannot participate in the game of the market, be it childhood, unemployment, incapacity to work, sickness or old age. In some cases these everyday risks can be insured via the market, for instance, in private health insurance schemes. In other cases these risks cannot be insured. Other, non-market institutions, are necessary to handle, for instance, cases of indigence and distress. There was a long-lasting debate, whether in such cases there was a duty of the state to intervene or to abstain from any social policy measures. According to the German neo-liberals the former liberal schools favoured, in principle, that individuals should be responsible for making provision against all possible contingencies for themselves and their families and that in cases where this did not work, relief should be left only to spontaneous private charity. Contrary to this view the neo-liberals argued that employment opportunities may shrink, personal disasters may occur in the form of accidents and ill-health, old people and children may be the victims of other people's negligence; in such cases, and in many more after two destructive wars and ruinous inflation, private charity could not be sufficient to prevent distress[3]. Of course, the German liberals were aware of the indisputable fact that the necessary redistributive measures themselves might have a negative impact on the recipients' willingness to work and the tax-payers' readiness to create wealth. But, on the other hand they were convinced that in a market economy the strong incentives to produce would overcompensate the welfare losses caused by social policy. Additionally, the German liberals argued that men living in a free society would not be rational, egocentric wealth - maximizers, as they are modelled in the economic text-books, but moral personalities not opposing redistributive policies to prevent poverty. In Hayek's words: "In the Western world some parision for those threatened by the extremes of indigence... due to circumstances beyond their control has long been accepted as a duty of the community" (Hayek 1960, p. 285).

But on what principles should a social order for the free society be built? Here the German liberals relied heavily on the subsidiarity principle in which state measures are only legitimate, if private charity proves to be inadequate. After impoverishing wars redistributive policies had to exist on a larger scale than in peace-time with quickly growing wealth.

But, how should the normal risks of life such as sickness, old age and incapacity be managed? There is a powerful externality argument for compulsory insurance. Otherwise, those who neglect to make provisions could become a burden to the public (cf. Hayek 1960, p. 286). Compulsory insurance does not automatically imply membership in a unitary organisation under state control. An alternative is the creation of independent self-governing bodies. This evolves out of the liberal conviction that social questions of normal life risks are not primarily a duty of the state. At first glance, these

---

3 For details of the Anglo-Saxon debate see ROBBINS (1976, p. 127).

independent bodies might appear to be a purely technical detail. But, in the great debates on the foundation of a social state a hundred years ago the old liberals fought for a state-free social insurance system. They rightly feared that a state-run national health service or old-age pension system would become an instrument of vote-maximizing political behaviour. They were successful insofar as the German social security system is self-governing from legal point of view.

At this point it should be stated that an important difference exists between the welfare state and the German conception of a social state. For instance, contrary to the British National Health Service, which is run by the state, the German system is built upon a club-like basis such as health schemes for companies, corporations, communities, etc. In principle these institutions are all autonomous, the members (delegates of the employers associations and deputies of the employees) elect their representatives to the governing boards. Starting from the ideal of a free society, it was self-evident that the autonomy of these bodies should be strengthened, thereby placing the social security system beyond the reach of politicians. Those insured in the respective clubs should be encouraged to control their administration, decide on the benefits they wish to insure for themselves, and also fix the level of their contributions.

II. The Influence of the Social Market Economy Programme on German Economic Policy

This rather superficial sketch of West Germany's post-war liberalism leads to the difficult question, of whether the "Social Market Economy" Programme has impacted German economic policy during the last decades? Already, in the early seventies a member of second generation German neo-liberalism, Hans-Otto Lenel, posed the question: does Germany still possess a Social Market Economy? (Lenel 1971, p. 261). At that time Karl Schiller, then Minister of Economic Affairs, presented his model of an "enlightened" economic policy. According to this concept, micro-economic relations should be under the control of competition via markets. Simultaneously, the macroeconomic relations should not follow the rules of the "invisible hand", instead they should be steered with the assistance of non-compulsory planning for the entire economy, the so-called planification (Globalsteuerung) - to use a French term. Global targets were set for the whole economy like growth rates, inflation and employment goals, as well as balance of payments objectives. The main instrument to reach such aims was the so-called Concerted Action, in which the heads of the unions and employers associations gathered together. There the Minister of Economics presented wage-guidelines and informed both groups about future government plans, especially with respect to fiscal policy. From the stand-point of a "Social Market Economy", this represented unacceptable interventionism, despite the fact that some of its leading members (Müller-Armack, Röpke) advocated business-cycle policies under certain conditions, while criticising Keynesian recipes for full-employment as counterproductive (for details see Bernholz 1989, p. 203). The macro-economic policy of Karl Schiller, in which the ideas of J.M. Keynes played a crucial role, failed under his successors and led in the mid-seventies to Germany's first serious recession.

Since the collapse of the Schmidt-government in 1982 and the new coalition between Christian and Liberal democrats, the term "Social Market Economy" has been used to describe official government policy. But, whether this actually signals a self-commitment to the principles laid down by the founding fathers of the liberal tradition is an open question.

Looking back on the forty-year period of West-German economic policy - i.e. the time before the German-German reunification (1990) - it cannot be claimed that the economic policy of the country has been simply the product of the "Social Market Economy" Programme. But, the important complement to the 1948 currency reform of the Western Allies was the scrapping of countless price regulations at one blow by Ludwig Erhard, and later a genuine institutional revolution, which has led Germany on the path towards a market economy. Despite many interventions into the economic order since then, the growth of redistributional coalitions (Olson) and many government measures against the market, it can be said, that Germany is still a market-oriented country with a rather successful record in its economic performance. In the years immediately following the end of the war, the possibility existed that another economic path could have been chosen. A good example is Great Britain, where under the Fabian critique of capitalism, a mild form of a welfare state was introduced together with full-employment policies which handicapped the economy for decades. Also, socialist experiments - perhaps not totalitarian but social-democratic - were pushed through by left-wing groups. That the path to a market economy was chosen, was the result of a courageous decision of Ludwig Erhard, who at that time - before the foundation of the Federal Republic of Germany (1949) - maintained powers allowing him to act as an quasi economic dictator. His decision was backed by the theories and conceptions of the Ordo-liberals and the proponents of a "Social Market Economy". And, Erhard himself was a prominent member of that group. Erhard's decision was not fundamentally changed. Since then and during his fourteen years as Economics Minister, he introduced step-wise the rules of a market economy into a framework, which under the Nazi government had been organised along the principles of economic planning.

The Ordo-liberal vision of a free society also sparked a much deeper understanding of the problems of an economic order. For instance, a market order cannot be combined with all sorts of restraints on competition or collective property as the promoters of market socialism believe. The market system can only function smoothly under a system of private property rights and personal responsibility for decision-makers. Therefore, privatisation in a very broad sense is a constituting principle of a "Social Market Economy".

But, what happened in the three fields mentioned as core elements of the "Social Market Economy"? The recommendation that competition policy is necessary to protect individual freedom led to a long discussion about the appropriate rules for the competition game. The outcome was the 1957 Law Against Restraints of Competition, which was a political compromise (for details see Möschel 1989, p. 143), and a Monopolies Commission Act. The Ordo-liberal view entered also Article 86 of the EC-Treaty. And presently, there is a sharp debate, whether industrial policy should replace or coexist with competition policy based on the rule of law. The answer goes without saying.

The desirability of a stable value of money is undisputed in Germany. Free international trade and unrestricted convertibility have strengthened the German mark, which is now one of the three leading world currencies. Compared to nearly all other currencies, the German mark has preserved its value as the relatively most stable currency. Its purchasing power has fallen more than sixty per cent since the early fifties, which compared to the nineteenth century gold standard is a rather meagre result.

In the field of social policies, even the most optimistic German liberals are dissatisfied. No use of the opportunities for an extension of personal freedom within the social insurance institutions have been achieved. A reform in the capital-backed pension system to a pay-as-you-go system in 1957 gave Konrad Adenauer an unprecedented election victory through a high increase of the old-age benefits. Since then, social policy is one of the main playing fields, upon which political competition takes place. Today the whole social security system is the battlefield for income redistribution. The rapid decline in birth-rates, since the mid-sixties, questions the possibility of financing the system in the years to come. Of course, the state-controlled monopoly for old-age pensions is not the only possibility for financing benefits, and there are fierce debates, as to which solution would best fit into the framework of a free society.

A Short Bibliography of Important Texts on the Social Market Economy in English and German

BARRY, N. P.: "Political and Economic Thought of German Neo-Liberals", in: A. PEACOCK and H. WILLGERODT (Eds.): *German Neo-Liberals and the Social Market Economy*, London 1989.

BERNHOLZ, P.: "Freedom and Constitutional Order", *Zeitschrift für die gesamte Staatswissenschaft*, Vol. 135 (1979).

BERNHOLZ, P.: "Ordo-liberals and the Control of Money", in: A. PEACOCK and H. WILLGERODT (Eds.): *German Neoliberals and the Social Market Economy*, London 1989.

BOEHM, FRANZ: *Wettbewerb und Monopolkampf. Eine Untersuchung zur Frage des wirtschaftlichen Kampfrechtes und zur Frage der rechtlichen Struktur der geltenden Wirtschaftsordnung*, Berlin (Carl Heymanns Verlag) 1933, reprinted in 1964.

BOEHM, FRANZ: "Die Ordnung der Wirtschaft als geschichtliche Aufgabe und rechtsschöpferische Leistung", Series *Ordnung und Wirtschaft*, Vol. 1, Stuttgart and Berlin (W. Kohlhammer) 1937.

BOEHM, FRANZ: "Die Idee des Ordo im Denken Walter Euckens", *Ordo-Jahrbuch für die Ordnung von Wirtschaft und Gesellschaft*, Bd. 3 (1950), pp. 15-64. (The Ordo yearbook was published by Helmut Küpper in Düsseldorf and Munich from 1948-74; from 1975 it has been published by Gustav Fischer in Stuttgart.)

BOEHM, FRANZ: "Left-wing and Right-wing Approaches to the Market Economy", *Zeitschrift für die gesamte Staatswissenschaft*, Vol. 135 (1979).

BOEHM, FRANZ: "Rule of Law in a Market Economy", in: A. PEACOCK and H. WILLGERODT (Eds.): *Germany's Social Market Economy: Origins and Evolution*, London 1989.

ERHARD, L.: *Germany's Comeback in the World Market*, London 1954.
ERHARD, L.: *Prosperity Through Competition*, London 1958.
ERHARD, L.: *The Economics of Success*, Princeton 1963.
EUCKEN, W.: "On the Theory of the Centrally Administered Economy: An Analysis of the Geman Experience", *Economica*, London, Vol. 15 (1948).
EUCKEN, W.: *The Foundations of Economics*, Edinburgh 1950 (Translated by Terence W. Hutchison).
EUCKEN, W.: *This Unsuccessful Age*, Edinburgh - London - Glasgow 1951.
EUCKEN, W.: *Grundsätze der Wirtschaftspolitik*, ed. by Edith Eucken and K. Paul Hensel, Bern and Tübingen (Francke and J.C.B. Mohr [Paul Siebeck]) 1952.
FISHER, A. G. B.: *Economic Progress and Social Security*, London (Macmillan) 1945.
FRIEDMAN, MILTON: *Capitalism and Freedom*, Chicago (University of Chicago Press) 1962.
GIERSCH, H., PACQUE, K.-H. and SCHMIEDING, H.: *The Fading Miracle*, 1991.
HAYEK, F. A. v.: *The Road to Serfdom*, London 1944. German translation: *Der Weg zur Knechtschaft*, Erlenbach - Zürich 1945.
HAYEK, F. A. v.: *The Constitution of Liberty*, London 1960.
HAYEK, F. A. v.: "What is Social? What does it Mean?", in: F. A. v. HAYEK: *Studies in Philosophy, Politics and Economy*, Chicago 1967, pp. 237-249.
HUTCHISON, TERENCE: "Notes on the Effects of Economic Ideas on Policy: The Example of the German Social Market Economy", *Zeitschrift für die gesamte Staatswissenschaft*, Tübingen, Vol. 135 (1979).
JOSEPH, Sir K.: *Why Britain Needs a Social Market Economy*, London (Centre for Policy Studies) 1975.
LENEL, H. O.: "Evolution of the Social Market Economy", in: A. PEACOCK and H. WILLGERODT (Eds.): *German Neo-Liberals and the Social Market Economy*, London 1989.
LENEL, H. O.: "Does Germany Still Have a Social Market Economy?", in: A. PEACOCK and H. WILLGERODT (Eds.): *German Neo-Liberals and the Social Market Economy*, London 1971/1989.
LITH, U. van: *Der Markt als Ordnungsprinzip des Bildungsbereichs*, Munich 1985.
LUTZ, F. A.: "The German Currency Reform and the Revival of the German Economy", *Economica*, 16 (1948), p. 122ff.
LUTZ, F. A.: "The Case for Flexible Exchange Rates", *Banca Nazionale del Lavoro*, Vol. 7, Rome 1954.
MESTMAECKER, E. J.: "Macht-Recht-Wirtschaftsverfassung", in: H. K. SCHNEIDER and CHRISTIAN WATRIN (Eds.): *Macht und ökonomisches Gesetz, Schriften des Vereins für Socialpolitik*, Vol. 74/I, Berlin 1973.
MESTMAECKER, E. J.: "Competition Policy and Antitrust: Some Comparative Observations", *Zeitschrift für die gesamte Staatswissenschaft*, Vol. 136, Tübingen 1980.

THE SOCIAL MARKET ECONOMY: MAIN IDEAS

MISES, L. von: *Human Action. A Treatise in Economics,* Edinburgh and New Haven, Connecticut 1949, reprinted in 1963.

MISES, L. von: *The Anti-capitalistic Mentality*, Princeton, New Jersey 1956.

MOESCHEL, W.: "Competition Policy From an Ordo Point of View", in: A. PEACOCK and H. WILLGERODT (Eds.): *German Neo-Liberals and the Social Market Economy*, London 1989.

MUELLER-ARMACK, A.: *Wirtschaftslenkung und Marktwirtschaft*, Hamburg 1946, reprint: *Wirtschaftsordnung und Wirtschaftspolitik,* Freiburg (Rombach) 1966; second ed. published by Paul Haupt in Bern and Stuttgart, 1976.

MUELLER-ARMACK, A.: "The Principles of the Social Market Economy", *German Economic Review*, Stuttgart, Vol. 3 (1965), in this volume pp. 255-274.

MUELLER-ARMACK, A.: "The Social Market Economy as an Economic and Social Order", *Review of Social Economy*, Milwaukee, Wisconsin, Vol. 3 (1978).

MUELLER-ARMACK, A.: "The Meaning of the Social Market Economy", in: A. PEACOCK and H. WILLGERODT (Eds.): *Germany's Social Market Economy: Origins and Evolution*, 1989.

OLIVER, H. M.: "German Neo-liberalism", *Quaterly Journal of Economics*, Cambridge, Massachusetts, Vol. 74 (1960).

PEACOCK, A. T.: *Structural Economic Policies in West Germany and the United Kingdom,* London (Anglo-German Foundation) 1980.

PEACOCK, A. and WILLGERODT, H.: "Overall View of the German Liberal Movement", in: A. PEACOCK and H. WILLGERODT (Eds.): *German Neo-Liberals and the Social Market Economy*, London 1989.

POPPER, K. R.: *Die Offene Gesellschaft und ihre Feinde* (The Open Society and its Enemies), Bern (7th edition) 1993.

RICHTER, R.: "Currency and Economic Reform. West Germany after World War II", *Zeitschrift für die gesamte Staatswissenschaft,* Vol. 135 (1979).

ROBBINS, L.: *Political Economy: Past and Present. A Review of Leading Theories of Economic Policy*, London 1976.

ROEPKE, W.: "Staatsinterventionsmus", in: *Handwörterbuch der Staatswissenschaften*, Jena 1929.

ROEPKE, W.: "International Economics in a Changing World", in: *The World Crisis*, London 1938.

ROEPKE, W.: *The German Question*, London 1946.

ROEPKE, W.: *Internationale Ordnung*, Zürich 1945. English: *International Order and Economic Integration*, Dordrecht, Holland 1959.

ROEPKE, W.: *The Social Crisis of Our Time*, Edinburgh and Chicago 1950.

ROEPKE, W.: *Welfare, Freedom and Inflation,* London (Pall Mall Press) 1957.

ROEPKE, W.: *Economics of the Free Society* (translated into English by Patrick M. Boarman), Chicago 1943.

ROEPKE, W.: *A Humane Economy: The Social Framework of the Free Market*, London and Chicago 1960. German: *Jenseits von Angebot und Nachfrage*, Zürich and Stuttgart (Eugen Rentsch) 1958.
ROWLEY, C. K. and PEACOCK, ALAN T.: *Welfare Economics: a Liberal Re-statement*, London 1975.
RUESTOW, A.: *Das Versagen des Wirtschaftsliberalismus*, Düsseldorf and Bad Godesberg 1950.
SCHILLER, K.: *Preisstabilität durch globale Steuerung der Marktwirtschaft*, Tübingen 1966.
SCHMIDTCHEN, D.: "German "Ordnungspolitik" as Institutional Choice", *Zeitschrift für die gesamte Staatswissenschaft*, Tübingen, Vol. 140 (1984).
STOLPER, W. and ROSKAMP, KARL W.: "Planning a Free Economy: Germany 1945-60", *Zeitschrift für die gesamte Staatswissenschaft*, Tübingen, Vol 135 (1979).
STREISSLER, E.: "Kritik des neo-klassischen Gleichgewichtsansatzes", in: ERICH STREISSLER and CHRISTIAN WATRIN (Eds.): *Zur Theorie Marktwirtschaftlicher Ordnungen*, Tübingen 1980.
SOHMEN, E.: "Competition and Growth: The Lesson of West Germany", *American Economic Review*, 49 (1959), pp. 986-1003.
WALLICH, H. C.: *The Mainsprings of the German Revival*, Frankfurt/Main 1955.
WATRIN, C.: "The Principles of the Social Market Economy - its Origins and Early History", *Zeitschrift für die gesamten Staatswissenschaften*, Bd. 135 (1979), pp. 405-424.
WATRIN, C.: "The Social Market Economy", in: *The Konrad Adenauer Memorial Lectures 1978 - 1982. Delivered by Karl-Günther von Hase, Hans Peter Schwarz, Christian Watrin. Introduction by Anthony Nicholls.*
WATRIN, C.: "Towards a More Humane Society?" in: A. PEACOCK and H. WILLGERODT (Eds.): *Germany's Social Market Economy: Origins and Evolution*, 1989.
WISEMAN, J.: "Genesis, Aims and Goals of Social Policy", *Public Finance and Social Policy* (Proceedings of the 39th Congress of the International Institute of Public Finance), Detroit, Michigan (Wayne State University Press) 1983.
WISEMAN, J.: "Economic Efficiency and Efficient Public Policy", in: H. HANUCH, K.W., ROSKAMP and JACK WISEMAN (Eds.): *Staat und Politische Ökonomie Heute*, Stuttgart and New York (Gustav Fischer) 1985.
WISEMAN, J.: "Social Policy and the Social Market Economy", in: A. PEACOCK and H. WILLGERODT (Eds.): *German Neo-Liberals and the Social Market Economy*, London 1989.
ZWEIG, K.: *The Origins of the German Social Market Economy*, London and Virginia (Adam Smith Institute) 1980.

Discussion Summary

NORBERT F. TOFALL

Paper discussed:
CHRISTIAN WATRIN: The Social Market Economy: the Main Ideas and Their Influence on Economic Policy

The discussion was opened by a comment about the peculiarities and differences between the ordo-liberal theory of the School of Freiburg, *Freiburger Schule,* and the concept of the Social Market Economy as it was developed by Alfred Müller-Armack (AVTONOMOV). Then, the dilemma of practical social policy was discussed. On the one hand, the concept of the Social Market Economy means that limits are set to the free market by social elements. On the other hand, there is always the danger that the practice of social policy reduces the performance and functional order of the market and therefore the success of the whole Social Market Economy (AVTONOMOV).

That there are fundamentally different concepts of social policy can be clarified with the historical reference to the German Reich in the seventies of the 19th century. With his social welfare legislation, the German chancellor Bismarck pursued the aim to decrease the power of the political leaders of the working class. The *Sozialistengesetze* (laws banning political actions by the Socialists [SPD]) and the introduction of the social insurance system by the law are different instruments of the same policy against the Social Democrats (WATRIN).

The debates in the German *Reichstag* (parliament of the German Reich) about the form of the social policy show that the liberals strictly fought against a state-run social policy. The German liberals fought for a social policy, which was based on the principle of self-administration, to minimize the state influence - which they considered as heteronomy - on the economy and on the individual citizens. At that time as well as nowadays, self-administration in the social insurance system means, that each of the individuals, who are affected by the same social risks, join and administer the system by themselves for the purpose of helping a member - only a member

DISCUSSION SUMMARY

and only if necessary - out of the fund which is built up by the members' contributions. A social policy, which aims at guaranteeing self-administration and the liberty of the persons affected, must always be based on the insurance principle. In this, one can find the historical roots for the fact that in Germany private and non-state-run health insurances exist beside the public insurances (WATRIN).

The discussion about the dilemma of the practical social policy is surely directed at defects of the system of the Social Market Economy which arise when the social policy is not organized in an economic way. Today the German social insurance system has gone out of control because enormous governmental interventions have lifted the insurance principle off its hinges and replaced it by the principle of redistribution. On the other hand, Alfred Müller-Armack has always pointed out that the social insurances ought to be supported by their members through their membership contributions and that the social insurances have only to pay the social services for their members and for nobody else. Redistribution cannot be a part of a working social insurance system (WATRIN).

To the historical reference to the German Reich, it was objected that beside the Bismarckian intentions for introducing the social insurance system, the German-Prussian monarchs had quite different intentions. The monarchs Wilhelm I and Wilhelm II were very Christian and therefore they saw in the introduction of the social insurance system a part of their Christian responsibility. Wilhelm II explicitly wanted to establish a social kingship (NÖRR).

It was replied, that this form of a Christian responsibility was often felt as Prussian dominance. In the 19th century, the German Reichstag had essentially fewer rights and competencies than the West-European parliaments. This correlation has to be taken into account by viewing at the practical policy (WATRIN). It was admitted that the idea of a social kingship certainly was a patriachal one (NÖRR). However, one cannot mistake this idea for pure power politics.

With regard to different speeches of Bismarck, PETER KOSLOWSKI agrees with the latter. Bismarck held the opinion that nobody ought to make profit with the poverty of human beings. Furthermore Bismarck's social insurance system was unique in Europe. Some of the patriarchally minded Christian conservatives in Germany did not vote for this social insurance system because they feared that the private charity could be decreased by this system.

DISCUSSION SUMMARY

Referring to Bismarck's speeches in the German Reichstag, it was replied ironically that Bismarck simply was a brilliant speaker and politician (WATRIN).

The thorough discussion of Watrin's paper shows that there must be a long tradition of the Social Market Economy in Germany. However, today the question is important whether the concept of the Social Market Economy is something like an international trend and if it is possible to use it successfully in other countries (LIAKIN).

The discussion about the Social Market Economy must be regarded in its correlation with the discussions of the German economists in the *Verein für Socialpolitik* (Association for Social Policy) in the last century, which were shaped by the Historical School of Economics, especially by Gustav Schmoller. Undoubtedly, Müller-Armack stands in the tradition of Gustav Schmoller. It is, therefore, possible to call the Social Market Economy a typically German idea (WATRIN).

To the question whether the Social Market Economy is an international trend and whether it is possible to use it successfully everywhere, it is firstly referred to as the positive economic development in the last hundred years. Secondly, in all Western countries social insurance systems exist today. Thirdly, the Social Market Economy is the answer to the failed socialism. Socialism with its direct governmental planning and with its permanent interventions into the free actions of the individuals was not able to solve the social and economic problems of the people. Fourthly, it is most important that we never forget the initial question which should guide our scientific work: How can the individual freedom of human beings be saved? And this question is not only the question for East Europe and Russia, it is also the question for the USA and especially for Germany, where we have a rate of the state control over the gross domestic product of more than 50 per cent (WATRIN).

Chapter 2

The Idea of Economic Order in Contemporary Russia

KONSTANTIN S. PIGROV

I. Introduction. The Destiny of the Terms "Order" and "Ordnung"
II. The Concept of Social Order
III. The Concept of Economic Order
IV. The Being of Economic Order and its Idea
V. The Duality of the Idea of Economic Order
VI. Modifications of the Idea of Economic Order
VII. Conclusion: The Economic Order as an Ecological Order

I. Introduction. The Destiny of the Terms "Order" and "Ordnung"

The terms considered in the present paper do not seem to be generally accepted. They have not appeared yet in dictionaries and reference literature. Before starting the discussions of economic order, it must be necessary to point out that the basic concept has not been defined yet.[1] Besides, the usage of the terms in German and Russian scientific communities differs both in contexts and in connotations. That is why the methodological and terminological basis of the presented research seems to quite essential.

---

1 See for example: V. ALTUKHOV: "O Smene Poriadkov v Mirovom Obchestvennom Razvitii" (On Changes of Orders in the World Social Development), *Mirovaya Ekonomika i Mezhdunarodnye Otnoshenia* (World Economy and International Relations), 4, Moscow (Nauka) 1995, p. 57.

THE IDEA OF ECONOMIC ORDER IN CONTEMPORARY RUSSIA

The destinies of the Russian word "poriadok" (order) and of the German word "Ordnung" are quite different, which should be relevant for the conference under the title "Theory and Ethics of the Economic Order in Russia and Germany". Encyclopaedias provide a surprising complexity of German terminology associated with "Ordnung". Brockhaus Encyclopaedia cites five terms in different fields (besides the common meaning), that is, in Philosophy, Sociology, History of Religion, Mathematics and Biology. It seems that for the German ear the word "Ordnung" is associated primarily with the social sphere (Ordnungsbehörden, Ordnungsmittel, Ordnungsstrafen, Ordnungspolitik, etc.). In Russian the word "order" is associated with the social sphere too, especially in everyday usage. But this is not expressed in terminology. At the same time, the Great Soviet Encyclopaedia cites ten (!) mathematical terms "order" besides its other usage in sciences (order of interference, order of reaction).[2]

Thus, one can assume that the basic foundation of the Russian mentality is manifested by the fact that the Russian word "order" lacks a certain connotation and that the term "order" used in Russian social sciences is a borrowing acquired through translations of foreign works.[3] I suppose that is the reason why there cannot be a common theory of economic order in Russia and Germany. But there may be pointed out at least four interpretations of economic order which can be described as follows:
- the Russian theory of economic order in Russia,
- the Russian theory of economic order in Germany,
- the German theory of economic order in Germany,
- the German theory of economic order in Russia.

One can assume that the Russian mentality does not comprehend the social world in terms of order, or not only in terms of order, that is, as opposite to chaos, anarchy, undifferentiated unity, or plurality) but it comprehends it somehow differently, in some other words. Besides, even if the term "order" appears in Russian social, economic and political texts, it is just an external

---

[2] See: BROCKHAUS: *Enzyklopädie in Zwanzig Bänden*, B.16, (F. A. Brockhaus Wiesbaden) 1991; BOLSHAYA SOVETSKAYA ENTSYKLOPEDIYA, Third Edition, Moscow (Sovetskaya Entsyklopediya), vol. 20, 1975, pp. 405-406.

[3] See for example: JAN TINBERGEN: *Peresmotr Mezhdunarodnogo Poriadka*, Moscow (Progress) 1980. Original: *Reshaping the International Order: a report to the club of Rome*, in: National Union Catalog 1973-1977, New York (Dutton) 1976.

application of a Western (say, German) concept of order to the Russian reality.

II. The Concept of Social Order

As we fail to find the definition of the general usage of the term discussed, it is necessary to formulate a working definition, which is assumed to be not the final one, but just the one allowing to start the analysis. By social order we shall mean some steady system of relations inside a society, which implies orderliness (that is, a certain consistence) of the elements of the society; further, of a particular element with the whole; and finally, the consistence of the whole with its elements. Social order implies, therefore, *solidarity, loyalty, legitimity.* (All the three concepts are understood in the broadest meaning).

The concept of social order is close, first of all, to the well-known and widely used in Russia concept of social structure which was defined 25 years ago as a "network of orderly and interdependent connections between the elements of a social system",[4] where the forms of social organisation, social activities, character of functioning of social institutions are established. Second, the concept of social order can be comprehended by the contemporary Russian consciousness in a close connection with the term "social law" which was interpreted in the official historical materialism as "an objectively existing, necessary, essential, repeating chain of phenomena of social life."[5]

Third, the concept of planning should be taken into consideration. S. L. Frank devoted a special chapter to planning and spontaneity in his work on social philosophy. He pointed out that as "the form and the structure of the social unity, being an incarnation of some ideal content, on the one hand, imply conscious and intentional, planned realization of an idea, on the other hand, they imply a certain spontaneous, direct, naturally emerging expres-

---

4 YU. LEVADA: "Structura Sotsialnaya" (Social Structure), in: *Philosophskaya Entsyklopediya*, vol. 5, Moscow (Sovetskaya Entsyklopediya) 1970 p. 142.
5 G. ANDREEVA: "Zakonomernost Obshchestvennaya" (Social Appropriateness), in: *Philosophskaya Entsyklopediya*, vol. 2, Moscow (Sovetskaya Entsyklopediya) 1962, p. 153.

sion of the real process of life."[6] The concept of planning which was close to that of social order, was much discussed in the Soviet social-economic theory, since it was of extreme ideological importance. It was used in arguing for "the advantages of the socialist production relations".

All the above terms (social structure, social law, planning) do not have specifically Marxist meaning. Their content was formed within the framework of the "first" positivism and was adopted by the official Soviet social theory.[7]

III. The Concept of Economic Order

In the present paper the economic order is understood as a moment, an aspect of social order, which is a steady system of economic relations in a society. Solidarity, loyalty and legitimacy of the economic order are of specific meaning, related to the production, distribution and consumption of material and spiritual goods.

Solidarity in the context of economic order first of all implies the division of labour, which was considered to be the key concept in the classical political economy. Let us recall that A. Smith saw the meaning of civilization in the division of labour: "...without co-operation and support of thousands of people, the poorest dweller of a civilized country could not live the way he lives now, the way we consider quite simple and common."[8] The same idea was later often repeated by F. Engels.[9]

---

6   S. L. FRANK: "Dukhovnye Osnovy Obchestva. Vvedenie v Sotsialnuyu Filosofiyu" (Moral Foundations of a Society. Introduction to Social Philosophy), in: *Iz Istorii Russkoi Sotsialnoi i Pravovoi Mysli. Russkoe Zarubezhie*, Leningrad (Lenizdat) 1991, p. 418.
7   See, for example: N. I. KAREEV: *Sushchnost Istoricheskogo Protsessa i Rol Lichnosti v Istorii* (The Essence of the Historic Process and the Role of a Personality in History), Moscow (Mamontov) 1914.
8   A. SMITH: *Issledovanie o Prirode i Prichinah Bogatstva Narodov*, Moscow (Sotsecguis) 1962, p. 26. Original: ADAM SMITH: *An Inquiry into the Nature and Causes of the Wealth of Nations,* London (World Lock &Co.) 1812.
9   See for example: F. ENGELS: "Proiskhozhdenie Semyi, Chastnoi Sobstvennosti i Gosudarstva", in: K. MARX, F. ENGELS: *Sochineniya*, 2nd edition, vol. 21, p.

. Loyalty means a relation and motivation to labour, ability, striving and readiness to participate in the public production.

Finally, legitimacy as related to economic order means the activities of the authorities (state) designed to reach certain common goals of production, for example, to ensure employment, just wage commitments, etc.

The concept of economic order implicitly existed both in the mentality of people in the Soviet period, and in the official social-economic theory. The concepts and ideas have not that much changed since then, though, of course, the terminology has, and quite essentially. The closest to the "economic order" are the terms like "production relations" (economic relations, technological relations), "social economic formation", "mode of life".

IV. The Being of Economic Order and its Idea

The economic order exists objectively, that is, a steady system of economic relations exists independently from an observer. It was already mentioned that in the official Soviet historical materialism, the "objectivity" was of great ideological importance, because this objectivity implied the necessity of the transition from the capitalist formation to the communist one. That is why they spoke not of a flexible, moving, unreal existence based on the opinions and relations of people, their "first order construct", but about the being, social being, which has an ontological significance implied in its definition and absolutely determines social consciousness.

Besides an objective economic order, there is an idea of it which is not objective, but more or less successfully explained by theorists. The idea of economic order is close to the social ideal in the Russian philosophical tradition.

Not only the idea of economic order, which can be realized out of the dumbness of the world by the theoretician, but the objective economic order itself are fully dependent upon the theoretician. His "second order con-

---

173-174. Original : *Der Ursprung der Familie, des Privateigentums und der Staats.* Im Anschluss an Lewis H. Morgans Forschungen von Friedrich Engels, Hoeffigen-Zuerich (Verlag der Schweizerischen Volksbuchhandlung) 1884.

structs" being expressed, multiplied through mass media, change the economic order. That is why the theoretician takes a significant part in building it. Besides, considering the economic order abstracting from the existing theory and ideologies, within the framework of the "first order constructs only", one can see that it does not exist without the co-ordination of sense of human behaviour, which is realized by the consciousness.

At least two approaches concerning the interaction of the idea of the economic order and its objective being are known. These two approaches are rooted in the very ontology of the problem: if there is an idea and its objective existence, then, there is a possibility to place first either idea, or its objective existence.

The approach called materialistic (nominalistic, naturalistic) in the common terminology, is not, generally speaking, necessarily connected with Marxism, especially in the 20th century. In the framework of such an approach, the being of economic order is determined by natural, anthropological, technological and other factors of this kind. This objective being is reflected in the notion of economic order and in its turn determines it. Of course, the materialists of this kind do agree that the very idea of an economic order functions as a more or less active regulator. The relationship of the being of an economic order and its idea can be described in terms of cybernetics and the theory of automatic regulation:

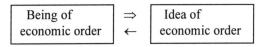

Being is the object of regulation, the idea is its regulator.

We see also the other approach, which was quite clearly formed in Neo-kantian social economic theory.[10] It is characteristic of Russian philosophical idealism. Thus, it can be called an idealistic (realistic) one. According to it, the idea and ideals do not only determine the being of economic order, but form its deep structure. Of course, idealists agree that the real world modifies

---

10 See for example: R. SHTAMMLER: *Khoziaistvo i Pravo s Tochki Zreniya Materialisticheskogo Ponimaniya Istorii (Sotsialno-Filosofskoye Issledovanie)*, vol. 1,2, St.Petersburg (without publisher) 1899, 1907. Original: R. STAMMLER: *Wirtschaft und Recht. Nach der materialistischen Geschichtauffassung. Eine socialphilosohische Untersuchung*, Leipzig (Veit) 1896.

ideas. Thus, the above scheme is in force. But the role of being and of idea are inverse now.

The two described approaches to the interaction of the being of economic order and of its idea presuppose orientation towards essentially different values. The materialistic approach is explicitly or implicitly based upon the highest value of individual survival and satisfaction of the individual's basic material needs. The idealistic one is based upon the highest value of the transcendental, where it is quite natural to sacrifice the wealth and even life of an individual.

In contemporary Russia (and probably in Germany, too) the two above approaches and the corresponding value systems coexist, interact, compete, turn into each other. They imply two ideas of economic order which are complementary to each other. Materialists take care of the earthly life, idealists remind of the ideal one and demand that the economy at least should not prevent from the hard thinking of the transcendental. Distinct and undivided, these two ideas represent the spiritual basis which is the subject of this paper.

V. The Duality of the Idea of Economic Order

Materialistic aspect. As it was stated above, this is the aspect in the idea of economic order which is determined by the materialistic view on the relationship between the being of the order and its comprehension in the idea. This view implicitly contains the model of the "economic man" and also the model of the "purpose rational behaviour". This view expresses general attitudes of the "disenchanted world" and is closely connected with the technogenic modern European civilization. It is implied in both the Western understanding of economic order and in the Soviet Marxist interpretation of it. It should be underlined that, notwithstanding essential differences, the Western and Marxist ideas of economic order are growing from the same root and are similar to each other in a number of essential positions. These positions are based primarily on a high estimation of the production forces and their development, on the conviction that by means of "slyness of the mind" it is possible to get from the nature everything humankind needs for life.

THE IDEA OF ECONOMIC ORDER IN CONTEMPORARY RUSSIA

This is the fundamental modern European idea. The founding fathers of the Modern European civilization, F. Bacon and R. Descartes assumed that it is the technological development, with its wide spread in industry that would accomplish the soteriological task.[11] It is well-known that Protestantism also made a significant contribution to this ideology.[12]

Production forces are of the highest value for society since they guarantee its survival and a certain welfare for its members (those loyal towards the economic order), too. Besides that, the production forces constitute the very economic order, since it promotes their progress. As for the present condition of production, the economic order is much dependent upon communication means. The economic information flow grows much faster than the amount of services rendered. That is why the economy needs the accelerated development of communications. This is possible only in the form of computerization. Thus, the transition from written to typed forms of supporting the economic order is implied in the value basis of the materialistic approach to the economic order.

The official Soviet Marxism preserved the primacy of the development of production forces irrespectively of the designed goals. This accounts for the fact that the transition from the attitudes appropriate for the planned economy to those specific to the market economy took place so painlessly in the USSR. Indeed, the state is legitimate in respect to the economic order if and only if it is capable of organizing the economy on the basis of the progressive development of the production forces. The political regime that we had up to 1985, was not legitimate from this point of view, since it was not capable of securing such a progressive development of the production forces as it was the case of the Western countries. This infringement the of economic order brought the Soviet power to collapse along with the Soviet Union. The "500 Days" programme elaborated by the Shatalin-Yavlinsky working group starts with the reference to this illegitimacy of the Soviet system. According to this group, the transition to the new system (that is, to the market model) will "resolve the most strained, accumulated over decades problems of this country, it will organically unite our economy with the

---

11 See an intersting analysis: J. NETOPILIK: "Zur Subjet-Object Beziehung im Sozialismus", *Deutsche Zeitschrift für Philosophie,* 2 (1972), p. 1454.
12 M. WEBER : "Die protestantische Ethik und der Geist des Capitalismus", in: M. WEBER: *Gesammelte Aufsaetze zur Religionssoziologie,* Bd. 1, Tübingen (J. C. B. Mohr) 1920.

world economy, it will provide the growth of the production to satisfy the needs of the people and thus it will create the social orientation of the economy, liquidate deficit, and will make all the achievement of the world civilization available to the citizens."[13] These are those values which could not be met by the Soviet economic order but which are considered to be primary from the materialistic point of view.

The state legitimity in terms of economic order is understood in a similar way in the sphere of international relations. Joining the Russian Federation by any ethnic formation is legitimate from the point of view of the economic order, if this promotes progress of the production forces for this ethnic formation.

The behaviour of an individual is loyal in terms of the materialistic aspect of the economic order if it is directed towards economic progress. This results in a high estimation of diligence and the correspondent concept in the Soviet ideology: labour as the first vital need, labour as "the need of a healthy organism".[14]

Finally, in the framework of such a conception of the economic order, the individual should be capable of co-operation, of labour consensus, of participating in the division of labour. This results in a high evaluation of professionals and in moral condemnation of dilettantism. A dabbler is bad not because he is bad in doing his business, but because he attempts to do what is not his business and breaks the established order of the division of labour. Man should not only feel a propensity to working, but also strive to work "in the team", where he is performing his job well as a part of the job performed by the others.

Everything regarding the co-operation of individuals can be, to some extent, applied to the co-operation of different peoples, national economies.

---

13 *Komsomolskaya Pravda,* November 1, 1990, special issue.
14 In the Soviet period some interesting investigations were conducted. They are almost unknown in the West. For example: R. I. KOSOLAPOV: *Kommunisticheskiy Trud: Priroda i Stimuly* (Communist Labour: The Nature and the Stimuli), Moscow (Mysl) 1968; G. S. GRIGORIEV: *Trud - Pervaya Chelovecheskaya Potrebnost. Dialektika Protsessa Truda* (Labour as the First Human Need. The Dialectics of the Process of Labour), Perm (Kn. Izd.) 1965; M. I. ZAITSEVA: *Tvorchestvo kak Tsennost i kak Motiv (na Primere Truda Ingenerno-Tehnicheskih Rabotnikov)* (Creativity as a Value and as a Motive), Moscow (Soviet Sociological Association) 1979.

But more complex problems arise here. The international co-operation is impeded by national myths, ethnic ambitions. Calls for co-operation, for distribution of the spheres of activity are sometimes emotionally perceived as a "national humiliation" or "national offence". The up-to-date task of the theoretician is to be above this mythology, to be able to make clear the rational basis of the international co-operation.

The materialistic idea of economic order for Russia is of a Western meaning, mainly that of German. Its original model was constructed along with other attributes of the Western civilization. And this idea was initially assimilated by the elite (Peter the Great, for example), and only after that it was adopted "below", transforming itself and becoming deformed and eventually losing its identity.

In this context it is important that mutual ethnic values are defined by the extent to which people resist the economic order which the elite is trying to impose. Joseph de Maistre gave some definitions of the Russian character which seems to be quite offensive: "Two inconveniences of the Russian: inconsistency and mendacity. The spirit of distrust and cheat is running in all the veins of the state...Theft, such as plundering, is rare in your country...you are courageous but mild...; however, theft, such as swindling, is permanent. You buy a diamond, it is with a stain; you buy matches, they lack sulphur. All the ways of management are contaminated with this spirit and it is tremendously ruinous."[15] At first sight this sounds like a strong offence; but this is just an emotional reaction of a Western man to another type of economic order. After the First World War, a Russian philosopher ironically wrote: "Of course, under the Germans we shall be better off. They will put everything in order, 'as in Riga'. They will establish police, departments. Let us admit that this is run so badly and stupidly by us. Administration will operate. They won't take bribes, - what a relief! ...Oh, besides: eventually, the Germans will teach us Russian patriotism, as it was done by the wonderful Wigel and Dahl..."[16] In general, this subject ("to surrender" at the mercy

---

15 J. DE MAISTRE: "A Letter to Mr. P. B. Koslovsky about the Russia of 1815", in: *Russkii Archiv. Istoriko-Literaturnyi Sbornik*, Moscow (Chertkov's Library Edition) 1866, pp. 1502-1503.
16 V. V. ROSANOV: "Apokalipsis Nashego Vremeni" (The Apocalypse of Our Time), in: V. V. ROSANOV: *Uedinennoe* (The Secluded), Moscow (Sovremennik) 1991, pp. 90-91.

of civilized nations) can be found everywhere in the Russian culture and is always expressed more or less ironically.

If the theorists will surrender to such emotions, this will hinder an efficient international co-operation. Emotions disarm a partisan of the materialistic idea of the Western order; he is not anymore fitting the framework of purpose rationality of behaviour.

Idealistic aspect. Generally speaking, it is opposite to the materialistic aspect. It implies that the idea of economic order defines its existence, whereas the existence of the transcendental is of the highest value.

In general, it sometimes seems that the 'economic man' himself is not considered in the idealistic approach. Of course, it is assumed that some earthly welfare is necessary but it should not divert us from preparing for the eternal, from difficult and tenacious thinking of the transcendental. Can we speak of "order" here, since the term is borrowed from Western languages? Is it not too artificial? For example, maybe, one should speak of economic harmony rather than of economic order? The words of a poet: "The Land of ours is rich, But so far lacks order", can be interpreted as an assumption of the impossibility of any foreign Western order but not as a desire to establish it.

The idealistic point of view on the economy implies not the purpose rationality model of behaviour but rather some synthesis of the value rationality model and the traditional models. (Perhaps, for the elite it would imply the value rationality model, for the mass the traditional one?) The subject of such an order could not be conceived of as the "economic man". The honesty of the "economic man", his meticulous and conscientious approach would be perceived just as a formalism, pettiness. Bribery could be conceived of as a natural donation, an expression of favour. From the point of view of the modern European culture, such an "economic harmony" is connected with the society of a traditional type, not only Russian.

The values of the world, that still remains "enchanted", actively constitute the economic harmony. This was convincingly shown by S.N. Bulgakov in his religious interpretation of the economic sphere. In every part of economic activity he discovers the "Sofia roots".[17]

In the idealistic point of view, the power is legitimate as far as it is related to the economic order only if it provides the communication of the

---

17 S. N. BULGAKOV: *Filosofia Khozyaistva* (Philosophy of the Economy), in: S. N. BULGAKOV: *Sochineniya* (Works), vol. 1, Moscow (Nauka) 1991.

people and of every individual with God. When M. Gandhi criticizes the Western civilization, he first of all points out that this "civilization is the rejection of religion, and it has so grasped the peoples of Europe that they seem to be partly insane..."[18] A progressive development of production forces is not at all obligatory here. L. Tolstoi writes that "all this external culture, which is considered ... to be an especially important result of the efforts of the Christian mankind, is in fact something absolutely unimportant and so miserable that the Japanese, who are not characterized by any specific spiritual merits, when it became necessary, learned all the scientific wisdom within some decades..."[19] Further, Tolstoi opposes Christianity to European culture: "The Japanese ...have a great advantage...they are not Christians."[20]

It is not even implied that the authorities should regulate and manage the economy. The authorities are *a priori* legitimized by Providence, and consequently, they are designed for the accomplishment of the destiny rather than for management. The point is not the legitimacy of power but the "legitimacy of the epoch". The sacrally legitimized power experiences the same fate that is experienced by the people. There is no question about the evaluation of the legitimacy "from below", by the people: the democratic mechanisms accomplishing such an evaluation, are initially rejected.

The reaction of many Russian philosophers to the First World War provides a lot of examples of this kind. The economic catastrophe of the population was interpreted according to Apocalyptic patterns as the period of spiritual enthusiasm and was opposed to the "dim epoch", "routine epoch":

> "During another, even dimmer epoch, we shall not have this exclusive perception and attentiveness, which we possess today, in the period of the spiritual revival that we are experiencing... During the routine epochs the supertemporal fades, the feeling withers and the very thought sometimes loses the elevation and force of its flight.

---

18 M. K. GANDHI: "'Hind Svaradge', ili Indiiskoe Samoupravlenie" (Hind Svaradge or Indian Self-Government), in: M. K. GANDHI: *Moya Zhizn* (My Life), Moscow (Nauka) 1969, p. 442. Original: M. K. GANDHI: *An Autobiography; or, the Story of My Experiments with Truth*, Ahmedabad (Navajivan Publishing House) 1948.
19 L. N. TOLSTOI: *Gibel Tsivilizatsii i Predstoyatschii Perevorot (Iz Byvshih pod Zapretom Sochinenii L. N. Tolstogo o Nashem Vremeni)* (The Downfall of the Civilization and the Coming Coup), Riga (Without publisher) without year, p. 6.
20 *Ibid.*

> Then the attention is absorbed by the particular and the general is forgotten; the great historical whole is covered by discord of the opposite forces, insignificant details and occasional daily problems, whereas the unique meaning of life is lost and disappears in the flashy chaos of events, as it were."[21]

It is evident that from the materialistic point of view, the war is a destruction of economic order; but from the idealistic one, it is a revelation of the higher law of Providence. On the contrary, routine epochs, when the economic order seemingly dominates, appear as the "flashy chaos of events".

Correspondingly, the loyalty of an individual towards the whole in the Russian consciousness of such a type, as a rule, is not fixed upon one's economic behaviour, but reveals itself as "spirituality", humility, fear of God. Let us continue reading V.V. Rosanov where he says that "the Germans will establish order". It is followed with an unexpected inversion:

> "We shall take possession of their soul so faithfully and warmly, as it was in the case of Wigel, Dahl, Wetenek (Vostokov) and Guilferding... The subjugation of Russia by Germany will be actually, both internally and spiritually, the subjugation of Germany by Russia. We shall eventually turn them (the best of them) into something resembling human beings, not Stallmeisters...Secretly, we shall be their masters, and they will be our nurses, loving and obedient. They will serve us, serve in the material sense. And we shall educate them spiritually."[22]

These words express the weakness of facing the Western civilization, an attempt to compensate for it in the elusive, difficult to define sphere of "spirituality".

The idealistic loyalty (beyond the emotional and ironical but inefficient utopia of V. V. Rosanov) emerges here as different forms of asceticism. I shall again quote E. N. Trubetskoi:

> "And now, in the days of the great trial with fire, Russia expresses contempt towards its wealth and extremely strongly feels the pettiness

---

21 E. N. TRUBETSKOI: "Otechestvennaya Voina i Yeyo Dukhovnyi Smysl" (Patriotic War and its Spiritual Meaning), in: E. N. TRUBETSKOI: *Smysl Zhizni* (The Purport of Life), Moscow (Respublika) 1994, p. 381.
22 ROSANOV: *op. cit.*, p. 90-91.

of material welfare...Now when masses of people sacrifice themselves and a voluntary death is an everyday event, it appears shameful to take care of comfort." [23]

And finally, solidarity, agreement, as an aspect of economic harmony (economic order) is determined in the idealistic view through *Sobornost*, community[24].

Thus, we have tried to present both the aspects of the idea of economic order. Now, let us consider some essential modifications of them, their transformation.

VI. Modifications of the Idea of Economic Order

The two fundamental primary meanings of the idea of economic order described above are subject to modification. This is especially important, when we take into account that in the contemporary "disenchanted" world the idealistic model does not dare to present itself in its most authentic, purely theocratic model.

We have already pointed out that the model of the "planned economy" seems to be at first sight a version of the materialistic approach to the idea of economic order. In reality, it is not so. The value of the "communist tomorrow" is sacral and plays in this model the role of the Absolute. Thus, the model of the "planned economy" is essentially an idealistic aspect of the economic order but, put in "materialistic" language, alien to it. This accounts for the fact that the opposition of the market and the planned economy turned into a hard ideological conflict over the principles.

Besides the communist form, the idealistic model can take the form of the "national idea". We have already seen above how the conflicts in the sphere of the idea of the economic order are rationalized into forms of interethnic conflict (J. de Maistre, V. V. Rosanov). It is not occasional that Gennady Ziuganov, the present leader of the Communist Party of Russia, actively used the national idea in his electoral campaign, striving to defeat the "democrats" whom he called "cosmopolites". Reactionary political regimes

---

23 TRUBETSKOI: *op. cit.*, p. 393.
24 See, for example, FRANK: *ibid.*

of the 20th century have actually realized a hypertrophied idealistic model of economic order; in other words, the idealistic model, taking on communist or nationalist clothes realized itself in the reactionary political regimes. One cannot say that relapses are impossible. On the contrary, the more complex the conditions of mankind are, the more probably such relapses are. But permanent theoretical reduction of communist and nationalistic ideas to their adequate, properly idealistic model, which they are trying to conceal, gives us hope that relapses (at least, in the same form) will be impossible.

VII. Conclusion: Economic Order as an Ecological Order

Let us proceed to the main factor of modernity which not only modifies the two aspects of economic order, materialistic and idealistic, but, through synthesis of them, sets the question of transcending them. It is the ecological factor.

In the first half of the 20th century, people thought, that all major problems of human survival could be resolved with the progress of science, technology and production forces. Up to the 1980s, the classical idea of the modern European civilization dominated.[25] If some nations are rich whereas others are poor, this is accounted for by the fact that the former have secured welfare by hard work in the disciplinary framework of the rational economic order. The poverty of others results from the fact that they have not participated in this kind of order. That is why the common assumption was that the materialistic view of the economic order is the most appropriate. When the South takes after the North, global welfare will emerge.

---

25 See: I. RUVINSKY: "2000 God Glazami Shestidesyatyh i Vosmidesyatyh" (The Year of 2000 Seen by the 60s and 80s), *Znanie-Sila*, 12, Moscow (Molodaya Gvardia) 1984. It was shown in this paper how naive, enthusiastic, full of uncoditional faith in the absolute might of science the authors of the 60s were. And the CPSU Programme of 1961 was also full of enthusiam over the scientific and tehcnological progress. It was this enthusiasm that allowed to promise to accomplish building material and technological basis of communism by 1980. The matter was not only in the voluntarism of N. S. Khrushchev. This was the general prevailing mood both here and in the West.

THE IDEA OF ECONOMIC ORDER IN CONTEMPORARY RUSSIA

But in the second half of the 20th century the ecological problem came forth. The economic order became more and more determined by the ecological order.[26] The Arabian kingdoms are so rich not owing to hard work of their population, but owing to their resources. Scientific and technological progress, as well as that of production forces do not only resolve global problems but aggravate them. The dominant opinion of the present moment is that the economic growth after the Second World War is caused not by the new technologies, not by the Western economic order, but by the opportunity to manage the richest resources of the Near and Middle East. It is not work based on the patterns of the Western economic order, but it is the cheap oil with a low level of contamination "that has put industrialisation at its present height."[27] Thus, the inevitable exhaustion of resources will bring up the catastrophe of the industrial development. The economic order can do nothing about it.

The Western economic order is often understood not as a way of conquering the nature but as a plunderer's violence and as a way of concealing the violence of the rich over the poor nations.[28] The progress of production forces appears to be not a realization of the rational part of man but of one of the elements of the nature which "uses" mankind as its agent: "...mankind is more and more submitted to the mighty and spontaneous geological process, Technogenesis."[29]

The forms of technical development we know about are war-oriented, based upon Galilean science and they destroy the belief in the rationality of the Western economic order. It becomes clear that the technical development is not able to save human labour. Technology can accumulate and redistrib-

---

26 D. H. MEADOWS, D. L. MEADOWS, J. RANDERS, W. W. BEHRENS: *The Limits to Growth,* New York (Universe Books) 1989.
27 V. TAYLOR: "The End of the Oil Age", *Ecologist,* 8/9, vol. 10, Wadebridge (1980), p. 303.
28 FIDEL CASTRO RUZ: *La crisis ecoonmic y social del mundo. Sus repercusiones en los paises subdesarrollados, sus perspectivas sombrial y la necessidad de luchar si gueremos sobrevivir,* La Habana (Oficio de Publ. De Conseijo de Estando) 1983. Another apporach, but the same thesis: I. SHAFAREVICH: "Dve Dorogui k Odnomu Obryvu" (Two Roads to the Same Precipice), *Novyi* Mir, 7, Moscow (Izvestiya) 1989.
29 R. K. BALANDIN: *Geologgicheskaya Deyatelnost Chelovechestva. Tekhnoggenes* (Geological Activities of Mankind. Technogenesis), Minsk (Nauka i Tekhnika) 1978.

ute labour but it cannot replace it. In a general way this was demonstrated by Z. Staikov.[30] The same results were obtained by V. V. Kocheryguin. In 1971-1975 in the national economy of the USSR, the increase of the productivity of labour resulted in saving the labour of 20 million people. At the same time, the growth of fixed capital, which accounts for the growth of production and the growth of productivity of labour, was achieved with the labour of 36 million people.[31] This was not because the planned economy was inefficient at that time. The USA data show the same tendency in another form: in 1974 - 1984 in the USA, notwithstanding automation and, to a great extent owing to it, there were created 18 million additional jobs.[32] New types of technology create more jobs than they liquidate.

All this is very important taking into account that the Western economic order is losing its soteriological significance. The adoption of it, as it appears now, is not able to secure welfare, it is not even able to secure survival. The legitimate power is not that which fixes upon progress of production forces but that which is capable of defending (and maybe seizing) the diminishing natural resources. It is natural in this context that the idealistic aspects in the economic order become more active. (Maybe again in the nationalistic or communist version.) The Western economic order seems to be legitimate only as long as it is producing arms, because it is not labour but nature that is the main factor of welfare and of national survival.

What, then, is the role of the international solidarity which is one of the components of economic order? As a conclusion, let us try to find the essential alternative for the world development. Is national egoism the most relevant strategy for the national survival, or, on the contrary, is it the international economic (and ecological) solidarity since solidarity within a nation alone is not sufficient? One can suppose that the national survival needs the

---

30 Z. STAIKOV: "Nauchno-Tekhnicheskata Revolutsiya - Sotsiologicheski Problemy" (Science and Technology Revolution - Sociological Problems), *Sotsiologicheski problemy*, 3, Sofia (1976), pp. 15-27.
31 V. V. KOCHERYGUIN: "K Voprosu ob Effectivnosti Zameny Zhivogo Truda Mashinnym" (On the Efficiency of Using Machine Labour Instead of Human Labour), *Izvestiya Akademii Nauk SSSR. Ekonomicheskaya Seriya*, 5 (1982), p. 41-53.
32 W. F. MILLER: *New Developments in Technology and Their Implications for Developed and Developing Countries*, (SRI International) 1985.

world economic order, which would be the world ecological order. In particular, this holds true for the economic order in the system "Russia and Germany". The task of theorists is to elaborate an efficient programme of overcoming the national egoism.

Chapter 3

Has the Market Economy Still a Chance? On the Lack of a Disciplining Challenge*

MANFRED E. STREIT

I. Loss of a Disciplining Challenge
II. Decay of Style in Economic Policy
III. Causes of the Decay
IV. The Principle of Social State
V. Damaging Effects on the Economic System
VI. Chances for Reforms

I. Loss of a Disciplining Challenge

1. The question raised in the title may sound peculiar, the more so, if we remember how the two antagonistic social and economic systems have been developing. It seems that one of those systems finally turned out to be what competent analysts, like Ludwig von Mises and Friedrich August von Hayek expected on the basis of arguments which were neglected or played down for a long time, namely a blind alley in societal evolution. Within a dramatically short period of time practically all socialist systems have crumbled. The heritage they left was poverty, decay and potential conflicts, so that even the most hard-headed socialists in capitalist countries were at least temporarily dumbfounded. However, for systems based on a democratic political constitution and a market oriented economic constitution, the loss of the socialist challenge may aggravate immanent dangers. Von Hayek warned us about

---

* My answer is based on a number of earlier studies, the list of which is given at the end. Further references can be found in the studies listed.

HAS THE MARKET ECONOMY STILL A CHANCE?

these dangers almost five decades ago in his political book "The Road to Serfdom". And it was not a matter derision when he dedicated the book "to the socialists of all parties". For him socialism as a model of society enjoying much sympathy in the West had already discredited itself a hundred years ago after the appearance of the Communist Manifesto. But soon after his book had been published, during the post-war economic boom, he feared that socialism would be replaced under the influence of social reformers propagating a "hotchpotch" of inconsistent goals under the label of a welfare state or a social state. Hence he argued that reform proposals should be carefully scrutinised as to whether their consequences would not be quite similar to those of a mature socialism.

2. Actually it was already Alexis de Tocqueville who in the first half of the last century envisaged with surprising insight the development described by von Hayek, though for him it was impossible to make a direct comparison between democracy and the market economy on the one side and socialism on the other. For him the democratic nations were in danger of being subjected to a new kind of despotism. As compared to its historic predecessors, this despotism, according to de Tocqueville, was "milder and more flexible, and it would humiliate people without torturing them". His description of man in the custody of the state, yielding to the loss of freedom and being exposed to isolation, surprisingly agrees with, for instance, warnings of the German sociologist Helmut Schelsky concerning the "improvement of social justice" at the price of personal freedom. There is no lack of telling examples. A particularly abusive case in point is the politically much praised extension of the social insurance system in Germany by introducing a special insurance supposed to cover cases of nursing. Taking into account how such cases are identified and categorized, it is amazing that the German citizens - without apparent protest - accept the fact that they must expose their existence in every, even most intimate detail to public servants, who have to evaluate, categorise and computerise them. Raising no objections, they submit to this humiliating procedure only to gain a deceptive hope for a total dependence on the custody provided by the state.

3. In Germany these aforementioned warnings may be considered as farfetched by those adherents of the "social market economy" who refer to this policy concept in political speeches. However, what has been achieved in practice by emphasizing the social element of the concept has to be considered with concern. Growing doubts are raised in the debate upon Germany as a location for investments when assessing its competitiveness within and

outside the European Union. Hence it seems expedient to consider briefly how the relationship between the "social market economy" as a concept and the political practice changed during almost five decades. Thereafter reasons for this change will be explored. Then I shall turn to deficiencies of the economic order which are characteristic of this change before assessing the chances of the market economy.

II. Decay of Style in Economic Policy

4. Right at the beginning it should be mentioned that the "social market economy" as a policy concept was based on preceding scientific work on economic systems to an extent which is exceptional on an international scale. During the first one and a half decades the politically binding force of this concept was due to special circumstances. The basic decision regarding the economic order was taken for the West Germans, and not by themselves. After the war, the majority of their politicians and trade union leaders considered the market economy obsolete. Their judgement was based on the experience related to the interwar period, but also on ideological positions. The adoption of the "social market economy" as a concept of economic policy has been much more a case for some convinced proponents and for pragmatists with a good sense for political attraction during the election campaign of 1949 than the result of a wide consensus in the later ruling parties. Only the success of an economic policy initially guided by the concept produced a binding force. Temporarily the concept gained almost the status of a political credo. However, it did not go so far that the deviations from the concept, more or less justified at the beginning, were eventually eliminated (e.g. housing policy, agricultural policy).

5. The growing approval by the population of the policy guided by the concept was not based upon a corresponding knowledge of the functioning of a market system and its constitutive elements. Then, as well as now, it seems appropriate to argue like the economist and economic journalist Wolfram Engels who once so aptly characterized the attitude of the general public towards the market economy: "Experienced, though unappreciated". What mattered at first, was the experience of transition from the general loss of orientation and from the agonising general shortage administered by ration-

ing to a rapidly emerging order of social and economic affairs, and also to new chances of earning an income. This open and complex system of a market economy was gradually experienced "... as a state of affairs in which a multiplicity of elements of various kinds are so related to each other that we may learn from our acquaintance with some spatial or temporal part of the whole to form correct expectations concerning the rest, or at least expectations which have a good chance of proving correct." (Hayek)

The quick shaping of an order in this sense can be easily explained. There were still sufficient possibilities to revitalise those rules of a society based on private law, which are conducive to a market economy. Similarly, the values supporting the rules were still shared by the majority. This is what distinguished the Federal Republic of Germany of the late 40s and the 50s from many countries undergoing transformation today.

6. In the 60s the binding force of the concept faded away. The "synthesis of the Keynesian message and the Freiburg imperative" propagated by the economist and then Minister of Economic affairs Karl Schiller by far exceeded the business cycle policy originally envisaged by the concept of the "social market economy". At the same time it was an expression of a constructivist optimism regarding the possibilities to steer the economy in accordance with macroeconomic policy objectives. Later on, the synthesis turned out to be what at least a few German economists - in the first place Hans Besters, Erich Hoppmann and Egon Tuchtfeldt - expected right from the beginning, namely, as a costly failure. This was not only due to the actual political handling of macroeconomic policy but also to its scientific foundation. The experience made supports the hypothesis that the presumed business cycles were largely a product of economic policy itself. To use the terminology of Besters, they were intervention cycles.

7. Since the 70s the political actors predominantly employ merely the epithet "social" when describing their initiatives. Thereby they tend to take it for granted that the economic system functions sufficiently well to cope with the side effects produced by the interventions which correspond to such initiatives. The "social component" has become a sort of trademark for an ephemeral legislation. Its basic objective is redistribution. At least illusions regarding redistribution are permanently nurtured. Similarly, it is part of the decay of style in economic policy, that the conditions for the application of policies in accordance with the so-called stability law establishing a business cycle's policy in 1966 were neglected for the last two decades. As for the policy concept, one can agree with the economist Norbert Kloten: "The

institutional framework of the social market economy has turned out to be not strong enough to contain tendencies towards a politicisation of elements of the economic order...".

III. Causes of the Decay

8. The political opportunism regarding the economic order may be deplored. But on an international scale it is commonplace. In its genesis it can be considered sufficiently explained by political economy or public choice. Opportunism points to the "institutional framework" and thereby to the constitutional character of the prevailing forms of democracy. If in this context a specifically German trait should exist, it would have to refer to a widespread image of the state. It is a traditional perception which manifested itself already in the "social kingdom" of Prussia. The state is assigned the role of a kind of father of the family. It is the task of the state to produce equity of individual incomes and to secure existing opportunities for earning an income. Fairness of distribution in accordance with merit and need as well as protection of the gained socio-economic positions - these are the dominating preconceptions of the values shaping the understanding of the role of the state. Expectations based on such an understanding give birth to "the mirage of social justice" (Hayek). It is a delusion because the moral and social concepts which are characteristic of and can be established within a small group are transferred to the society as a whole.

9. The delusion is based on false conceptions regarding market processes as well as political decision-making. Market processes are judged from the perspective of the Aristotelian Oikonomia, i.e. the closed household economy. The permanent and open process of self-co-ordination and self-control in the market is experienced. However, the market economy remains unappreciated as an unplanned, spontaneous order reflecting Adam Smith's "invisible hand". The Aristotelian understanding leads to an overestimation of the possibilities of a purpose-oriented control over the self-organising market system. This, in turn, is connected with an underestimation of undesirable side effects of attempts to establish such a control. In turn, these side effects may again give reasons to complain about social injustice. The image of political decision-making represents wishful thinking. It reflects a norma-

tive theory of democracy which has already been sharply criticised by Joseph Schumpeter as "the classical doctrine of democracy". It is a preconception of political actors, pursuing well-knowingly and well-meaningfully the interests of their constituencies. This has nothing in common with real political processes.

10. The intellectual fathers of the "social market economy" as a policy concept were probably not aware of the delusive consequences. But they saw, above all, that this concept was conceived as a compromise, and therefore related to a basic conflict. A brief formulation by the economist and secretary of state, who coined the term "social market economy", Alfred Müller-Armack, according to which it is necessary "to combine the principle of freedom in the market with social equity" accurately describes the problem. What the intellectual fathers probably underestimated, was the political dynamics related to the social component of the concept. At least for some of them "social equity" was both a political concern and a concession to win support for the concept. This holds true for Müller-Armack's "social irenics" and Rüstow's "vital politics", as well as for Röpke's "economic humanism". But it should be noted that soon Röpke and Rüstow, like the leading figures of the ordo-liberal Freiburg school of law and economics, Franz Böhm and Walter Eucken, opposed the political practice labelled "social market economy". The intervention criterion of "conformity to the market" was intended to secure a reasonable compromise. But as early as 1954, the criterion was unequivocally rejected by the Federal Constitutional Court as a valid reason for appeal in order to revise interventionist legislation.

IV. The Principle of Social State

11. Whereas the Court considered the constitution "neutral" regarding a specific economic system, the principle of social state (Sozialstaatsprinzip) as a constitutional norm assigned to politicians an "unqualified authorisation", as formulated by Ernst Benda, a former judge of the Federal Constitutional Court. According to him, the state is authorised to carry out "socially constructive activity". The extreme bias of the compromise between free-

dom in the market and social equity or social justice which was practically struck by political actors has several reasons:

(1) The constructive mission implies a variety of meanings which cannot be delimited in a stringent way. This permits to justify permanently new interventions by referring to the ever-changing material and social conditions.

(2) It is this authority that politicians use as a tool for pursuing goals of their own when competing for positions and when responding to the pressure of vested interests.

(3) Those measures considered most suitable for gaining electoral support are usually the least compatible with the functional conditions of a market system.

In other words, the conflict is almost all the time resolved at the expense of individual freedom and responsibility.

12. From the viewpoint of conformity to a market system the fundamental conflict arises because the rules which are constitutive to market processes in the majority of cases are different from those legitimised by objectives of the social state. On the one hand there are general, abstract (universal) rules, on the other the rules tailored to satisfy the interests of certain groups. The latter reflect intentions to redistribute income and wealth or to protect socio-economic positions. The disillusioning results of numerous studies analysing the implementation of the principle of the social state permit to draw, above all, two conclusions:

(1) The estimated cost-benefit ratio of measures to implement the principle tends to become most unfavourable when those costs are taken into account which arise from compensating undesirable side effects of the original measures.

(2) The actual measures taken can be too easily explained by opportunistic policy making without any reference to the idea of social justice.

13. Alongside with measures aiming at social justice an ethical reorientation of the private law can be observed in legislation and jurisdiction. Traditional rules of private law serve to guarantee freedom of action. Freedom of action is linked to personal responsibility. Personal responsibility also means looking after one's own interests when engaging in market activities. Taking care of one's own interests includes also decisions regarding expenses on transaction costs in order to discover alternative opportunities. The greater the propensity to incur transaction costs on both sides of the market, the more intensive will be the competitive control of market rela-

tions. In this respect competition is based on personal responsibility when making use of the freedom of action. Insofar as this personal responsibility is not limited due to health problems and comparable reasons, and the freedom of action is not illegally restricted by others, contracts based on private law essentially draw the guarantee of their authenticity from the freedom of action. An ethical re-orientation takes place, above all, by reinforcing the protection of that party to a contract which has been assessed by the legislature as the weaker one, or by imposing additional obligations upon the party considered the stronger one. Regarding jurisdiction, the consequence of this ethical re-orientation is an assessment of the material as opposed to the formal quality of legal transactions. Because of the protective requirement the guarantee of authenticity becomes questionable. The practice of judicial assessment of the material content, e.g. regarding contracts of employment in Germany, led to peculiarities which are markedly influenced by considerations of social justice. This kind of jurisdiction should have induced specialists in law within parliament to take a closer look at the quality of the corresponding laws they had passed. This is also true for the observation that the protection of the party declared the weaker one frequently brings more harm to it than good. An excessive protection of one side of the market induces restrictive reactions on the other side. This aggravates or even creates anew those problems whose prevention had been the objective of legislation. But legislation supposed to serve social justice is not so much guided by economic insights than by political necessities as identified by political actors.

V. Damaging Effects on the Economic System

14. Comparing the concept of "social market economy" with the political practice, I would like to emphasise three deficiencies which make themselves felt more and more clearly. The first deficiency refers to a lack of conformity of the practised social justice with the functional requirements of the economic system. It reflects a misuse of social policy and emerges from the process of political competition. This misuse also represents a misapprehension of the market economy being an unplanned, spontaneous order. Such an order does not completely exclude establishing elements of a social state but it requires a reorganisation of a number of a arrangements suppos-

edly to serve social justice and a withdrawal of group privileges. For example, concrete proposals have been developed on how to provide a basic pension for everybody instead of nurturing the illusion of an all-embracing social security. In the same vein it is possible to establish a less costly system of taxation and redistribution. If group privileges were withdrawn, which is a key element of all proposals aiming at deregulation, including those related to the labour market, also protectionism in international trade would have to be abandoned. It is the poorest in the world community who are harmed most by restrictions of trade. Refusing to give the less developed countries a chance to earn an income by engaging in trade reflects a scandalous attempt to secure socio-economic positions in developed countries in the name of social justice. Given this, so-called development aid amounts to bribing the less developed countries to accept protectionism. And experience has shown that development aid tends to produce more harm than good. Furthermore, protectionism turns out to be self-damaging in the long run, being a policy directed at conserving industrial structures instead of benefiting from change.

15. The second deficiency results from poor policy responses to emerging problems. Environmental problems can serve as an example. In this case the heart of the matter is not a market failure, the importance of which should be determined by the efficiency criteria which could only be made operational by using more knowledge than there is to know. What really matters is that the system of rules governing the market process has to be amended by taking into account externalities, referring in this case to effects of using the environment. The scope of amendments depends upon the extent to which the use of the environment as a productive resource and as a depository of pollutants is considered acceptable. There is no way in determining this scope in an objective and stringent way. Like the extent of redistribution it is a matter of collective decision making. The only thing science can do is to enlighten such a decision by pointing out the consequences which the various choices are likely to have. Considering the spectrum of basic possibilities in environmental policy, ranging from legal rules to incentive oriented control, the state of the art is well advanced. There is no doubt that the problem of acquiring concrete steering knowledge is ever present. However, problems going beyond that are mostly consequences of political halfheartedness and of escapism. Be it, for example, agriculture, energy production or transportation: in these cases much could be done to respond to the environmental problems. However, political opportunism is

HAS THE MARKET ECONOMY STILL A CHANCE?

ever present. It is the special treatment which these sectors receive that is an obstacle from the environmental point of view. No conflict exists between the market economy and the environment. The heart of the matter is a recurrent, general problem of the welfare state. And the problem becomes obscured, if not tabooed, when employing ethical statements as it is frequently the case in the debate upon environmental issues. The problem is political opportunism reflected by attempts to accommodate special interests of sectors like those just mentioned.

16. At the same time political opportunism reflects a third and fundamental deficiency, namely the institutional framework of the prevailing form of democracy. In a moving speech before the German Economic Association (Verein für Socialpolitik) in Dresden in autumn 1932, Alexander Rüstow hit the crucial point regarding the political surrender to vested interests: "What is now going on here, has a motto: 'The state as booty'". It has been shown again and again how small the chances are that politicians would remove that deficiency on the basis of their insight and free will. For example, the proposals of the joint constitutional commission, formed according to the German unification treaty of 1990 would have led to even larger deficiency in this respect. On the level of the European integration, the same holds true for the Maastricht treaty if it is compared with the Treaty of Rome which gave birth to the European Economic Community. Hence there is little chance that the political actors themselves are prepared to prevent a surrender to vested interests by binding themselves with corresponding constitutional rules.

VI. Chances for Reforms

17. Reforms according to the motto "more market" or even "more constitutional state" could, at best, provoke politicians to give the verdict of "not feasible". The reluctance of political actors to undertake even those reforms which have been clearly identified as necessary, can easily be explained by employing the theory of public choice. The political mechanism which leads to a perpetual growth of privileges for specific groups works also as a ratchet against reforms. A political reversal in economic and social policies would require to take away privileges in distribution and security from their respective groups. This would trigger their protest. Since the de-

sirable positive effects of reforms on the economic system tend to be widespread and difficult to identify they are not likely to recruit political support for the reformers which would offset the losses of support from special interest groups due to a manifest withdrawal of privileges. And as public opinion polls usually indicate, the conflict between political practices in the name of the social state and economic necessities either goes unnoticed or is pushed aside. Hopes are still high that the bill for the provision of privileges will be paid by someone else - be it with taxes or duties, or with unemployment of others.

18. Hence, the principle of "voice" (Albert O. Hirschman) which is characteristic of democratic decision making processes turns out to be a one-way traffic lane when considering chances for reforms. However, pressure to remove costly privileges and to reorganise social services may come from another principle, namely "exit". This principle does not only govern the shadow economy within a country but also competition between countries for mobile resources. Exit from the official economy into the shadow economy not only stands for ways to avoid or evade the growing burden of taxes and of social insurance contributions. It also signifies that labour markets could be more flexible and more responsive to unemployment if only unions, employer organisations and the state which is frequently backing up their agreements would make it possible. Part of the shadow economy are also private initiatives to offer social services. These offers signal that willingness to become involved in charity is still alive in society. It could be even promoted to ease the pressure on the collective systems of social security which, as anonymous mass organisations, simply cannot live up to the expectations permanently raised by politicians.

19. The second force of "exit" mentioned above and referring to competition among governments for internationally mobile resources represents an important aspect of the on-going discussion of Germany as a location for investments. The basic reasoning underlying this discussion runs as follows: The attraction of a country as a location for investments also depends on its institutional framework. The framework can influence the competitiveness of private actors in international trade, for example, by differences in taxation, labour laws, consumer protection, administrative procedures etc. To the extent to which the framework is produced by the legislature and the jurisdiction it can be employed to improve the attraction of the country in question. Corresponding decisions have to receive parliamentary consent. Hence the resulting competition among suppliers of institutional systems is a com-

plex phenomenon, comprising competition between national political actors responding upon actual and potential decisions of private competitors. In other words competition among systems implies a linkage between the two principles, "voice" and "exit". From the point of view of reforms, it can have a disciplining effect on political actors, making them more aware of a reasonable balance between measures which supposedly foster social justice and requirements of a competitive private sector. And beyond the public debate in Germany there is sufficient evidence that the improved international mobility particularly of capital does not go unnoticed by political actors.

20. However, the relevance of the two mechanisms of "exit" for actual reforms should not be overestimated. Ultimately elections have to be won at home and political actors as well as the electorate may not necessarily arrive at an economically convincing diagnosis of the competitiveness of the domestic economy. What appears to exert pressure to revise policies, though not always in the best possible way, are symptoms of the shadow economy and of the competition among systems, namely negative effects on public revenue. Not only in Germany it is the empty public purse which in one way or the other asks for remedial action. It becomes increasingly difficult to sustain policies which "buy time" for adjustment and gloss over deficiencies in the capacity of the economic system to adjust and to innovate, deficiencies which have been produced by ill-considered legislation and corresponding policies. This may also be the time when "voice" in terms of public resentment can be transformed into electoral support for reforms as it has happened in several countries. Taking up the question raised in the title, I can now give an answer: Even within an ageing Western Europe the market system has still a reasonable chance to survive, though it may well be possible that the chance will be used only after having gone through a process of pathological learning.

MANFRED E. STREIT

References

BOEHM, F.: "Privatrechtsgesellschaft und Marktwirtschaft", *Ordo,* 17 (1966), pp. 75-151.
DEREGULIERUNGSKOMMISSION: *Marktöffnung und Wettbewerb,* Stuttgart (Poeschel) 1991.
ENGELS, W.: "30 Jahre Soziale Marktwirtschaft - erlebt aber unverstanden", *Vortragsreihe der Landesbank Rheinland-Pfalz,* Heft 6 (1977).
HAYEK, F. A.: "The Results of Human Action but not of Human Design" in: F. A. HAYEK: *Studies in Philosophy, Politics and Economics,* London und Henley (Routledge & Kegan Paul) 1967, pp. 96-105.
HAYEK, F. A.: *Recht, Gesetzgebung und Freiheit. Band 1: Regeln und Ordnung,* Landsberg am Lech (mi-Verlag Moderne Industrie) 1973/1986.
KLOTEN, N.: "Der Staat in der Sozialen Marktwirtschaft", *Walter Eucken Institut: Vorträge und Aufsätze,* 108, Tübingen (Mohr [Siebeck]) 1986.
KRONBERGER KREIS: *Bürgersteuer - Entwurf einer Neuordnung von direkten Steuern und Sozialleistungen,* Schriftenreihe, Bd. 11, Bad Homburg (Frankfurter Institut) 1986.
KRONBERGER KREIS: *Das soziale Netz reißt - Vorschläge zur Rettung des Systems der sozialen Sicherheit,* Schriftenreihe, Bd. 16, Bad Homburg (Frankfurter Institut) 1988.
MUELLER-ARMACK, A.: "Soziale Irenik", in: W. STUETZEL u.a. (Hrsg.): *Grundtexte zur Sozialen Marktwirtschaft,* Stuttgart und New York (Fischer) 1950/81, pp. 417-432.
MUELLER-ARMACK, A.: "Soziale Marktwirtschaft" in: *Handwörterbuch der Sozialwissenschaften,* Stuttgart et al. (Fischer et al.) 1956, pp. 390-392.
ROEPKE, W.: *Civitas Humana - Grundfragen der Gesellschafts- und Wirtschaftsreform,* Bern (Haupt) 1944/79, 4. Aufl. 1979.
RUESTOW, A.: *Ortsbestimmung der Gegenwart,* 3. Bd., Zürich (Eugen Rentsch) 1957.
STREIT, M. E.: "Entstaatlichung der Wirtschaft - Eine ordnungspolitische Notwendigkeit", in: *FiW, Beschränkung des Staatlichen Einflusses in der Wirtschaft,* FiW-Schriftenreihe Heft 155, Köln (Heymanns) 1993, pp. 1-10.
STREIT, M. E. (1994a): "Das Leitbild der Sozialen Marktwirtschaft - Konsens, Konfliktfelder, Defizite, Reformchancen", in: *Markt mit Moral - Das ethische Fundament der Sozialen Marktwirtschaft,* Gütersloh (Verlag Bertelsmann-Stiftung) 1994, pp. 203-214.
STREIT, M. E. (1994b): "Westeuropas Wirtschaftsverfassungen unter dem Druck des Systemwettbewerbs", *LIST FORUM für Wirtschafts- und Finanzpolitik,* 20 (1994), pp. 111 - 124.

HAS THE MARKET ECONOMY STILL A CHANCE?

STREIT, M. E.: "Dimensionen des Wettbewerbs - Systemwandel aus ordnungsökonomischer Sicht", *Zeitschrift für Wirtschaftspolitik,* 44, 2 (1995) pp. 113-134.

VAUBEL, R.: "Der Mißbrauch der Sozialpolitik in Deutschland: Historischer Überblick und Politisch-ökonomische Erklärung", in: G. RADNITZKY und H. BOUILLON (Hrsg.): *Ordnungstheorie und Ordnungspolitik,* Berlin, New York, Tokyo (Springer) 1991, pp. 173-201.

Chapter 4

The Chances for Economic Order in Post-Soviet Russia

SERGEY A. NIKOLSKY

I. The Will to an Economic Order
II. The Example of the Agrarian Sector
III. Prospects for the Future

The central conception of the paper is "order" (*poriadok*). One of the definitions of this term given in V. Dahl's dictionary describes "order" as "correct organisation, adherence to proportion, to sequence, to certain arrangement of things". The derivative conception, "orderliness", (*poriadochnost*) adds to the main conception a moral connotation[1]. It is in these two contexts - rationality and morality - that the term will be applied in this paper.

I. The Will to an Economic Order

Organisation and reorganisation of the social and economic entity may take place in the situation of either "disorder" or "order". It is obvious, that the destruction of social economic systems (for example, the break-up of the Roman Empire) is a transition from a certain order to disorder, chaos. As for

---

1 VLADIMIR DAHL: *Tolkovyi Slovar Zhivogo Velikorusskogo Yazyka* (Explanatory Dictionary of the Great-Russian Spoken Language), Vol. 3, Reprint Moscow (Terra) 1995, p. 327.

the emergence of new social formations, they are possible both in the situation of order and the situation of chaos.

Was, for example, the construction of the USSR following the distruction of tsarist Russia in the beginning of the 20s of the 20th century a phenomenon of order? The papers of the theorists of bolshevism, written both before and after the October revolution of 1917, present a logical system describing the principles, the structure and the mechanisms of constructing the communist society. In these papers the necessity and historic inevitability of the formation of a new social and economic organism are rationally grounded. But as man is not only a rational, but also an ideological and moral being, which was well understood by the leaders of bolshevism, in their papers we can also find an attempt to create a new morality[2]. It is in these two contexts (which were to a certain extent artificial and anti-human) that one can speak about the construction of socialism in the USSR as of a phenomenon of order.

What creates the prerequisites for a new economic order in the initial stage of its formation, in other words, what makes it possible? (From now on I shall refer in my analysis to the Soviet and to the post-Soviet society of the period starting from mid-eighties, that is, from the moment when Gorbachev came to power, and up to the present time.)

First, **a fairly large part of the society was inclined to accomplish changes which imply order**. In fact, in the beginning of the "perestroika" there were social groups of this kind in different layers of the Soviet society. In the rural society this layer was represented by the executives, specialists and qualified agricultural workers of agricultural production complexes (APC). Due to their previous life style (under the dominance of an administrative-commanding system operating according to the canons of a planned economy) they were inclined to favour the regulated, gradual measures creating a new order. At the same time, the morality according to which they really lived, due to its contents could play an essential role in the possible formation of a new order, although in some of its aspects this actual morality was different from the officially declared communist morality.

---

[2] I demonstrated this by referring to the distruction of the old and the creation of the new agricultural system in Russia in 1917 - 1933 in S. NIKOLSKY: *Vlast i Zemlya. Khronika Utverzhdeniya Byurokratii v Derevne Posle Oktyabrya* (Power and Land. The Chronicle of Establishing Bureaucracy in the Country After the October Revolution), Moscow (Agropromizdat) 1990.

SERGEY A. NIKOLSKY

This part of the society partly expected and partly demanded changes to be accomplished by the power of that time represented by the leaders of the CPSU who were of a reformatory disposition - M. Gorbachev, A. Yakovlev, E. Shevardnadze and some others. But M. Gorbachev's caution and hesitation which were beyond common sense did not allow to employ this source of rational orderly social reformation. As for the other rationally thinking politicians of the highest level, they were either initially oriented towards chaos, considering it to be the most efficient way of breaking the old order and constructing a new one, or - due to their habit of acting only in the framework of the old order, that is, of obeying the will of the higher executive, - kept "waiting for the command" to start creating a new order. (This fact has been confirmed by their memoirs.)

Second, **the ideology of economic reforms based on order should be developed** when the reforms are at their initial stage. Partly it may certainly contain the critique of the previous economic and social order doomed to destruction. (As it is known, in the USSR in the second half of the 1980s, the critique of the communist ideology was widely spread.) But at the same time, along with the critique there should have been developed a positive ideological content of the new social and economic order. And, to my mind, this new ideology ought to be consistent with the social expectations ideologically not yet formed, but existing within the part of the society that is most active and willing to have changes. Unfortunately, this did not happen in the USSR during the last years of its existence.

For instance, the emergence and gradual fading away of farming in Russia is considered to be a well-known economic phenomenon. In 1992 it was obvious that the ideology of farming in agriculture became very popular among the urban intellectuals. Nothing inspired a certain part of Russian intelligentsia so much as the opportunity to call for the dispersion of the collective farms and the imposition of individual farms. It happened this way because the very ideas of the individual based solely on the private property farming were not consistent with the social disposition of the wide layers of the rural society. More over, it partly happened this way because people who, due to various reasons, defended collective farming were ideologically persecuted, and there was formed a negative rather than a positive attitude to farming in the country.

For establishing a new economic order at the initial stage of its development, there should also take place a profound reform of the structures governing the society. Without this profound reform a new order (as far as we mean its rational gradual introduction "from above") cannot be established. The activities of the representative and legislative power and of mass media should also be focused on the course of establishing a new order. In the sphere of the economy, there should be reformed the system of finance, be created a working monetary system, be introduced free price formation, efficient control of monopolies, etc.[3]

Everything mentioned above comprises the prerequisites of the emergence and development of a new economic and social order.

II. The Example of the Agrarian Sector

The total critique of the Soviet society and de-ideologisation of the social life in the period of the "perestroika" and the stagnation of the governing bodies of the state and the party, which occurred up to August of 1991, caused such a situation, that the most active part of the society, including the one that had been previously inclined to accomplish the social and economic reforms for establishing order, chose other - disorderly and often dishonourable - forms of social conduct. The point was in the seizure of a part of the social wealth, conducted as fast as possible, in a legal, semi-legal or illegal way, and in turning this part of the state property into the private property without prior permission. The huge capital of the so-called "new Russians", made within a couple of years, are known to be based on the three sources: credits received from the state at a small rate of interest (while the inflation rate was much higher than the interest rate), licenses for imports donated by the state (first of all, import of food) and licenses for export (raw materials).

In the agrarian sector of economy, the domination of disorder over order, that is, at the initial stage, the destruction of the old order was, to a great extent, the result of a lack of ideology and policy that were consistent with the condition of the agrarian sector. Now, five years after the first government acts on agrarian reforms were adopted, it is possible to see those real

---

[3] To my mind, these issues are considered systematically and in detail by H. LAMPERT in: *Sotsialnaya Rynochnaya Ekonomika. Germanskij Put* (Social Market Economy. The German Way), Moscow (Delo) 1994.

grounds that inspired the authors of the project of the accelerated modernisation of the Russian village, the project that eventually was rejected by reality.

The first ground - their trust in the efficiency of private property of the means of production and, first of all, land, as it is considered to be the main powerful factor of agrarian modernisation that starts operating immediately.

The second ground - their prior and, as time has proved, main attention to the issues of internal economic reform with nearly absolute lack of attention to the problems of interaction of agricultural producers with the processing enterprises, trade, maintenance structures (supply, procurement, sale).

The third ground - their disregard of social issues, that is, of the whole sphere of life-maintenance of the rural population, which became possible first of all due to the personal attitude to the peasantry as "second rate" people. (This was proved by the persecution of the executives of big collective farms who were shown as "red landlords" in the "liberal" press in 1992 - 1993.)

It is natural, that the reform, understood so narrowly and at the same time officially suggested for fulfilment, could not win the support of the agrarian producer, and of the rural population in general. That is why, on the one hand, these reforms were not wide spread, and, on the other hand, where they were introduced, they were essentially transformed.

First of all, it concerned the issue of property of the means of production and land resources. Lack of land cadastre and of a wide system of land committees with a sufficient quantity of qualified staff at the regional level made this idea unfeasible all along. Besides, seeing, that the economic reform every year became less and less oriented towards the production interests in general, and those of the village in particular, the peasants, owing to their traditional caution and common sense, did not hurry to put land into market circulation, land being a fundamental economic and life resource.

Due to the mistakes made in the course of privatisation of complexes of processing, maintenance and trade, these complexes became absolutely controlled by their staff, and agricultural producers turned out to be barred from the participation in the privatisation, which caused the isolation and contradiction of interests of these natural partners of the agricultural production complexes (APCs)[4]. As a result, the peasants lost the impetus to increase the

---

4   According to the data of Vice Head of the Department of Agrarian Policy of the Ministry of Agricultural Production of Russia, V. NOVIKOV, about 90% of the processing complexes were privatised on the basis of this scheme by November

volume of production, as the processors and the trade artificially cut the transfer prices, while increasing to maximum the prices at which the goods were sold to the consumers. (The last also worked against the peasantry, as the high prices could be afforded only by a small number of the consumers, thus decreasing the number of consumers.)

Five years of agrarian reforms of 1992 - 1996 resulted in serious degradation processes in farming, and today there can be distinguished the following main groups of agricultural producers.

First, the formerly strong farms that accomplished the reforms only to that extent to which it was necessary for reaching the optimum production efficiency under the present economic conditions.

Second, the farms that in the past could be described as "average" in efficiency and that managed to adjust only partly to the new unfavourable economic reality - that is, some changes took place there and some (the best) part of the peasantry and specialists managed to survive and to get adjusted to the new reality. As for the rest, they either to some extent interact with the former, or are not included in the process of large scale commercial farming, either being engaged in natural farming, or simply degrading.

Third, the farms the members of which, having no resources and leaders, distributed among themselves (mainly sporadically) the means of production and became absolutely engaged in natural farming on their private plots. It is natural that the processes of economic and social degradation here are the strongest.

It is obvious that at present no one is able to assess quantitatively the ratio of these three types of farms. Although it is clear that, taking into account the lack of any reasonable well-thought of strategy of agrarian reforms during the past five years, the first group of farms cannot be numerous. At the same time, the number of people pushed into natural farming, as well as pushed out of normal life, is large. (It should be noted that for Russia this is really a serious problem, as in 1995 in the countryside there lived 40 million people, 10 million of them engaged in agriculture.)

It should be also noted that the described state of affairs emerged only two years ago and that is why it has not been yet followed by the reaction of those "pushed out", and what took place has not been yet comprehended

---

1996, in 80% of them the controlling block of shares turned out to belong to the staff members of the complex: *Ekonomika i Zhizn* (Economy and Life) No 47 (November 1996).

completely either by the victims or by their children. And it should not be doubted that this is sure to happen and the reaction to this new violence of the power of the government (inactivity that caused such deplorable consequences) is sure to follow in this or that form. The forms may be either passive or active, but in either case they will negatively affect the further social and economic development.

It is natural that what has taken place in the agrarian sphere cannot be described as order with its moral constituent. And the reformers, including those who may replace the "radical-liberals" of the beginning of the 90s, will have to bear the responsibility for this.

Were the authors of the radical reforms aware of the fact that the economic disorder was not desired, did they take it as a concomitant inevitable evil, or was it their conscious course? These questions are far from being idle. They imply the degree of historic responsibility for the caused chaos.

Let us consider the conception of Ye. Gaydar, who was the author of the radical reforms of the years from the end of 1991 until 1992. His interpretation of the market emergence in Russia claims that with the absolute power of the nomenclatura, the property during the transition period will still remain in its, the nomenclatura's, hands. The possibility of another way of owning property, of another form, of another owner is not discussed. Under these conditions, the market mechanism ought not to be regulated for getting started, it ought to be absolutely free, unconstrained. This is the only means to prevent the nomenclatura from keeping the power, it still owning the property. Gaidar's text runs as follows: "Russia cannot and should not be taken from nomenclatura by force, it may be 'redeemed'. If the property is separated from power, if a free market emerges in which the property will anyway constantly move, obeying the law of competition, this is the optimum solution. Let the nomenclatura initially hold the strongest positions in this market, this is just a guarantee of the continuity of property rights. Later, each owner will have to confirm his positions by his deeds. In any case, such an exchange of power for property would mean a step forward, away from 'imperialism' to a free open market, from the 'Asian way of production' to the European one. It would mean the end of nomenclatura itself as a stable, lifelong, inherited political economic elite, not subjected to the laws of the market".[5]

---

[5] YEGOR GAIDAR: *Gosudarstvo i Evolutsia* (The State and the Evolution), Moscow (Evrasia) 1995, pp. 143-144.

ECONOMIC ORDER IN POST-SOVIET RUSSIA

The past years proved that instead of the free capitalism intended by the radical reformers, as they admitted themselves, there emerged a criminal capitalism, with which the state attempts to fight, and that does not add any freedom to the model of the market economy which was thought of at the end of 1991. Why did it happen and are there still any chances for transition to the orderly construction of an efficient economic system?

III. Prospects for the Future

A brief answer to the question concerning the discrepancy between "the emerged", "the actual", and "the intended", "the proper", should take into account that such a mechanism is not adequate and hence not feasible in essence when there is no totalitarian society and state (and no intention to create it). The intentional destruction of the state management system that was of little efficiency, but still worked, without attempting to re-orientate it towards the constructing reformation, was a mistake. In agriculture, for example, this might consist of purposeful attempts to re-orientate the state governing bodies to the processes of the reformation of the whole system of the agricultural production complex (APC), to the creation of market infrastructure, to price regulation both inside the APCs and among the APCs and other sectors of economy. As for the prices, such a regulation did take place: low prices are dictated to the producer by the natural economic partners - processors, dealers, maintenance structures. Among those the most influential are Mafia structures engaged in importing food and monopolistic provision the agrarian producers with the resources.

And still, an efficient economic system in Russia has chances, this has been proved by some tendencies in the development of the APCs. The point is that the place of the state, deprived of all regulating functions and, in fact, removed from the governing system, which seriously damaged the APCs, is being taken by those entrepreneurial and financial structures that are oriented not to the export of capital from the country thus turning the country into the raw adjunct of developed states, but to the efficient production and recovery of the economic potential of Russia. First of all, these structures, which is natural, turned to the most efficient and quickly recoupable projects in the sphere of furnishing with resources the agrarian producer, processing and sales of his products. This gave the initial results, but soon it turned out that the efficiency of the final links in the chain "producer - processor - structures furnishing the resources - trade" depends on the efficiency of the first link.

Due to this, at present in Russia, there started a new stage of the movement of the entrepreneurship into the agrarian sphere. One of the evidences of this is the fact that the largest and quite inefficient bank operating in the field of agriculture - "Agroprombank" - was turned into a partly state owned bank. One of the largest Russian banks operating with the deposits of the citizens - "Savings Bank of the Capital City" ("Stolichny Bank Sberezheny") ("SBS") - not a long time ago (November of 1996) won the competition for the right to join "Agroprombank" with the formation of a new banking structure "SBS - AGRO". "SBS" gets more than 1200 local branches of "Agroprombank" with the compulsory depositing of large funds in the resources of the new bank, the state considerably participating in the aggregate capital of the new structure. It may be assumed that the credit policy of the new private-state banking structure will prove to be more efficient than the former one, which was orientated exceptionally towards the state credits.

At the same time, there are quite a few spheres in the APCs where the private capital will flow only if it has to (due to low and long-time return of the investments). This, for example, concerns the improvement of land resources, measures on natural resources conservation, social policy, the restructuring of inefficient farms of agrarian producers. The problem of affordable consumer prices on agricultural products (essential commodities should have low price lest they should shake the trust in the reforms or cause social upheaval) and the problem of the intersectorial balance cannot be solved only by means of private capital. These should be taken care of by the state, embedded into its agrarian strategy.

Thus, after five years of transformations in the post-Soviet Russia, the issue of creating economic order is still crucial. This implies creating an economic order that would be consistent with the interests of the most active and worthy (honest) part of the population of Russia, an economic order that would have efficient economic and acceptable social prospects significant for the whole society, while the state would collect its strength to do what only it should do in the interests of the country.

Chapter 5

The Social Market Economy: Social Equilibration of Capitalism and Consideration of the Totality of the Economic Order
Notes on Alfred Müller-Armack

PETER KOSLOWSKI

I. The Social Market Economy and the Post-Marxist Theory of Capitalism
II. Social Equilibration, Totality of the Conditions of the Economic Order, Critique of Doctrinaire Liberalism
III. Social Market Economy and Neo-Liberalism
IV. A Synthesis of Social Equilibration (*Ausgleich*) and of the Guarantee of the Free Working of the Market Forces
V. Social Objectives and Tasks of Social Policy in the Social Market Economy
VI. The Social Market Economy as a Means of Social Peace-Making
VII. The Social Market Economy and Economic Reconstruction
VIII. Conclusion

The theory of the social market economy developed in the German tradition of economics particularly in the years after the end of World War II is a theory of the market economy and of capitalism that responded to the critique of capitalism in the Marxist and other traditions by taking up some of the points of this critique, by refuting its general critique of the market, and by reforming and extending the theory of the market.

The theory of the social market economy accepts from the analysis of the theory of capitalism that there are dialectical developments in the market process and the formation of capital possible - but not as Marxism assumed necessary. As a result, the theory of the social market economy contends that it is necessary to analyze and counterbalance or equilibrate certain processes in which negative side effects or externalities of the market process might accumulate. This equilibration of the market process is, however, done without giving up the general and basic orientation of the economic order and process upon the model of the market economy. The theory of the social market economy tries to develop, in contrast to the utopian ideal of pure capitalism, an institutional framework for the social equilibration of capitalism without abandoning the concept of a capitalist order with its emphasis on private property, utility and profit maximization, and co-ordination by markets.

I. The Social Market Economy and the Post-Marxist Theory of Capitalism

Alfred Müller-Armack as the leading theorist and inventor of the term "social market economy" has repeatedly emphasized that the theory of the social market economy developed from the research into the origins and nature of capitalism in the post-Marxist theory of capitalism of the years 1900 to 1930. The theory of the social market economy is grounded in the theory of capitalism. Müller-Armack writes in 1973: "The present field of thought of the social market economy has been prepared by scientific analysis that has had as its object the rise of our modern industrial society from the 16th century. I mean the post-Marxist research and theory of capitalism of the years 1900 to 1930. An astonishing fact: this period of economic and social science has been almost forgotten today."[1] Müller-Armack mentions

---

1   A. MUELLER-ARMACK: "Die wissenschaftlichen Ursprünge der Sozialen Marktwirtschaft" (1973), p. 179: "Das heutige Gedankenfeld der Sozialen Marktwirtschaft wurde durch wissenschaftliche Analysen vorbereitet, die das Entstehen unserer modernen Industriegesellschaft seit dem 16. Jahrhundert zum Gegenstand hatten. Ich meine die in der Zeit von 1900 bis 1930 zu hoher blüte gelangte nachmarxistische Kapitalismusforschung. Eine bemerkenswerte Tatsache: Diese Periode unserer Wissenschaft ist heute fast dem Vergessen anheimgefallen. (All translations from the German language and from Müller-

THE SOCIAL MARKET ECONOMY: NOTES ON MÜLLER-ARMACK

the works of Werner Sombart, Max Weber, but also of Jakob Strieder on the genesis of modern capitalism as well as the works of the Historical School of Economics, of Gustav Schmoller and Karl Lamprecht.[2]

What is the result of this post-Marxist analysis of capitalism of the years 1900 to 1930[3] and its impact for the theory of the social market economy? Müller-Armack himself gives a list of nine points central for the development of the social market economy:

1. On the ground of neutral scientific research, the successful critique of the economic content of the Marxist theory had been developed. The developmental laws of capitalism, the heart of the Marxist theory, with its elements of the theory of value, the theory of accumulation, the theory of exploitation, the law of the tendency of the rate of profit to fall, have been subjected to an extensive examination that resulted in the fact that very little was left of the Marxist approach. It also has had the effect that Marxist theory turned from the elder Marx the economist to the younger Marx of the critique of culture and alienation.

2. The primitive theory of the capitalist mode of production has been replaced by new ways of conceptualizing the market economy in terms of economic systems, styles, constitutions for which historical research produced an enormous material for historical comparison and classification.

3. The theory of the social market economy owes to the tradition of the post-Marxist tradition of the theory of capitalism, particularly to Max Weber, but also to Werner Sombart, the insight into the importance of the mental, scientific and religious factors in the economic history of modern times. The materialist theory of history which remained a postulate of the Marxist philosophy of history and tried to avoid being scrutinized by historical research

---

Armack's texts in this paper are by P.K.). Cf. also A. MUELLER-ARMACK: "Der humane Gehalt der sozialen Marktwirtschaft" (1973), pp. 168 f.

2 Cf. for the Historical School of Economics P. KOSLOWSKI (Ed.): *The Theory of Ethical Economy in the Historical School* (1995).

3 Cf. for the post-marxist theory of capitalism in the German tradition of economics P. KOSLOWSKI (Ed.): *Economic Ethics and the Theory of Capitalism in the German Tradition of Economics* (forthcoming). For a critique of Marxism-Leninism cf. P. KOSLOWSKI: *Nachruf auf den Marxismus-Leninismus* (1991). Russian translation with additional four essays "Outline of the Alternative of a Personalist Philosophy": *Proshchanie s marxizmom-leninizmom. Ocherki personalistskoi filosophii* (1997).

has been refuted by a theory of history which acknowledged the effects of the mental factors in the social and economic history.

4. The critique of the planned economy and the analysis of the problems of economic calculation developed by Ludwig von Mises gave new impulses for the economic analysis of a competitive economy in the years before World War II.

5. The possibly most valuable and long lasting idea in Marx's theory, his attempt to explain the social and economic dynamics of capitalism, has found its successor in Schumpeter's theory of economic development which was freed from the Marxist presuppositions and has led to a new theory of economic growth.

6. Schumpeter also added the analysis of the genesis of social classes to the analysis of economics and economic sociology which offered a new approach for overcoming the Marxist sociology of classes.

7. Schumpeter's sociology of imperialisms also tried to refute the exclusively economic approach to the theory of imperialism and offered a much deeper understanding of the phenomenon of imperialism and the politics of imperialism and traced it back until the late 19th century.

8. The post-Marxist theory of capitalism offered a more realistic analysis of the motives and functions of the entrepreneur as the dynamic person in the process of competition emerging in modern times. Particularly Max Weber, Sombart and Schumpeter are here the central authors.

9. The economic history of that time, particularly in the very realist analysis of the Rhenish economic historian Bruno Kuske, provided the social sciences with a more fact-oriented theory of the making of the modern worker and replaced the emotionally coloured reports of Friedrich Engels about the social history of the early 19th century by a realist account.[4]

Müller-Armack summarizes the indebtedness of the theory of the social market economy to the post-Marxist theory of capitalism and the research of the Historical School as follows: These traditions gave the theory of the social market economy the insight into the totality of the economic style of an epoch, a style in which mental, economic, social and political factors form a synthesis. In the Historical School of the 19th century, however, these styles of an economic epoch remained economic and historical facts that had to be taken as given. It was the task of a later time, of the first decades of the

---

4   A. MUELLER-ARMACK: "Die wissenschaftlichen Ursprünge der Sozialen Marktwirtschaft" (1973), p. 180-181.

20th century, to analyse the economic style of an epoch as the result of a consciously developed formation of a style.

Müller-Armack mentions that he himself wrote a book *Entwicklungsgesetze des Kapitalismus* (Laws of Development of Capitalism), that was published in 1930 in which he tried to draw the conclusion from the post-Marxist theory of capitalism and its theory of economic stages.[5] He remarks that it might have been the right way to avoid the word "capitalism" and to replace it by the more neutral notions of the industrial economy or the market economy since the capitalist calculation is not restricted to the capitalist economy only but is known in the socialist economy, too. He also concedes that the term capitalism is often used in a pejorative and denunciatory way which does not aim at understanding the phenomenon of capitalism but originates in the aggressive wish to defame the present economic order.

Müller-Armack, nevertheless, leaves no doubt that the social market economy is a form of capitalism - although that form of capitalism that has learned from the Marxist, post-Marxist and other theories of capitalism like the one of the Historical School of Economics about the dialectics of the accumulation processes of a capitalist order and tries to compensate the insufficiencies of a purely capitalist order by a social framework.

II. Social Equilibration, Totality of the Conditions of the Economic Order, Critique of Doctrinaire Liberalism

The results of these analyses of capitalism are three major insights of the social market economy:

1. the insight into the need for the equilibration or counterbalancing of specified accumulation and dialectical processes in capitalism which result in also clearly specified insufficiencies of the economic system.

2. the idea that the theory of the social order cannot be described by economic theory in the narrow sense only, i.e. by neo-classical equilibrium analysis. The proper understanding of the economic order of the market rather presupposes the insight that the market is embedded into the "totality of the economic order" which comprises more than the mere exchange and co-

---

5   *Ibid.*, p. 181.

ordination process of the market. It presupposes, first of all, a legal order and an order of social policy. The idea of the "totality of the economic order" or "*wirtschaftliche Gesamtordnung*" points to what has later been called the interdependence of the orders of politics and economics and represents the liberal analogue to the idea of political economy developed in the Marxist tradition. It is right to say that the theory of the social market economy is also a "political economy" since it conceptualizes the interdependence of the economic and political elements of the social order and their dependency on each other although it changes completely the material content of the interdependence of the political and economic order. Whereas in Marxism this interdependence is conceptualized as the interdependence between the political order of the dictatorship of the proletariat and central economic planning, the interdependence between the political and the economic order in the market economy is one between democracy and the market economy, between democratic voting and the mediation of supply and demand in market exchange.

3. The third insight that the theory of the social market economy gained from the post-Marxist theory of capitalism and its critique of Marxism is not formulated literally in the Müller-Armack's paper "Die wissenschaftlichen Ursprünge der Sozialen Marktwirtschaft" of 1973 but can be derived from his other scientific papers. It is the insight that the totality of the economic order cannot be derived from one principle only since processes of negative side effects and critical masses can lead to results of the economic order that are neither politically nor economicly desirable and must be corrected. The theory of social market economy by its dual principle of efficiency and of social equilibration avoids the mistake of doctrinaire liberalism to expect that the market process always leads to an equilibrium or even optimum.

The theory of the social market economy is clearly a theory of a capitalist order but it is a theory of the capitalist order that does not fall into the errors of doctrinaire liberalism to believe that the market process is completely self-corrective and will always lead to a state of equilibrium without external intervention. Müller-Armack is here very outspoken in his book *Wirtschaftslenkung und Marktwirtschaft* (Economic Direction and the Market Economy) of 1946. He criticizes the doctrinaire liberalism and the concept of a liberal market economy by saying that it overlooks that it is a task of the state to secure competition and to avoid the formation of monopolies and trusts by anti-trust legislation. Doctrinaire liberalism overlooks that economic competition is a sociological organisational means aiming at the lowering of costs and prices in the interest of the common weal. It is founded on the conviction that economic competition is more than only the expression of formal freedom of contract.

Monopolies that try to eliminate competition have always used successfully the argument and the legal institution of formal freedom of contract for their goals of monopolizing the economy, contends Müller-Armack[6]. He also criticizes that doctrinaire liberalism did not succeed in conceptualizing the totality of the order of life and in providing for the conditions of preservation of the market economy.

He summarizes his critique of the liberal market economy as follows: "The mistakes and omissions of the liberal market economy lie in the end in the narrowness of the economic weltanschauung that liberalism defends. It induced liberalism to overlook the instrumental character of the order it conceptualizes and realizes and to take by mistake the market economy for an autonomous world. The market economy may, however, not at all claim to be the complete regulation of all of our life. It needs significant social and political guarantees as well as measures of land-developing and town-planning and of stabilization of the business cycle. The market economy seems to us today as an instrumental means whereas liberalism has been tempted to make it the idol of its weltanschauung. As an instrumental means, however, the market economy continues to be for us the very efficient and up to now irreplaceable means and the only way to organize the economic life of mass cultures without sacrificing for this goal the last rest of our human dignity."[7]

The social market economy avoids the dangers of doctrinaire systems by emphasizing the instrumental character of the economic order and by maintaining that the last criterion of economic systems is the improvement of the consumption of all individual consumers. Müller-Armack repeatedly points to the fact that in the market economy it is consumption that directs, by the expression of the estimates of the consumers in prices, the processes of production.[8] The teleology of the economic order in individual private consumption, the fact that private consumption is not only the goal but also the criterion of the economic process, and the fact that the market economy is instrumental on this aim avoid the fallacy of the doctrinaire theories of eco-

---

6   A. MUELLER-ARMACK: *Wirtschaftslenkung und Marktwirtschaft* (1946), p. 105.
7   *Ibid.*, 107.
8   *Ibid.*, p. 91.

nomic systems to place the criterion for the shape of the economic order or economic system in the purity of the system principles (*Systemprinzipien*), be they central planning in socialist economic systems or the general equilibrium of the market in the theory of the market economy.[9] The final criterion for an economic order is not the purity of its system principles or the monism of its system structure but the degree of consumer satisfaction and consumer wealth it yields.

In this sense all the more recent critiques of the concept of the social market economy from the "pure liberal theory of the market process" that the theory of the social market economy does not remain within the neo-classical orthodoxy seem to be beside the point.[10] The theory of the social market economy has never been monistic or pure. It was non-monistic from its beginning. It has not been critical of the idea of a total economic planning only but also critical of the idea of a totalization of the market as the only means of co-ordination in the social order.

III. Social Market Economy and Neo-Liberalism

In the modification of the concept of capitalism by the affirmation of the need for social equilibration, by the conceptualization of the totality of the economic order, and by the awareness of the possible insufficiencies or fail-

---

9 The critique of doctrinaire theories of the economic order in the theory of the social market economy is an application of the larger problem that all thinking in systems faces: How can the systematicness of the system be reconciled with the freedom of humans in and from the system? How can the new and unforseeable be thought in a complete system with fixed system principles? The problem of system and freedom has first been discussed when the totalist philosophical systems of German Idealism realized that freedom either blows up the closed system or the system principles make freedom within the system impossible. Cf. H. KRINGS: "System und Freiheit. Beitrag zu einem ungelösten Problem" (1975); and P. KOSLOWSKI: "Überlegungen zur Dialektik von System und Freiheit" (1979).
10 Cf. for such a critique H. KLEIN: "Freispruch für Alfred Müller-Armack. Der Erfinder der Sozialen Marktwirtschaft hat immer vor demokratischem Sozialismus gewarnt" (1997), p. 15.

ures of the system principles like market failure or market monopolization, the social market economy is distinguished from neo-liberalism. Müller-Armack clearly states that although "it is not incomprehensible, but it is wrong to regard the Social Market Economy only as a variety of neo-Liberalism".[11] The neo-liberal and the social market economy concept of capitalism share some origins and some basic ideas but the two concepts diverge in their basic ontological concepts. Whereas neo-liberalism regards the machinery of competition as the sole principle of organisation, the concept of social market economy has grown from different roots since it does not rely solely on the mechanical rules of competition but also on the order of the state and of society. The social market economy is not exclusively a theory of competition, rather it is a theory of the *wirtschaftliche Gesamtordnung* (comprehensive economic order).[12] The theory of the social market economy is a "*ausgearbeitete und durchdachte Theorie der gesellschaftlichen Gesamtordnung*", an "elaborated and fundamental theory of the totality of the social order".[13]

IV. A Synthesis of Social Equilibration *(Ausgleich)* and of the Guarantee of the Free Working of the Market Forces

The guiding idea of this theory of the totality of the economic order is the *Synthese von sozialem Ausgleich und freier Wirkungsmöglichkeit der Marktkräfte*, "the synthesis of social equilibration and of the guarantee for the possibility of the free working of the market forces".[14] Central to the concept of a capitalist order developed in the social market economy is the idea, that the market forces by themselves may not always lead to a general equilibrium of society. Even if they reach economic equilibrium in the mar-

---

11 A. MUELLER-ARMACK: "The Principles of the Social Market Economy" (1965), p. 91. In this volume below pp. 257-258.
12 A. MUELLER-ARMACK: "Das Grundproblem unserer Wirtschaftspolitik: Rückkehr zur Marktwirtschaft" (1946), p. 39.
13 A. MUELLER-ARMACK: "Vorwort zu" (Preface to) *Wirtschaftsordnung und Wirtschaftspolitik* (Economic Order and Economic Policy) (1965), p. 11.
14 A. MUELLER-ARMACK: Article "Soziale Marktwirtschaft" (1956), p. 248.

ket, the result may not be a social equilibrium. Since the economy depends on the stability and performance of the totality of the social order it is not sufficient for the entire society to be "in equilibrium" if only the economy is in equilibrium. The society as a whole must be in a state of equilibration.

The concept of equilibration, or in German *Ausgleich*, is central as well for the conditions of the working of the market as for the relationship between the economic order and the other orders of the society. Alfred Müller-Armack mentions different dimensions of the concept of equilibration. The social market economy equilibrates on the basis of a competitive economy between the free initiative of the individuals and social progress measured also in terms of social security. This socio-economic progress is guaranteed by the very economic performance and efficiency of the market economy.[15] The social market economy further equilibrates between the right to freedom of contract and the exigencies of anti-trust policy, between the freedom of enterprise and the demands of zoning and other kinds of economic regulation. Müller-Armack emphasizes that it is the very synthesis of social equilibration and equalization with the free working of the market forces which must be realized not only in the German economy but also in the process of European economic integration. The task of the economic order is the synthesis of economic competition, technical progress, and social progress.[16]

The idea of "Ausgleich", of equilibration, has become so dominant in the German concept of the economy that the Federal Republic of Germany even founded a "Deutsche Ausgleichsbank" (German Bank for Equalization and Equilibration). This government banking institute has been designed to counterbalance the shortcomings of the market process by financing economic measures to be taken to counterbalance detrimental effects and insufficiencies of the market process. The idea behind this institution is that it is the task of the state to secure an equilibration of the burdens and the rewards between the members of society and to balance between human needs, the needs of the environment or the ecology, and the working conditions of the competitive market.

The idea of *Ausgleich* or equilibration in the charter of this government bank assumes that there is a permanent ethical and political need for equalizing and equilibrating the economy in several fields. In the social market economy, the government must equilibrate between the individual economic

---

15 *Ibid.*, p. 245.
16 *Ibid.*, p. 247.

THE SOCIAL MARKET ECONOMY: NOTES ON MÜLLER-ARMACK

interests in economic growth and consumption on the one hand and the protection and preservation of the natural environment on the other hand. The state must further equilibrate between the requirements of economic freedom, efficiency, and growth on the one hand, and the need for social justice in the distribution of income and wealth and for social security on the other hand. It must equilibrate between the rights of property of the old owners and heirs of capital as well as between the rights of new entrepreneurs to an access to capital for their enterprises etc.. In this view, the market creates a permanent ethical and political task of balancing, a task of equilibration for those acting in the market as well as for those responsible for the actions of government, for its economic and political interventions into the market.[17]

In the theory of the social market economy, the idea of balancing, equilibration, or compensation is central in three fields: in the field of the access to capital for medium and small sized enterprises, in the compensation for market insufficiencies with regard to the ecology and protection of the environment, and in the fulfilment of tasks of social policy that are needed as a compensation for the risks of the industrial mode of production and as an insurance against the contingencies of severe personal misfortune and situations of need.

The German word *Ausgleich* comprises six aspects of balancing:
1. counterbalancing,
2. equilibration,
3. right reciprocation,
4. compensation,
5. equalization,
6. levelling.

Müller-Armack's concept of the social market economy centres on the positive connotations of the term balancing, like counterbalancing, equili-

---

[17] The founding charter and the description of the tasks of the "Deutsche Ausgleichsbank" as a financing institution founded originally for the compensation paid to individuals for damages and losses during and immediately after World War II, make the statement that the bank is founded for "equalizing and equilibrating the social market economy in those situations of the economic process where important economic tasks are realized only insufficiently by the free market forces". (DEUTSCHE AUSGLEICHSBANK: *Deutsche Ausgleichsbank: Kreditinstitut des Bundes für Mittelstand, Umweltschutz, soziale Aufgaben*, p. 7.)

brating, securing right reciprocation and compensation, and not on the more "socialist" connotations of the concept like equalization and levelling.

The concept of the social market economy affirms the central and indispensable role of the market as a means of social co-ordination and of the price system as the co-ordination measure for supply and demand according to the needs and wishes of the consumer. The concept of the social market economy acknowledges, however, the possibility of market insufficiencies. The term "market insufficiencies" might be more appropriate than the term "market failure", since the latter gives the wrong impression of a total market collapse and of the availability of a failure-proof alternative assumed to be the state.

The concept of the social market economy is aware of the fact that state failure and misconceptions of the economic reality by government decisions are as frequent as market insufficiencies or failures. It is also aware of the fact that government failures have an even more critical impact on economic efficiency than partial market failures or market insufficiencies. There is a considerable asymmetry between market and state failure: market failure is correctable by the state, state failure is not correctable by a higher order institution in society since there is none above the state and, therefore, only correctable with more difficulty than market failure. Since the state is the highest order institution it can only be corrected by itself. Self-correction, however, is always a difficult task.

The idea of *Ausgleich*, of balancing claims for making peace, is also central for the philosophy underlying the social market economy since Alfred Müller-Armack considered the social market economy to be an irenical or peace-creating formula. The concept of the social market economy includes the idea that the economic system pursues social objectives of social security and of social equilibration in the sense of reducing extreme income differentials.[18]

---

[18] A. MUELLER-ARMACK: "The Principles of the Social Market Economy" (1965), p. 94f.: "The Social Market Economy not only embraces an economic order coordinated by the market; the adjective 'social' also indicates that this system also pursues social objectives."

V. Social Objectives and Tasks of Social Policy in the Social Market Economy

In an early paper, Müller-Armack describes the social objectives and tasks of social policy in the social market economy as follows:[19]

1. *The creation of a social order of the firm* in which the worker is valued as a human being and co-worker. This social order of the firm gives him a right to economic co-determination without narrowing the entrepreneurial initiative and responsibility of the entrepreneur.

2. *The realization of an order of competition* as a task for legal and government action. The legal order of market competition is thought to be a political task. In fulfilling this task the government must direct the striving for profit of the individual in a direction that is useful for the common weal.

3. *Anti-trust policy*. The government and legislative must engage in an anti-trust policy in order to fight the abuse of economic power.

4. *Stabilization policy*. The economic policy of the government must stabilize the business cycle. The realization of a stabilization policy must aim at procuring security for the worker against the detrimental effects of economic recessions or of the instability of the entire business cycle on his income and family.

5. *The equilibration of income differentials* in a way that is compatible with the market order (in German: *marktwirtschaftlicher Einkommensausgleich*). The government must aim at equilibrating the differences in income by abolishing unhealthy differences in income and wealth by means of taxation and of transfers to families as well as by subsidizing child care in families and by subsidizing housing of the needy.

6. *Zoning policy and subsidies for inexpensive homes*. The government of the social market economy should be responsible for the zoning of cities and support the construction industry to be able to build less expensive appartments (*sozialer Wohnungsbau*).

7. *Transfer of capital to small and medium sized firms*. The government should ease the access of small and medium size firms to capital in order to enable them to compete in the market with large and capital rich firms (*Mittelstandsförderung*).

---

19 A. MUELLER-ARMACK: "Vorschläge zur Verwirklichung der Sozialen Marktwirtschaft" (1948), pp. 100ff.

8. *Introducing and strengthening the co-operative elements in the market economy by the government.* Müller-Armack advocates governmental efforts to increase the elements of co-operative self-support in the economy, e.g. in housing co-operatives.

9. *Further development of social security.* The social market economy should further develop social security.

10. *Town planning.*

11. *Minimum wages.* The social market economy should determine minimum wages and secure individual wages by tariffs that are reached in free bargaining processes.

It is obvious that this is a rather extensive catalogue of state measures or interventions to be taken into the economy which would find only critical acclaim by neo-liberals.

VI. The Social Market Economy as a Means of Social Peace-Making

The idea of "Ausgleich", of equilibration, so central to the concept of the social market economy in its emphasis on the relationship between market efficiency and the system of social security has, for Müller-Armack, even a metaphysical or religious meaning. The idea of the social market economy is considered to be a concept that will reconcile the different kinds of weltanschauung, of ideologies and religious denominations.

In his paper "Ways of Social Peace-Making" or "Social Irenical Ways" (*Soziale Irenik*)[20], Müller-Armack examines whether it is possible to develop an idea of the social order, a *Sozialidee*, that might reconcile the different ideologies and religious denominations. He calls the term "Social Market Economy" coined by himself "an irenical formula".[21] Behind his idea of an equilibration or *Ausgleich* of the ideologies, there is a far-sighted analysis of the pluralistic society and of its problem how to cope with the fact that the different traditions of social teaching like Catholic social teaching, Protestant

---

20 A. MUELLER-ARMACK: "Soziale Irenik" (1950).
21 A. MUELLER-ARMACK: "Der humane Gehalt der Sozialen Marktwirtschaft" (1973), p. 173.

social teaching, socialism, and liberalism compete with each other and that each of them cannot expect to gain total control over the social order. Rather, all these ideologies must come to terms with the basically pluralistic character of modern society.

Müller-Armack's theory of the social market economy is a theory of the totality of the social order, of the style of living (*Lebensstil*)[22], of the common form of style (*Stilform*) of an economy and society.[23] Although it is a theory of the totality of the social order, it concedes that the character of modern society is pluralist.

It does not fall, however, into the dogmatic pluralism of the multicultural society. The idea of the social market economy rather maintains that, beyond the different kinds of weltanschauung, the free society needs a common concept of the social order that unifies the different ideologies. For Müller-Armack, the concept of the social market economy is the common ground on which Catholic and Protestant social teaching, the purified elements of socialism, and the best traditions of liberalism can meet.

The theory of the social market economy is derived from two sources, from the understanding of the price system and the mechanics of competition in the tradition of classical economics from Adam Smith and Ricardo on the one hand and from the tradition of the sociology of knowledge, the sociology of culture and of the humane sciences in the German tradition of the Historical and Cultural Sciences (*Geisteswissenschaften*), on the other hand. It is important to acknowledge particularly Müller-Armack's roots in the tradition coming from Troeltsch, Dilthey, Max Scheler, Plessner and Max Weber. Müller-Armack himself emphasizes how much he has learnt from the sociology in the tradition of the humane sciences. He mentions particularly the insight into the historical character of the economy.[24] This insight in the historical character of the economy has been widely lost in today's economics, and with it has been lost the insight that the economy can only be understood in its historical genesis.

By emphasizing the fact that economics as a theory is grounded in the historical and humane sciences, the theory of the social market economy can

---

22 A. MUELLER-ARMACK: "Stil und Ordnung der Sozialen Marktwirtschaft" (1952), p. 237.
23 A. MUELLER-ARMACK: "Der humane Gehalt der Sozialen Marktwirtschaft" (1973), p. 172.
24 *Ibid.*, pp. 168 ff.

counterbalance the tendencies of present economic science to visualize its theory as an unhistorical natural science that is applicable without historical modifications to the economies of all cultures and historical periods. The insight of the social market economy into the historical character of its object, the market economy, and particularly into the historical nature of the institutional framework that must accompany a market is of particular interest to the countries that are like Russia in the process of transition from a communist to a liberal market order.

In the concept of the social market economy, the synthesis of the unhistorical equilibrium concept of the price system as an equilibrating mechanism between supply and demand and the insight into the historical nature of the social order being the frame of the market process prevent two errors common to both extremes of economic utopianism, the error of believing in a timeless unhistorical self-equilibrating market and the error of the belief in the unhistorical validity of a central planning of the economy. Both utopias, the utopia of a market perfectly self-adjusting and in permanent equilibrium as well as the utopia of central economic planning, underrate human freedom, its realization in history, and humankind's ability to co-ordinate individual actions by markets *and* by political deliberation and decision making.

VII. The Social Market Economy and Economic Reconstruction

The theory of social market economy has not been developed, according to Müller-Armack, as a response to the devastating effects of a lost war in Germany, and it was not a response to these devastations only. It has been - right from its beginning in the years 1945-49 - a response to the errors and mistakes already made before World War II. The social market economy is the critical response to the idea of mobilizing the economic forces by planning and socialism common to the ideologies of these decades, to socialism, communism and national socialism. In the idea of a "Total Mobilization"[25]

---

25 The programme and mood of the years 1925 to 1933 is well described in two books of ERNST JUENGER published in this period: *Die totale Mobilmachung* (The Total Mobilization) (1928) and *Der Arbeiter* (The Worker) (1932).

and of the "Labour State" (*Arbeitsstaat*), bolshevism and national socialism agreed. Both ideologies conceptualized themselves as the forces overcoming the "anarchy" and "slowness" of the market economy that was falsely assumed by them to be obsolete and outdated.

The economic crisis to which the concept of the social market economy responded is the crisis caused in the first half of the 20th century by the shift to planned economies and by the obstructions to and even abolition of the working of the price system. For Müller-Armack, it is not the destruction of the factories and machines for production, but the obstructions to economic organisation, co-operation and co-ordination, the lack of a true co-operation between the factors of production that is the fundamental cause of the economic problems that Europe faced at the end of World War II.[26] The thoroughness of the crisis of the economic order in Europe and the growing state interventionism in the years between 1914 and 1945 is the reason why a new concept of a liberal order and social market economy has to be developed at the end of World War II.[27]

The universality and deepness of this crisis in Europe has also caused, according to Müller-Armack, that the social market economy has not been and is not only a specifically German concept, but a generally valid idea and theory of the economic order and of the way how the destructions of World War II can be overcome. The destruction of Europe after two world wars has not been only the consequence of the wars, but also of the shift to the planned economy in most parts of Europe in the first half of the 20th century. The social market economy is not a "specifically German form of overcoming the problems of reconstruction",[28] but is a concept for all of Europe.

Müller-Armack concedes that, in the initial stage of the elaboration of the concept of the social market economy, he regarded the social market economy to be a specifically German form of coping with the situation of destruction and the need for reconstruction. In the historical process of the European unification he learnt, however, that the social market economy

---

26 Cf. A. MUELLER-ARMACK: "Das Grundproblem unserer Wirtschaftspolitik: Rückkehr zur Marktwirtschaft" (1946), p. 36.
27 A. MUELLER-ARMACK: *Wirtschaftslenkung und Marktwirtschaft* (1946), p. 22.
28 A. MUELLER-ARMACK: "The Principles of the Social Market Economy" (1965), p. 103. In this volume p. 272.

might serve as a means to find the platform for the different traditions of the market economy in Europe.

Since the concept of the social market economy as a synthesis has a dynamic and non-static character it might serve as the formula for finding a new dynamic synthesis of the different economic systems that prevail in the countries of Europe.[29]

VIII. Conclusion

According to our knowledge of history, a purely capitalistic society, built exclusively upon private property, maximization of utility and profit, and coordination by way of the market and price system, without any state activity for guaranteeing the legal order and certain measures of social security has not yet been reality. As a societal model, the pure model of the market economy and of capitalism bears utopian, counterfactual features; it is itself a social utopia.[30] Its utopian character always becomes evident when its defenders seek to immunize it against their opponents' objections with the incompleteness argument, that is, by pointing out that the "real" market economy has never been realized in its pure form and that its shortcomings can always be traced to exogenous influences. Such a procedure is, however, not justifiable.

The theory of the social market economy is an attempt to give the answer to these shortcomings. As a social theory it adjusts itself to the reality of the totality of the economic order and takes into account its place in history and the historical conditions of its realization. In contrast to the social market economy, the neo-liberal theory of the market remains a "pure" theory that pretends to present a superior model, superior to the "impure and compromising" model of the social market economy. A theory, however, that presents a model taken to be superior due to its systematic closeness but that can never be realized due to exogenous influences or non-producible precondi-

---

29 *Ibid.*, p. 104. In this volume p. 267.
30 Cf. PETER KOSLOWSKI: Ethics of Capitalism and Critique of Sociobiology (1996). Russian translation: Etika kapitalizma. Evolutsia i obshchestvo (1996).

tions is a bad utopia. It remains, as Hegel ironized it, in the "precariousness of the ought to be".

As a theory of society, the pure market model or pure capitalism cannot suffice because it is essentially an economic theory of production, exchange, and economic co-ordination. As an economic theory, it must neglect essential aspects of social action and political integration. By making freedom and efficiency the sole guiding values in its ideal of co-ordination, the theory of the pure market economy evades the problems of social equilibration as well as of the totality of the economic order and gains its most impressive comprehensiveness in general equilibrium analysis.

The problem of weighing the goods and values of a society against one another, however, cannot be avoided. This can be demonstrated at the question of how the sacrifice in the fulfilment of one societal goal versus the gain in the realization of another goal should be weighted against each other. How are sacrifices of liberty for the sake of increases in efficiency, or sacrifices of efficiency for the sake of social equilibration, and vice versa to be evaluated?

It also turns out that the maximization of profit and utility as the economic motive and the free disposition over private property assume a characteristic abstractness when they lay claim to unlimited social validity. The maximization of profit and utility can only be admitted as motives under constraints; otherwise they reduce the wealth of human motivation to abstractions of rationality and ignore the social embeddedness of the pursuit of goals. The same is true of rights of disposition over private property. The coordination of the individual actions in the market must occur within a social framework which the conditions of this co-ordination - private property, maximization of profit and utility, and the price system of the market - do not adequately determine, but rather presuppose.

The limits of capitalism and of the pure market economy as a social theory are that the co-ordination ideal does not comprise the whole of a society's guiding ideas and that the form of one's economic action does not fully comprise the substance of one's social action. As a social theory, capitalism is *materially underdetermined* and incomplete. It must be complemented by a comprehensive social-philosophical theory concerning the framework within which capitalism can activate its advantages as a method of co-ordination. It must be supplemented by a theory of the social genesis and normative justification of preference formation (social psychology and ethics), by a theory of the social institutions this framework consists of (family, churches and religious communities, state), and by a theory of the political compensation for capitalism failure (market failure, the limits of subjectivism, and consideration of substantial life interests).

The necessity of such a framework becomes evident in the dialectic proper to the three structural characteristics of capitalist market economy. In all three characteristics a change-over from quantity into quality and from form into content is observable. The unlimited accumulation of private property leads, from a certain point of control of a market to a qualitative jump and to a problem of power. Unlimited pursuit of profits and benefits leads to a change-over into greed, miserliness and a loss in the wealth of human purposes. The co-ordination of production and the assignment of social status exclusively by way of market success, that is, successful anticipation of demand and willingness to pay, leads to an exaggerated subjectivism and the neglect of more substantial purposes.

The concept of the social market economy responds to the challenge of this dialectics of capitalism by the social equilibration of capitalism. This is a concept that is still convincing and unrefuted by the recent developments of the globalisation of the economy and by the increased competition on a world-wide scale.

The actual individuation of what social equilibration of the market means in a certain period might change but the basic structure of the conceptual solution of the social market economy remains valid. It might become necessary to sacrifice parts of a social security system that have become obsolete, wasteful, or simply too extensive and expensive. It might also be necessary to give up "social slack" in the system of the social equilibration of the market. It remains, however, necessary to equilibrate the workings of the market with the demands of social integration and social security.

The social market economy is not a closed system of principles or an unchanging doctrinal body that determines the extent of the social equilibration once and for all. Rather, it is an open set of principles and theoretical tools that help to analyse the totality of the economic order and the conditions under which it guarantees efficiency and the good life. It is also a theoretical tool for the practical task of economic and social policy to analyse and recognize the changing requirements for social equilibration as they arise from the workings of the market process.

THE SOCIAL MARKET ECONOMY: NOTES ON MÜLLER-ARMACK

References

DEUTSCHE AUSGLEICHSBANK: *Deutsche Ausgleichsbank: Kreditinstitut des Bundes für Mittelstand, Umweltschutz, soziale Aufgaben,* Schriftenreihe Heft 1 (German Bank for Equalization and Compensation: Federal Credit Institute for Middle Sized Enterprises, Environmental Protection, Social Tasks; Series of Brochures, Vol. 1), Bonn without year.

HAVER, P.: *Leitbilder der Gerechtigkeit in den marktwirtschaftlichen Konzeptionen von Adam Smith, John Stuart Mill and Alfred Müller-Armack* (The Guiding Idea of Justice in Adam Smith's, John Stuart Mill's and Alfred Müller-Armack's Conceptions of the Market Economy), Frankfurt am Main (Lang) 1991.

KLEIN, H.: "Freispruch für Alfred Müller-Armack. Der Erfinder der Sozialen Marktwirtschaft hat immer vor demokratischem Sozialismus gewarnt", *Frankfurter Allgemeine Zeitung,* 26 April 1997, Nr. 97, p. 15.

KOSLOWSKI, P.: "Überlegungen zur Dialektik von System und Freiheit" (Reflections on the Dialectics of System and Freedom), in: H. M. BAUMGARTNER (Ed.): *Prinzip Freiheit* (The Principle of Freedom), Freiburg, München (Karl Alber) 1979, pp. 231-253.

KOSLOWSKI, P.: *Nachruf auf den Marxismus-Leninismus* (Obituary on Marxism-Leninism), Tübingen (J.C.B. Mohr [Paul Siebeck]) 1991. Russian Translation: *Proshchanie s marxizmom-leninizmom. Ocherki personalistskoi filosofii,* St. Petersburg (Izdatelstvo Ekonomicheskaya Shkola) 1997 (=Eticheskaya Ekonomia. Issledovanie po etike, kulture i filosofii khoziaistva, Vol. 3).

KOSLOWSKI, P. (Ed.): *The Theory of Ethical Economy in the Historical School. Wilhelm Roscher, Lorenz von Stein, Gustav Schmoller, Wilhelm Dilthey and Contemporary Theory,* Berlin, Heidelberg, New York, Tokyo (Springer) 1995 (= Studies in Economic Ethics and Philosophy, Vol. 7).

KOSLOWSKI, P.: *Ethics of Capitalism and Critique of Sociobiology.* Two Essays with a Comment by James M. Buchanan, Heidelberg, Berlin, New York, Tokyo (Springer) 1996 (Studies in Economic Ethics and Philosophy, Vol. 10). Russian translation: *Etika kapitalizma. Evolutsia i obshchestvo,* St. Petersburg (Izdatelstvo Ekonomicheskaya Shkola) 1996 (=Eticheskaya Ekonomia. Issledovanie po etike, kulture i philosophii khoziaistva, Vol. 1). German original: *Ethik des Kapitalismus* 1982, 5th ed. 1995, *Evolution und Gesellschaft* 1984, 2nd ed. 1989, both books with Mohr Siebeck, Tübingen.

KOSLOWSKI, P. (Ed.): *Economic Ethics and the Theory of Capitalism in the German Tradition of Economics: Historism, Ordo-Liberalism, Marxism, Critical Theory, Solidarism,* Berlin, Heidelberg, New York, Tokyo (Springer) forthcoming in 1998 (= Studies in Economic Ethics and Philosophy, Vol. 13).

KRINGS, H.: "System und Freiheit. Beitrag zu einem ungelösten Problem" (System and Freedom. A Contribution to an Unsolved Problem), in: D. HENRICH (Ed.): *Ist systematische Philosophie möglich?* (Stuttgarter Hegel-Kongreß 1975), Bonn (Bouvier) 1988, pp. 35-51.

MUELLER-ARMACK, A.: *Wirtschaftslenkung und Marktwirtschaft* (Economic Steering and Market Economy) (1946), reprinted in: A. MUELLER-ARMACK: *Wirtschaftsordnung und Wirtschaftspolitik. Studien und Konzepte zur Sozialen Marktwirtschaft und zur Europäischen Integration*, Bern/Stuttgart (Paul Haupt) 1976, pp. 19-170 (= A. MUELLER-ARMACK: *Ausgewählte Werke*, edited by Ernst Dürr, Harriet Hoffmann, Egon Tuchtfeldt, Christian Watrin).

MUELLER-ARMACK, A.: "Das Grundproblem unserer Wirtschaftspolitik: Rückkehr zur Marktwirtschaft" (The Basic Problem of Our Economic Policy: Return to the Market Economy) (1946), reprinted in: A. MUELLER-ARMACK: *Genealogie der sozialen Marktwirtschaft. Frühschriften und weiterführende Konzepte* (Genealogy of the Social Market Economy. Early Papers and Conceptions Developing Developing Them Further), Bern/Stuttgart (Paul Haupt) 2nd edition 1981, pp. 33-50 (= A. MUELLER-ARMACK: *Ausgewählte Werke*, edited by Ernst Dürr, Harriet Hoffmann, Egon Tuchtfeldt, Christian Watrin).

MUELLER-ARMACK, A.: "Vorschläge zur Verwirklichung der Sozialen Marktwirtschaft" (Suggestions for the Realization of the Social Market Economy) (1948), reprinted in: A. MUELLER-ARMACK: *Genealogie der sozialen Marktwirtschaft. Frühschriften und weiterführende Konzepte*, Bern/Stuttgart (Paul Haupt) 2nd edition 1981, pp. 90-109.

MUELLER-ARMACK, A.: "Soziale Irenik" (Social Irenics) (1950), reprinted in: A. MUELLER-ARMACK: *Religion und Wirtschaft. Geistesgeschichtliche Hintergründe unserer europäischen Lebensform* (Religion and Economy. The Foundations of our European Form of Life in the History of Ideas), Bern/Stuttgart (Paul Haupt), 3rd ed. 1981, pp. 559-578 (= A. MUELLER-ARMACK: *Ausgewählte Werke*, edited by Ernst Dürr, Harriet Hoffmann, Egon Tuchtfeldt, Christian Watrin).

MUELLER-ARMACK, A.: "Stil und Ordnung der Sozialen Marktwirtschaft" (Style and Order of the Social Market Economy) (1952), reprinted in: A. MUELLER-ARMACK: *Wirtschaftsordnung und Wirtschaftspolitik. Studien und Konzepte zur Sozialen Marktwirtschaft und zur Europäischen Integration* (Economic Order and Economic Policy. Studies and Concepts on the Social Market Economy and on European Integration), Bern/Stuttgart (Paul Haupt) 1976, pp. 231-242.

MUELLER-ARMACK, A.: Article "Soziale Marktwirtschaft" (Social Market Economy) (1956), in: *Handwörterbuch der Sozialwissenschaften*, edited by E. von Beckerath et al., Stuttgart, Tübingen, Göttingen 1956, Bd. 9. Reprinted in: A. MUELLER-ARMACK: *Wirtschaftsordnung und Wirtschaftspolitik. Studien und Konzepte zur Sozialen Marktwirtschaft und zur Europäischen Integration*, Bern/Stuttgart (Paul Haupt) 1976, pp. 243-248.

THE SOCIAL MARKET ECONOMY: NOTES ON MÜLLER-ARMACK

MUELLER-ARMACK, A.: "Vorwort" (Preface) (1965), in: A. MUELLER-ARMACK: *Wirtschaftsordnung und Wirtschaftspolitik. Studien und Konzepte zur Sozialen Marktwirtschaft und zur europäischen Integration*, Bern/Stuttgart (Paul Haupt) 1976.

MUELLER-ARMACK, A.: "The Principles of the Social Market Economy" (1965), in: *The German Economic Review. An English Language Quarterly on German Economic Research and Current Developments*, 3 (Stuttgart 1965), Nr. 2, pp. 89-104. In this volume below pp. 255-274.

MUELLER-ARMACK, A.: "Die wissenschaftlichen Ursprünge der Sozialen Marktwirtschaft" (The Scientific Origins of the Social Market Economy) (1973), reprinted in: A. MUELLER-ARMACK: *Genealogie der sozialen Marktwirtschaft. Frühschriften und weiterführende Konzepte*, Bern (Paul Haupt) 2nd edition 1981, pp. 176-184.

MUELLER-ARMACK, A.: "Der humane Gehalt der sozialen Marktwirtschaft" (1973) (The Humane Content of the Social Market Economy), in: A. MUELLER-ARMACK: *Genealogie der sozialen Marktwirtschaft. Frühschriften und weiterführende Konzepte*, Bern (Paul Haupt) 2nd edition 1981, pp. 167-175.

STARBATTY, J.: "Alfred Müller-Armack's Beitrag zu Theorie und Politik der Sozialen Marktwirtschaft" (Alfred Müller-Armack's Contribution to Theory and Politics of the Social Market Economy), in: *Soziale Marktwirtschaft in vierten Jahrzehnt ihrer Bewährung* (The Social Market Economy in the Fourth Decade of its Trial), Stuttgart/New York (G. Fischer) 1982.

Discussion Summary

NORBERT F. TOFALL

Paper discussed:
PETER KOSLOWSKI: The Social Market Economy: Social Equilibration of Capitalism and Consideration of the Totality of the Economic Order
Notes on Alfred Müller-Armack

The discussion was opened by asking whether there exist good and bad types of capitalism and what is the difference between social equality and social equilibration (ZIMBULI).

There are no good and bad types of capitalism. There are different types of capitalism which depend on the historical and political situation. The terms *good* or *bad* only make sense in the meaning of adequacy to the special historical and political situation, not in the meaning of a general judgement about capitalism. To the second topic it is pointed out that the difference between social equality and social equilibration is crucial for a free society. For a free society, social equality cannot be a value. people always act in different ways under different goals and have different abilities and skills, so that in a free society the results of individual action are different. Social equality as a political goal would destroy the results of freedom. Social equilibration means something different. It is a kind of compromise between different interests, not a general levelling (KOSLOWSKI).

However, there are a lot of causes which make an equilibration impossible. For example, it is impossible to find an equilibration between community and society (PIGROV).

The social market economy is a dynamic theory in which a particular equilibration does not ever exist. In a crisis, it is necessary to find a new equilibration between the different social interests. Today the Japanese and East-Asia competition leads to the necessity of a new social equilibration in Western Europe. There is no end of history (KOSLOWSKI).

DISCUSSION SUMMARY

It is important to look at the capitalist theory by being aware that capitalism is a utopia or something like a regulative idea which can only be successful if it is socially safeguarded. In this meaning, the social market economy is an idea which has become reality. In Russia the idea of capitalism ought to become reality, but this is only possible in the long run. Perhaps one can say that the metaphysic idea of freedom can only become reality in the form of a socialism which is based on the liberalism (SOLOVIOV).

However, Immanuel Kant did not initiate the social market economy by his regulative ideas. The social market idea of Müller-Armack is a meta-order for reconciling different ideologies and religious denominations. In a pluralistic society, it is not tolerable that one of the social teaching schools gains total control over the society. And it is typical for Germany that there are two powerful different schools of social teaching, Catholic and Protestant social teaching, but also socialism or liberalism. The social market economy as a meta-order for a pluralistic society is a typical German model of political theory after World War II. The social peace in Western Germany for nearly half a century is not thinkable without this meta-order. In Europe, however, the different religions play an even more important role for the differences in the political arena. It is, therefore, even worse that an integrating social idea of Europe does not exist. Thus, the task is: Imagine Europe! (KOSLOWSKI).

Section II

The Ethics of the Economic Order

Chapter 6

The Ethics of Business in Russia

SVETLANA V. SIMONOVA

I. Introduction
II. On the Axiology of the Russian Culture: General Remarks
III. The Peculiarities of the Russian Culture and the Ethics of Capitalism
IV. The Communal Economy Serving Capitalist Relations
V. Conclusion

1. Introduction

What is traditionally associated with the Russian soul is far both from ethics and entrepreneurship. Ilia Iliich Oblomov became a typical representative of the Russian personality due to the wide-spread intelligentsia myth about his lazily contemplative nature. It is not clear, whether this common idea is correct, however, it is quite true considering the investigations of our culture: we appear to know incredibly little about the specific character of the Russian ethos. Therefore, being aware of the necessity of the future analysis of the chances of the establishment of the capitalist entrepreneurship on the Russian soil at present, I shall dwell here upon more local and controllable issues.

THE ETHICS OF BUSINESS IN RUSSIA

Before discussing Russian morals in the sphere of entrepreneurship, it is necessary to start with at least general axiological cultural analysis of the Russian culture. Paraphrasing the well-known saying of Wilhelm Dilthey, it is possible to say: "what the Russian culture is can be learnt not by reflections on it but only from its history". The history of the Russian morals concerning the social and property aspects of the definitions of man will be dealt with in this paper. The paper will also concern the history of business in Russia.

Chaadayev was to some extent right in his observation that in Russia there was a paradoxical combination of education (in the European sense) and tyranny. In all reflections on the specific character of Russia, no matter if they belong to Slavophils or Westerners, the thinkers stated: the Russian soil is quite different from the Western soil and this has been proved throughout the Russian history. This is a painful issue as well as any conversation concerning national peculiarities, but we have the right to raise it, for it will depend on the way this issue is resolved, whether the Russian entrepreneurship will follow the route from a teleology of destruction to ecological rationality.

If we accept as normal and consistent with the traditions and customs of the Russian culture the variety of ethical norms dominating in the sphere of business relations today, when after a number of enormous social shocks all the customs and values accumulated over centuries of cultural construction were several times seriously shattered, we shall inherit the errors of the initiators of those shocks and, maybe, we shall share with them their sins. No one in the world - except God - begins from zero; we, those living in the culture with all its peculiarities, go on. This refers to the Russian entrepreneurship, too.

II. On the Axiology of the Russian Culture: General Remarks

I do not think it is necessary to prove here that the Orthodox church traditions, rituals determined the Russian ethnos in the Middle ages. It was the Orthodoxy that out of many nationalities living in the territories from the Urals to the Carpathians formed the Russian character, the Russian mentality. The analysis of the values of culture of the Russian Middle Ages should include the attitude of people to the labour, wealth and its accumulation, usury, since these attitudes form the background of ethics of entrepreneurship of the market economy.

The investigations prove the existence of a fairly complex Orthodox doctrine on man, which was formed within the tradition of the Eastern monasticism. The ideal of monastic life in the cultural life of the Orthodoxy had such an impact that the energetic anthropology, the doctrine of the fervour of the soul became spread a long time before St. Gregorios Palamas formulated it in terms of theology and defended it in council acts (1341-1351). "Hesychasm* had penetrated in the Old Russia long before the disputes on the nature of the Favora light between the arch-bishop of Solun, Gregorios Palamas, and the Calabrian monk Barlaam. It rendered a vital impact on our spiritual and cultural life " - writes a modern researcher of the religious culture of Russia[1]. The features of the Russian anthropocentrism and its influence on the Russian culture are investigated by a well-known Catholic scholar Tomas Spidlik as well[2]; his conclusions do not differ at all from the words of the Russian researcher.

Rooted in the traditions of the Orthodox energytism, the morality of the Russian Middle Ages was not a rigid mechanism, regulating the behaviour structures. Energytism in anthropology could be simply described by means of the term "soteriological functionalism"; but this term is not applicable to the Middle Ages, it belongs to the modern philosophical vocabulary. Energytism means man has not a single sinless ability: everything has a seal of decay, of the transient, temporary. However, directing all his abilities to God, man hoped to become godlike. Thus, man can be similar to God in his aspirations, while human qualities are not valuable at all, man is not substance, but energy. The world of values emerged as a result of this kind of understanding of god-likeness: God replied to the summons of man and a saint appeared in the world. I shall not dwell upon the popular at present

---

* (Translator's note: Hesychasmas was an ascetic mystical practice by which the mystic hoped to see the light of the transfigurated body of Christ.)
1 IOANN EKONOMTSEV: *Pravoslavie, Vizantiia, Rossiia* (Orthodoxy, Byzantium, Russia), Moscow (Khristianskaya Literatura) 1992, p. 168.
2 TOMAS SPIDLIK: *L'Idee Russe: une autre vision de l'homme,* Troyes (Abilgraf - Editions Fates) 1994.

THE ETHICS OF BUSINESS IN RUSSIA

subject of the Orthodox anthropology; I shall refer instead to the main book which gives the major bibliography on the issue.[3]

A saint - like material objects, on which Grace rests, one of God's energies - is, speaking figuratively, the territory of paradisiacal closeness of God to man, the place of their intimate communication. This is how the ideas of the values of the icon, church, book penetrate in the world of the Old Russia. The saint was an ideal, a model of man. Neither money nor manual labour - the main components of the economic wealth of a nation - were blamed, but they were not encouraged in the cultural world of the Middle Ages in Russia.

Energytism in respect to axiology means denial of the unconditional values, a sort of nihilism. It sometimes resulted in comical and ugly phenomena in the Russian culture associating together a great righteous person and a terrible sinner (however, is it not characteristic of Christianity which allocated a robber in Paradise). Ivan the Terrible was known as a dissipated person, but he was also the author of books on morality, where the evil was condemned, and of spiritual poems and music. This bloodthirsty tsar was reprimanded straightforwardly (by Vasiliy the Blessed, for example; after that however, he remained to be a spiritual authority for the tsar. The tsar bore the coffin with the body of the dead saint). However, no vice could shake the people's trust in given by God "Dearest Tsar Ivan Vasilievich". Because of the denial of the absolute, independent of God values, the idea of *jus naturale* appeared to be revolutionary in Russia, the Russian rulers tried to implement this idea since Alexey Mikhailovich. Peter the Great enforced these ideas directly and severely (which contradicted the traditional in Old Russia *jus divinum*). In fact, the establishment of "eternal" values as we shall see, does not result in anything except for nihilism in Russia.

The lack of absolute values resulted in an extremely primitive social structure of Old Russia, a certain uniformity of the social mechanism. The attitude to man in the Old Russian language was so eccentric that no definitions were accepted as inherent except for maybe definitions of kinship (as the facts of the social and cultural development of Russia suggest, this primitiveness should not be associated with backwardness). The annals and other written documents demonstrate that social and property definitions were not essential for characterising this or that person (only after Peter one can find the decisive influence of property relations on the relations between

---

[3] S. S. KHORUZHII: *Posle Pereryva. Puti Russkoi Filosofii* (After the Break. The Roads of the Russian Philosophy), Saint Petersburg (A-cad) 1994.

people and a steady lexicon of property distinctions). Although it is surprising, this is a fact, that "in Old Russia we actually do not know a word designating a person known for his wealth", writes a researcher of Russian books V. V. Kolesov.[4] That is, if a medieval writer wanted to point out somebody's wealth, he had to use the epithets describing the relation of the person to the church or temporal power.

The defender of "old piety", archpriest Avvakum, in his book of Psalms interpretations once explained the meaning of the equality the way it was understood in the period of the Russian Middle Ages. The "Nikonists" introduced a new system of titles, new names for the patriarch and the tsar to be said in the prayers: "Most Holy Patriarch", "the Most Pious, Most Powerful, Greatest Tsar". This was opposed by Avvakum: "Before the dean and the priest would say to everyone: 'God remember you in His Kingdom' and to the Tsar they would say: 'God remember your Honour for all time'; and to the Patriach they would say: 'God remember your Grace in His Kingdom'".[5] No one can be called the holiest without sinning. It is not someone who is holy, it is the place he occupies in the hierarchy of the clerical or temporal power. In this negative sense all people were equal.

One cannot say that the ancient Russian writers did not mention money at all. On the contrary, even in hagiographic works they positively described money and other little joys of life. Money in itself is neither an obstacle or assistance for salvation. (When young St. Seraphim Sarovsky used to work in his father's shop, in his homilies he often used "money" metaphors.) A. S. Demin gives a number of examples of an "aesthetic attitude to money" in the Russian medieval prose. For example, an hagiograph wrote about the life of St. Ioann of Novgorod, "he loved money and did not conceal it." The author of *The Story of Tochtamysh's Invasion*, summarizes the results of the devastation in terms of money. "There was not anything in the plots to make the authors necessarily mention counting money; apparently, the authors

---

4   V. V. KOLESOV: *Mir Cheloveka v Slove Drevnei Rusi* (The World of Man in the Word of Ancient Russia), Leningrad (Izdatelstvo Leningadskogo Gosudarstvennogo Universiteta) 1986, p. 183.
5   AVVAKUM PETROV: *Zhitie Protopopa Avvakuma, im Samim Napisannoe i Druggie ego Sochineniya* (The Life of Priest Avvakum, Written by him, and his Other Essays), Arkhangelsk (Severo-Zapadnoye Knizhnoye Izdatelstvo) 1990, p. 103-104.

themselves considered these operations important."⁶ In this respect it seems typical that in the Russian medieval law "the term 'crime' was not known. Instead of it, such words like 'offence' are used. 'Offence' did not mean abuse of honour, it denoted both a murder and not paying a debt, primarily designating damage. Thus, the material aspect of crime prevails"⁷ over the moral and other aspects.

Labour in the works of Russian medieval authors also acquired some value only in addition to the course of salvation: the medieval authors called for working with a prayer, any result being considered as a gift of God, like the Grace sent by God upon the saints. This explains the following peculiarity of the Russian culture: many words denoting holiness also mean labour. The Greek word 'praxis', translated as 'doing', 'deed' also meant 'praying' accompanied with 'theoreia', that is, 'contemplation'. 'Sophia', wisdom, was one of the key words of the Russian spiritual culture, from *Sermon on Law and Grace* up to Dostoyevsky and our days. This word has typical 'business' connotations. Vladimir Toporov writes that the paradox of "the fullness of Sophia which is realized as plurality...'transcends' the antithetic character by some infinite creative energy...due to the creative character of Sophia movement of self-development." In his opinion, "the response of Sophia to createdness and mortality, to entropy of the world is multifruitfulness". The word 'holiness' is derived, according to the author, from the preslavic 'svet' which meant 'to increase', 'to swell': "Taking into account the contexts and analogies of typological character,...some benefactory growing, flourishing of a invigorating substance was meant, which led to the ripening of the *fruit*,...to the maximum fertility, income."⁸ The image of the spiritual holiness was formed on the basis of this extreme prosperity adopted in the Orthodox Christianity. The Saints in the Russian tradition are symbols of So-

---

6 A. S. DEMIN: ""Imenie": Sotsialno-Imushchestvennye Temy Drevne-Russkoi Literatury" ("The Estate": Social-Property Issues of Old-Russian Literature), in: *Drevnerusskaya Literatura: Izobrazhenie Obshchestva*, Moscow (Nauka) 1991, p. 30.

7 M. DIAKONOV: "Russkoye Pravo" (Russian Law), in: *Rossiia: Entsiklopedicheskii Slovar*, Leningrad (Lenizdat) 1991, p. 526.

8 V. N. TOPOROV: *Sviatost i Sviatye v Russkoi Dukhovnoi Kulture* (Holiness and the Saints in the Russian Clerical Culture), Moscow (Gnozis-Shkola "Yazyki Russkoi Kultury") 1995, pp. 80,480.

phia, denoting the excess of divinity in some location (Saint Land) or at some time (Christmas-tide).

The process of spiritualization of the saint in the connection with the adoption of supermundane ideals of Christianity was not painful to Russia. At least, a great expert of the Russian culture Rosanov, who opposed the fecund saint to the eunuch spirit of Christianity, often spoke about the popular concept of holiness using the same terms.

Various popular proverbs and sayings are associated with "sanctified" labour, the labour meant above: "With the prayer in the mouth, with work in hands", "God loves work", "God's creature works for God", "That who is early up, gets from the hand of God", "A bee works, a candle for God will be good", "Man cannot work successfully, unless God helps."[9] St. Fiodor Studit, a well-known Byzantine writer, the author of the monastic code, read by the worldly Orthodox Christians, calls the monks to work: "...everybody's need is satisfied by God...but we shall not lie in bed, we shall work and sweat to satisfy the monastery's needs. Since God is prone to be merciful when He sees His order being executed by the whole community together, and then he sends the means of provision from the invisible sources."[10]

Taking into account the fact that the request for fruits was addressed to God, it is difficult to say how highly developed the culture of labour was in the medieval Russia, and to judge how the contracts were fulfilled. In addition to the well-known facts demonstrating the responsibility and precision of fulfilling contracts in the entrepreneurship of the period before the October revolution, I managed to discover an interesting agreement, showing a high level of honour contracts among the merchants. Twice a year the herring is shipped up the Volga from the Caspian Sea. If one blocks the lower part of the river with nets, the rest of the river will have no fish. There was a rule among the merchants, according to which the merchants of the lower

---

9   V. DAHL: "Poslovitsy Russkogo Naroda" (The Proverbs of the Russian People), *Sbornik V. Dalia v Trioh Tomah*, Moscow (Russkaya Kniga) Vol. 1, 1994, p. 63. Ibid., Vol. 2, p. 404.
10 FIODOR STUDIT: "Podvizhnechiskie Monakham Nastavleniia" (Admonitions of Ascetism to Monks), in: *Dobrotoliubie*, Moscow (Svyato-Troitskaya Serggiyeva Lavra) Vol. 4, 1992, p.208.

THE ETHICS OF BUSINESS IN RUSSIA

Volga started fishing one and a half weeks after the fish had started going up, so that the higher Volga would not be left without fish (though no punishment would follow the violation of this rule). This tradition disappeared after the October revolution, when the religion was repressed... At the same time the merchants, whose duty of honour was to fulfil this rule, disappeared, too.

The words of Christ condemning money-grabbing seem to be understood in the Orthodoxy not literally, their interpretation is restrained by the functionalism described above. St. Nil Sorsky and other non-grabbers treated with understanding the monastic property, reprimanding surplus, grabbing as one of the passions, and not as a fact of possessing. The problem of the struggle between non-grabbers and Iosiphlists is rooted in the modernisation of the medieval history as far as it is considered as the problem of property and possession. Non-grabbers did not deny property. The documents demonstrate that they meant the extent of the necessary in the monastic life, which implies various opinions among the believers.

All this can be supported with the material found in the books written by medieval authors. In *A Message to a Monk* the famous ecclesiastical medieval writer Maxim Grek denies the concept that the human destiny is controlled by Fortune, a blind law. He is sure that the fate is designed by God: "God makes you poor and rich, makes you feel humble and elevated". He writes that God is the only master of destinies in the world. He is also the source of wealth and poverty (according to what is better for a particular person for his salvation). Of course, Maxim Grek is far from accepting wealth as the seal of God's grace on man, he is far from Protestantism, as it was understood by Max Weber. But in the words of Maxim Grek there is nothing regarding wealth as evil, as a useless aspect of life contradictory to Christianity.

Some indifference in the Russian culture towards any steady, constant value led to its negation, which happened to be so popular in the 19th century. Property was not understood in the energetic anthropology as something inherent and inalienable to man. In general, except for striving to be similar to God, according to the Eastern Orthodox anthropology, man becomes a radical cynic and nihilist and gradually loses all values (see the proverbs in Dahl's dictionary: "After us, eat wolf grass!", "That, who drinks, sleeps, that who sleeps, does not sin", "Amen does not knead", "Oh my God, kill to death him who has got money and whose wife is good"[11]). In the proverbs (often knavish and mocking the ideas of the divine), a desire is reflected to relate God's gifts - His response to man - to human efforts ("God gave you health, you have to get money on your own!", "God gave you hands, you have to make ropes yourself"[12]). This process, the slogan of which Dostoyevsky formulated like this: "If there is no God, everything is allowed!", is less frightening in the Western European cultural world where the values are traditional not only in their relation to God, but on their own, too. In Russia, any abstract considerations concerning the morality, the necessity to be adherent to the values irrespectively of the requirements of the specific human actions, as a rule, caused evil and anarchism.

In addition, in case the property is recognized in its legal definition specific to Modern history, the oriental version of Christianity should be rejected. This idea is supported by the talented writer V. F. Ern who seems to be too categorical in his judgements: "First, the recognition of private property contradicts the Christian teaching of grace. According to this teaching, all the positive that we possess, belongs not to us, but to God. Second, owing the private property is either idolatry or atheism."[13]

It does not mean, as I have mentioned, that there was no respect to private property in the Russian popular proverbs ("Your own shirt is your own width, and your own tightness"[14]). This just means that the value of property was not understood as unchangeable and inalienable positive value inherent to man. That is why the Russians were indifferent to expropriations. They lived in the world where the expropriation was usual at the end of human life, and the major expropriator was God. Probably, something like that happened with the attitude to serfdom: the phenomenon of serfdom was rarely understood by the serves as being somebody's property. In the proverbs created by the serfs there are complaints concerning changes of the fate, bribery of the priests, injustice of the managers, hard work, but never the chains of 'serfdom'. "He who possesses himself and controls himself cannot be in any way made subordinate," teaches Ioann Zlatoust.

---

11 V. DAHL: *Ibid.*, Vol. 2, p. 395; Vol. 3, p. 614.
12 V. DAHL: *Ibid.*, Vol. 2, p. 398.
13 V. F. ERN: "Khristianskoe Otnoshenie k Sobstvennosti" (Christian Attitude to Property), In: *Russkaia Filosofiya Sobstvennosti (XXII-XX)*, Saint Petersburg (Nauka) 1993, p. 202.
14 V. DAHL: *Ibid.*, Vol. 2, pp. 626-629.

THE ETHICS OF BUSINESS IN RUSSIA

Finally, it is surprising that in the traditional Russian morals, lenders were sometimes more respected then debtors ("Gathering money means breathing heavily", "Lending is like throwing down, getting back what is owed to you is like throwing up", "Do not feel sad he who borrows; feel sad he who lends"[15]). And it is beyond any doubt that lenders are not condemned by the Church morals. *The Domostroi*, an encyclopaedia of the household of XVI, recommends usury among other household activities.

A beggar, a poor person, a peasant, a noble, a merchant, a lender, a debtor were equally Church people and shared Orthodox ethical values (it held true at least till the period of the Split).

III. The Peculiarities of the Russian Culture and the Ethics of Capitalism

Does it mean that Weber's assumption that Protestant ethics is indispensable for a successful development of capitalism is not relevant for Russia? And if not, is it true that nothing stood in the way of capitalist relations in Russia in the sphere of morals?

Before answering this question, it is necessary to point out that the capitalist development in Russia was not so victorious and easy, both in the sphere of state and in the sphere of society. Some capitalist characteristics were steadily rejected by the morals of the Russian society.

Capitalism is characterized by the following: the domination of money - goods relations and private means of production (which existed in Russia at the period of the beginning of capitalist reforms, except for land property), a highly developed division of labour, the growth of the public character of production, the market of labour force (it emerged in Russia after serfdom was abolished). Which traits of the ethics of capitalism were unacceptable for the traditional morals of the Russian society?

Marx demonstrated that one of the characteristics of capitalist production was striving to new goals: "A simple turn-over of the goods - selling for the sake of purchasing - is a means for achieving the final goal beyond the turn-over - for acquiring the use value, for satisfying the needs. On the contrary,

---

15 *Ibid.*, p. 452.

the flow of money as capital is the goal in itself, because the increase of the value can be achieved only in the framework of this permanent movement. That is why the capital flow has no limits."[16]

Unlike the previous forms of the economy, capitalism has no limits of the growth of accumulation; in many respects this was the basis of its successful development. Maybe, Marx's analysis of capitalism is just rendering the Arisotelian distinction between economy and chrematistics and the definition of the priority of chrematistics, that is, the priority of such an economy that strives for an infinite accumulation of money and has neither any measure, nor any goal. It was this infinity of the accumulation of money that the traditional Christian ethics, including the Orthodox version, was against.

The wealth of a well-off person, a merchant, was encouraged in the traditional ethics as far as he was moderately, reasonably rich. "But in spite of all the respect to the 'possession' and money," - writes a researcher of the ancient Russian literature Demin, - "the writers disapproved of significant and, moreover, of excessive profits. A very rich character in literature became a negative character." Further, the researcher comments on the following excerpt from *The Story about Luka Kolochsky*: "..and he got a lot of wealth...and became purposeless and shameless." At the same time, in the story about a rich virtuous man, the wealth is limited "to the constraints of conscience".[17]

Ioann Zlatoust (Ioannes Chysostomos) says: "Do not wish more and you will not lose everything; and do not gather more than necessary and you will not lose the necessary; do not trespass the established limits and you will not lose all your property, but cut off the excess in order to be rich in the necessary."[18]

This also confirms that counting the 'virtuous' money as it was understood by medieval man, that is, gifts to the prince or to the tsar, the description of wealth of the overseas churches was meticulous and ended with an exact or approximate but often extremely long list of valuable things, whereas the wealth which was acquired dishonestly was considered by the

---

16 K. MARX, F. ENGELS: *Izbrannye Sochineniia* (Selected Works), Moscow (Politizdat) Vol. 7, 1987, pp. 146-147.
17 A. S. DEMIN: *Ibid.*, p. 32.
18 IOANN ZLATOUST: *Sobranie Pouchenii Izbrannyh iz Tvorenii Izhe vo Sviatyh Otsa Nashego Ioanna Zlatoustogo* (The Selected Works of our Father Ioann Zlatoust), Moscow (Posad) Vol. 1, 1993, p. 244.

writers as 'infinite' and 'uncountable'. In *The Story of Tochtamish's Invasion*, summarizing the results of the tragic event, the author says: "If it be possible to count all the losses, mishaps and tortures, I cannot say, methinks, it would be thousands of thousands roubles."[19] The vicious infinity is used here in the negative sense.

IV. The Communal Economy Serving Capitalist Relations

What constrains the anti-values of chrestematics, inherent to capitalist entrepreneurship and what could humanise them, for example, in the Russian culture? I would not like to consider the variety of values in subcultures, which emerged after the fall of the Russian Empire. Eventually, all of them are rooted in the *Pax Russica*.

It seems that only the rejection of infinity and of the unconstrained economy - if the value factors opposing the entrepreneurial activities are limited by the axiology - could be in the way of establishing specific capitalist values in the economy and entrepreneurship in the Russian culture.

First of all, I shall discuss the issue, which was not touched upon when discussing the relation of ethics to profits. This is a problem of the distribution of the benefits resulting from labour.

A monk, as it is well-known, makes an oath of submission and non-grabbing. A monk did not own even the fruits of his own labour. But the values acquired as a result of his labour became the property of the community. The community justifies both the property and the acquisition; it is difficult to show the limits of the necessary in the life of the community. Even the family is not such a serious economic formation as the community: the family (especially such a family where the husband is the head of everything) is closer in the sphere of decision-making and in the allocation of the benefits to a proprietor. The words of Christ concerning non-grabbing, being addressed to everyone, are vague as related to the community, since one can restrict himself to the necessary in his personal life, but cannot make others do the same. Personal asceticism reduces personal needs but how is it possi-

---

19 A. S. DEMIN: *Ibid.*, p. 29.

ble to reduce communal needs? It is as a result of communal life that the immensely rich decoration of churches emerges, and the community ensures the prosperity of monastic works and lands (sometimes encouraging the sin of grabbing). The requirements of non-grabbing are restricted by the communal relations: the monasteries were rarely accused of in the medieval culture, and even if they were, it was within the framework of anticlerical movements (Strigolniki, for example).

There is a rich historiography of the Russian agricultural community. The land problem was one of most painful problems of the modernisation of the Russian household, and it has not been still resolved.

As to the other forms of communities, the bibliography on this issue is very poor. The interest of the researchers to land property was suppressed by the interest to the religious community in general, which was of greater importance than the communal land property. There were town religious communities, fraternities, other types of religious organisation, based upon mutual trust of its members and often upon common property.

In the time of Peter I, which fairly damaged the Russian traditional way of life, the traditional Russian community united around the parish, lost the absolute significance it used to have in the Russian life. Although before Peter, the community was the primary element in the structure of the social self-government. And (which is very important, though was ignored in all the previous investigations) the Russian community was based not on the sort of activity (like the guilds of Western European Middle Ages) but exclusively on religious grounds. Although the people of one profession preferred to settle together (the community formed around a church, a parish) in a town, a parish could unite and actually united various representatives of the town infrastructure. I shall not mention here the contribution of such a community to the morals, but it had serious advantages for emerging Russian capitalism.

In Russia, besides peasant agricultural communities, there remained Old Belief communities, a kind of preserves of pre-Peter life-style. It is in these Old Belief communities that the Russian capitalist entrepreneurship flourished.

The agricultural community, even taking into account all the positive aspects related to its activity in Russia, that is, social protectionism concerning the poorest households, the cultivation of the spirit of self-government, was very much restrained by very useful, but monotonous peasant labour which was supported and approved of by the community (the goal of economic activities of the peasant community was "just" satisfaction of the needs of its members). The common property, the opportunity to manage the money of the community could not be designed for reaching the goals different from those of the community (in general, there always were exceptions to the rule - millionaires, who preferred buying a trade license to paying off a large redemption and then annual merchant contributions. Eventually, they won the competition with families of merchants). And this probably prevented the peasant community from getting adjusted to the dynamically developing capitalism. But the town community which was not preserved as such in the "Nikonian" Orthodoxy, played the first role in the emerging capitalist relations.

I shall give the account of the advantages of the town Old-Believers community. First, the common property enabled the Old-Believers, while the other conditions being equal, to have a bigger starting capital than the individual merchants. Second, a member of the community was not constrained by the traditional sort of activity, as it was the case in the villages. Third, the community was a voluntary religious community; its members worked thriftily, led by conscience and not by fear. And finally, there were no moral restrictions on the profits for communal entrepreneurs: many Old-Believers had great incomes, controlled them, but did not formally possess them. In fact, the demands of the manufacturers to their employees were often so unreasonable because they were sanctioned by the community and not by their personal will.

The Old-Believers got used to the scheme Money-Goods-Money much more easily than their individualist colleagues who did not have the natural need in capital formation. We observe the similar processes when many directors of previously state owned enterprises, who became millionaires overnight, are quite satisfied and use the old styles of management, since they are not forced to take care of their enterprises. They and their families became rich without it.

The centre of Old-Believers of priestless trend (Bespopovtsy) in Moscow was Preobrazhensky cemetery; Popovtsy met at Rogozhskoye cemetery (the communities meeting at these cemeteries were the centres of socially active Old-Believers). As a result, in Moscow almost the majority of merchants was formed by Old-Believers.

For the Popovtsy the service was conducted by fugitive priests, later (in 1853) this religion got its own metropilos. Bespopovtsy, sticking to the traditions of the Russian Middle Ages, of worshipping icons, did not accept the service of the "Nikonian" church. Bespopovtsy were the most radical among the Old-Believers. The Guchkov family, to which a known reformer politician A. I. Guchkov belonged (Chairman of the Duma, Chairman of War Industry Committee, Military Minister of the Provisional Government, "Octiabrist"), were Bespopovtsy. One of the sources of the wealth of this family was the fact that the forefather was the treasurer of the communal fund: when the Old-Believers were scared by state repressions, this merchant was in charge of 12 million roubles.

The founder of the dynasty M. Ryabushinsky was also an Old-Believer, one of Popovtsy. His grandchildren were among the leaders of the progressist party. It is worth noting that so far the religious and property background of the political struggle of the main bourgeois democratic parties in Russia has not been studied; while it is obvious that the Old-Believers influenced the political scene of pre-revolutionary Russia very much.

The famous Nizhnii Novgorod merchant N. A. Bugrov, who in the 80s was invited to a ball by Alexander III for his contribution to the Russian economy, who was also the organizer of the river traffic on the Volga, distributed incredible profits among his fellow countrymen Old-Believers.

The list of the names of Old-Believers, the founding fathers of the Russian entrepreneurship, is long. Here are just some of them: the Soldationkovs, the Sherygins, the Treumovs, the Pavlovs, the Morozovs.

The mentioned above advantages of the town community during the period of transition to capitalism confirm that only the members of town Old-Believers community became capitalists. The Old-Believers living in the country, however rich they might be, did not organize capitalist enterprises.

But even not mentioning the Old-Believers (who never formed the majority of the Russian entrepreneurship), the business activities of individual merchants usually tended to transform into communities. Although the enterprises were called joint-stock companies, they actually "belonged to a narrow circle of relatives-shareholders".[20] Most often, the sons took over their father's business. Even if the founder of a big capital was an individual, his followers lived as a community, where the money management was collegial, both for the production and personal needs. For example, the most wide-spread form of the enterprises was a partnership. At the end of the 19th

---

20 A. BAIKINA, L. DODONOVA: *Ocherki Istorii Rossiiskogo Predprinimatelstva i Blagotvoritelnosti* (The Essays on the History of Russian Entrepreneurship and Charity), Tiumen (Belyi Parus) 1994, p. 93; DEMIN: *ibid.*, p. 29.

century, there existed two types of partnerships, partnerships based on trust and limited liability partnerships, depending upon the level of the liability of the partners: in the first case the partner was liable with all his property, in the second case the partner was liable only according to the amount of his share.[21] It should be noted, that there were different types of participation in the enterprises of the first type: the organizers risked all their property, other partners and shareholders were liable only according to their contribution. The majority of Russian businessmen organized community enterprises of this type: the Morozovs, the Prokhorovs, the Mamontovs, the Khludovs, the Yakunchikovs, the Alexeyevs, the Guchkovs, the Abrikosovs.

The significance of the name of an enterprise is very remarkable: the names of companies often contained the names of the organizers (Eliseyev's Shop, Philippov's Bakery, Morosov's Manufacture, Zinger plant). Using the name of the businessman in the name of firm demonstrated that the name guaranteed the quality and the success of the business. Everybody in Russia knew the names of the proprietors of the two competing Volga steamer companies *Samolet* and *Caucasus and Mercury*.

V. Conclusion

The analysis of the attitude to entrepreneurial activities in the Russian culture helps to destroy the myth claiming that the traditional ethics of Orthodoxy constrains the business activities. And it is also wrong to think that it promotes this activity. In the Church ethics, the submission of the values to the course of the salvation demands to stick to the necessary, and this constrains the accumulation.

But the Church ethics has an important exemption (which reflects the soteriological functionalism of "energetic" ethics) which enables capitalist relations to develop on the Russian soil. It involves an opportunity of a compromise of the spirit of personal asceticism with the needs of the economy of the mixed town community traditional in Russia. It is on the basis of the

---

21 *Ibid.*, p. 120.

town Old-Believers collective businesses that the capital of the prospective mighty entrepreneurial dynasties was started. The permission of the collective accumulation in the ethics of Old-Believers was a successful adjustment of the traditional ethics to the unlimited accumulation of capitalism.

In the cases when an individual businessman became successful, his business also tended to the collective type of business. This tendency resulted in the wide-spread activities of partnerships, that is, businesses uniting the capital and the efforts of several capitalists who either were relatives or belonged to one confession.

Chapter 7

One's Own, Proper
What Is Property in its Essence?

VLADIMIR V. BIBIKHIN

I. The Situation
II. Seizure of the World
III. The Most Familiar
IV. Freedom of Property

I. The Situation

Privatisation, which is said to take place or to have taken place in Russia, is called criminal, Mafia-ridden, immoral, a menace to the rest of the world. More seldom are its positive evaluations. There is no need to align oneself with either opinion. The promptitude of judgement solidifies the principal and in the long run the decisive feature of the situation: the fact that property reforms are conducted blindly. There is no difference of opinion in this respect. An important or leading activist of the privatisation, recently sacked, has expressed his wish that it be conducted in a more thoughtful manner. The belated character of the wish confirms that the amplitude of unthoughtfulness in the whole affair is itself unthought of. Understandably, one is inclined to believe that a more detailed planning could have produced more success. Yet it is most probable that the process which started moving ten years ago takes place in a depth unattainable for any plan or project. It is not a mere coincidence that the preceding socialist volte-face in Russia, too, took a haphazard stance. A theorist of the state and historian, Nikolai Alekseyev, observed in 1928: "Wonderful as it may seem, the majority of contemporary socialists, while proposing a reform of property and calling for the abolition of the latter, wander in complete darkness and do not know for sure what they are striving at"[1].

II. Seizure of the World

Today's privatisation is a direct continuation of the seventy years of "socialized property" in Russia, not for the reason that it is conducted by the same nomenclature, but because it goes on, using more effective means, in the line of the same seizure of the world, which at the beginning of the century demanded concentration of all available forces into a collective fist. Let loose by depersonalization, liberated from religious constraint, new resources of the collective remained nevertheless handicapped by the collectivist ideology and haphazard ethics, a remnant of the former religious piety. The dumping of both ideology and ethics today facilitates greatly the seizure, and restores its original acuteness.

Neither this seizure of the world nor its particular intensity these days is a novelty of the 20th century. The global seizure of the world is not a new or a local event, it exhibits an ancient face. Evident or obscure, preoccupation with conquering, mastering or taming the world has never loosened its grip on man. Perhaps Heraclitus had this in mind when he suggested: one should know this, the War is general, and truth is contest, and all comes to be in battle by seizure[2]. Right now, when even the so called cultural heritage is also an object to be seized and academic science is being swept to rubbish, amid that what seems to be wild disorder, unprecedented in the eyes of a nervous observer, philosophy gets a unique chance to remind itself of its early beginnings and its initial essence. The primary meaning of *sophia,* to be heard yet in its Aristotelean definition as "the vigour of technique"[3], is dexterity, clever grasp, cunning. Seizure of the world is not a passing obscuration of people forgetting shame, decency and their own long-running inter-

---

[1] N. N. ALEKSEYEV: "Sobstvennost i Sotsializm" (Property and Socialism), in: K. ISUPOV, I. SAVKIN (Eds.): *Russkaya Filosofiya Sobstvennosti,* Saint Petersburg (SP "Ganza") 1993, p. 346.
[2] HERACLITUS: *Fragm. 80* (Diel Kranz) = *Fragm. 28* (Marcovic).
[3] ARISTOTELES: *Eth. Nic.*, VI 7, 1141 a 9.

WHAT IS PROPERTY IN ITS ESSENCE?

ests, but the very element of early thought. Now, at a brusque turning point, in a fracture, Russia has distinctly shown the hard core of the eternal relation of humans to their world.

The bolder the seizure, the more urgently the world proposes itself as the target of activity. It is evident at the level of everyday talk. Russia *must* enter the world community, take its place in the world level in its economy, in its banking business. Small enterprises, too, set to no greater task than attaining world standards in technology and communications. Science follows more openly world patterns than before. Everywhere chairs of world culture have emerged. In its omnipresence, the world, of course, has not become closer or more comprehensive, it sinks rather more surely into its elusiveness. The world is, as good as ever, closer in its strange intimacy to human beings than anything, as all things are introduced to us by what they are in. We primarily find ourselves in the world and try to secure our place in it. The first to be grasped, the world is the last thing to give an account of; one invariably looks for it to take one's bearings, yet nothing is harder to fix. In the world of things and in the world of mind, human enthusiasm creates changing patterns. Invariably, the ultimate target, the *whole*, remains equally out of reach for the shrewd and for the slow.

Frequent proposals of abstaining from efforts to seize the world, calls of self-limitation, of renunciation abstract from fundamental realities. We see the seizure as *the* clue to the contemporary situation, political, economic and intellectual. At the same time, it is safe to trace the seizure up to the natural desire to see, which, according to Aristotle, is common to all human beings. What is simply seen, may seem far away from being appropriated, yet seeing unobtrusively turns into overseeing. Inadvertently, long before any seizure of land, oil, buildings, positions begins, that primary seizure takes place, when observation becomes control. As soon as this elemental seizure occurs, any consequent material seizure, which is usually much more naive and controllable than the primordial one, cannot fail to follow the first. It lacks sense completely to claim that the first seizure is unjustified or that the slide of *seeing* into *overseeing* may be immoral. A metamorphosis of what is properly seen into overseeing of property occurs too early, as if in a dream, to be timely grasped or formulated.

Seeing turns over into overseeing and possession so suddenly that the most acute analysis fails to grasp the pattern of transition, or even the difference between the two. Yet it is this difference that deserves most attention. The early origins of property cannot be a matter of jurisdiction. The latter has to do with material seizure only. Formally, the all-powerful *vedomstva*, departments, literally "seeing bodies" (*ved-* 'understand' from *vid-* 'see'), "inspections" in socialist economy, were and also are now by no means proprietors of what they control(led), but they exercise(d) powers unimaginable with a private proprietor. Privatisation now limits the former unlawful authority of a class which nominally possess(ed) within the nationalized economy no more than a man in the street.

At the same time, seizure is an act of one who is seized himself, too, as in enthusiasm, passion, or fascination. It is usually difficult to establish by what exactly one is seized, as the state of being seized hinders elucidation. It rarely is eager, in its rush, to define itself. On the contrary, both seizure and the corresponding state of being seized prefer to hide. The history of the Russian language shows connection of seizure (*zahvat*), cunning (*hitrost*), stealing (*hishsheniye*) and enthusiasm (*voskhishsheniye*). What seizes most, has the nature of cherished secrecy. Nothing is more severely guarded than hidden motives of our behaviour. In every act and word one is guided primarily by what one is least of all inclined to analyze.

While looking into this seizure of the world, we should have in mind our being seized by its mystery, too. Our epoch, or at least the present situation in Russia, is often called unprecedented in various respects. To our mind, it is unprecedented, indeed, but only as far as never before this reverse of the coin, this inevitable dependence of our aggression, in that it always follows suit to the grip of the world *on us*, was so thoroughly neglected. We usually pose as authors of all our initiatives. The world is understood as an object of human endeavour. Human activity is thought to be spontaneous, and the criticism of its excesses presupposes unilaterality of our onslaught. However, the latter is never one-sided. We belong to our world with an intimacy we are never fully prepared to acknowledge, least of all today. While perfecting our grasp of the world, we always lack attention for the manner the world in *its* early grasp dictates us our steps. Any research here faces cunning of a very intricate kind, the grasp of *sophia*.

The world is always mine. It strengthens its grip on me precisely by the fact of being invariably my own. Each epoch faces the changing world with the same belief, although with greatly varying readiness to accept the reciprocity of possession. In his pursuit of material things, contemporary man is much less than in earlier, more "idealistic" epochs, inclined to locate the stimuli of his initiatives outside his body and his psyche. Still the challenge comes, as always, from the world as an evasive whole. Its early grip has determined us long before we started our operations.

That is why, in regard of the fresh seizure that let itself go in our country, justification or accusation is out of place. What evades notice in all this seizure, is uniquely important, namely the decisive provocativeness of the world as the frame of our being.

III. The Most Familiar

In its primary seizure (in our being seized by its seizure) the world remains the principal orienting point, horizon and limit, unseizable and indeterminable in itself, as a whole. In all disputes about property the only stable fulcrum to firmly rely upon is also presented by the world as the ultimate target of all possession. Possession of the whole world looms of course too large and far, yet all other ways of establishing the limits of property lead nowhere, unless by decree. Anyway, human being cannot find itself but in the world. Almost everything in our country may become, if the destiny of Russia does not determine otherwise, alien private possession. Yet in an important sense this immediate world, my world, my country, will remain mine. But in what sense?

The avid pursuit of private property today has its firm foundation in the former nervous hope of idealistic communists to have in their collective possession what earlier belonged to the tsar and other proprietors. In 1927 in his poem *Very Well!* V. Mayakovsky tried to hypnotise himself: "The street is mine, the houses are mine... My co-operation is beginning to feather... My militia takes care of me..." Necessarily, this desire to see the whole country (and in the long run the whole world) as one's possession opposed itself in a very explicit manner to former habits of ownership. Of course, both property and socialization were far from being properly understood. It could not have happened otherwise. Reformers thought they were guided by the perfect (*wise*, cf. *sophia*) scientific theory. The ultimate goal was to show the way to humanity to change the face of the earth. Transformation was expected to spring out necessarily of the effort of the collective, armed with all the ways and means to change the world. Mayakovsky drew his inspiration from the supposed feelings of a compact human mass on its march towards paradise.

Socialization, into which the country was drawn, being intensively taught new collectivist norms, bitterly failed. A similar failure is expecting the present "capitalism", self-murderously careless of its roots. The attraction of *one's own*, when obeyed in a blind or careless way, makes ethics look obscure, obsolete or non-existent. Naturally, this invites in turn the mechanisms of social control, which in similar situations exhibited severe features in Russia.

Any regulation of property is likely to drift. This should have been clear well before the experiments with property began. It is enough to listen attentively to what the word *property* says in order to understand that property has to do with being proper, correct, normal, natural. Property presupposes some effort to achieve something like an elucidation of some true nature or destination of things. It is erroneous to see here only an example of vexing polysemanticity. What is detected by lexicography, is only the upper part of an iceberg. The constant tendency to affirm, fixate, confirm, formalise material and even intellectual property by legal procedures shows to what extent the hope that it will stand on its own feet is feeble. Property always goes along with an effort to establish its status. Otherwise it is at least dubious. Its slipperiness is universally felt. "The notion of property is shifting like sand"[4]. The process of establishing property, or establishing what is property, has no end. The roots of property touch depths where definitions are powerless. With its new projects of property, the self-relying revolutionary conscience is stuck firmly in an intricate net it has no chances to unknit or even to understand. The new revolutionary conscience is guided unconsciously by a dream that somewhere, at a magical point, the two contrasting meanings of property would melt together. It can be safely said that many experiments with property are misguided by a word and are involved in a grammatical exercise.

Property, as what is juridically ascribed to a certain person, is definitely different from property as natural quality of something. At the same time, juridical property presupposes some proper way of possession. When, in their revolt against private proprietors, the Bolsheviks chose to remain deaf to the unfathomable depths of *owner*ship, they had driven themselves to the shallows. When our contemporary privatisators try to establish a new system of possession by decree, they remain deaf, too, to the fact that property is null and void if not animated by the fascination of *one's own, suum* in Latin,

---

4 N. N. ALEKSEYEV: *ibid.*, p. 348.

WHAT IS PROPERTY IN ITS ESSENCE?

svoyo in Russian. This fascination of *one's self*, although deeper than ethical norms, in its roots has nothing to do with selfishness.

Nothing exercises a greater demand on us than *our own*, in the sense that we are occupied with our own business, have our own mind, and know our time. Apart from this source, all ownership is relative or conditional. In as far as ownership is serious enough to reach its origins, it evades juridical or any other forms and makes the task of giving an account of it a puzzle. Latin expression *suo jure* is usually translated as *in one's right* and is misplaced in the context of individual rights, but originally it meant *by rights, on a solid foundation,* as *suum* was understood in the sense of ultimate raison d'être. *Suum esse,* literally *to be one's own*, equalled to *be free*. The Russian word *svoboda*, freedom, is akin to *suum* not in the sense of my property, but in the sense of my being properly myself. My proper self is the initial property, without which any other property is a *qui pro quo*. The ancient Greek name for being, οὐσία, originally meant *property*. In Heidegger, the word for *event* as manifestation of being, opens up in the direction of property (Ereignis - eignen, eigen).

One could reasonably ask if all technical, economic and scientific exploits are really enough to satisfy human desire for what is one's own. In a novel by Francis Fitzgerald, the hero was able to acquire enormous possessions, only to see himself as far as ever from his own self. The same discrepancy between property and what is properly one's own makes it very easy to raise "the question of property" and very difficult, if not impossible, to solve it. Even a limited success in a purely lexical operation of defining property within academic discourse cannot be achieved without first taking property in a limited sense.

Our world, as mentioned above, is at the same time the fascinating ultimate target of every seizure and the closest neighbour, intimate and familiar, closer to us even than our closest surroundings, which we feel alienated when our world darkens. In the history of the word, the Russian *mir* (meaning *world, peace, society*) is akin to the Greek *philia*, friendly disposition. When Vassily Rosanow invokes God as "the centre of the world's endearing", he treads the way already prepared by our language, where *mir* is etymologically connected to *milyi*, dear[5]. In our encounter with our world,

---

5 *Svoyo* in present-day Russian gradually loses the meaning of "intimately kindred" and "good", which belonged to the same root *su* in Sanskrit. But the same links persist due to etymological filiation between *svoyo* and *syn* (son) and

our subsequent acceptance of things is foreshadowed in a decisive manner. It is this perspective that intrudes imperatively upon any discussion of property.

One's own, the most familiar, involves the intimate, as sex, family, then the society, the state, while our experience of the "world" directs the progress of involvement and sets the ultimate target for it, as said above. In my world *my own* coincides with the universal. All these magnitudes, each of which stubbornly eludes definition, haunt the problematic of property. The unknown hero of the present-day manipulation with property in our country is philosophical enterprise, a subconscious effort to elucidate, by conventional practical means, the whole situation. But what is proper and what is actually our own, is never easy to grasp. Our self is the last thing to possess, and to know oneself is a prerogative of gods, according to Plato.

Almost everything in our country is said to be already in someone's hands. If nobody knows for sure in whose one's, it is not because of secrecy of possession, as if the new proprietors were hiding themselves, but because of the substantial impossibility to know otherwise than in legal terms, what is properly seized and, properly speaking, by whom. Similarly, in 1918, when it became universally clear that almost all property had been either seized or liberated, it remained in the long run and even up to our days unknown what exactly happened. There is an atmosphere of fright and in the vicinities of property these days in our country, undisclosed murders are being constantly reported. The origin of tension is not the confidence of new proprietors standing up firmly in defence of their rights. On the contrary, general uncertainty prevails, and makes new "trials" inevitable because of the difficulty to establish, who is finally the proprietor of what.

We surely can "have" the world, the ultimate horizon of property, only as a theme or the theme of questioning[6]. Moreover, to the question, who are *we*, properly speaking, the only proper answer is a description of our relations to the world as *the* event of our history. Sobered after blind fights for property, people inevitably come back to the school of *sophia*. Human beings can never be satisfied with finding niches in their surroundings, they

---

      also in the prefix *z*(from *su*)-*dorovye*, meaning "health" (literally, "good wood", "good matter"). The same link exists between the German *das Kind* (child) and the English *kind* with its two principal meanings of "breed" and "friendly".

6 V. V. BIBIKHIN: *Mir* (World), Tomsk (Vodoley) 1995.

burden themselves, in some way or other, in theory or more often in practice, with the problem of the whole. On the other hand, they know about the whole necessarily least of all. The science of not knowing, an ability to leave the world alone belongs to the art of life. "Some degree of sane unconsciousness... is as necessary for any society, as for a sane organism it is necessary that the brain... should remain unconscious of the functioning of internal organs"[7].

Unseizability of the seizure of the world makes all definitions of possession questionable, which provides a solid foundation for all sorts of criticism. Attractiveness of the own, the proper, in no way leads to harmony and order. The most cruel conflicts occur among close neighbours about the closest things (religious, civil wars). The reason why we, a product of biological evolution, cannot live in peace within our environment, is a theme apart. Efforts to ultimately elucidate property relations exhibit the face of apocalypse. In Christian faith, the Last Judgement comes from God to open the truth, severe but salutary, about the human being in what its proper self is. When a human judge, a leader or a collective, tries on his own to do the job and accomplish apocalyptic elucidation (e.g. *purges* under totalitarian rule), severity of judgement, as a rule, is guaranteed, but the process cannot end in the triumph of the truth for the reasons mentioned above. *Weltgeschichte* both ways turns to be *Weltgericht* (Hegel), all depends on whether the judging instance possesses the knowledge of what human being properly speaking is. In order to be cruel in their disputes over property, people do not need to know what property is, or to whom it belongs; on the contrary, some degree of anxious uncertainty on the subject is quite enough.

IV. Freedom of Property

In his idea of abolishing the state Marx was by no means more radical than his master Hegel. Hegel could not aspire to see the state die, because his seemingly unconditional acceptance of the state presupposed its *lifting* (Aufheben). A *lifted* state becomes a pure idea. On the contrary, publicist, and Marxian, criticism of the state, its "revolutionary" criticism and the so

---

[7] E. SAPIR: *Selected Works,* Moscow (Progress) 1993, pp. 609-610.

called criticism by means of arms only serve restoration of the state through its reorganisation. In general terms, criticism of any institution is thematization of the latter, that is to say, attraction of efforts, attention and means to it. For Hegel, the only worthy effort is that of free thought. Thought, in Hegel, is an intimate penetration into what is uniquely, concretely *one's own*.

"Internal property of the mind" is defined by Hegel as possession of one's body and spirit, acquired by culture, school, habitude. The act of coming back to one's self is hindered by *alienation*. Alienation is an important word in Marxism. The Soviet experiment followed the Marxist programme of abolishing alienation through socialization of property. Discarding the seventy years of the socialist experiment, present-day activists follow their revolutionary forerunners, who reduced all previous human history to a sort of preparation for their enterprise.

Marx' optimism draws energy from the Hegelian idea that a free rational will eventually re-establishes all things in their essence. The rights of free will are immense. It is a cow, according to Hegel, who, while grazing the grass in the meadow, proves that the destiny of the grass is not to be left as it is. The reasonable will so much more helps things fulfil their destiny. One's own body is also subject to one's will, otherwise it remains foreign (alien) to one's self. Human being is much more than a body, and much less seizable. As the free will is situated in another dimension than things and objects, freedom in Hegel excludes levelling of seizable property, both in the form of privation and in the form of forced allotment. Forcing property on those who refuse it, perhaps because they dedicate their efforts to a higher cause, equals its *limitation*. In this respect, too, Marx was much less radical than his teacher. As for Russian socializers, they fell short even of the Marxist theory and forced on everybody such forms of obligatory property as a "guaranteed" workplace. In our latest reform, forcing "privatisation cheques" on every citizen was an intrusion inadmissible even in Marx.

As justification of property lies in the necessity to help things regain their proper state, he who does right by a thing may consider himself its full proprietor, and in this case any purely legal claims to it are null and void, so thinks Hegel. He takes in a strong sense the postulate of the Justinian property legislation, according to which actual usage may turn into juridical possession, and introduces *freedom of property, Freiheit des Eigentums*, as a norm for the times to come. When Marx announces that "means of production", including land, belong to those who use them, a factory to the worker, a field to the peasant, he felt himself firmly established on paragraph 62 of

WHAT IS PROPERTY IN ITS ESSENCE?

Hegel's "Philosophy of Right": "About one and a half thousand years ago *freedom of person* began to blossom through Christianity and became a universal principle among, it is true, a small part of mankind. As for *freedom of property*, it has, so to say, only yesterday been accepted in certain places as a principle. An example from the world history of how much time the spirit needs to make a step forward in its self-consciousness - and against impatience of opinion". Purely legal possessor incapable of restoring what he possesses in its proper nature, not using it according to its destination, is an "empty lord" *leerer Herr*, and must cede his rights.

In Marx the principle is both obscured and complicated by the introduction of collective ownership, that is to say, of a novel juridical and authoritative mechanism. In Hegel the idea, not bearing the burden of its revolutionary enforcement, is ready to patiently sail until the moral climate is ready to accept it. Yet even Marx is still attentive, even somewhat superstitiously, to "social conditions". It was a fault of Russian Marxists that they were not stubborn enough to insist upon a careful reading, by the socialist government, of what was acknowledged by the latter to be its Bible. Now, after the failure of the Marxist (in fact, Hegelian) project, the country has swayed against the direction forecast by Hegel and being realized now in the social market economy. There are no reasons to doubt the correctness of Hegel's prediction. "In the face of freedom nothing really matters... There is nothing in the world higher than Right, its foundation is residence of the divine in its proper self"[8].

In § 65 of Hegel's "Philosophy of Right" the theme of alienation (*Entäusserung*) is introduced. We are already prepared to run into difficulties in what concerns property. It is not hard to agree that the "holy" right to property remains at the same time "to a considerable degree subordinated, it may and should be broken" giving way to rights of the people and the state. Still what follows a definition of "true alienation" (it is "an announcement of my will that I will no longer regard the thing in question as mine") is unexpected: "Alienation is a true seizure of possession (die Entäusserung ist eine wahre Besitzergreifung)". This is presupposed, however, by the freedom of property. A thing belongs to him who returns it to its true self according to its idea. The latter may include its absolute freedom from myself. Then I make the thing mine by honouring its independence from me.

---

8 G. W. F. HEGEL: *Die Philosophie des Rechts,* ßß 29-30.

Things also may be transformed according to their value into goods and in this case all their individuality is evaluated by a unified measure, money. The possibility to reduce things to the simplicity of their universal value is a great achievement. Money is a more "clever" form of property than merchandise. Money opens up the whole world of goods. Instead of cleaving to this parcel of land and becoming its appendix, I am free to possess its almost immaterial equivalent. Money means alienation of natural possession to acquire ideal property which is truer than any manual seizure.

The next step alienates me from money. I come off the money just as I got loose from material nature before. Now I am in full possession of my "unalienable substantial definitions", I come back to the "internal property of the spirit", to the essence of my self. Hegel proposes a criterion to distinguish conditional property from that of the spirit: independence from time. What a certain neighbour owned to my grandmother is lost for me. But the fact that I had been for long years unable to speak out freely does not mean that my right to speak lapsed to those who had deprived me of it. Free speech is my most proper property. Alienation seems impossible here.

Or is it still possible? Nobody remembers who were the authors of ancient epic poems. The achievements of archaic genetics are now completely depersonalized. It turns out that everything, in the long run, comes to be alienated. It is forgotten who was the author of the world. Hegel's criterion of the lapse of time unveils itself as not absolute, although useful in its field of application. A person may fully give itself away to what is properly *its own* to such a degree that all that was partial and private disappears in the "general", belonging to human being as a genus. A person has no right to take away its own life; yet the state can take it. The "internal property of the spirit" is not mine, after all; the *people* in its idea, the genus claims its right on it. All property as belonging to a person vanishes, only property in the sense of what is proper affirms itself. Alienation covers first everything in natural economy, then merchandise, next money, intellectual property later on, and finally individuality itself. Property concentrates to something that makes idle the question to whom it belongs. It is *its own*. The "generic" triumphs, not in the sense of some generalisation, but on the contrary, as a victory of what is most unique, as unattainably unique would have been a person capable to possess all attributes of the genus.

Freedom of property, whether acknowledged or not, effectively carries itself into practice in a *negative* way. In times of war and revolution, drastic or even annihilating measures are taken to curb private proprietors. Less conspicuous, although hardly less effective are ideological measures in the form of disclaimimg property as immoral, "a theft" (Proudon). Another phenomenon, showing the underground work of the idea, is the frequently observed easiness with which people accept a loss of property. Well known is the readiness of Russian "capitalists" to give away their possessions to revolutionaries. "If private property in Russia so easily, almost without resistance, was swept away by the whirlwind of socialistic passions, it was only because the belief in the *truth* of property was too frail"[9].

There are no serious grounds to think that by the end of the 19th century our mentality has greatly changed. By our refusal to accept as our true history what has happened and what happens to us now we prepare ourselves for a new political turn, which can hardly fail to be as abrupt as those that we have already had in this century. It is also by no means excluded that at this turn little will remain of the precocious "capitalism" in Russia[10].

---

[9] S. L. FRANK: "Sotsializm i Sobstvennost" (Socialism and Property), in: K. ISUPOV, I. SAVKIN (Eds.): *Russkaya Filosofiya Sobstvennosti*, Saint Petersburg (SP "Ganza") 1993, pp. 311-312.

[10] The theme is developed in the article: V. V. BIBIKHIN: "Svoboda Sobstvennosti" (Freedom of Property), *Put* 7 (1995), p. 154.

Section III

The Repersonalisation of Socialized Property

Chapter 8

Privatisation in the New Lands of the Former German Democratic Republic

WOLF-DIETER PLESSING

I. The Treuhandanstalt (Privatisation Agency)
II. The Results of Privatisation
III. Privatisation Procedure
IV. Experiences

I. The Treuhandanstalt (Privatisation Agency)

The Treuhandanstalt was the most significant institution created to manage the economic unification of Germany. Its principal aim after June 1990 was the rapid privatisation of eastern German industry, of real estate, of farmland and of forests.

In its short but turbulent history it grew from nothing into an organisation with 3,000 staff members, split between Berlin Head Quarters and 15 regional offices throughout eastern Germany. It was an independent agency established under the public law, acting as an enterprise and reporting to the Ministers of Finance and of Economics. It was closed down at the end of 1994, when most of its tasks had been completed.

The Treuhandanstalt was conceived in March 1990 by East Germany's last semi-communist government. Three months later all the state-owned property and enterprises were transferred to the Treuhandanstalt. For this

PRIVATISATION IN EASTERN GERMANY

purpose these enterprises were converted by law on July 1st, 1990 into West German style corporations - either limited liability companies/GmbHs or stock companies/AG's.

It quickly turned out that the companies were in a very bad condition, due to the following reasons:

The former Communist government had established large vertically integrated conglomerates, or "combines", which tended to be highly self-sufficient in their trading patterns. They turned out to be uncompetitive in their existing structure, unlike the mostly small and medium sized enterprises in the West, which were much more flexible.

The GDR had not invested enough in its state-owned enterprises.

About 21 per cent of industrial machinery in the old East Germany was more than 20 years old, compared with only 5 per cent in West Germany. 29 per cent was 11 to 20 years old. The companies were overstaffed and their productivity was insufficient.

East German companies lost most of their clients when, immediately after the monetary union, superior West German goods flooded into their domestic market. This was the effect of the immediate abolition of tariff restrictions, of the adoption of West German economic laws and of the introduction of the West German D-Mark. But East German companies also lost their Eastern bloc export markets as a result of the shortage of hard currency there.

The Treuhandanstalt executives were therefore initially side-tracked into keeping the shell-shocked eastern German companies afloat. A total of DM 20 bn in liquidity credit was handed out in the first three months after the currency union, merely to ensure that the companies could pay their wages.

It was clear that eastern German industry could only stay competitive in the united Germany if the companies were thoroughly restructured. The Treuhandanstalt could not have done this restructuring as a centralised institution. That would just have revived the old state economy of the former GDR. Instead, there was a firm conviction that privatisation is the best way of restructuring. Responsible private owners can do this job better than the state. Against this background, the Treuhandanstalt followed the strategy:

- to privatize wherever possible,
- to restructure companies with a view to later privatisation,
- to close down those companies which have no chance of surviving in a market economy.

The Treuhandanstalt was also charged with breaking up the larger combines.

II. The Results of Privatisation

At the end of 1994, the Treuhandanstalt had privatized some 15,000 companies in the form of share deals (approx. 6,600) or asset deals (approx. 8,000). In addition, about 4,400 expropriated companies were returned to their former owners. Small shops, hotels, restaurants, chemists etc. accounted for a further 25,000 privatisations; the Treuhandanstalt had set up a subsidiary for this, the "Company to privatize trade". Together with a large number of sales of land and buildings for new businesses, the Treuhandanstalt succeeded in privatizing more than 90,000 units by the end of 1994.

In this way, the initial stock of just under 14,000 companies at the end of 1990 was reduced to a small remainder within four years, as can be seen from the table given below.

Of the 192 remaining companies, the 63 which belong to the Management Limited Commercial Partnerships (MKGs) as well as two additional firms and three companies being phased out and their participating interests have been assigned to a special successor company of the Treuhandanstalt, the BMGB. In addition, 10 real estate companies have been assigned to the state owned privatisation company (TLG). The TLG, the BMGB and the Deutsche Kreditbank AG are under the auspices of the federal government.

PRIVATISATION IN EASTERN GERMANY

Gross and net holdings as of December 31, 1994:

TOTAL PORTFOLIO	13815
Dissolved by a split-up or merger	328
Rights/privileges to mining property	502
Parts of assets	484
THA interest being examined	1
Other companies not in the gross holdings	146
GROSS NUMBER OF COMPANIES	12354
PRIVATISATIONS	6546
Companies completely privatized	6321
Companies where majority privatized	225
Privatized parts of companies	8054
COMPANIES RETURNED TO FORMER OWNERS	1588
Companies completely returned	1588
COMPANIES TRANSFERRED TO MUNICIPALITIES	310
Companies completely transferred	265
TRANSFERS OF PROPERTY	45
LIQUIDATIONS/closings	3718
Company liquidations in process	3561
Company liquidations completed	157
NET NUMBER OF COMPANIES	192

For the remaining companies, privatisation had been started by December 31, 1994 and was for the most part - such as in the case of the central German polyolefine complex - completed with a signed contract in the first half of 1995; there remained, however, some minority THA interests and companies held by the Federal Agency for Unification Tasks (BvS) which were not intended to be privatized because their purpose - and consequently their existence - was limited. They will be closed down till 1998.

III. Privatisation Procedure

In general Treuhandanstalt offered its companies to as large public as possible in open and unconditional bidding procedures.

The Treuhandanstalt required a written offer before any decision could be made to privatize a company. In addition to the bidding price, the offer had to contain a carefully elaborated concept for the continued operation of the firm. A concept generally comprised:
- a business, investment and financial plan,
- an employment plan,
- envisaged business relations with suppliers and customers.

The investors acquiring the companies generally had to enter into a contractual commitment to ensure that the number of jobs and the amount of investment promised in the company concept during the period covered (usually 3 to 5 years) would be actually realized. If the commitments were not fully met, financial penalties as stipulated in the contracts had to be paid. Some 1.5 million jobs and investment totalling DM 211 billion were promised on this basis in contracts with the Treuhandanstalt.

The Treuhandanstalt did not hunt out investors for its companies only in Germany, but also made great efforts to attract interest from abroad. It succeeded in finding a total of 860 foreign investors for the eastern German companies, creating approximately 155,000 jobs and investing almost DM 26 billion.

3,718 of the total of 13,815 Treuhandanstalt companies proved to be non-viable and had to be closed down. Closure took the form of bankruptcy in only about 10% of these cases. The vast majority of these companies were liquidated in such a way that the Treuhandanstalt was able to hive off parts of the company and save about one-third of the original jobs.

Another important field of activity for the Treuhandanstalt was transferring to the municipalities those assets like roads, public transport, sports facilities, kindergartens, schools, etc. which had previously been held by companies. Some 40,000 assets, including 310 companies, were assigned in this way to the municipalities.

In financial terms, the work of the Treuhandanstalt turned out to be very expensive. The agency spent almost DM 200 billion on debt-relief, interest payments, restructuring, and so on. In contrast, the revenue from the privatisation amounted to DM 37 billion, leaving a deficit of DM 163 billion to be shouldered by the state.

IV. Experiences

In order to establish the market economy in Eastern Germany, the main steps were:
- to strengthen the role of the market,
- to transfer the state property together with the task of restructuring the company to new owners and
- to create a competitive market.

This presupposes a minimum of legal and institutional reforms and also a minimum of infrastructure ranging from a capital market to transport planning mechanisms. The fact that the tried-and-tested legal system of the Federal Republic of Germany was extended to cover the former GDR in the course of German unification was undoubtedly an advantage for the privatisation process in eastern Germany.

But experience has also shown that a sophisticated legal system is not all that matters. The complexity of long-established Western laws often makes them virtually impossible to understand and to apply for those who are unfamiliar with them. They are, after all, the result of decades of fine-tuning. In other East European countries the choice between perfection and speed of implementation should go against perfection.

One has to abandon the illusion that privatisation can mean a big increment in terms of revenue. The decisive "profit" or benefit to be gained is an innovative entrepreneur who is willing to invest in the company and make it competitive on his own account and under his own responsibility. This explains why the Treuhandanstalt aimed at rapid privatisations and why its revenues had been so modest.

To make the market economy fully operational, there is a need to attract new and active entrepreneurs as soon as possible. Such entrepreneurs bring with them their management know-how and business concepts which, together with the associated capital and technology transfer, will give the companies and the people working in them positive prospects for the future. In all its invitations to bid for acquisitions, therefore, the Treuhandanstalt required that the potential investor should have creative ideas, a sense of entrepreneurial responsibility and business know-how, and should also give binding assurances to make the investments which will pave the way for the company's survival and growth in a social market economy. These assurances on investments and job guarantees were often more important to the Treuhandanstalt than maximizing the selling price.

Privatisation work should be as decentralized as possible. Treuhandanstalt Head Quarters were located in the capital, Berlin, and 15 regional branch offices were set up in the main cities of the new federal states. The head office was responsible for basic policy decisions and for the larger companies. The regional branch offices were responsible for the smaller companies, and they had a large degree of autonomy in this respect. This organisational structure providing for regional branch offices proved to be viable. It permitted the necessary local contacts, facilitated communications with the companies, and also prevented the procedural hurdles associated with overcentralized bureaucracy.

A set of tools and techniques of privatisation had to be developed. At the outset there was a need for an honest inventory: data and facts. This was achieved by having opening balance sheets and business concepts drawn up. Then the workable principles needed to be developed to put a valuation on companies and real estate.

The privatisation itself took place via public invitations to tender. Wherever possible, the invitations to tender were published internationally. Possible buyers for bigger enterprises were sought out by international investment banks.

It was very important that the privatisation process was accepted by the population. The Treuhandanstalt therefore developed a model of selling the company to its own management - the management buy-out model. For their own self-esteem it was important that individuals were able to become actively involved in a social market economy. This model gave them a say in the business decisions of the company.

A scheme of support measures such as investment allowances, tax advantages, equity capital programmes, loan programmes, government incentives etc. was offered to give the largest possible sections of the population an opportunity to set up or acquire their own business.

Today with the end of the privatisation period, half of the way of restructuring Eastern Germany is gone by. We are just on the second part of this way, where the newly established enterprises and the new leaders of the former state owned companies have to prove their viability and competitivity under market conditions. This is not true in all cases. Some 10 to 15 % of the restructured companies have to overcome serious problems to survive. In case of their bankruptcy, other enterprises may take over their assets and thus constitute a new economic tissue in Eastern Germany.

Not all the problems are resolved until now, but the results achieved so far show, that Germany has good chances to manage the deep structural change from a socialist central planned system to a free and market oriented economy.

Discussion Summary

NORBERT F. TOFALL

Paper discussed:
WOLF-DIETER PLESSING: Privatisation in the New Lands of the Former German Democratic Republic

In Russia, a grave problem of economic crime exists. It is asked in which scale or extent economic crime was a problem of the reunification of Germany and of the privatisation in its Eastern part (GROMOVA).

For the judgement about the extent of crime in the process of the German reunification it is necessary to look at the dimension of the privatisation task and at the size of the *Treuhandanstalt* (Fiduciary Board [for Privatisation of Nationalized Property in the Former German Democratic Republic]), where more than 3000 professionals worked. In addition to this staff, more than 3000 persons were indirectly involved into the privatisation process. Within this circle of persons there were only very few who must be called economic criminals (PLESSING).

KONSTANTIN PIGROV doubts that it was successful to educate the people in Eastern Germany by the measures described in Plessing's paper. The education of the people should have been the real goal for the *Treuhandanstalt*.

It is asked for the concept and the principles which formed the basis of the privatisation in Eastern Germany. Why and how was the so called nationalized property transformed into private ownership? Privatisation is not a purely technical affair. Therefore, a description of the situation in Eastern Germany is not sufficient. The rationality of actions can only be analysed by knowing something about the principles and values which formed the basis of the actions. Furthermore, which different forms of privatisation were used? (KOSLOWSKI)

PLESSING points out again that the performance of the *Treuhandanstalt* cannot be judged if one does not take into account the bad and disastrous conditions of the East German economy. To the question about the princi-

DISCUSSION SUMMARY

ples, values and technique of the privatisation PLESSING develops the following points:

Firstly, it was necessary to set up *DM-Eröffnungsbilanzen* (opening financial statement in DM-currency). The evaluation and accounting of the East German firms were necessary to get information about the status of the firms. No private person will buy a firm, if he does not know exactly the assets, price-earnings ratios etc. of the firm in question.

Secondly: The *Treuhandanstalt* wanted to reduce the power of individual big firms and combines because of their negative repercussions on competition. It was its goal to guarantee as much competition as possible in the new East German market. It tried, therefore, also to gain foreign entrepreneurs and investors. The privatisation policy of the Treuhandanstalt was oriented at international standards taking into account the globalization of economic action and competition.

Thirdly: It was most important that the East German people should accept the measures taken by the *Treuhandanstalt*. One tried to get it by the following actions:

- The workforce and the staff of an enterprise could buy the enterprise by themselves (management-buy-out).
- If the prices for enterprises were too high, special conditions were offered to the workforce and the staff.
- Better tax rates of writing off assets were granted, so that lower taxes had to be paid.
- In addition to the granted write-off rates, the government paid investment subsidies. An enterprise, which does not make profit, has no advantage from write-offs. So direct payments to them were necessary.
- Loans at very low or zero interest rates were given for building up new enterprises (*Existenzgründungsdarlehen*).

All of these measures were based on the general goal to establish a market which would work. This required to build up a market with as much competition as possible (PLESSING).

The biggest problem was to make investments in East Germany more attractive. Therefore, one looked at two objectives by each measure of privatisation: safeguarding jobs and securing investments. The latter means that the *Treuhandanstalt* checked whether the buyers of an enterprises had really invested money in the enterprise. The fulfilment of these two objectives was checked every 6 months. The checks revealed that in general the goals of

DISCUSSION SUMMARY

securing jobs and of the volume of the investments were exceeded by partly up to 120 per cent (PLESSING).

LIAKIN doubts that it is possible for Russia to perform in the same manner as Germany. For Russia it is simply too expensive.

Nobody in Germany had thought that the privatisation would be so expensive for Germany. In the beginning one even made calculations on the basis that the *Treuhandanstalt* could earn profits, which could be used for the new lands of East Germany. The high loss of the *Treuhandanstalt* is also a piece of very strong evidence for the fact that the socialist East German economy had been in a bad and disastrous state at the moment of reunification (PLESSING).

KOSLOWSKI emphasized that foreign entrepreneurs in the Russian market are most important for securing competition and for overcoming nomenclatura capitalism. In the long run Russia cannot isolate itself from the world market although opening the market contradicts strong Russian traditions.

Chapter 9

Reprivatisation and Economic Transformation in the Countries of the Former Soviet Union

ALEXANDER I. LIAKIN

I. The Formation of the Concept of Privatisation in Russia
II. Forms and Results of the Small Privatisation
III. "Big" Voucher Privatisation and the Distribution of Property
IV. The Money Stage of Privatisation
V. The Possibility of Deprivatisation in Russia.

The privatisation of the state and municipal property in the Russian Federation has become a unique state programme of the period of market reforms in Russia. The fact that its accomplishment has become possible, means that it won the support or at least neutral attitude of socially active layers of the population. The privatisation taking place in the country is of such a large scale, that it has been influencing essentially the economy of Russia, and it is evident that it will have impact on it in future.

At the same time, economists and various political groups have different opinions concerning the results of this process; the opinions range from an enthusiastic recognition of the privatisation, considering it one of the main achievements of the reforms, to considering it an economic catastrophe. The report on the results of the voucher stage of privatisation by the Property Management State Committee was not submitted to the State Duma and, as a consequence, an official evaluation of it was not given. As a whole, the voucher stage of privatisation was considered by the President of Russia as an essential element of the success of the market reforms[1]. However, the recent dismissal of Vice-Prime minister A. Chubais may be considered as a preparation for a possible change of evaluations.

I. The Formation of the Concept of Privatisation in Russia

It is necessary to consider privatisation in the general context of the capitalist transformation of the Russian economy. The necessity of privatisation of the state property was discussed in the close connection with the market transformations which were being accomplished in the country. There were offered various forms, terms and scales of such a privatisation. The radical character of the privatisation depended to a great extent on the radical character of the market reforms in general.

The active discussion of the question of the necessity of privatisation concerned the reform of the economic system in 1987 and the transition to market relations. The increasing disproportions in the national economy, the fall of the efficiency of production and the collapse of the consumption market, which were going on along with the assimilation of market relations in the Soviet Union, were accounted for by the incompatibility of the market management of the economy with the domination of state property.

Besides, the state property was considered to be the basis of the political system and therefore, the private property was to become an economic guarantor of democracy. Therefore, the privatisation in Russia was not only an economic, but also a political process.

It was supposed that the scheme of privatisation to be elaborated should meet the following three criteria:

the creation of an efficient proprietor,

the shortest possible terms of realization,

the observation of the principle of social justice[*].

---

[1] For example, in addressing the staff of the *Property Management State Committee*, the Russian Federal Property Fund, the local committees and property funds on the occasion of completing the voucher privatisation, President of the Russian Federation B. Eltsin finished with the words: "Thank you for what you have done".

REPRIVATISATION IN THE FORMER SOVIET UNION

The schemes of privatisation proposed became more and more radical.

The first project of privatisation was proposed by the Academician I. Bunich and was partially implemented in the Soviet *Leasing Law*. According to it, the staff could buy out the state property on terms of leasing. After the final payment for the leased property the leased enterprise could be transformed into any form of corporate property with the distribution of the shares among the staff.

This type of privatisation was very time-taking, the opportunity for paying for the state property was given only to the staff and the subsequent redistribution of the property could take place only after the total payment, or as a result of the secondary emission or of bankruptcy, or through the workers' selling their shares.

The second scheme of privatisation was implied in the Soviet Law on the privatisation of the state property. According to it, the right of priority of the staff to buying out was also provided; the property was to be evaluated in current prices, taking into account the inflation. Long term payments were provided.

The long duration of the process, the appraisal of the property in real prices, the right to buy the property given to the staff only, the opportunity to use the income of the enterprise for this were assumed in both cases. In addition to these variants of privatisation, there was an appropriate system of measures providing the transition to the market economy: a gradual price liberalization and liberalization of foreign trade activities, an active state investing policy, preservation of a rigid state control over the sphere of distribution, a gradual formation of the market infrastructure.

Such an approach assumed a long evolutionary way of the formation of capitalism, the development of private capital in the new sectors of the economy, a gradual privatisation of the state property on the basis of leasing contracts, as well as the bankruptcy of state enterprises and recovery procedures.

The scheme of privatisation finally adopted in Russia was essentially different from the both described variants. The main difference was the issue of specific securities, the privatisation voucher, which permitted to accomplish privatisation in the shortest time possible. The privatisation voucher made the

---

* The slogan of social justice was from the very beginning a utopia and, to a certain degree, was caused by populism. Even before the realization of the programme had started, it was obvious, that such a large scale of the process of the division of the state property could not be socially fair.

Russian privatisation unique and different from the similar processes in the advanced as well as in the developing countries.

The boosted privatisation was an element of the general policy of "shock therapy", the Russian variant of the theoretical schemes of J. Sachs and the Russian adherents of the Harvard school. The accepted scheme of privatisation can be considered in the connection with price liberalization, total liberalization of foreign trade activities, introduction of a uniform rate of the rouble, and the rejection of direct interventions of the state in the economic processes.

For the further discussion of the features of the Russian privatisation, it is necessary to pay special attention to the initial conditions under which this process began.

1. By 1991 (just before the privatisation processes in Russia began) the share of state enterprises in the industry was 93.9 per cent, they provided 97.1 per cent of the output. The cost of the main production assets only in the economy (balance cost in the end of the year) was 1,361 billion roubles[2].

2. The distributive mechanism of the socialist economy reproduced personal incomes of households to the extent sufficient for current consumption only. Even the increased currency of the period of reorganisation, having resulted in the collapse of the consumer market, caused accumulation of 216 billion roubles, and it was only an insignificant part of these savings that the population was ready to spend on buying property, that was incomparable with the amount of the state property to be sold.

3. The differentiation of incomes between the top and the bottom 10 per cent of the population was less than five to one. There was no legal private capital (at least, significant) in the country. The accumulation of capital by means of resales of the goods of the public sector at free prices, the export of raw materials, the import of computers and office equipment, cashing the money funds of state enterprises and other spheres of the initial money accumulation of the Russian private capital just started to emerge.

4. As the structure of prices was deformed, it was an extremely difficult task to define the cost of the property to be privatized in a particular situation. An appraisal based on the accounting reports contained price distortions

---

2 *Narodnoye Khosiaistvo Rossiiskoy Federatsii 1992: Statisticheskii Ezhegodnik* (THE National Economy of the Russian Federation 1992: Statistical Year-Book), Moscow (Goskmstat Rossii) 1992, pp. 11,68.

accumulated over a long period of time. The market appraisal was not possible due to the absence of the market of capital.

5. For the society, the attention of which was focused on the problems of the privileges of the nomenclatura, the problem of social justice was very painful. If there is no legal capital, who is capable of buying the state property? Besides, why should people purchase what had been created at the cost of their unpaid work?

The introduction of the privatisation voucher seemed to be able to resolve all these problems: the suggested legal tender the cost of which was equal to the cost of the property to be sold; the conventional price of property with the conventional legal tender, and the free voucher flow and the opportunity to evaluate the property in liquidity. And finally, the privatisation voucher was granted free to everybody, and therefore everybody could receive a part of the property which was to be given away. Formally, all the people in the country were in the equal starting conditions before the "entrance to capitalism".

The officially declared goals of privatisation were formulated in the programme as follows:

1. The increase of the efficiency of production owing to the proprietor motivation*.

2. The formation of a wide layer of the middle class, possessing property and supporting the reforms.

3. The solution of budget problems at the expense of the sales of the state property.

4. The attraction of foreign investments.

5. The creation of a competitive economy.

As it was already stated above, the programme was fulfilled in terms of the quantity. The issue to be discussed is to which extent the goals of the privatisation were achieved. The estimation of the process in terms of quality is the most complex issue and the opinions concerning it differ very much.

---

* They spoke of the "proprietor feeling" in the publications of the Soviet period, and somewhat later the politicians started speaking about it from the beginning of perestroika. In particular, the growth of the efficiency of production was assumed to happen as a result of leasing, and later as a result of privatisation, because the worker considering himself a proprietor would presumably do his best, stop stealing (what is the point of stealing one's own?).

It is necessary to mention that the generally used term "privatisation" denotes three quite different processes:
- small privatisation;
- voucher privatisation, that is, turning the state enterprises into joint stock companies;
- money privatisation, including both the turning of state enterprises into joint stock companies (those not privatized at the first stage) and the sales of the shares, given over to the state at the voucher stage of privatisation.

Each of these processes has peculiar forms of realization and results.

II. Forms and Results of the Small Privatisation

Small privatisation (as far as this process actually was finished) consisted in the sale of property at auctions and through competitions. By December 1, 1994, 74.8 per cent of the 100,690 state enterprises of Russia in the sphere of trade, household service, and public catering were privatized (69.32%, 72.22%, 69.32% respectively).[3] The buyers could be either companies or individuals (the former under the condition that the share of the state property is less than 25 per cent of the authorised capitals). The small privatisation was compulsory for the enterprises with the number of workers up to 200 persons and the value of the fixed capital up to 1 million rb. on the balances of January 1, 1992. Big enterprises, with the number of workers up to 1000 persons and the value of the fixed capital up to 50 million rb., could choose the direct sale as a form of privatisation (the decision was to be made by the staff).

The adopted form of selling the state and municipal property allowed to establish market prices irrespectively of the inflation factor. When the privatisation vouchers were partially used for payments, the relation between the auction price and the voucher rate could be clearly traced.

The "efficient proprietor" for the small privatisation had already been prepared by the previous development. On the one hand, the capital had been accumulated by the co-operative movement (and, as it was frequently the case, a member of a "guild" of illegal businessmen from the period of

---

3   *Panorama Privaizatsii* (The Panorama of Privatisation), 1 (1995), p. 60.

REPRIVATISATION IN THE FORMER SOVIET UNION

the planned economy was the source of this capital); on the other hand, a former director of the state enterprise, who had also been much experienced in the "non-formal" business, became the owner. As a result of the formation of private property, the relations which had existed before, were just made legal. The obvious positive aspect of the legal registration of private property was the economic responsibility for decision-making: one could not anymore compensate for his own miscalculations at the state's expense. Where the buyer could not organize normal operation, the problem was resolved through the bankruptcy procedures with the subsequent change of the proprietor, reorientation of the production, etc. Bankruptcy in this sector does not imply, however, serious economic and social consequences and, therefore, occurs rather regularly.

The problem of the formation of the competitive environment was relatively simply resolved here. As far as the tenders, trusts, management centres, other managing structures, which controlled the activity of shops, of enterprises of communal services in the territories of regions and cities, were liquidated, the newly formed independent private enterprises were forced to fight for consumers, to search for independent wholesalers, etc. Besides, the increasing competition on the part of the enterprises of this sector, which originally emerged as private enterprises, had an impact on the situation.

Now in this sector a network of flows of goods and services of a market type, including retail trade oriented to consumers of different groups of income, wholesale and jobbing trade has been formed. The number of intermediaries was reduced, the effective demand influences the growth of the turnover, keeping constant and even reducing the trade margin.

Certainly, during the small privatisation there were infringements: the selling prices were forced down, the access of the participants to the information concerning the objects to be privatized was unequal; the privileges of the staff became an almost official way of reducing the selling price, etc. But the main purpose, that is, the increase of the efficiency, was achieved, which is clearly demonstrated by the trade network today. Privatisation is not to be blamed for the significant reduction of the system of communal services and catering services affordable by the average consumer. The rapid decrease of the incomes of the population as a result of the crisis has decreased the demand for the services in these sectors and they, in any case, could not be run without considerable state financing, which is just a fantasy under the present conditions.

It is difficult to say how much the small privatisation was connected with the criminalization of the economy. We lack any trustworthy and complete data. But there is no direct link traced between these two processes: both the small enterprises to be privatized and the initially private ones and the small state enterprises can get under the control of criminal groups. The entire variety of causes connected with the peculiarities of the emergence of the market in Russia is effective here.

To finish the discussion of this form of privatisation, it is necessary to point out that it has not created a significant number of new proprietors. Eighty thousand enterprises, even if the significant part of them are partnerships, are now represented by one to two thousand proprietors.

III. "Big" Voucher Privatisation and the Distribution of Property

"Big" privatisation means turning state enterprises into joint-stock companies with the subsequent selling of shares to individuals and companies, the state share being no more than 25 per cent. The voucher stage of the big privatisation was the most difficult and ambiguous process in the Russian privatisation. The evaluations of it were various.

During two years from July 1992 to July 1994, 24,934 enterprises out of 32,757 registered enterprises became joint-stock companies; more than 16 thousands of them were sold at check auctions[4]. On the one hand, the unification of the procedure allowed the enterprises to prepare for privatisation and to depend too much on the officers in charge of it; on the other hand, the uniformity of the procedure did not permit to take into account the interests and characterics of particular objects and did not insure against abuses. (In 1993, there were found out 7088 violations of law in the privatisation sphere[5].) In the Economic periodicals there was often expressed a concern whether the quantity of liquidated vouchers equalled that of the issued ones.[6]

---

4   *Panorama Privatizatsii*, 7 (58) (1995), p. 36.
5   *Rynok Tsennyh Bumag* (The Market of Securities), 23 (1995), p. 9.
6   See, for example, *Kommersant*, 25 (1994) p. 55.

REPRIVATISATION IN THE FORMER SOVIET UNION

The privatisation process was regulated not so much by law but rather by presidential decrees. Almost a year after the adoption of the law *On Privatisation of State and Municipal Enterprises in the Russian Federation* the real shifts were rather insignificant. The process became rather activated after the President's decree No 721 which, on the one hand, simplified the procedure, on the other hand, offered the following alternative to the managers of enterprises: either to get privatized according to their own wish, or to be privatized by the Property Management Committee.

The hyperinflation experienced by the country since 1992 considerably accelerated privatisation. The rouble cost 30 times less by the end of the year than in the beginning of 1992. At the same time, the appraisal of the property to be privatized was based on the prices of the preinflation period, before re-evaluation of the fixed capital. Further re-evaluations of 1992 and 1993 were not taken into account for estimating the registered capital of an enterprise which was supposed to be turned into a joint-stock company. The price of a privatisation voucher was close to the face value only for a short period at the end of November - beginning of December, notwithstanding all rate changes. After this period it fell down to four thousand rb. and then reached the face value only in September 1993. As a result, in January 1993, the face value of the privatisation voucher compared with the share of an enterprise to be privatized was 60 times less. Though, the rate of the voucher slowly grew, its maximum value equalled four face values, whereas the rouble in June 1994 cost about 500 times less than in December 1991.

The third cause of the acceleration of the privatisation was the system of privileges for the staff, which gave the top managers an opportunity to become the proprietor of the enterprise.

According to the privatisation programme, the staff could choose one of the three offered versions of the privileged distribution of shares:

1. 25 per cent of the privileged shares were distributed free of charge; 10 per cent might be bought by the staff with a 30 per cent discount; 5 per cent of common shares could be bought by the top managers at the face value;

2. 51 per cent of common shares might be bought by the staff at the price which could be 1.7 of face value;

3. 20 per cent of common shares is bought by the staff at a 30 per cent discount; 20 per cent is given in trust with the right to repayment at the face value to a group which takes the responsibility for the bankruptcy of the enterprise during a year. This group is liable with its property for fulfilment of its obligations.

ALEXANDER I. LIAKIN

Each of these versions represented different approaches to seeking the "efficient proprietor"*. In the first version the proprietor could emerge as a result of buying the shares at the secondary market, in the second version, this chance was given to the top managers; in the third, the efficient proprietor was supposed to be formed at the stage of the primary distribution, besides, he was not supposed to be by all means one of the director's group. At the stage of voucher privatisation, the second version overshadowed the others. It was chosen by 73 per cent of the enterprises to be privatized.

The voucher stage of the Big privatisation did not and could not resolve any of the declared problems. Under the condition of a fall of production 50 per cent breaking off the established economical connections, the fall of the consumption market, it is difficult to achieve efficiency of production in any form of property. The influence of privatisation on efficiency is the subject of a special research; in the present paper, one can express some general assumptions only.

It is obvious that for the increase of efficiency one should take some organisational and technical measures: changing the management staff, changing the management, creating new forms of labour motivation, etc. All these measures demand more or less significant material expenditures. The exchange of vouchers to shares could bring neither money nor real contribution in the enterprise. Thus, formally, it was not connected with real production. But for the accumulation of vouchers, one needs money. And this money was in different ways taken from the production circles. Vouchers were bought for the profits of the state enterprises, fake firms were created, which accepted the resources belonging to these enterprises. Finally, the budget investments were spent for this purpose. The scandal caused by the privatisation of Nizhnii Novgorod GAZ (GAZ - Gorkovskii Avtomobilnyi Zavod - Gorki Car Plant) is very characteristic in this sense. At the first meetings, where external shareholders participated, every tenth general director was replaced. This could be interpreted as both a desire of new proprietors to

---

* The origin of the term "efficient proprietor" is very interesting. "Efficient proprietor" means a shareholder capable of exercising influence on the decisions of the corporation since he has a big portfolio of his corporation. And it also implies that there are other shareholders, who acquired their shares free of charge, and who are not able to participate in the management positively, being not aware of the long-term interests of the company.

establish order in the management, and a conflict between the interests of the new shareholders and the previous administration.

It should be mentioned that the problem of personification of property as a result of privatisation is the most difficult task. In the developed countries, big fortunes were either formed over centuries or connected with exclusive entrepreneur abilities of a certain personality, and therefore, the proprietors are known to everyone. In Russia, big private fortunes were formed over a decade, but their proprietors and origin are known to a few. The voucher allowed not only to distribute the property among everybody, but also to concentrate it in the hands of few, rapidly, latently and relatively painlessly.

According to the results of the first, voucher stage of Big privatisation, we can distinguish five major groups of proprietors:

administration of former state enterprises,
banks,
voucher investment funds,
commercial structures,
staff.

At the first stage it was very rare that foreign investors intervened in the process of distribution, whereas the part of shares of the common people who acquired them at voucher auctions is so small that may be disregarded.

Each of these groups of proprietors has its own motivation and certain advantages in the acquiring of shares, or in the later realization of the rights of proprietorship.

As it was already mentioned, there is no available, secure and systematic information about the distribution of property in Russia. At the present moment, the first publications devoted to the analysis of this issue start to appear. The information concerning the structure of the ownership of capital shares, its distribution among different groups of proprietors in Russia is almost unavailable, and personification is just impossible. There exist legal restrictions on such information (in accordance with the Law *On Joint-Stock Companies,* the data from the register of shareholders can be given only to the shareholders possessing more than 1 per cent of shares), whereas to get this information from the registerholder is even more difficult. The data cited below were obtained through the polls administered by the state structures and research groups.

Changes of shares of the most significant groups of shareholders in the share capital in 1994 - 1995, average values, per cent of the registered capital[7]

	April 1994	December 1994	March 1995	June 1995	June 1996
Insiders, all	62	60	60	56	51
common workers	53	49	47	43	35
top managers	9	11	13	13	16
outsiders, all	21	27	28	33	45
major	11	16	17	22	32
minor	10	11	11	11	13
State	17	13	12	11	4
All	100	100	100	100	100

The information cited above does not offer a complete picture of the distribution of the share capital because it is impossible to take into account the hidden concentration of shares. The system of trust management of shares, the institution of the nominal shareholder, buying up shares through figure-heads, creating lots of intermediary structures, holding shares of each other, devaluate the primary available information concerning shareholders. For example, the estimation of the participation of the staff seems too high, because the administration usually buys up shares through figure-heads. Minor outsiders are often the representatives of the administration or of a group of interconnected persons. Thus, speaking of the new proprietors in Russia, one should rely upon personal intracorporate information and draw conclusions about the most general tendencies only.

The staff, which got a significant part of shares as a result of closed subscription, rapidly gets rid of the shares. The second variant of privileges appeared to be favourable for the further consolidation of blocks. This part of

---

[7] A. RADIGGIN, V. GUTNIK, G. MALGGINOV: "Postprivatizatsionnaya Structura Aktsionernogo Kapitala i Korporativnyi Kontrol: 'Kontrrevolutsiya Menedgerov?'" (Post-Privatisation Structure of the Capital of a Company and Corporate Control: "A Counter-Revolution of Managers?"), *Voprosy Economiki*, 10 (1995), p. 53.

proprietors is eroded from two sides: the enterprise administration and the outside investor. The administration and the outside investor can act together, having co-ordinated their interests, but they also can compete for buying the working control. Each of them uses special methods, not always usual in terms of traditional understanding.

The struggle for the working control is usually clearly reflected on the secondary market. The prices of shares of such a company steadily grow; the number of operators buying the securities grows too and this goes like that till one of the parties gets the working control. Right after that, the rate price rapidly falls, as well as the liquidity.

The process of the reduction of the part of the staff is quite fast, but it is limited by the creating of the working control. The shares which were not bought by the staff are of no interest any longer.

The Director's control over the enterprise in case of the second variant of privatisation happened to be quite unreal. The staff, as it was noted above, easily sells the shares and the administration faces the problem of increasing its own block. In the most cases, this requires co-operation with some external investor, the so-called "strategic" investor. In some cases, the problem is resolved without the participation of the latter, by means of an intensive "beating out" the shares from the staff, buying the shares through a figurehead company where the financial means of the enterprise are somehow transferred to, by means of making one block out of all shares through the formation of joint-stock companies of the "closed type" with the participation of the staff, which brings to the registered capital the shares acquired by closed subscription.

Banks form the most promising group among the external Russian shareholders. Buying vouchers took place in the "golden age" of the Russian banking system. The growth of loan rates under the conditions of hyperinflation, the growth of hard currency rates, the utilisation of state loans helped banks to raise rapidly their own funds. The turnover capital was concentrated in the banks. The devaluation of the voucher (from the promised two "Volgas" up to five dollars) permitted to accumulate big blocks without great expenditures. Although there were different approaches to buying shares (from buying all the shares "for the cases of emergency" to creating portfolios with strict branch priorities), creating the blocks of shares of privatized enterprises allowed banks to have real influence.

More or less big investing projects are financed by banks under the condition of the control over the corporation, to which the financial resources are to be given. The process of the formation of financial-industrial groups (FIG), which was started in 1994, demonstrates the transition to the essentially new relations in the real sector based upon mutual financial interests. The interbranch complexes, connected technologically, having mighty financial centres in the form of banks, have real opportunities for growth.

Voucher investing funds, different types of financial companies, which collected the vouchers, are different in their content, in the capital exercising control over them and the prospects of further development. Some of them are unsteady formations, operating on the verge of breaking the law. Having acquired vouchers from the population by means of aggressive advertising, having invested them without any projects in different enterprises, they gradually resell the most profitable blocks and give up managing the property. The most serious and significant funds are reorganised into investment companies, making money from both speculations and control over enterprises.

The interests of commercial structures, which have taken part in the privatisation are quite various: from the speculations with the securities bought, to buying real estate and to establishing control over the production in their sphere of interest.

Foreign investors, who took part in the first stage of privatisation are very few. Even fewer of them are more or less serious firms. Direct investments are started, as a rule, at the second, money stage of privatisation. The expenditures on getting the working control are considerably increasing and the rules of the game become clearer. The opportunity of buying a big block at an investment competition or auction definitely means getting a certain control. And there is no need of playing with the staff, administration, operations at the secondary market.

It is evident that the privatisation did not create the middle class. Moreover, the growing income differentiation results in disappearing that strata which could be considered as the Soviet middle class. This is proved by the recent elections to State Duma. Those 40 million proprietors which A. Chubais spoke of, actually voted against the forms and methods of the transformations which turned them into proprietors. It was mentioned above that the number of shareholders from the staff decreases, whereas people, who invested their vouchers in Voucher Investment Funds, being formally shareholders, do not probably seriously think of themselves as proprietors.

At the same time, it seems that the main negative aspects of the voucher privatisation are different. Social justice cannot be achieved in the process of distribution. The most socially just measure would be that of the efficient selling the property. The process of its distribution through voucher privatisation attracted great capitals from the real sector. Meanwhile, the uncontrolled division in no way guaranteed against the criminal capital which probably was involved in this process. Even such an inefficient measure as the income declaration was not enforced. The primary distribution did not create proprietors able to manage the property, and thus, it was accompanied with a very expensive process of further purchases and blocks consolidation. The presence of additional securities amounting to 1,480 billion rb. could not help to influence the inflation process of 1992-1993. The further purchase of vouchers from the population and the staff of the enterprises also turned the investment resources of firms into the additional demand. But discussing these and other negative consequences of the completed process is just of an academic interest. Maybe, it will help to answer the question "Who is guilty?", but not the question "What is to be done?"

However the process of voucher privatisation might proceed, at the present time it resulted in the radical change of the mechanisms of the economy. Now in Russia a stock market has appeared, although imperfect, it can resolve the major problem, that is, the transfer of financial resources to the spheres of the most efficient placement. As a result of its functioning, the capital cost appraisal becomes possible. One can establish easier financial connections and transfer capital more flexibly.

IV. The Money Stage of Privatisation

The money stage of privatisation has switched from the principle of social justice to that of economic efficiency. The opportunity of the participation of individuals, both staff members and outsiders, is limited. The staff members retain all the former privileges, and therefore, they can even buy out the working control. But since the price of shares now is determined by the cost of the assets as of the first balance date before the moment of making the decision, buying some significant quantity of shares is impossible for the staff. The aforementioned process of the distribution of property was changed into its selling at market and sometimes even higher prices. Under such conditions, there are fewer than before of those who want to pay real money for the shares with dubious opportunities.

The forms of selling the shares left after a closed subscription at the enterprises have not much changed.

Specialised auctions for selling shares imply selling them at a uniform price to all participants. All those who applied without having negotiated the price get at least one share. But the past voucher auctions convinced people that buying one or two shares does not mean anything for a small holder. Consequently, even this form of sales does not result in splitting the blocks. Sociological researches show that the potential demand of the population for the securities of privatized enterprises can account for 14.6 per cent of the aggregated demand for shares. Only banks and foreign investors can demand for more, 29.8 per cent each. But this number is dubious because the estimated aggregated demand of the population for shares, according to the poll, is 4 times that of the population's savings.[8]

Money auctions imply the concentration of shares in the hands of big investors in the process of primary selling. Besides, the prices of the blocks to be sold can differ even at one auction.

The money stage can resolve the tasks of privatisation as such. The distribution of funds acquired by selling the state property is realized between budgets of different levels and the enterprise. 51 per cent of these funds is given to the enterprise as a primary investment, and this does not depend upon the fact whether the enterprise belonged to the federal or municipal property. Moreover, a special form of selling shares at investment competitions was developed, permitting to invest money. The seller offering the biggest amount of investment becomes the winner.

Foreign capital becomes a bit more active at the money stage of privatisation. Now one can say that new rules of the game have been established.

Recently a number of scandals, related to the money privatisation have burst out (first of all, here securities auctions are meant). There were illegal discounts, unfair conditions for different participants, breaks of the rules of application process, etc. This proves the necessity of improving the procedure, enforcing control, but not at all the inefficiency of the process.

---

8   *Panorama Privatizatsii*, 14 (1995), p. 6.

V. The Possibilities of Deprivatisation in Russia

The future of privatisation, taking into account upcoming presidential elections is quite uncertain. In Russia, politics was always a "concentrated economy", and the process of turning to the left was demonstrated by the previous parliamentary elections. How can communists' and the other left political groups' coming into power influence privatisation as well as share property and securities market at all? The comical publications are full of such predictions.

If one considers the ongoing political changes, however, not as an effect of Providence but as a result of some interaction of social and economic factors (among which privatisation is not the least), the possible shifts in the property distribution should be looked upon taking into account the restrictions imposed by the economic and social conditions.

The perspectives of privatisation under the condition of a turn to the left are determined by its peculiarities.

As for the small privatisation, no one can believe that this process could be revised. On the one hand, it did not involve the basic economic forces. On the other hand, it appeared to be efficient under the present conditions. And it is difficult even to assume that the state control will be soon established over hundreds of thousands of small enterprises.

The question is to what extent the results of the great privatisation and, first of all, its money stage, can be revised. In this context, one should consider the existing social and economic restrictions which limit the scope of possible decisions.

The changes in the social structure resulting from the privatisation did not create a broad layer of proprietors (and could not do it). It is worse that they have not so far resulted in the improvement of the situation of the people. The social tension increased because of the growing differentiation of property and income. That is why there will be no serious protest against the revision of the results of the privatisation. At the same time, striving to the order and stability, as it is shown by all recent polls, prevails in all social layers. It seems that the turn to the left is connected with those striving to stability and order. That is why somewhat radical decisions concerning the nationalisation of property do not seem possible.

The restrictions imposed by the economic situation are as follows:

ALEXANDER I. LIAKIN

1. Over the years of the reforms, the basic funds of the country have been mostly spent. This keeps the consumption at a level higher than critical at the fantastic fall of production over the last five years. But this means that great investments are needed in the nearest future, and thus, there are no resources sufficient for the growth of the current consumption, nor for the social experiments like buying out the privatized property.

2. The system of the centralised branch management of the economy is destroyed, and its reconstruction will take a lot of time. The increase of centralisation and the state intervention in the economy can be realized by means available and acceptable for the market economy in the following ways: budget, loan, financial, customs policies and administrative import restrictions. These measures do not demand radical steps towards the nationalisation of industries.

3. The intensification of ties of the economy of Russia with the world market, the growth of its external debt prevent from accomplishing such measures which would break the above ties with the world market.

Taking into account these restrictions, it is possible to outline the future of the privatisation and nationalisation in Russia.

Two different variants are possible:

1) The present conditions are accepted as they are. A new executive power only can change them after the adoption of appropriate laws.

2) The privatisation is declared illegal; the property is nationalized and the central planning system of the economy is restored.

It seems that both ways are not probable[9], though there are some possibilities for the second one ensued from the form of the voucher privatisation itself.[10] A radical shift in the economy, the second one within a decade, would just result in ceasing the production process, which has already lost a half of its usual volume. The Russian economy would not survive a second radical experiment.

The most probable is the intermediary variant of events. The results of the privatisation will be disputed in particular cases of the transactions in accordance with the law, valid for the moment of these deals (moreover, we have

---

9 See, for example, the interview with the leaders of large opposition parties (both of the left and right orientation) concerning the prospects of the securities market in Russia: *Securities Market*, 23 (1995), pp. 2-11.

10 See: K. ZHUKOV: "Illiuzii Pobediteley" (The Illusions of the Winners), *Expert*, 1 (1991).

already witnessed the examples of the kind: the privatisation of the hotel Astoria in St.Petersburg was disputed and the hotel was returned to the state). Taking into account the scale, a complete revision of the results of the voucher stage of privatisation is impossible. Probably, the attention will be paid to some leading enterprises and to the strategic spheres: mining industry, metal industry, arm industry. The least dangerous situation will be for the Western investors. Legitimacy of the capital in this case cannot be doubted, the transactions meet the requirements of law and there is no need to strain the relations with the developed countries.

The possibilities of the deprivatisation of property will depend upon results of the privatisation campaign.

There should be changes in the procedures of privatisation. The money privatisation will be less rapid; there will be a ban for selling blocks of shares of some companies (first of all, in the "strategic" branches). The initial auction prices will grow; along with the privatisation, the process of increasing state participation in the share capital of some companies will be started by means of state investments and in some cases there will be the nationalisation resulting from bankruptcies.

There will be imposed stricter restrictions on the deals with securities which would result in taking over the working control of companies. There will be a structured control over foreign investments and actions of foreign investors in the controlled Russian enterprises.

It seems, however, that the key direction of the activity of the new government in case of the victory of the left at the elections will be not the privatisation but the budget, finance and protection of the Russian high-tech enterprises.

The corrections of the present economic policy in this aspect will be introduced by any government. The radicality of the measures taken can differ. As for the privatisation itself, the correction will be performed by any government irrespectively of the responsibility for the measures already taken.

Section IV

The Privatisation of the Agricultural Sector

Chapter 10

Independent Family Farms Versus Hierarchical Forms of Organisation

Spontaneous Emergence of Property Rights Structures in Russian Agriculture

SILKE STAHL

I. Introduction
II. Property Rights, Organisational Structure, and Optimal Farm Size
III. Optimal Farm Size as an Organisational Problem
IV. An Alternative Model
    1. The Basic Idea
    2. Stability of Agricultural Organisational Forms
V. The Explanatory Power of the Model
    1. Assessment Taking into Consideration the Background of Conventional Models and Their Critique
    2. Explanatory Power Taking into Account the Background of the Russian Property Rights Tradition
VI. Resume

INDEPENDENT FAMILY FARMS IN RUSSIAN AGRICULTURE

I. Introduction

When in the former Soviet Union in 1990 within the framework of the thorough reorganisation of state and society and in consideration of the catastrophic supply problems it was decided to restructure the agricultural sector as well, the decision-makers were led by the model of agriculture both in Western Europe and the United States where only 2.4 per cent of all farms are not run by peasant families (C. F. Runge 1987, p. 35).The aim was to establish an agricultural system based on family farms and equipped with private property rights to land and other means of production which are not subject to interference by the state (I. Silajev cited in D. Van Atta 1993, p. 75).

During the following period the corresponding legal preconditions were created. These legal preconditions concerned the restructuring and potential dissolution of collective farms and the development of a free market for land (see S. Wegren 1994, p. 222ff). Meanwhile, even Western experts considered the legal framework, though still being afflicted with some shortcomings, especially with regard to the registration of property in the land register, as de jure appropriate for privatisation (R. L. Prosterman/L. J. Rolfes/R. G. Mitchell 1995, p. 175). Nevertheless, the aspired wave of foundations of private peasant farms did not come to happen. Compared with the 1000 peasant farms existing in 1991 the number of private farms rose with the result that today 6 per cent of all agricultural workers are engaged in private farming. But this trend has come to a stop and in some regions the share of private farming has already started to sink (Agra-Europe 36/21 22.5.1995).

Under these circumstances there is no telling yet when private agriculture will be able to become the mainstay of agricultural production which is going through a deep crisis at the moment, was characterized by a decrease in yields of 20 per cent in 1994 (Agra-Europe 36/19 8.5.1995) and brought in the worst harvest for 30 years in 1995 (Finansovyie Izvestiya 5.9.1995). To a certain extent this is also owing to the fact that among the 6 per cent of private farmers there are quite a lot of "weekend farmers" who pursue their primary occupation in the towns and, due to the insecure and meanwhile also expensive commercial supply of food, have taken the production of food for personal purposes into their own hands.

Looking back into Russian history, it becomes evident that this resistance to efforts to carry through individual-private structures in the agricultural sector is not a new phenomenon at all: when, after the first Russian revolution in 1906, prime minister Stolypin tried to defuse the poverty in the countryside by facilitating the conversion of communal property into private property, up to 1914 only a minority of farmers separated themselves from their village communities. (P. Lyashchenko 1949, p. 747). Rather, one can observe that the rural population went spontaneously over to communal structures of village organisation in moments of crisis. Thus, the enormous population pressure which, in the first half of the 19th century, caused a deep crisis in the Russian countryside, led to the spread of practices of regular land redistribution. This redistribution of land according to the changing needs of the population could always been found in some regions of central Russia, but only during this time of crisis it became a widespread practice and was also adopted in Western Siberia and the southern steppes. (D. Atkinson 1983, p. 9).

After the October Revolution a similar phenomenon could be observed: in a situation that was characterized by the juxtaposition of relatively much political freedom on the one hand and massive economic pressure owing to grain confiscations and the raise of rural population as a result of the migration of town-dwellers and soldiers returning home on the other hand, almost all peasants who, during the Stolypin reforms, had separated from the village came back into the traditional community and the traditional redistributional practices were re-established (D. Hoffmann 1994, p. 639f).

This phenomenon obviously contradicts the orthodox position in the transformation debate. According to that position, the construction of a system of property rights according to Western principles, which is a prerequisite for the development and the functioning of a market economy, is considered as being in principle possible. (O. Blanchard et. al 1991, D. Lipton/ J. Sachs 1990). In following such an argumentation two aspects have been left out of consideration: on the one hand, it starts from the assumption of a strong central state being able to influence and force the transition process. It has the power not only to commit laws down on paper but also to implement them practically, something which requires strong and incorruptible executive organs. On the other hand, the argumentation is based on the conjecture that the majority of the population supports the transition process and prefers private property rights to collective forms of ownership.

Those representatives of the New Institutional Economics who occupy themselves with the transition problem (see for example J. Myhrman 1989, M. Reichhard 1995) tackle the problem from a somewhat different perspective. They investigate explicitly under which preconditions rational individuals choose certain rules, for example property right regimes. It is usually assumed that the regime that shows the lowest transaction costs will emerge. Very often within this context the argumentation is based on a rather implicit assumption that historic development is characterized by a movement toward undiluted private property rights (see H. Demsetz 1967, p. 350f).

The strength of this approach can be traced back to the fact that individual choice is made explicit. Furthermore it focuses on the role and the interplay of external and internal institutions (see F.A. Hayek 1988, pp. 11-28), especially property rights around which the transformation debate finally centres. The problem with the approach, as it becomes evident in the concept of the choice of institutions which are minimizing transaction costs, is that it starts from rational individuals knowing all the alternative choices and being able to choose the alternative which minimizes transaction costs. The role of social aspects in the emergence and change of institutions is left out of the discussion and it is not made clear how, as a result of individual choices, a structure on the societal level can develop.

In the following paper the attempt to investigate the change of property right regimes and organisational structures in Russian agriculture shall be made from a somewhat different perspective. Therefore, in chapter 2 the interrelationship of property right structure, organisational form and optimal farm size will be discussed. In chapter 3 a model which explains why, in the long run, an agricultural property rights structure based on family farms should emerge will be presented. As reality, as explained above, shows us a different picture, in chapter 4 an alternative model will be developed which also allows for the development of communal property right regimes. Chapter 5 will discuss the applicability of this model to the development of property right regimes and organisational structures in Russia. The paper finishes with an outline of future possibilities to broaden the model.

SILKE STAHL

II. Property Rights, Organisational Structure, and Optimal Farm Size

In the preceding chapter it has already been mentioned that there is a strong interdependence between the property rights regime and the organisational structure. This interdependence shall be clarified in this chapter.

Discussing property rights in the agricultural sector primarily means discussing property rights in land as land constitutes, apart from work, the most important factor of production. It is possible to distinguish between four components of property rights in land: the right to use it (*usus*), the right to use its products (*usus fructus*), the right to let it lie fallow or use it in a way which does not correspond with the original purpose (*abusus*) and, finally, the right to sell or bequeath the land or to give it as a present without interference from the outside (*transfer*). These rights need not necessarily be united in one person. Undiluted property rights exist only if all four components can be attributed to the same person. If an individual is not allowed to sell the land or if he is told how to use the land, the property rights are diluted; they are not private but communal. Decision-making concerning land as a production factor lies rather in the hand of the community, not of the individual.

What does this classification of different kinds of property rights mean for the organisational form? In this paper "organisational form" will be interpreted as the way the decision-making process concerning the use and the transfer of the resource is organized. It follows that the way the different components of property rights are attributed determines the organisational form: if, within a group, all components are attributed to the same person there are no problems because the same person makes the decision and carries it out as well; within the respective group we have the case of a decentral form of organisation. If, by contrast, one individual is attributed only the right to use the land and to decide over its product, there must be some authority that decides the way how, for example, the resource is used or transferred.

Which form of organisation results from such a splitting of competence depends on whether those rights which are not attributed to the individual are either attributed to another individual of the group or the group as a whole or whether they are "administered" centrally. In the first case (co-ordination of property rights on the group level) the situation can be described as a horizontal hierarchical form of organisation, in the second case as a vertical hierarchical form of organisation (J. Hirshleifer 1995, p. 48). In chapter 4 it will be shown that a decentral form of organisation can be principally unstable and that, as a result of this, one of the two hierarchical forms of organisation mentioned will emerge.

To summarize, we can state that there is a duality of organisational form and property rights. Decentral forms of organisation are characterized by the almost complete attribution of decision rights and therefore also of property rights to the individual, in this case the farmer, whereas hierarchical forms of organisation leave only a limited number of property rights to him/her. The use of the resource is determined by "chains of instructions".

It appears to be possible to find real world equivalents in the agricultural sector for all these rather theoretical forms of organisation: the European family farm is the classical example of a decentral form of organisation. Co-operatives, the traditional Russian village community or kibbutzim can be understood as horizontal hierarchies. Vertical hierarchical forms of organisation can be found in history, for example in the form of the *Gutswirtschaft* (ownership of an estate). Also socialist collective state farms such as the Russian *sovkhosy* can be described as vertical forms of hierarchy. If, in the course of privatisation, one of the former collective farms only changed its label by restructuring itself into a joint stock company, that means if the old structures principally persist, these newly created companies can be categorized as vertical hierarchies as well.

As a next step the relationship between optimal farm size and organisational form has to be made explicit. This appears to be important as the inefficiency of the large Soviet type state farms is often put down to their size. However, one can often hear the reproach that European farms are too small and can only survive in the world market because they are heavily subsidized. At the same time, especially in the developing countries, co-operatives are extraordinarily successful and large plantations guarantee a well-being for their owners. In the course of history at certain times there have been systems of small and independent family farms, one might think of the Germanic social structure, and at other times large estates being farmed by slaves. Obviously sometimes larger, at other times smaller structures were able to catch on.

In neo-classic economic theory a number of articles about the optimal farm size can be found. Thus, Yoav Kislev and Willis Peterson (Y. Kislev/W. Peterson 1982) for example explain the optimal farm size over the ratio of machine costs to opportunity costs of labour. Thereby they are able to explain the emergence and stability of smaller family farms. They also realize that their findings are somehow contradictory to the existence of large plantations especially in the developing countries. For this reason they argue that, as opposed to the farms in developed countries, where possibilities for reinvestment in the industrial and service sector exist, in developing countries the owners of plantations are forced to reinvest in the agricultural sector and by doing so consciously accept diseconomies of scale. This explanation appears to be rather unsatisfactory as it seems to be more sensible in whatever the case to raise consumption, something which can be observed empirically as well.

Therefore, one has to ask, whether farm size really is the decisive factor for analysing the stability of agricultural structures. The following two chapters are devoted to this question. In both of them the argumentation will centre around the problem of organisation and thus, as explained above, also around the problem of property rights. As the first step, a connection between the question of the optimal farm size and the form of organisation will be created.

III. Optimal Farm Size as an Organisational Problem

Apart from neo-classical explanations of the optimal farm size also representatives of the New Institutional Economics had a critical look at the question of optimal farm size. Unlike the neo-classicists they focus on the control problem. One example for such a reasoning is the work of Mancur Olson (M. Olson 1985). Starting from the empirical fact that, compared to industry, one can only find small (in terms of value added) and at the same time space-intensive enterprises in US-agriculture and this even though in the 19th century there were attempts to erect large "Bonanza Farms" along the railway lines in the middle west which were to be managed like industrial enterprises (H.L. Briggs 1932), Olson concluded that the small surviving enterprises must have been the efficient ones and thus must have the optimal farm size.

Why their size can be interpreted as optimal Olson explains with the help of the underlying organisational structure as follows: as has already been mentioned, agricultural enterprises, compared with industrial ones, are characterized by high spatial intensity. That means, in order to achieve a roughly equivalent turnover they need much more space than an ordinary industrial enterprise. This includes, as Olson makes it explicit, the following decisive problem: how shall workers in such enterprises be controlled and co-ordinated? This is a problem because employees work far away from each other and an inspector would need to have several square miles under surveillance. This means that as soon as an enterprise has reached a critical size and new workers have to be employed, an enormous control problem arises which will lead to diminishing returns to scale. Large agricultural enterprises are no longer competitive if they face smaller production units and will have to leave the market while the smaller ones will gain a foothold.

Starting with Olson's argumentation one can find a number of further arguments for family farms as the better organisational form in the literature. Thus, K. Hagedorn (K. Hagedorn 1992a) for example showed that an agricultural enterprise is not only confronted with the problem of space intensity but also with the problem of the diversity of decisions: different soil conditions, various microclimates and a large number of agricultural products call for a large number of management decisions. Therefore the cost of management personnel will rise rapidly and the advantages of the cost digression of capital goods will be overcompensated. But Konrad Hagedorn does not regard the lower co-ordination costs due to a smaller span of control to be the only advantage of small agricultural enterprises. Rather, he argues, being socialized in a farmer's family leads to a work ethics that minimizes transaction costs.

At first glance this explanation seems to be satisfactory. On the one hand, it can be made clear that the survival of agricultural enterprises is more a question of organisation than a question of the optimal farm size, on the other hand, it can be considered as a departure from the assumption that individuals consciously choose those institutions that minimize transaction costs. Instead, it will be shown how those institutions that are best adapted will be selected by the environment. Moreover, by stressing the integrative function of the farmer's family, the role of informal rules, i.e. rural culture for example, is picked out as a central theme. Especially this aspect is very often neglected.

Nevertheless this way of reasoning shows some deficits as well: it is supposed that in the long run a decentral form of organisation will gain a foothold. How then is it possible to explain that, as explained above, hierarchical forms of organisation could be successful in history as well?

In order to answer this question it appears appropriate to discuss the failures of the approach. In his argumentation Olson refers to the historic case of the decline of the large bonanza farms in the American middle west which are said to have disappeared due to high co-ordination costs. If one has a close look at the source cited by Olson (H. L. Briggs 1932) it becomes obvious that the high co-ordination costs were only an indirect cause of the decline of the bonanza farms. Rather the monoculture of the large farms (itself possibly being a result of the high co-ordination costs) made them vulnerable for crop failures and changing market conditions. The large farms mainly growing wheat lost the basis of their existence when the wheat prices fell continuously during consecutive years, while smaller farms were less afflicted by this development and were thus able to survive. This was due to the fact that wheat was only part of their production and that these farms, unlike the large bonanza farms, could live off their own, much more diversified, products so that they were less sensitive to the price fluctuations of grain.

Moreover, in his extension of Olson's theory Hagedorn stresses the role of traditional rural values when explaining the superiority of family farms. By doing so he implicitly refers to the values that can be found in Western societies. The question of what happens if other values are prevalent, for example if the integrative function is not attributed to the family but, as can often be found in developing countries, to the village community as a whole is left open. The fact that Olson as well implicitly refers to the traditional Western values as a basis for his argumentation becomes evident if one has a look at how the small farmers being competitors to the large bonanza farms are characterized:

> "... immigrants from the agricultural districts of northern Europe who were looking for opportunities to establish themselves. They were ambitious to become farmers and land owners." (H.L. Briggs 1932, p. 28).

Yet, the biggest problem with the approach presented lies in the fact that on the one hand it presupposes functioning market structures and on the other hand it takes the rule of law, especially concerning property rights, for granted. But what happens, if distribution channels are underdeveloped or some suppliers have better access to markets than others? In which respect

INDEPENDENT FAMILY FARMS IN RUSSIAN AGRICULTURE

will the investigation need to be changed, if agricultural enterprises are forced to devote a large part of their resources to enforce their own rights themselves instead of devoting them to production because the state is too weak to secure that the rights of the individual have to be sometimes if at all defended at comparatively low costs, as the individuals can rely upon a well functioning juridical system?

A model that takes these considerations into account will be presented in the following two chapters. In chapter 4 it will be developed without reference to any particular problem. In chapter 5 it will be discussed in as far the model is suitable to describe the current problems concerning property rights in Russian agriculture.

IV. An Alternative Model

1. The Basic Idea

In order to analyze the question of whether and under which circumstances certain property rights regimes and organisational structures develop in spontaneous processes, i.e. if there is no superior authority that influences individuals' choices, we shall fall back upon a model originally presented by Jack Hirshleifer (J. Hirshleifer 1995). Its basic idea stems from biology and explains territoriality in animal behaviour. But it is also designed to find application in other fields for example the struggle for control of the globe's free resources or the development of a (private) property rights regime during the gold rush in California.

The main question pursued in the model is whether anarchy, in our case we will identify this situation with a decentral form of organisation, is able to be a stable structure of organisation in society. It will be asked which factors determine this stability resp. instability and which organisational structure will emerge if the decentral form of organisation should be unstable. There are two potential candidates for alternative organisational structures: horizontal and vertical hierarchies.

In order to apply the model to the problem of agricultural development in Russia in the following chapter it first appears to be necessary to clarify the concepts of "anarchy" which, without referring to any value judgement, describes the decentral form of organisation, and "hierarchy" which refers to a more centralized form of organisation. In ordinary usage "anarchy" is associated with a notion of disorder or chaos while the meaning of "hierarchy" is rather characterized by strong dominance. The definition of these terms will be somewhat different in this paper.

Under "anarchy" we want to understand an organisational form that, though not being consciously created, is not chaotic or in total disorder. Patterns of interaction emerge without being intended. Anarchy is characterized by the fact that the individuals have to devote their budget, i.e. their resources, to two different activities: either they devote it to competitive activities - this appears to be necessary in order to retain an appropriate stock of resources for the next period - or they use it for production, that means for the creation of - abstract, not necessary pecuniary - income in order to facilitate survival. Generally speaking, anarchy appears to be a stable form of organisation if under certain external conditions an equilibrium between competitive activity and productive activity can be achieved.

If, by contrast, it is impossible to reach this equilibrium, a hierarchical form of organisation will gain a foothold. Under this organisational form decisions concerning the use of the resources will no longer be made individually. Rather it will be replaced by a hierarchical decision structure. In the better case a horizontal "agreement" underlies the hierarchical decision structure. This means that the handing over of competence is based on a more or less democratic decision. But it is also possible, that the vertical case, hierarchical dominance, i.e. a kind of dictatorship, emerges.

To a large extent the stability of a decentral social arrangement is contingent on the way resources are devoted to the two different uses and the income that can be gained in one period. Both variables will be determined - as it is usual in "classical" microeconomic theory - with the help of an optimization algorithm that leads to an equilibrium. That means that they are static in a certain sense. Yet, as the results are characterized by potential instability and owing to the fact that the sources and consequences of this instability are examined this approach contains a dynamic component. One weakness of the model is that within its framework it is not possible to show how the transition between the different organisational forms will take place.

Whether the results determined by the optimization algorithm are stable or not depends on the specification of certain decisive parameters, namely the conversion costs, the production coefficient and the decisiveness parameter. Conversion costs describe how "expensive" it is to devote a re-

INDEPENDENT FAMILY FARMS IN RUSSIAN AGRICULTURE

source to one of the two activities possible or, expressed differently, how much of the resource is needed in order to realize one unit of the activity. This means that the conversion costs are an expression of the shadow prices of competitive and productive activity respectively. The production coefficient does not diverge from the usual microeconomic concept and is chosen in a way that the production function shows decreasing returns to scale. Finally, the decisiveness parameter expresses the fierceness of the competitive activity, for example it shows whether the individuals pursue a rather defensive or a more offensive strategy.

As a first step the analysis will be carried for two identical enterprises. But, as will be shown, it is possible without any loss of generality to enlarge the analytical framework to N enterprises or to include different characteristics of the enterprises, may they be varying behavioural parameters, may they be behavioural assumptions expressing asymmetries.

2. Stability of Agricultural Organisational Forms

In this chapter the conditions under which the alternative agricultural organisational forms emerge will be investigated. The main feature of the environment in which the investigation will take place is the absence of a strong state which is able to influence the direction of the organisational development in a substantive manner and which has the power to define property rights and is able to put the resources necessary to secure and defend property rights at the individuals' disposal.

The organisational forms being discussed can be described as decentral on the one hand and hierarchical on the other hand. In order to capture the phenomena we shall choose a relatively small agricultural area as a unit of investigation. In this area either one large agricultural enterprise or a variety of small private family farms or a somewhat smaller large agricultural enterprise together being in competition with some family farms can be found.

The first case, obviously, is a hierarchical form of organisation, the second a decentral one, whereby there is symmetry between the competitors. The enterprises are able to devote their resources either to production for the market or use them for competitive activities and to push through their own rights with regard to other competitors. This embodies, apart from "classical" competitive activities such as the creation of markets, but also the directed influencing of the bureaucracy which is not able to act according to the directives of the legislative organs due to the fact that the directives themselves are contradictory or because the legislative organs do not exist at all as they are just in the process of being restructured. In such a situation the executive organs will probably decide on the basis of "the better arguments" or just in favour for those enterprises that are able to corrupt them. The third case, finally, refers to a decentral organisational form with asymmetries concerning the large agricultural enterprise. The fact that this large enterprise is hierarchically organized itself is irrelevant, as we are discussing the organisational level which is above the firm level. Moreover, the problem of hierarchy afflicts, although to a much smaller degree, not only the large agricultural enterprises but the family farm as well; yet, as mentioned above, not on the overall organisational level but on the firm level.

As a first step we want to model the simplest version with two enterprises. The resources R_i, being at an enterprise's i=1,2 disposal - we are discussing labour, capital and land, the classical factors of production - can either at conversion costs a_i be transformed into one unit of productive activity E_i or at the conversion cost b_i into one unit of competitive activity F_i:

(1)
$$R_i = a_i E_i + b_i F_i$$

The corresponding production intensities e_i and competitive intensities f_i are defined as

(2)
$$e_i = \frac{E_i}{R_i} ; \quad f_i = \frac{F_i}{R_i}$$

and the share one enterprise i has in the whole resource R which has to be split up between the two enterprises is given by

(3)
$$p_i = \frac{R_i}{R}$$

The way the resources being at the enterprises' disposal are shared out largely depends on the decisiveness parameter m, 0<m<1. This parameter describes the fierceness of the conflict. The sharing out of the resources is shown in the success function:

(4)
$$\frac{p_1}{p_2} = \left(\frac{F_1}{F_2}\right)^m$$

INDEPENDENT FAMILY FARMS IN RUSSIAN AGRICULTURE

By combining (2), (3) and (4) we get

(5)
$$p_1/p_2 = \left(f_1/f_2\right)^{m/(1-m)}$$

From the aspect of the sharing out of the resources which is described in (5) we can analyze the conditions under which the system is able to survive, that means under which circumstance a decentral form of organisation will gain a foothold. This is obviously the case if there is no striking unequal distribution, that means if p_1/p_2 is not very close to 0 or ∞. If, instead, it is probable that one enterprise appropriates all resources, the juxtaposition of independently operating enterprises will break down. Whether this will happen or not depends on the decisiveness parameter m: If m is approaching 1, i.e. the fiercer the competitive activities, then in the case of $f_1 > f_2$ enterprise one will finally dominate entirely as p_1/p_2 is approaching ∞. If $f_1 < f_2$ then enterprise 2 will be successful as p_1/p_2 is approaching 0. Owing to the instability of the decentral form of organisation a more hierarchical form will become predominant and this will probably be its vertical variant because m expresses the readiness to subordinate the other to one's will.

What exactly determines the value of **m**? As has already been mentioned, m describes the determination of the parties in the conflict, the readiness to subjugate the opponent totally. In as far this readiness can be found in a population largely depends on the cultural framework. The attitude toward aspiration to dominance is of crucial importance. If the successful are held in high regard m should be much higher than in a society in which the successful are stigmatised and egalitarianism predominates as the leading value.

A decentral system based on private family farms might be unstable for a further reason. This is the case if the sharing out of the resources does not directly lead to a hierarchical situation but the incomes Y_i are so low that they lie under the minimal income Y which is necessary in order to guarantee survival. The resulting existential crises will cause the enterprises concerned to search for new possibilities also in the organisational structure in order to facilitate survival in the following periods.

As will be shown, this case will occur in the case of high conversion costs **a**, high decisiveness parameter **m**, and increasing numbers of population **N**. An increasing number of population might result in an increased number of farmsteads due to partitions because of inheritance. In order to determine the equilibrium income we will first develop a production function

(6)
$$Y_i = E_i^h = ((e_i R_i))^h =$$
$$((e_i R(p_i)))^h =$$
$$\left(e_i R \frac{f_i^M}{f_i^M + f_j^M} \right)^h$$

with
$$M = \frac{m}{1-m}$$

whereby **h**<1, that means there are decreasing returns to scale. This should be realistic in the kind of agriculture we are investigating here because agricultural production, as could already be shown by Turgot, is characterized by decreasing returns to scale due to decreasing quality of additional units of soil. In addition, there are the control costs already described in chapter 3. These two factors should overcompensate possible scale economies if one regards the comparatively low degree of automatization that characterizes agriculture in an environment in which property rights are insecure.

As we analyze the symmetrical case, all parameters are equal for all enterprises. Moreover, we argue within a framework of Cournot behaviour, i.e. within a framework in which both enterprises optimize and take the behaviour of the other as given. They maximize the production function under the condition of total use of resources $a_1 e_1 + b_1 f_1 = 1$. We have to formulize the corresponding Lagrange function for both enterprises. Due to the symmetry property this will be shown for one enterprise only.

(7)
$$L(e_1, f_1,) = \left\{ \left(e_1 R \frac{f_1^M}{f_1^M + f_2^M} \right)^h - (a_1 e_1 + b_1 f_1 - 1) \right\} \max!$$

If this function is differentiated and rearranged* we will get the reaction function

---

* The first order conditions are
$$\frac{\partial L}{\partial f_1} = \{h( )\}^{h-1} \left\{ e_1 R M \frac{f_2^M}{(f_1^M + }\right.$$

INDEPENDENT FAMILY FARMS IN RUSSIAN AGRICULTURE

(8)
$$\frac{f_1^M}{f_2^M} = \frac{M}{b_1 f_1} - (M+1)$$

As both functions are symmetric, enterprise 2 has the analogous reaction function

(9)
$$\frac{f_2^M}{f_1^M} = \frac{M}{b_2 f_2} - (M+1)$$

In order to determine the equilibrium income it is necessary to derive the competitive intensity **f**. This will be achieved by supposing (owing to the symmetry assumption) uniform f_i, b_i and a_i. Therefore equations (8) and (9) reduce (under the omission of index **i** as the enterprises are regarded as symmetrical) to

(10)
$$f_1 = f_2 = f = \frac{M}{b(M+2)} = \frac{m}{b(2-m)}$$

If this result is inserted in the original production function one yields as equilibrium income

(11)
$$Y^* = \left[\frac{1-m}{a(2-m)} R \right]^h$$

$$\{(f_2^M)^2\} - b_1 = 0$$

$$\frac{L}{e_1} = h(\cdot)^{h-1} \frac{R f_1^M}{f_1^M + f_2^M} - a_1 = 0$$

$$\frac{L}{\cdot} = a_1 e_1 + b_1 f_1 - 1 = 0$$

By division of the first two equations one yields
$$\frac{f_1^{M+1} + f_1 f_2^M}{e_1 M f_2^M} = \frac{a_1}{b_1}$$

Combined with the third equation we will get
$$\frac{f_1^M}{f_2^M} = \left(\frac{M - M b_1 f_1}{b_1} - f_1 \right) \frac{1}{f_1}$$

A decentralized system of independent family farms will be stable, if the subsistence level Y is met, i.e. if $Y^* \geq Y$. Instabilities arise, if the conversion parameter a increases such that the subsistence level can no longer be met. For example this is the case if there are inefficiencies due to the lavish use of resources. The diminishing of the resource basis R and of the production coefficient h owing to worsened climatic conditions, soil deterioration and erosion has similar consequences.

A further source of potential instability can be found if one expands the investigation to N enterprises. In order to do that the equation (1) to (11) have to be enlarged. Then the maximization problem can be presented as

(12)
$$L(\{e_1\}, \{f_1\},) = \left\{ \left[\frac{\{e_1\} R \{f_1\}^M}{\{f_1\}^M + \{f_2\}^M + ... + \{f_N\}^M} \right] \right\}^h - (\{a_1\}\{e_1\} + \{b_1\}\{f_1\} - 1) \max!$$

and analogously to the case of two enterprises one gets an equilibrium income of

(13)
$$Y^* = \left[\frac{1-m}{a(N-m)} R \right]^h$$

It is evident that Y will fall under Y^* if the population increase, i.e. raising N, is not accompanied by an increasing resource basis R. This is the case if $R=R(N)$ is not valid. The resulting increasing instability can only be stopped by a corresponding fall of a or increase of h. If it is not possible to compensate this development with the help of the parameter a and h it is very probable that the organisational structure will develop into a hierarchical form. Contrary to the case with a high decisiveness parameter this need not necessarily be a vertical hierarchy. Rather it might be a horizontal form of hierarchy which is characterized by egalitarianism. Which form of hierarchy will emerge in the end will depend upon how the individuals perceive their environment and this is dependent on the respective cultural background. What such a perception and cognition mechanism might look like will be discussed in the following chapter.

Yet, before we come to this point it is necessary to outline case 3 - enterprises among which, due to their history, longer time of existence, and size asymmetries can be found. These asymmetries find their expression in diverging conversion costs **a** or **b** respectively or differing production functions due to varying specifications with the production coefficient **h**.

There will be a divergence in conversion costs if one side, usually this is the larger one, has easier access to or better influence on the bureaucracy that regulates land allocation problems or is more successful in organizing the supply with inputs. Then this side will need less resources in order to influence decisions in its favour or to reach an advantageous competitive position by a better supply with means of production. There are varying production coefficients if the efficiency of the enterprises is not the same. This may be caused by different incentive structures or distinct agrotechnical knowledge. A dissimilar development of the enterprises' income is the consequence of the asymmetries. It is possible to derive this result by simulations which will not be shown here. It is intuitively evident that relatively small conversion costs and comparatively high productivity will lead to a higher income of one enterprise.

Enterprises with different incomes can coexist as long as both earn an income that is above subsistence level. Yet, if the incomes are so different that the smaller enterprises permanently earn an income $Y^*<Y$ and the large enterprise is just able to hold the subsistence level, then the situation will become unstable and it is probable that either the small enterprises will start to cooperate and band together as a hierarchical form of organisation, for example a co-operative, or they are incorporated into a large enterprise. The result of such a merger of individual small enterprises is the concentration and thus the reduction of the price of competitive activities. Owing to the fallen parameter b more resources are devoted to production and income can rise so that it will possibly be above subsistence level in the end.

The results of this chapter can be summarized as follows: three different constellations of organisational structures have been analyzed regarding their stability. Those parameters which can cause an instability have been made explicit; particularly, the decisiveness parameter **m**, the conversion costs **a** and **b**, the production coefficient **h** and the population size **N** are named. In the following chapter the explanatory power of the model will be judged.

SILKE STAHL

V. The Explanatory Power of the Model

1. Assessment Taking into Consideration the Background of Conventional Models and Their Critique

The conventional approaches have mainly been criticized as they have not been able to explain the historical persistence of organisational structures in agriculture that are not based on independent family farms. This was mainly due to the fact that they assumed perfect market structures and well functioning property right systems as well.

The model presented is able to overcome these shortcomings as its scenario is characterized by uncertainty concerning the property rights (thus) to be defended and the state has only limited influence on shaping the society. At the same time it appears to be possible to integrate a strong state into the model by having a low conversion parameter b. This means that less resources are needed for the protection of individual rights. Nevertheless, there will always be controversies and even if there is a strong state it might be possible that a decentral organisational form appears to be unstable. Cultural aspects can be included in the analysis by an appropriate specification of the parameters. Thus, the model is able to illustrate a situation in which the decentral form of organisation is unstable. In the long run a distinct organisational form will become predominant.

One might criticize the model because on the level of the enterprise optimizing, rationality and complete information are assumed. This critique becomes relatively insignificant if one considers that optimization appears only on the enterprise level; on the societal level the organisational form is not chosen consciously according to an optimization algorithm. The transition from one organisational form to another might be explained by trial and error or by the imitation of organisational clusters nearby. The set of organisational forms being "tested" depends up to a large extent on cultural preconditions (see discussion in S. Stahl 1996). Thus, within this model we have no collective rational choice of institutions.

A further problem that should be mentioned is the question of whether the model is dynamic or static. Regarding the underlying optimizing procedure one might assume that it is more static than dynamic. Yet, with the help of the model it is possible to analyze historical and thus dynamic developments and the variability of the parameters allows for an, even though exogenous, dynamic element.

INDEPENDENT FAMILY FARMS IN RUSSIAN AGRICULTURE

2. Explanatory Power Taking into Account the Background of the Russian Property Rights Tradition

In this part of the paper we shall try to use the structure of the model for the explanation of the property right problem we can find in Russian agriculture. It will be possible to show that the aim of the transition process, a system of independent private family farms, might be unstable under certain conditions. The explanatory power of the model will be tested by confronting it with two historical situations: the spread of communal practices in the 19th century and today's transition problems in the agricultural sector.

If we want to apply the model to the organisation problem prevalent in the 19th century, as a first step it is necessary to investigate whether there was a weak state and thus only relatively insecure property rights at this time. It seems to be self-evident that under the communication conditions during this time the state's influence in the countryside was only weak. Instead, administrative and legislative structures were institutionalized at a local level. Since 1863 we can find the semstvo, a self-governing body, at a district (rayon) level (R. Wortmann 1976) and since 1861 the mir already had political functions in the villages. In the countryside legislation was decentralized to a large extent and did not know a uniform codified law as a jury which was composed of peasants passed judgements according to human understanding and the regional customs (L. Zakharova 1991).

Property rights were extremely insecure. To a certain extent this was because the notion of property was underdeveloped. The peasants were convinced that land could not belong to anyone else other than God and that man could only take possession of it for a limited time as long as he cultivated it. (S. Nikolsky 1994, p. 10). Thus, demarcations between the land of the lord and the peasant could seldom be found and land conflicts were the order of the day.

In those regions where redistributional practices were not prevalent at first, the starting point can be described as decentral as the family farm was the dominant organisational entity. Yet, this organisational structure broke down: the village community distributed resources according to aspects of need and thus a horizontal hierarchical structure emerged. In the context of the model presented this means that the parameter m and b as well as the population size N and the size of the resource R being at the population's disposal first guaranteed a stable decentral structure. But with the time there must have been changes in these values which let the system become unstable. Which changes were these? One might think of an increase in the decisiveness parameter m. Taking the central egalitarian value of the peasants into consideration this does not seem to be very plausible. Moreover, an increase in m would rather have led to a vertical hierarchical organisational structure than to the horizontal one that actually emerged.

Thus, we have to analyze whether the factors which determine the equilibrium income changed in a way that the actual income fell under the subsistence level. One can assume that the conversion costs were quite high as the peasants could not rely on the administration if a land conflict occurred. Furthermore, it was not usual at all that peasants appealed to the administration or a court in order to solve a conflict. Yet, there is no reason why conversion costs should have risen over time.

Thus, high conversion costs can not be made responsible for the change of the organisational structure but only for the general low income near the subsistence level. This means that the crucial factors are the population development on the one hand and the size of the resource land on the other: during the first half of the 19th century Russia experienced an enormous population increase which took place mainly in the countryside as industrialization was still in its beginnings. While the population rose by 60% during this time, only 6% of this increase was absorbed by the cities (W. Blackwell 1982). Furthermore, in the course of the breaking up of the demesnes and the peasants' land the lord received 20% of the land which before had been cultivated by peasants (A. Gerschenkron 1968, p. 168, B. Mironov 1985).

The model can not tell us how the transition to the new organisational form took place. Yet, outside the model we can make conjectures. Thus, it is reasonable to assume that the shared values that can be found in a group determine the way the environment and especially the organisational alternatives are perceived (A. T. Denzau/D. C. North 1994). Only a small fraction of all the possible alternatives are taken into consideration and the judgement of the members of the group concerning an organisational innovation is more or less the same. This facilitates the transition from one organisational form to another. In the case considered the choice was mainly influenced by the predominant rural egalitarianism and conservatism. An organisational form that promised a just distribution was chosen. It was a conservative organisational form as it had already been practised in some regions since time immemorial.

Not only this historical situation but also today's problem of an insufficient willingness to operate independently in the framework of a private

INDEPENDENT FAMILY FARMS IN RUSSIAN AGRICULTURE

family farm can be explained with the help of the model presented in chapter 4: again the external conditions are characterized by a weak state - the government is unstable, independence is demanded in the regions and the semstvo movement is coming back with a vengeance (Agra-Europe v. 10.4.95, p. 29) - and insecure property rights. This insecurity results from an ever changing legal situation, not very reliable land records (V. Renard 1994), incompetent and overtaxed administration, and finally from the open future of the privatisation efforts which has vividly been demonstrated by the fact that the Duma is preparing a law concerning the renationalization of enterprises at the moment (*Frankfurter Allgemeine Zeitung*, 16 February 1996).

The situation corresponds with case 3 of the analysis in chapter 4 - one large enterprise being in competition with several small family farms. Hoping for higher incomes in the future these people took the risk of becoming independent farmers. The problem is that the small farms and thus the whole organisational structure cannot survive at the moment. This has two consequences: those thinking of becoming independent farmers will become more and more hesitant and existing private family farms will be given up. The consequences are the stagnation described in the introductory chapter and even a real retrograde step back from the establishment of a private agricultural sector.

Looking for the reasons for this development one has to assume that both groups, the (former) collective farms as well as the newly created independent family farms, operate near subsistence level. This means that small deviations from the parameters determining income will lead to an advantage for one of the two organisational forms. Thus, we have to analyze, in as far as there are deviations in the parameters **b** and **h**.

The parameter **b** describes how many resources are needed in order to produce one unit of competitive activity. This parameter is definitely biased in favour of the collective enterprise as it still has the old connections to administration and suppliers at its disposal and thus needs less resources in order to bribe and convince whereas the small family farms face a somewhat suspicious administration. A further factor is that owing to the cultural continuities the population has a negative orientation toward private enterprise and thus property is less respected. All this leads to a comparatively high parameter b. That large enterprises are more successful if they try to realize their interests can be derived from two figures: their share in all the subsidies is higher than their share in the land used for agriculture (K. Hagedorn 1992b) and 16% of all private enterprises that ceased operation indicated as the main cause that they had problems with large former collective farms in their neighbourhood (S. Wegren 1992); thus, they devoted so many resources to competitive activity that in the end they were ruined.

Differences in the size of the production coefficient h can also be made responsible for a diverging income situation. Yet, it is difficult to evaluate which organisational form is more efficient and shows a higher production coefficient. The motivation to engage in a small enterprise is certainly higher than in a former collective farm but in the latter the productive capital might be more favourable. Moreover, it appears possible that due to specialization employees in the large agricultural enterprises are better qualified. If one also considers that the private farmers very often received low-quality soil (R. L. Prosterman et al. 1995) it appears to be obvious that also the coefficient **h** is biased in favour of the large former collective enterprises.

Thus, an organisational form characterized by a juxtaposition of private family farms and former collective farms is unstable. Many farmers who became independent gave up. The original aim of agricultural transition - a system based on private family farms - has lost its attractiveness. The low attraction is reflected in the diminishing share of private farms and the diminishing number of starting of new private agricultural enterprises. Not a system of independent family farms is the attractor of the development but rather the large agricultural enterprises that resulted from the restructuring of the old collective farms and are organized like industrial enterprises: there are command hierarchies and - even though the members of these enterprises are shareholders and thus de jure owners of the means of production - most characteristics of property rights, especially *usus* and *abusus*, are allocated to the management.

VI. Resume

A model has been developed in this paper, in order to explain why structures which are based on a system of family farms can be unstable. It could be shown that this model has explanatory power if it is confronted with historical material.

Yet, this model is only the first step and we shall delineate in this last section in which direction it can be developed further. On the theoretical level one should analyze how the resulting changes if not decreasing but constant or increasing returns to scale are supposed. Furthermore, it appears possible to integrate the modified behavioural conjectures as for example satisfying or melioration. Also the endogenization of the population size appears to be useful.

As a further step not only the decentral but also the hierarchical form of organisation should be tested for stability and the mechanism that underlies the transition between the different organisational forms should be made explicit. The model presented by Denzau and North offers a promising clue.

As regards contents two points should be mentioned: in order to make the model more accessible for empirical investigations a system of indicators for the several parameters could be developed. Yet, this could prove to be quite difficult as the data base for the historical situations is very incomplete and unreliable. This would mean that the indicators are rather qualitative than quantitative. The other point is that one could test whether the model is also applicable to the situation in developing countries.

References

ATKINSON, DOROTHY: *The End of the Russian Land Commune 1905-1930*, Stanford (Stanford University Press) 1983.

BLACKWELL, WILLIAM: *The Industrialization of Russia*, Arlington Heights (Harlan Davidson Incorporated) 1982.

BLANCHARD, OLIVER et al.: *Reform in Eastern Europe*, Cambridge MA (MIT Press) 1991.

BRIGGS, HAROLD E.: "Early Bonanza Farming in the Red River Valley of the North", *Agricultural History*, 6 (1932), pp. 23-37.

DEMSETZ, HAROLD: "Toward a Theory of Property Rights", *American Economic Review*, 57 (1967), pp. 347-359.

GERSCHENKRON, ALEXANDER: "Russia - Agrarian Policies and Industrialization 1861 - 1917", in: ALEXANDER GERSCHENKRON (Ed.): *Continuity in History*, Cambridge MA (Belknap Press) 1968.

HAGEDORN, KONRAD (1992a): "Das Leitbild des bäuerlichen Familienbetriebes in der Agrarpolitik", *Zeitschrift für Agrargeschichte und Agrarsoziologie,* 40 (1992), pp. 53-86.

HAGEDORN, KONRAD (1992b): "Wirtschaftliche und politische Triebkräfte der Umformung einer sozialistischen Agrarverfassung", *Jahrbuch für Neue Politische Ökonomie,* 11 (1992), pp. 191-213.

HAYEK, FRIEDRICH AUGUST VON: *The Fatal Conceit,* London/ Chicago (University of Chicago Press) 1988.

HIRSHLEIFER, JACK: "Anarchy and Its Breakdown", *Journal of Political Economy,* 103 (1995), pp. 26-52.

HOFFMANN, DAVID A. J.: "Land, Freedom and Discontent: Russian Peasants of the Central Industrial Region Prior to Collectivization", *Europe-Asia Studies,* 46 (1994), pp. 637-548.

KISLEV, YOAV/PETERSON, WILLIS: "Prices, Technology and Farm Size", *Journal of Political Economy,* 90 (1982), pp. 578-595.

LIPTON, DAVID/SACHS, JEFFREY: "Creating a Market Economy in Eastern Europe", *Brookings Papers on Economic Activity,* 1 (1990).

LYASHCHENKO, PETER: *History of the National Economy of Russia to the 1917 Revolution,* New York (Macmillian) 1949.

MIRONOV, BORIS: "The Russian Peasant Commune After the Reforms of the 1860s", *Slavic Review,* 44 (1985), pp. 436-467.

MYHRMAN, JOHAN: "The New Institutional Economics and the Process of Economic Development", *JITE,* 145 (1989), pp. 38-59.

NIKOLSKY, SERGEY: "Peasant Consciousness and Agrarian Modernization of Russia", *Problems of Economic Transition,* 26 (1994), pp. 6-23.

OLSON, MANCUR: "Space, Agriculture and Organization", *American Journal of Agricultural Economics,* 67 (1985), pp. 928-937.

PROSTERMAN, ROY L./ ROLFES, LEONARD J./ MITCHELL, ROBERT G.: "Russian Agrarian Reform: A Status Report from the Field", *Communist Economies & Economic Transformation,* 7 (1995), pp. 175-193.

REICHHARD, MICHAEL: *Der Beitrag des Transaktionskostenansatzes zu einer Theorie der Transformation von Wirtschaftsordnungen,* Frankfurt (Peter Lang) 1995.

RENARD, VINCENT: "Emerging Land Markets in Eastern Europe", *Economics of Transition,* 2 (1994), pp. 501-513.

RUNGE, CARLISLE FORD: "Inefficiency and Structural Adjustment in American Agriculture", in: HARDWIGER, BROWNS (Eds.): *Public Policy and Agricultural Technology,* Houndsmill (St Martins Press Text) 1987.

STAHL, SILKE: "Transition Problems in the Russian Agricultural Sector. A Historical-Institutional Perspective", in: ASH AMIN (Ed.): *Beyond Markets and Hierarchies. Interactive Governance and Social Complexity,* Aldershot (Edward Elgar) 1996, forthcoming.

VAN ATTA, DON: "The Return of Individual Farming in Russia", in: DON VAN ATTA (Ed.): *The "Farmer Threat". The Political Economy of Agrarian Reform in Post-Soviet Russia*, Boulder/ San Francisco/ New York (Westview Press) 1993.

WEGREN, STEPHEN K.: "Trends in Russian Agrarian Reform", *RFE/RL Research Report*, 2 (1993), pp. 46-57.

WEGREN, STEPHEN K. (1994a): "Rural Reforms and Political Culture in Russia", *Europe-Asia Studies*, 46 (1994), pp. 215-241.

WEGREN, STEPHEN K. (1994b): "New Perspectives on Spatial Patterns of Agrarian Reform: A Comparison of Two Russian Oblasts", *Post-Soviet Geography*, 35 (1994), pp. 455-481.

WORTMAN, RICHARD: *The Development of Russian Legal Consciousness*, Chicago/London (University of Chicago Press) 1976 .

ZAKHAROVA, LARISSA: "Autocracy and the Reforms of 1861-1874 - Choosing Paths of Development", in: BEN EKLOF et al. (Eds.): *Russia's Great Reforms 1855-1881*, Bloomington, Indianapolis (Indiana University Press) 1994.

Chapter 11

Russian Law and Land Privatisation

EVGENI F. SHEPELEV

I.	Land Privatisation as a Part of Establishing Market Relations in Russia
II.	Legal Regulation of Land Privatisation in Russia
III.	Local Legal Regulation of Land Tenure
IV.	Economic Aspects of Land Privatisation in Saint Petersburg. Preliminary Conclusions

I. Land Privatisation as a Part of Establishing Market Relations in Russia

It is doubtless that land privatisation is one of the aspects of establishing market relations and economic order in Russia. Besides the economic and legal significance, this problem has an essential ethical aspect, as only the combination of these three aspects and the investigation of them in their interrelations and their mutual development can give the desired result for the most efficient development of the society. The concept of real estate, as it is understood in Western countries now, involves land and buildings and constructions on land. In contemporary Russia, land and real estate are not identical categories. Probably, this diversity resulted from the process of privatisation, when first the property of enterprises was bought, then the buildings were bought, and only after that the land plots were bought out.

The endeavour to establish by law the general concept of real estate in 1991 was not supported by the legislative acts, and that is why land and what is on it are considered and evaluated separately.

RUSSIAN LAW AND LAND PRIVATISATION

Buying out land by enterprises is logically the final stage of the privatisation process and there is no doubt that it influences the development of civilized market relations. Land privatisation allows an enterprise to involve in the economic cycle all the means of production (land, buildings, constructions, equipment) as a whole, which creates new opportunities for facilitating the entrepreneurship.

Before buying out a land plot an enterprise is supposed to estimate most efficient variants of its further utilisation taking into account various factors including its situation, distance to highways, communication opportunities, opportunities for developing adjacent land, etc.

Land is a unique category. It is a natural resource allowing to get additional returns. In the civilized world it is well known that the price of land is constantly growing due to the objective causes and that investing in land is one of the most profitable and secure ways of increasing capital.

Buying land plots is very attractive for landlords in terms of commercial land-tenure and getting financial profits which can be used for increasing fixed capital, activating capital flow, decreasing taxes.

The increase of fixed capital is accomplished by including in nominal capital the cost of the land plot and by additional stock emission equal to this amount, which allows the enterprise to get additional funds to be invested in the production.

The right to manage the property gives the proprietor of a plot an opportunity to cover the expenditures and to get additional returns. One of the opportunities is that of leasing a spare (not used) part of the plot for erecting buildings and constructions and then utilising. Depending upon the needs of the proprietor and the terms of the contract, the returns gained as a result of such a transaction can take the form of either leasing payments (from the premium for the right of signing a leasing agreement after an auction to the regular payments counted as percentage of income resulting from the business activities on the part of the plot taken on lease) or building new constructions for the enterprise, renovation of the equipment, buying the most important technologies at the cost of the future leasing payments.

Another opportunity is getting loans on the security of the whole plot or of its part. It is profitable in cases when the banking loan rate is less than the income rate of commercial land tenure.

The third opportunity is the development and implementation of new projects of the most efficient land tenure taking into account rational investments in the most prestigious parts of it, possible reconstruction of a part of production means. A kind of such a variant is the opportunity of creating affiliated enterprises, branches or joint stock ventures and passing over the plots as a contribution in the nominal capital of these enterprises.

Acquiring a plot relieves an enterprise from the necessity to pay big sums of money to the state for leasing it. This is very profitable because it saves money, but it is also possible to get profits when the plot is bought for a bank's loan and paying off this loan decreases tax payments.

The simplest way of managing land property is selling it at market prices. This was the way chosen by some enterprises of Saint Petersburg, which had plots in different parts of the city and in the suburbs besides the main territory, mainly under the buildings and constructions designed for cultural and social purposes. Having bought small plots at favourable prices and having sold them with buildings, but at market prices, the enterprises got an opportunity to accumulate liquidity for buying the plots under the major industrial constructions.

Thus, buying the land plots by privatized enterprises was in the majority of cases economically profitable and reasonable.

II. Legal Regulation of Land Privatisation in Russia

The legal basis for regulating land relations is formulated in Article 9 of the Constitution of the Russian Federation: "Land and other natural resources are used and guarded in the Russian Federation as the basis of life and activity of those living on the territory. The land and other natural resources can be private, state, municipal or other types of property." Article 36 of the Constitution reads: "Citizens and their organisations have the right to own land as private property. Possession, tenure and management of land and of other natural resources can be exercised freely if it does not damage the environment and does not violate the rights and legal interests of other persons. The conditions and norms of land tenure are defined in accordance with the Federal Law."

These articles form the legal basis for the coexistence of many forms of land property. Within a short period of time, dozens of legal acts were created which regulated land relations and the process of land privatisation.

RUSSIAN LAW AND LAND PRIVATISATION

Unfortunately, the basic document designed for the regulation of land relations, the Land Code of the Russian Federation, is still being discussed and worked on. The Land Code of the Russian Federation, adopted in 1991, is out-of-date and most of its articles are fully or partially revoked by the President's Decree No 2287 of December 24, 1993 *On Updating Land Legislation of the Russian Federation in Accordance with the Constitution of the Russian Federation.*

On January 1, 1995, the First part of the Civil Code came in force. But chapter 17 *Property Right and Other Rights to Land* will not come into force till the adoption of the new Land Code. This complicates the situation, though some articles of the new Civil Code (for example, 129, 209, etc.) have already defined the legal framework of land tenure in the Russian Federation and also a number of issues concerning registration of land transactions.

The above documents, however important they might be, are just the basis of the arising land relations but they do not solve and cannot solve all the problems related to the process of land privatisation. This resulted in a number of federal legal acts, President's decrees, legal acts of the Government, and also ministerial legal acts designed to solve the problems of land privatisation. The most important of them are the following: Russian Federal Law *On Payments for Land*, October 11, 1991, No 1738-1; Russian Federal Law *On Addenda and Amendments to Articles 6, 8, 12 of Russian Federal Law On Payments for Land*, February 14, 1992, No 2353-1; Russian Federal Law *On Addenda and Amendments to Russian Federal Law On Payments for Land of July 16, 1992,* No 331701; Russian Federal Law *On Addenda and Amendments to Articles 6, 8, 12 of Russian Federal Law on Payments for Land, of August 9, 1994,* No 22-F-3; President's decrees: No 631 of June 14, 1992, *Establishing the Order of Selling Land Plots During the Privatisation of State and Municipal Enterprises, Additional Construction on the premises of These Enterprises, also Used by Individuals and Organisations for Commercial Purposes*; No 1767 of October 27, 1993, *On the Regulation of Land Relations and Development of Land Reform in Russia* (with amendments of December 24, 1993); No 1535 of July 22, 1994 *On Major Articles of State Programme of Privatisation of State and Municipal Enterprises in the Russian Privatisation after July 1, 1994*; No 478 of May 11, 1995, *On Measures for Securing Budget Incomes Involving Returns From Privatisation*; Government's Regulation No 1204 of November 3, 1994, *On the Order of Land Standard Price Estimation*; Roskomzem letters *On the Order of Land*

Standard Price Estimation of December 28, 1994, No 1-16./2096 and *On Standard Price of Land Occupied by Privatized Enterprises* of June 2, 1995, No 2-16/1120.

The process of land privatisation in Russia was actually started after Presidential Decree No 1535 of July 22, 1994. The Intensity of purchasing land plots by privatized enterprises depends upon many factors: financial opportunities of an enterprise, the availability of the necessary set of documents and their quality, the level of the qualification of the staff of the city administration departments. Local peculiarities and especially the level of the development of the local legislative basis and the way it organizes the work of the administration from the moment of submitting the application for the purchase up to giving the proprietor the documents establishing his title to the privatized land plot.

III. Local Legal Regulation of Land Tenure

For Saint Petersburg, the main documents concerning selling land, are Mayor's decrees: No 69-p of 28.01.94 *On Registration Documents For Actual Land Tenure*; No 881-p of 22.08.94 *On the Order of Price Estimation of Land Plots Sold in the Process of Privatisation of Real Estate*, with Amendments of Decree No 830 of 05.09.95; No 225-p of 09.03.95 *On Registration of Documents on Title for Companies Utilising the Plots in Saint Petersburg and Related Territories*; No 1010 of 18.09.95 *On Registration of Documents on Title for Companies Utilising the State Owned Plots in Saint Petersburg and Related Territories*; No 1049 of October 19, 1994 *On the Order of Realization of Presidential Decree of 22.07.94 No 1535 Concerning Selling and Leasing Land Plots*.

Other documents are: Municipal Property Management Committee's Regulation: No 989-p of 13.12.94 *On Establishing the Order of Co-operation of Branches of the City Administration Selling and Leasing Land Plots*; No 236-p of 06.05.95 and No 308-p of 07.06.95, with amendments to No 989-p; Regulation No 153-p of 05.04.96 *On Registration of a Typical Contract of Selling and Buying a Plot,* amendments included by the Regulation No 500-p of 05.09.95.

RUSSIAN LAW AND LAND PRIVATISATION

City Property Management Committee's Regulation No 695-p of 18.12.95 establishes a new order of the interaction of the branches of the city administration in the process of selling land plots in Saint Petersburg. In other words, within two years, the legal foundation was created and from time to time amended; the privatisation of land plots was organized on its basis.

The seller of land plots in Saint Petersburg is the Property Fund. An enterprise or an individual wishing to purchase a land plot, in accordance with the procedures valid till December 27, 1995, was supposed to submit to the Fund the following documents:
- certified copies of foundation documents;
- documents certifying the title to all buildings, constructions etc. on the plot;
- three copies of the map of borders of the plot elaborated by the Construction and Architecture Committee;
- three copies of the map of the plot, elaborated and certified by the Land Reserve and Land Tenure Committee;
- a copy of the privatisation plan;
- a copy of the shareholders register, confirming that no less than 75% of nominal capital of the company is private property;
- a record of proceedings of the Shareholders Meeting or of the Board of Directors meeting discussing the purchase of the plot;
- a filled in application form.

When all these documents are submitted, the Property Fund registers the application. If the Buyer acquires a part of the plot without its actual division, (this applies to the retail trade, restaurants and communal services, placed at the first levels of buildings), the list of the documents to be submitted is much shorter, as there is no need in maps of borders and plots and shareholders register. Instead of the maps, the Buyer should submit a confirmation of the proportion of the share of the plot and of its standard price.

The Property Fund administrates a thorough control of the documents submitted, when necessary, it requires that the Buyer should produce additional evidence, and in case the Buyer is eligible, it sends letters of inquiry to the Land Fund and the Land Tenure Committee and to the State Inspection of the Historical and Cultural Monuments Protection (UGIOP). In case only parts of plots are bought, the letters are sent only to UGIOP.

The Committees and UGIOP prepare their statements concerning the plot to be bought and submit them to the Seller. The Land Fund and Land Tenure Committee also give a confirmation of the standard price of the plot.

After obtaining the reports, the Seller can decide whether to sell the plot. The application of the Buyer may be rejected if the law does not allow to sell the plot. If the decision is to sell the plot, the Seller draws up a draft of the Contract and gives it to the Buyer for reading and signing. The copies of the Contract, signed by the Seller and the Buyer, are submitted to the Land Fund and Land Tenure Committee. The Buyer is supposed to pay the total sum within 30 days. After the Property Fund receives the money, the Buyer gets one copy of the Contract with Appendixes and registers the title in the Land Fund and Land Tenure Committee.

If, in accordance with the valid law, the plot is not to be sold, or the Buyer changed his mind about the transaction. or did not follow the terms of the Contract concerning the payments, the application is void and the documents are to be sent to the archives.

IV. Economic Aspects of Land Privatisation in Saint Petersburg. Preliminary Conclusions

One of the essential aspects influencing the decision concerning buying a land plot is its cost. The tendencies of the changes of the prices of land plots from 1992 to 1995 are shown in the tables below. The references to legislative acts concerning land price are added. A comprehensive table of the tendencies of land price changes are given at the end of the present paper.

Rates of Land Tax and Standard Land Price in St. Petersburg in 1992-1995

Main Concepts
Land tax is a regular annual payment for a unit of area. The rate of the tax is set by the Government of the Russian Federation as an average rate in proportion with the population and the economic region of the city.

RUSSIAN LAW AND LAND PRIVATISATION

The average rates are defined by the city administration according to the value of zones. The borders of the areas are defined in accordance with economic appraisal of the territory and general city plans.

In St. Petersburg the borders of social and economic zones and recreation zones are set by the Minor Council decision of 23.06.92 No 177, Appendix 1.

These borders are annually reviewed:
- in 1993: by the Minor Council decision of 13.07.93 No 294;
- in 1994: by the Mayor's decree of 14.04.94 No 352-r.

Standard Land Price was introduced for relieving the economic control of land relations in the period of utilisation of land as a security and in case the title holder changes.

The standard land price is set by the Government of the Russian Federation.

The rates of the land tax and the rate of standard land price did not change in 1992.

The average rate of land tax for Saint Petersburg was 21 rb/sq.m. It was defined by:
- Federal Law *On Payments for Land* of 11.10.91 No 1738-1, Appendix 2;
- Federal Law *On Budget System of the RF for 1992* of 17.07.92 No 3331-3;
- Minor Council Decision No 177 of 23.06.92.

The Standard land price was 50 times of land tax rate. It was defined by: Government Regulation of 25.02.92 No 112:

Zone No	Land tax rates (rb/sq.m)	Standard land price (rb/sq.m)
1	46.0	2300
2	40.0	2000
3	38.0	1900
4	36.0	1800
5	34.0	1700
6	32.0	1600
7	30.0	1500
8	28.0	1400
9	26.0	1300
10	24.0	1200
11	22.0	1100
12	20.0	1000
13	18.0	900
14	16 0	800
15	12 0	600

The rate of the land tax and the standard price of land did not change in 1993.

The average rate of land tax for Saint Petersburg was 73.5 rb/sq.m. It was defined by:

- Federal Law *On Payments for Land* of 11.10.91 No 1738-1, Appendix 2;

- Federal Law *On Budget System of the RF for 1993* of 14.05.93 No 4966-1;

- Minor Council Decision No 294 of 13.07.93.

RUSSIAN LAW AND LAND PRIVATISATION

Standard land price was 50 land tax rates. It was defined by:
Government Regulation of 25.02.92 No 112:

Zone No	Land tax rates (rb/sq.m)	Standard land price (rb/sq.m)
1	161,0	8050
2	140,0	7000
3	133,0	6650
4	126,0	6300
5	119,0	5950
6	112,0	5600
7	105,0	5250
8	98,0	4900
9	91,0	4550
10	84,0	3600
11	77,0	3850
12	70,0	3500
13	63,0	3150
14	56,0	2800
15	42,0	2100

The rate of the land tax did not change in 1994. The standard land price changed twice during 1994.

In the period from 01.01.94 to 21.08.94 the average rate of land tax for Saint Petersburg was 525 rb/sq.m. It was defined by:

- Federal Law *Amendments to the Federal Law On Payments for Land of 09.08.94;*
- Federal Law *On Budget System of the RF for 1993* of 14.05.93 No 4966-1;
- Mayor Regulation of 08.08.94 No 834-r.

The standard land price was 50 land tax rates. It was defined by:
Government Regulation of 25.02.92 No 112.

In the period from 22.08.94 to 02.11.94 the average rate of land tax for Saint Petersburg was 525 rb/sq.m. It was defined by:

- Federal Law *Amendments to the Federal Law On Payments for Land* of 09.08.94;

- Federal Law *On Budget System of the RF for 1993* of 14.05.93 No 4966-1;

- Mayor Regulation of 08.08.94 No 834-r.

The standard land price was 50 land tax rates. It was defined by:
Government Regulation of 25.02.92 No 112.

Standard price of land is equal 50 land tax rate. Purchasing price is equal the standard price of land with the coefficient ranging from 1 to 3 depending upon the zone value. It was defined by:

- Government of the RF Regulation of 25.02.92 No 112;

- President Decree of 22.07.94 No 1535;

- Mayor's Decree of 22.08.94 No 881-r *On the Order of Estimation of Price of Land Plots Sold in the Process of Privatisation of Real Estate.*

In the period from 03.11.94 to 17.05.95 the average rate of land tax for Saint Petersburg was 525 rb/sq.m. It was defined by:

- Federal Law *Amendments to the Federal Law On Payments for Land* of 09.08.94;

- Federal Law *On Budget System of the RF for 1993* of 14.05.93 No 4966-1;

- Mayor Regulation of 08.08.94 No 834-r:

The standard price of land is equal to 200 times the land tax rate. The purchasing price is equal to the standard price of land with the coefficient ranging from 1 to 3 depending upon zone value. It was defined by:

- Government of the RF Regulation of 03.11.94 No 1204;

- President Decree of 22.07.94 No 1535;

- Mayor's Decree of 22.08.94 No 881-r *On the Order of Estimation of Price of Land Plots Sold in the Process of Privatisation of Real Estate:*

RUSSIAN LAW AND LAND PRIVATISATION

No	Tax land rate rb/sq.m	Standard price of 21.08 (rb/sq. m)	Purchasing price (rb/sq. m)					
			from 22.08.94 to 03.11.94			from 03.11.94 to 17.05.95.		
			increasing coefficient			increasing coefficient		
			1	2	3	1	2	3
1	1150	57500	57500	115000	172500	230000	460000	690000
2	1000	50000	50000	100000	150000	200000	400000	600000
3	950	47000	47000	95000	142500	190000	380000	570000
4	900	45000	45000	90000	135000	180000	360000	540000
5	850	42500	42500	85000	127500	170000	340000	510000
6	800	40000	40000	80000	120000	160000	320000	480000
7	750	37500	37500	75000	112500	150000	300000	450000
8	700	35000	35000	70000	105000	140000	280000	420000
9	650	32500	32500	65000	97500	130000	260000	390000
10	600	30000	30000	60000	90000	120000	240000	360000
11	550	27500	27500	55000	82500	110000	220000	330000
12	500	25000	25000	50000	75000	100000	200000	300000
13	450	22500	22500	45000	67500	90000	180000	270000
14	400	20000	20000	40000	60000	80000	160000	240000
15	300	15000	15000	30000	45000	60000	120000	180000

In 1995, land tax rates and standard price of land introduced since 03.11.94 were applicable for privatized enterprises till 17.05.95, that is, till the publication of President Decree No 478 *Measures for Providing a Guaranteed Budget Income from Privatisation,* item 7 of which defined the standard price as 10 tax land rates for a unit of area. It is necessary to point out that these rates were valid for privatized enterprises only, since the market prices had been so high that the majority of big enterprises could not afford buying out the plots of their premises. For other buyers, the coefficient rests the same that is, 200.

The situation was essentially changed by the St. Petersburg Law *On Land Tax Rates in St.Petersburg in 1995*. Firstly, the new borders of social-economic districts were set (the quantity of districts increased from 15 to 19), and secondly, the differentiation of land tax rates increased: from 122 rb/sq.m per year in zone 19 to 19850 in zone 1 (before this difference was:

300 rb per sq.m in zone 15 and 1150 in zone 1), the increasing coefficients 2 and 3 remained consistent with the Mayor's Regulation of 05.09.95 No 830.

With the changes of standard price, the attitude of the enterprises to land privatisation changed as well. For example, there were 40 requests in the Property Fund in September - October 1994. The majority of these enterprises sought recommendations. There were no applications. Since the moment of setting the standard price of land plots (200 times land tax rate), there was a "lull". Probably the enterprises were shocked by the high, in their opinion, land prices. But after some time, the Property Fund registered some applications, mostly concerning small shares of plots without real division, and also an application for buying out a territory by a privatized enterprise in the centre of the city. This enterprise was the first to buy its plot.

The "boom" of applications started in June, 1995, (to be more exact, in early June), when there were 600 applications registered. This was caused by two reasons:

1) the decrease of standard price down to 10 land tax rates and

2) the desire to submit an application before St. Petersburg Law *Land Tax Rates in St. Petersburg in 1995* was adopted.

But even after the introduction of the new land tax rates in St. Petersburg, the "stream" of applications did not stop, and by the end of 1995 Property Fund registered more than 1000 applications. It was most probably caused by a "fly-wheel mechanism" and by the fact that people had realized that the land will not become cheaper.

It is necessary to note that a number of enterprises applied "just in case", without having the necessary financial resources for purchasing the land plots. They probably hoped that the funds will be increased before they had to sign the contract.

The experience of the first sales of plots permits us to draw some conclusions:

1. Approximately 70 per cent of the contracts signed concern shares of plots without real division of the plot.

2. The average price of 1 sq.m of the privatized land depends on the increasing coefficient and is approximately from 8000 to 47000 rb.

3. The borders of social-economic zones, set by St. Petersburg Law *Land Tax Rates in S.Petersburg in 1995* have to be made more precise and more differentiated taking into account different factors (for example, the utilisa-

tion of adjacent plots, communications density, the prospects of development of the territory where this plot is situated, etc.).

4. It is not "socially just" to establish 200 land tax rates for secondary proprietors (that is, individuals and not privatized companies and the enterprises that built constructions on the plots at their own expenses).

5. It is necessary to sell spare land plots at auctions and on the basis of competition.

LAND TAX RATES AND STANDARD LAND PRICES IN ST. PETERSBURG (1992 -1995)

Zone	1992		1993		1994 -1995							
	Land tax rate	Standard price	Land tax rate	Stand. price	Land tax rate	Standard price	Purchasing price (rb./sq.m)					
							from 22.08.94 through 03.11.94			from 03.11.94 through 17.05.95		
	rb/sq.m	rb/sq.m	rb/sq.m	rb/sq.m	rb/sq.m	rb/sq.m	increasing coefficients					
							1	2	3	1	2	3
1	46.0	2300	161.0	8050	1150	57500	575000	115000	172500	230000	460000	690000
2	40.0	2000	140.0	7000	1000	50000	50000	100000	150000	200000	400000	600000
3	38.0	1900	133.0	6650	950	47000	47000	95000	142500	190000	380000	570000
4	36.0	1800	126.0	6300	900	45000	45000	90000	135000	180000	360000	540000
5	34.0	1700	119.0	5950	850	42500	42500	85000	127500	170000	340000	510000
6	32.0	1600	112.0	5600	800	40000	40000	80000	120000	160000	320000	480000
7	30.0	1500	105.0	5250	750	37500	375000	75000	112500	150000	300000	450000
8	28.0	1400	98.0	4900	700	35000	35000	70000	105000	140000	280000	420000
9	26.0	1300	91.0	4550	650	32500	32500	65000	97500	130000	260000	390000
10	24.0	1200	84.0	3600	600	30000	30000	60000	90000	120000	240000	360000
11	22.0	1100	77.0	3850	550	27500	27500	55000	82500	110000	220000	330000
12	20.0	1000	70.0	3500	500	25000	25000	50000	75000	100000	200000	300000
13	18.0	900	63.0	3150	450	22500	22500	45000	67500	90000	180000	270000
14	16.0	800	56.0	2800	400	20000	20000	40000	60000	80000	160000	240000
15	12.0	600	42.0	2100	300	15000	15000	30000	45000	60000	120000	180000

Section V

The Economic Order in Private and in Public Law

Chapter 12

Law and Economic Order in the Structures of Russian Everyday Life

BORIS V. MARKOV

I. Everyday Life as a Network of Orders
II. Economic Reforms and Disciplinary Spaces of the Russian Society
III. Law and Power in Russia

Any tourist, even the most honest one, "smuggles" something he himself is not aware of. It is the weight of his attitudes and expectations, conceptual apparatus, as well as the complex symbolical machine of perception and understanding of the reality observed. As for scientific concepts, they appear fairly quickly and are usually supervised. It turns out to be much more difficult to analyse value preferences, social and moral norms of different sorts, and legal and economic differences as well. They are discovered with the accumulation of experience of the comparison of "ours" and "somebody else's", and this requires quite a labour-consuming study of the structures of everyday life in this or other visited and observed country. Acts of consciousness, efforts to establish distinctions between the beautiful and the ugly, the evil and the good, the convenient and the inconvenient, the decent and the indecent, eventually determine other networks of distinctions and differentiations, on which a scholar relies.

I. Everyday Life as a Network of Orders

M. Weber who strove to value-free science admitted that attitudes and orientations were, however, a part of it:

> "Even the answers to such, seemingly simple questions - as, for example, to which degree the purpose justifies the means necessary for achieving it; or up to which limit we should reconcile with the side effects of our actions, arising irrespectively of our desire; or how to remove the conflicts between the deliberate or inevitable purposes, opposing one another at their specific realisation - deal with the problem of choice or compromise. There are no scientific (rational or empirical) methods, which can offer us the solution of problems of this kind, and our strict empirical science is the last thing to be applied for relieving the person of a similar choice; and consequently one should not think that it is in the sphere of its authority."[1]

The investigation of everyday life involves some prejudices as well. Scholars consider it too vague and prefer to distinguish in it symbolical, social, economic, moral, legal, political, ideological, and other aspects. The world of daily interaction not fitting the ideal models is considered to be rather as an obstacle than a basis for their realisation. It is not occasional that political revolutions, seeking to transform the society according to the ideal models, face the resistance of the conventional order. Ethnographers, sociologists, economists and even philosophers pay more and more attention to the world of daily interaction. If social sciences aim at revealing the steady structures of everyday life, the philosophical interest is caused by difficulties of the substantiation of knowledge, which either hangs in the emptiness of a logic circle or is based upon such evidence, which is not doubtful and at the

---

1 M. WEBER: "Smysl 'Svobody ot Otsenok' v Sotsialnoi i Ekonomicheskoi Nauke" (The Meaning of 'the Freedom of Evaluations' in Social and Economic Science"), in: *Izbrannye Proizvedeniya*, Moscow (Progress) 1990, pp. 566-567. Original: *Wirtschaft und Gesellschaft*, Tübingen (Winkelman) 1985.

same time cannot be proved by methods accepted in science. The reference to life is connected also with the protest against rationality, the repressive influence of which is more and more realized by people.

What is everyday life? This word (*Alltag, Alltäglichkeit*) designates:
-self-evident reality, facticity;
-the world of common life, where people are born and die, enjoy and suffer;
-structures of anonymous practices as well as daily business in contrast to festivity, savings as opposed to expenditure, routine and tradition as opposed to inventiveness. It is something between the high and the low, between the aspirations of the spirit and the falls of the body.

Classical philosophers defined it as the sphere of collision of various individual opinions and interests, where the true knowledge was impossible. In modern philosophy it is considered as something ordered, traditional and routine, depersonalizing, hindering one's freedom or, on the contrary, as something spontaneous, ensuring freedom of individuality, which is suppressed in the process of education.

Phenomenological sociology, especially after Scheler and Schütz, discovered complex psychic and symbolical orders of the living world. "From the very beginning, - wrote A. Schütz,- everyday life presents itself as a universe of meaning, a set of significances, which we should interpret in order to acquire a support in this world, to reach an agreement with it."[2] He comes close to the understanding of everyday life as the symbolical, as an object of the experience in the world, and not just as institutions and establishments.

An important aspect of the phenomenological approach to everyday consciousness is its discovery of a common horizon, in which various individual prospects "are equalised", brought together as one type: "The general thesis of a mutual future results in the ability to grasp objects and their aspects, actually known to me and potentially known to him as everybody's knowledge".[3] One should recognize this ability of everyday consciousness to

---

2 A. SCHUETZ: "Struktura Povsednevnogo Myshlenia" (The Structure of Everyday Thinking), *Sotsiologgicheskie Issledovaniya*, Moscow (Vysshaya Shkola) 1988, vol. 2, pp. 130.

3 A. SCHUETZ: "Zdravyi Smysl i Nauchnaya Interpretatsiya Chelovecheskoi Deyatelnosti", *Vestnik SPbGU*, 4, Saint Petersburg (St. Petersburg University) 1994, p. 46. SCHUETZ A. "Common Sense and Scientific Interpretation of Human Action", *Collected Papers*, Vol. 1, The Hague, 1962, pp. 3-15.

LAW AND ECONOMIC ORDER IN RUSSIAN EVERYDAY LIFE

connect natural, social and subjective worlds, to form a general field of understanding of their various meaningful interpretations. The reality of everyday life, described by the feeling of facticity, self-evidence and obviousness, acts as an order recognized by everyone.[4]

Everyday life is not only a surface, it is also depth. Its highest structures include reason, law, *Ordo Amoris*, economy or purposeful rationality. M. Scheler has shown that in the sphere of feelings and experiences ranked as the lowest and spontaneous, people act not according to spontaneous drives, but in accordance with the objective hierarchy of values. Freud discovered an order even in the unconscious, which had been considered before as a source of unrestrained desires and uncivilized drives. Having applied "the economic approach", he, similarly to Marx, discovered the laws of libido circulation. Everyday life is not to be reduced to consciousness, unconscious, ideas, feelings, morals, or economy; everyday life is the surface on which the ideas - inhabitants of the highest spheres - and feelings, experiences, desires, arising from the depth, collide and interweave. These interweavings will form the events, which like singular points in mathematics designate the moment of a bend or a crisis of lines of development. Everyday life involves not only ideas, feelings and desires of people. It is primarily an order fixed by institutes. The assumption that the centres of authority preserve order by means of negative sanctions is denied in the model of public life, in which the strong centre and the universal structure give their place to the flexible and changeable everyday life.

One can conclude that a study of everyday life involves using various techniques of phenomenology, hermeneutics, analytical philosophy, psychoanalysis and deconstruction. In contrast to a too pure phenomenological programme of studying the everyday life, we can offer a sort of "topic-economic" approach for considering everyday life structures:

- first, as a complex fabric of various interweaving orders, compensating the weakening or destruction of some of them at the expense of strengthening some other;

- second, as a network of disciplinary spaces organized by a special image, the role of which is played by, for example, church and market, school and factory. They form first of all the necessary type of the body, as well as the norms and rules of action, which can seem to be not rigid for a scholar,

---

[4] P. BERGER, T. LUCKMANN: *Sotsialnoye Konstruirovaniye Realnosti* (The Social Construction of Reality), Moscow (Medium) 1995 p. 44.

and a moralist can find them lacking moral principles, by which the person is compelled to be guided in life.

Mastering these rules, as L. Wittgenstein thought, looks like the taming of animals, i.e. it is performed with justification. The everyday behaviour is based not so much on the critical reflection, but rather on following the rule. In life people behave otherwise than in the sphere of science, where everything is subjected to verification and substantiation, where statements are perceived as true or false. At the level of the daily interaction the questions of the truth are of secondary importance. The language expressions function as promises, oaths, threats, orders, questions and are considered in the perspective of the speaker. "Living up to the rule" works, therefore, as the final arbitrator of any reasoning and justifications.[5]

Rules on which people act, are not prejudices, and errors, which are subject to critique and elimination. This kind of interpretation has dangerous consequences, for it is not that easy to get rid of them in general and by critique of the old ideology in particular. Certainly, the norms and values, rules and notions of people are discussed in open discussions, but the discussions render just a short-term effect on the matrixes of daily behaviour. In the light of these difficulties, it seems reasonable to turn to the study of everyday practices, in which diverse discourses interweave and coexist. For example, the criteria of a moral action and an economic action are different, but it does not mean, that the economy is always immoral, and the morals are economically inexpedient. Therefore the economists and philosophers should not identify discourses about person with the historical reality.

For example, in philosophy one speaks about "the Russian idea", the Chosen people and spiritual force. On the other hand, turning to the Russian everyday life, one observes something quite opposite: repressions and greed, irresponsibility; all this implies that the real person is not to be reduced to moral or economic components. It is in this sphere that the problem of reaching a compromise arises: an adoption of absolute moral values in the discourse of economy would be similarly to a bomb explosion. The famous *Fable of the Bees* by Mandeville reminds us of the consequences of it. It is clear, that the set of traditional virtues is rather obsolete today. But who will undertake the task of updating and correcting it? Moral discussions on or-

---

5   L. WITTGENSTEIN: *Philosophische Untersuchungen - Philosophical Investigations*, Oxford (Basil Blackwell) 1969, p. 199.

gans implantations, euthanasy, abortions etc. in medicine are a good example of the fact that everyone realizes the insufficiency of the conventional moral code of doctors in medicine (though incapable of changing it).

The liberation of the economy from the pressure of moral norms was an important step on the way to capitalism. At the same time, it has resulted in a number of negative consequences and the problem of business ethics arises, which is similar to that of the ethics of science. There is moral pressure on business, expressing the reaction of the society to class differences, unemployment, exhaustion of natural resources, etc. In this respect, there is a problem of the relationship between business and ethics. An attempt to establish the priority of the criteria of a moral action in relation to the economic criteria is not realistic. This results in the need to find a peaceful form of communication between things which are different and incommensurable. It is necessary to raise the question: under which particular conditions can moral and economic actions be complementary?

With the emergence and expansion of cities and with the formation of market spaces in them, some essential changes occur both in the production processes and in the theories, justifying the mission of man in them. If the Christian church cultivated unity, the market separated people. Autonomy, freedom, and individualism as the conditions of entrepreneurship, were transcended into the essence of man. At the same time it would be too simple to reduce the aspirations of the European civilisation exclusively to the competition, thirst for profit and autonomy. These tendencies really frightened the authorities and often brought up attempts of restricting the market, which cultivated, besides thirst for profit, alien values and customs, brought together with goods from other countries. The relief was seen in the restoration of the traditional and, first of all, Christian values. This conflict is well represented in "The Merchant of Venice" by W. Shakespeare. A Jew requires, according to the agreement which had been signed earlier a pound of flesh from a Christian merchant for failing to pay for the credit. Both the parties of the conflict are here brightly represented: the traditional values and the new economic rights and laws. Shakespeare insisted on the Christian justice, but actually the market was the winner. In the Modern period the motto "man is a wolf to man" becomes popular. At the same time, A. Smith calmed his contemporaries by saying that the market does not only separate, but it also unites people. Philosophy has reflected this moment in the concept of Reason, according to which free individuals can reach a public agreement, where the norm providing both freedom and survival will be obtained.

The dialogue between ethics and politics seems to be a reasonable resolution of the new problems arising today in the process of disintegration of economic and political spaces and the emergence of new problems. For example, recognizing the multicultural character of Russia and Russia's role in bringing Europe and Asia together, one cannot help noting that there are also specific interests of various states. Probably, it is the most important problem taking into account the amount of ethnic conflicts which require a new approach. On the one hand, the concept of solidarity ethics and peaceful coexistence seems to be the only acceptable concept, however, it is actually impossible to exclude independent efforts, directed to self-preservation. The condition of variety, multicultural character, multinationality and the presence of various forms of property have already extended so much within some countries and in the whole world, that one cannot speak of the attempts to establish a homogeneous order in the spirit of fundamentalism. The diversity is so closely connected that it cannot be eliminated without damaging the whole. What according to the ideological or narrow national criteria is regarded as alien or hostile, turns out to be necessary, for example, for economic prosperity. At present a new model of society is being built taking into account the heterogeneity of its components and, first of all, of the society, the economy, the state and the necessity of "equilibrating" them and reaching a balance. Therefore, an assumption, that "the economic ethics should be constructed as a dialogue of economy and ethics"[6] can be considered as a promising one.

II. Economic Reforms and Disciplinary Spaces of the Russian Society

A universal power, striving to establish a unified order through a certain idea and certain regulations, prefers a universal ideology consistent with the idea and tries to enforce it. In its essence, this strategy is a legacy of the Enlightenment project, which is strongly critisized. The process of civilization is not to be reduced to mass enlightenment in terms of knowledge, prin-

---

6   W. STEGMAIER: *Wirtschaftsethik als Dialog und Diskurs*, Stuttgart (Akademie der Diözese Rottenburg) 1992, p. 7.

LAW AND ECONOMIC ORDER IN RUSSIAN EVERYDAY LIFE

ciples of law, and rational ideas. The public order is built by masters of "social mechanics", which turns it into a real support for the real power, since they create real disciplinary spaces at the level of everyday life. Throughout the Russian history, the attempts of European modernization encountered resistance and did not bring the democratization of the society and an efficient economy. This was the result of the fact that the process of reform in Russia was as a rule performed at the level of consciousness and was restricted to enlightenment. Today the reformers place their hopes on capitalism. It is assumed that the market as such is something like a Watt's valve in the vapour machine, which distributes energy. The transition to the market proceeds along with the rejection of state regulation and social guarantees. It is not at all surprising that it results in a "wild market" which frightens even its authors.

Actually, compared to all the orders that ever existed, capitalism cannot be considered to be natural, it is the most artificial order in the world. It required not only the idea of freedom and autonomy of the individual, not only technical discoveries and trade, but also substantial changes in the forms of power and property and of places of labour and relaxation, ways of communication, city planning, etc. Many of the basic prerequisites of capitalism seem to be so natural that they are not noticed even by Western researchers; but without them it is just impossible to create a welfare state in an accelerated way. As M. Weber thought, the secret of capitalism is not in the nature of market relations, since the retail trade and speculation always existed and the specific character of the economic man includes not only thirst for profit and aggressiveness, but also the ability to be self-contained, internal discipline, thrift, prudence, etc. These traits of character were associated with the Protestant ethics, which made our philosophers search for a basis of the Russian capitalism in the Orthodox sect of the Old Believers.

Judging by the prescriptions of reforms designed for backward countries, offered by American economists, the experts themselves do not understand clearly the complex structure of the European civilization which is based not only on knowledge and ethics, economy and law, but also on the specifically formed and organized body. For example, the history of the working class is not just the history of the formation of its consciousness, it is a complex process of the organisation of special disciplinary spaces, in which the body of a peasant, used to the organic logic, turns into the body of a worker, controlled by the mechanical logic, ensuring monotonous, repetitive, automatic actions.

BORIS V. MARKOV

The Western culture and the achievements related to it are based on a gentle but firm network of interactions and interdependencies between different social strata which correspond to the system of norms, rules and values regulating behaviour at the level of consciousness. Many of these norms and values are not "written down", but the society itself watches whether they are observed. Accustomed at home to being irresponsible and cheating, our businessmen soon find out that in the West one can cheat not more than twice. After that the community boycotts the cheat. Behind the freedom and prosperity, one cannot help seeing different "mild" dependencies and restrictions concerning credits, insurance, pensions and so on. This disciplinary machine, invisible to a Russian observer of luxurious shop-windows, works much more efficiently than a police surveillance.

Thus, besides the police, different economic and social institutions, tax and credit departments, there is a well-developed structure of public opinion, accusing and boycotting people not living up to the generally accepted rules of social behaviour; this draws an impressive picture of a structured disciplinary space, which organizes life no worse than road signs for motor vehicles. Great efforts and time were devoted to creating this everyday life structure. And in comparison to that, the dreams of our reformer do not seem to be serious.

One of the causes of the failure of reforms and modernization programmes was evidently the strategic miscalculation of intellectuals who reduced their tasks to the critique of the former ideology and to the enlightenment of the population by abstract models from American economics textbooks. While to create a new society and even to destroy the old society one should know their structure. The reduction of the former regime to the totalitarian ideology is a great simplification. Actually the past and the present are the forms of life which are functioning in the channels of psychic passions, body drives, points of view and evaluations, which have their barriers and thresholds. The management of this living order does not involve only cheating or prohibition. It does not cheat, it turns people into what is required. The epistemological reflection and critique of ideology do not take into account that there is a will to have power. If it were not natural, nothing could trouble the existence of the repressive regimes. Considering the so-called perestroika, one could see that it arose from the common protest against the repressive character of the relations between people. This spontaneous movement towards liberation which became uncontrollable lacking internal restrictions, frightened the authorities. But overcoming the internal

LAW AND ECONOMIC ORDER IN RUSSIAN EVERYDAY LIFE

prohibitions and barriers in the people's consciousness deprives it of its support and without creating proper disciplinary spaces in people's consciousness at the level of everyday life, it will not be able to establish an order even by means of repression.

In our society everybody is enlightened in terms of ethics, justice, of healthy life including ecology, but irresponsibility and cunning, indifference to the nature and life became steady traits of the Russian mentality. All this reminds of the situation when the person, giving a speech on the danger of smoking, lights a cigarette during the break. Machines of wishes are stronger and more diverse than the critical analysis or enlightenment. Thus, just a local and regional protest against producing wishes, a practical deconstruction of repressive disciplinary spaces of the society can turn to be more efficient as a strategy of liberation, than a revolutionary political protest.

Considering the process of social liberation not as a result of the ideological criticism and revolutionary movement, but as a civilization process concerning changes of everyday order, one can describe some disciplinary practices in which the production of main components of the "human being" was performed. This does not mean that the role of rational and discursive practices is to be denied. On the contrary, in our approach their functions are essentially clarified.

It is well known that the history of Russia is interpreted as a struggle between "Westernizers" and "Slavophiles". And among the former the most interesting are those who are not only oriented towards the West but who also see common civilizing processes in the Russian history.[7] Among the advocates of the alternative point of view, the most perspicacious ones are those who do not restrict themselves to the Russian national ideology history but try to understand the peculiar foundation of it.[8] So, we can restore the interesting history of the interaction of not only the ideas but also the structures of everyday life. And the most important are the processes like those of creating in Russia a court society which was structured and bred up according to the European patterns of nobility. But unfortunately, in Russia

---

7 PAVLOV-SILVANSKI: *Feodalizm v Rossii* (Feudalism in Russia), Moscow (Nauka) 1988. P. N. MILIUKOV: *Ocherki po Istorii Russkoi Kultury v Trioh Tomah* (The Essays on the History of the Russian Culture in Three Volumes), Moscow (Progress) 1993.
8 N. YA. DANILEVSKI: *Rossiya i Evropa* (Russia and Europe), Moscow (Kniga) 1991.

the nobility was isolated from the people and did not have impact on it. Its fate turned to be tragic and therefore the problem of the elite is so acute today in this country. If in Europe the morality of the nobility was preserved and cultivated (for example, the bourgeoisie created salons which played the role of disciplinary places for the upbringing of the youth), in Russia this process was interrupted by the revolution. Today's attempts of renovating the institution of nobility seem to be naive. One cannot instil life into museum exhibits. Thus, the formation of the modern elite involves the synthesis of the former "nomenclatura" and of criminal structures. The intellectuals and the cultural leaders are mostly playing the role of a screen and do not influence the mode of life and, what is most important, the ethics of business.

The fate of the intelligentsia politically engaged in Russia was not less tragic. Its mentality was formed as a certain synthesis of Christianity and utopian socialism which prevented it from constructive work. The intelligentsia was as a rule opposed to the state and the authorities, but for the people it was a repressive rather than a liberating structure, since it made the people hostage of the revolutionary reforms. And even today the left wing intelligentsia considers itself a privileged part of the society whose mission is to think and decide for others.

Of course, the most fundamental part of the civilization process is changing the customs of life. The people is perceived by the intelligentsia as the "primary author" of history, politics or discourse, an object of enlightenment. Caring for the reason and the spirit of the people, the intelligentsia perceives life as an incarnation of the idea and it does not pay attention to the institutionalisation of the "third estate". It is not at all surprising that the ideology preserving the peculiarity of Russia today lacks foundations. The problem is that during the last century the soul and the body of the Russians underwent various changes. The history left its traces on them.

The art of the Great Terror period represents exulted faces of people. Referring to the repressions, one can interpret them as an ideological camouflage, or as a cheat. But as a rule, history does not tell lies, but it represents a distorted, deformed reality. People of that time were not simply cheated, they were turned into what was needed at the level of visual attitudes and the desires and needs of the body. The real power was made by those thresholds and differences which became the internal prohibitions and restrictions. This explains the strange fact that the majority of the repressed people considered themselves to be victims of errors since they believed in the communist idea and thought the established order to be just and reasonable. This explains the fact that the critique of the past in the course of the reforms was perceived by the elder generation as casting dark shadows on their own life.

How and in which disciplinary spaces was the production of man or rather of his various structures performed? Right after the revolution the authorities sought for and found the efficient disciplinary means for the mass body in the form of meetings and demonstrations. It was involved in searching for the new forms of the influence on people which resulted in the emergence of public libraries, clubs, which became ideological centres, in the development of mass media, etc. The structures of enterprises, factories, plants, scientific institutes were no less and maybe even more important. While in the West these are places of work, study and research, in this country they functioned as places of the production of new man as well. Inefficient in economic terms, they taught us to make not an equivalent exchange but a sacrifice, what one calls today "a gift". "A gift" and "a sacrifice" remain today maybe only in the sphere of love. But in the past they were imposed here as common attitudes to life. At the former Soviet enterprises, people did not only work they "sacrificed" themselves to the society and received for that rather "a gift" in the form of "the wage". That they functioned as life organizers is proved by the fact that it was there where flats, extra pays of different sorts, visits to resorts were distributed. But the most important, of course, were meetings (Komsomol, Party, labour, etc.) which discussed not only business issues, but mainly ideological, political and even family problems. Today they are missed very much and, who knows, maybe they will revive in the form of the "social state". So, the exulted faces and glowing eyes of workers in the pictures of the period of the first five-year plans are not lies, but they are the real result of the synthesis of Christian asceticism and the so-called "Communist attitude to labour" when people did not simply work but built their "fine future". In this regard, we can say that "perestroika" started not in 1985 but much earlier, with the gradual decay of this consciousness.

This process cannot be regarded only as a result of the ideological activity of dissidents and American intelligence service. The evolution of the forms of everyday life brought up changes in the mentality of people. The most important of its results is the people's moving out from communal flats to separate flats. The communal flat, this for the West rare form of cohabitation, was established in Russia not only as a result of the housing crisis, it was a result of the communal mode of life, of hostels and barracks widely spread in the period of the great enterprises of communism. These disciplinary spaces created specific collective bodies accustomed to openness, submitted to mutual responsibility when everybody is responsible for everybody: Concealing the intimate was perceived as a mortal sin. With the spread of separate flats, people acquired their own sleeping places and even separate rooms. Children managed to escape public control and the one of their parents and teachers, and got something like complexes described by Freud. Owing to this, the form of the power of parents over children fundamentally changed where the practice of sin and repentance is combined with the cognition and manipulation of the mode of life.

Another important change of disciplinary spaces in contemporary Russia was the evolution of city life. The process of urbanisation in this country dates far back but our cities were still like huge villages. After the October Revolution the city life was also structured according to the village life, that is, according to the communal pattern: a communal flat where like in a village people survey each other and together hold the house; a palace of culture where like in a house for public reading in a village the ideological and psychic unity were to be reached; a central square where like at a village meeting, people came to demonstrate their unanimity with the authorities. But today these things are gradually disappearing. Big cities do not have centres. Power is demonstrated not at the tribunes, it moved to the TV screens. Museums, universities, conservatories did not disappear, but they do not hold the monopoly of the Truth and the Beauty.

The unified order has fallen apart, but the city in some incomprehensible way manages the behaviour of its inhabitants. Though it is impossible to call them to a unanimous demonstration for or against the authorities, but this is what is supposed to please intellectuals, and not disappoint them. The differentiation of the previously homogeneous mass of the population into different groups and strata makes impossible the victory of a universal ideology. This decomposition of the unified order, fearful for the Conservative wing, threatening to destroy the social identity, should not frighten us. Which order is the conservative dream? The domination of a new myth, the unity and the unanimity. Actually, the new order spontaneously appearing in the everyday life is not any more based upon an ideological unity, intolerable to the alien, it is based upon the interconnection, interweaving of different interests, presupposing tolerance and mutual respect.

LAW AND ECONOMIC ORDER IN RUSSIAN EVERYDAY LIFE

As B. Waldenfels shows in his works, this process has been going on for a long time in all the big cities of the world.[9] This resulted in the inflation of generally accepted norms, values, standards of evaluation ("modernity crisis"). Things and events, deeds and experiences, affects and desires are not measured by one and the same scale, they are perceived in a concrete context.

Today many theorists speak of the crisis of rationality, but they forget about the repressive character, about striving to acquire the alien through "understanding", which is a form of colonisation. The modern structures of everyday life discover a new order which is not dictated from the centre but is realized at the local level. This presupposes certain changes in the forms of communication which are built not on the basis of a universal ideology or some privileged discourse of ethics, religion or science. The interaction and the order of the diverse is determined by topography or, as Husserl said, "transcendental geology" of the cultural space in which the person lives. It is to its structure that philosophy should direct its critique.

Decay and disintegration of this space is being observed in contemporary Russia, but they occur in the direction different from that of the West. The disintegration of the former unified economic, political and cultural space resulted in the development of the new force fields, which are Mafia clans. The archaization of life is going on and many processes demonstrate that. The analysis of wall inscriptions, the so-called "graffiti", demonstrates not a conscious rebellion of the teenagers against signs, like in the West, but a division of zones and territories between "ours" and the "aliens". The similar processes are going on in the adult world: the breakdown of the former administrative system resulted in independence, but both enterprises and individual citizens experience great troubles with the sales of their production. The so-called criminal structures take care of that. They actively participated in buying off the vouchers, in returning credits and receiving forepayments. Naturally, under the condition of the growth of such tendencies, Russia's return to the civilized community is delayed up to an unknown time.

---

9 B. WALDENFELS: *Der Stachel des Fremden,* Frankfurt am Main (Suhrkamp) 1991, pp. 243-260.

BORIS V. MARKOV

III. Law and Power in Russia

Comparisons of Russia and Europe suggest the following:
1. Russia is a specific country. Its westernization was started by Peter I. Having "hacked through the window to Europe", he deformed the body of Russia.
2. The destiny and the development of Russia are connected with Europe. Russia should join Europe and learn attentively its experience.
3. Russia was once a part of Europe and has to be its part again.
4. Russia is half-Europe, half-Asia.
5. Russia is a bad or corrupted Europe.

These approaches reveal the peculiarity of Russia. The Russian state was formed under the Norman, Byzantine, Mongolian and European (German, French etc.) influence. The consequences of it at the level of everyday life are still not studied, but it is evident that the Eastern way of collecting tribute is still the leading strategy in the centre-periphery relationship.

What does the word "reform" mean as applied to the changes in Russia? Strictly speaking, re-form is a return of the old. Since we are speaking of Russia's borrowing European forms of life, the word "innovation" would be more appropriate. Understanding reforms as a transfer of European institutions into the body of Russia, we should pay tribute not only to Peter the Great, after whom, according to Miliukov, Russia soon recovered , but to Katherine as well. It was she who consistently and persistently started the transformation of the state and the legal order. But unlike Peter, who still knew Russia-Mother with its patriarchal structure and thus tried to transform it in a violent revolutionary way and first of all by direct introduction of the borrowed European order into all spheres of life, Katherine, who understood the incompatibility of Europe and Russia, acted half-heartedly and indecisively. This was the result of the fact that she did not want to and could not break the established forms of life, since she saw the growing resistance of the people and dealt with Pugachev's rebellion. Katherine did not follow the bourgeois way of allocating equal rights to the whole population she followed a purely feudal way of distributing privileges and reforming the administrative institutions. According to N. Elias's criteria, Russia only created a high court society with the monopoly of power centres, when Europe already passed to the stage of the formation of bourgeois republics and national states. Those rights and liberties which in the West were allocated to everyone, were given only to the nobility in Russia. Instead of the third estate, medieval guilds were formed.

Creating the legal order for all the citizens of the Russian Empire was delayed. Alexander I tried to fulfil the plans of Katherine and permitted buying and selling of land to everyone except for the serfs. But the war with Napoleon and Decembrist's rebellion left Speransky's projects to get dusty in the archives. "The Great Reformer" of Russia, Alexander II, who freed the country of serfdom, made it too late and did not get any tribute for it: he was killed by the members of People's Will. Nikolas II seemingly fulfilled with Stolypin's assistance the liberal projects of his predecessors and started breaking the stamina of patriarchal Russia, the communal possession of land. But these projects were doomed to failure: the First World War started and then the revolution.

This short survey of the well-known pages of the history of Russia can lead to different conclusions. On the one hand, the consistence of the authorities' attention to the European patterns of performing the reforms of the society is wonderful. Seeing the doubtless advantages of the West, one cannot make another choice. The accomplishment of this desire is hindered by the resistance of the Russian collectivist mentality. Since our man is egoistic and anarchistic, there arises a question: what will connect independent individuals obsessed with the thirst for getting profits, if the traditional values, basic for the Russian conscience, disappear. These values were not actual moral values, but at least they functioned as a moral foundation for the power and as the legitimisation of it. Russian cordiality was always coexisting with and complementary to the repressions. Hunger and fear propelled the poor hungry mob and that is why the hopes of free individuals happened to be unfeasible.

Force and justice have been for a long time mediated by the law, and the rejection of its important civilizing role is one of the most unpleasant traits of the Russian mentality. It is characterized by the Orthodox Christian idea that the authority is a form of the realisation of power which does not provide justice. So, justice, being absolutely weak, cannot exist in our world. The dilemma formulated by F. M. Dostoyevsky in his well-known "The Legend of The Great Inquisitor" is still not overcome by the part of the Russian intelligentsia which still opposes the authorities. At the same time, this law is not only a mechanism of establishing the domination of the strong but of the restriction imposed on the arbitrariness. A force which expresses and justifies its pretensions in an open discourse establishes formal and generally accepted borders which have been defined in the process of the struggle of one force with another. So, the law is a certain compromise of force and justice owing to which the force becomes partially just and the justice becomes strong. This implies the importance of the development of law.

In the Russian literature there were no works similar to *Spirit of Laws* by Montesquieu, *Social Contract* by Rousseau and Hegel's *Philosophy of Law*. There were no public discussions similar to the European discussions about natural and historical rights or social security. The humanistic intelligentsia in Russia considers law to be a certain ethical minimum; politicians consider it a form of compulsion. Taking into account the lack of legal order at the level of everyday life, the common nihilistic attitude to law seems quite natural. As far as the state was unjust, people did not feel sorry when they broke the law, or as they say in this country, "evade" the law. The Slavophiles considered the disadvantage of the Russian legal consciousness to be an advantage. K. S. Aksakov thought that the fact that the Russian people avoided the state and the law meant that they sought for the "intrinsic truth". This conviction was inherited by the ideology of People's Will which was based upon the belief in the "opportunity of an immediate transition to a better higher order skipping through the middle stage of the European development, the stage of the bourgeois state."[10] One need not dwell upon the legal nihilism of Russian Marxists who, though aware of the importance of the political struggle for changes in the public life, did not understand the role of law and the constitutional state. The priority of revolution over democracy, the domination of force over law, all this has resulted in the proclaimed economic and political freedom which is not confirmed in the legal form or is violated.

The source of the legitimate character of power in contemporary Russia can be found either inside or outside the power relationships; the stable existence and the efficient functioning of the political system, the conviction of its consistence with the interests, values, traditions of the majority can serve as the criteria. The sacred foundation of power in modern societies cannot be sufficient, and just few symbols remind today of the divine source of power (for example, "Monomakh's hat"*). The source of the justification of power

---

10 N. K. MIKHAILOVSKI: *Polnoie Sobranie Sochineniy* (Complete Works), Saint Petersburg (without publisher) 1906, Vol. 4, p. 952.

* Translator's note: Monomakh's hat is a regalia of Russian grand dukes and tsars, a symbol of the Russian tsarist autocracy. According to a well-known legend,

lies outside the sphere of power relations: in the sphere which is called "civil society", including public norms, values and institutions relatively independent of the state and providing the basic needs of man. Therefore, the legitimity of a political regime is guaranteed by its public support. But there arises a question: which values are characteristic of the Russian society? The liberal-democratic tradition considers these values as freedom and independence of the private life from the state intervention. The social-democratic tradition assumes that the influence of power on the society is necessary for creating the institutions of free public life which could oppose the monopolisation of power.

In our literature one can read that the "liberal tradition of the functioning of the civil society does not correspond to the cultural, historical, national and spiritual traditions of Russia"[11]. Since the paternalistic state policy has become a norm, even today the public consciousness of the Russians rejects liberal and neoliberal values under the auspices of which the social reforms of 1990s were started.[12] At the same time, the liberal ideology in Russia is deeply rooted in history. The principles of personal freedom, legal order, the belief in the necessity of social progress and of reforming the society were defended by A. S. Khomyakov, K. D. Kavelin, B. N. Chicherin, P. I. Novgorodtsev, etc. Kavelin insisted on the autonomy of ethics, Chicherin insisted on the autonomy of law, Novgorodtsev insisted on the autonomy of politics. This seems to be rather important, for it can be considered as the evidence of the communicative understanding of the values which are not given by God or Nature but are worked out by the people themselves. But one should take into account the inconsistency of the liberalism of these scholars, their anti-democratic frame of mind, since they thought that the power should belong to the elite.

---

the hat was sent by the Emperor Konstantin Monomakh to the grand duke of Kiyev Vladimir II Monomakh.

11 S. M. YELISEYEV: "Razvitiye Grazhdanskogo Obchestva i Liggitimizatsiya Vlasti v Rossii" (The Development of the Civil Society and the Legitimisation of Power in Russia), *Sotsialnye Reformy v Rossii: Istoriya, Sovremennoye Sostoyanie i Perspektivy*, Saint Petersburg (Petropolis) 1995, p. 140.

12 *Dannye Sotsiologgicheskogo Oprosa. Rossiiskoye Obchestvo: Tsennosti i Prioritety* (The Data of the Public Poll. The Russian Society: Values and Priorities), Saint Petersburg (Polis) 1993, p. 6.

BORIS V. MARKOV

The transition from the power of force to the power of law is the most burning problem of Russia. Which shifts can be noted in the legal order at the level of everyday life? First of all, it is a gradual division of moral norms and laws. However strange it might seem, but the domination of the former over the latter is one of the causes of the legal nihilism. Considering the law as an instrument of power, the Russian person evaluated actions according to the moral criteria. Hence, there is a compassion with the outlaws incomprehensible for outsiders. Outlaws are perceived as people suffering from the unjust power. It is not true that the arguments of the defenders of human rights resulted in establishing an idea of the disciplinary role of law and understanding it as the condition of liberty and of the possibility of a civilized society at the level of everyday consciousness. But long queues in lawyers offices, lawsuits concerning violations of consumers' rights etc. demonstrate that in Russia there is a process of the formation of new disciplinary spaces which concern the equality of people and the formation of law consciousness. And this is the guarantee that in the future people will vote in the process of free elections.

In each particular society, the fabric of social relationships is woven with diverse threads and therefore it is rather impossible to construct a universal order for all countries. Even if the Russian people followed the European way of development, the direct borrowing of ideas appears impossible. It is not connected with the quantity of people acquiring these ideas. There are no one-for-all ways of the realisation of personal freedom, legal order, constitution, as well as there is no capitalism identical for all countries. Contemporary Russia is a very complex social organism which is impossible to manage either autocratically, as before, or according to the European patterns. It is evident that any legal order is accomplished in the field of unwritten rules which are formed at the level of everyday life. We mean by that not only moral norms but the knowledge which is an important and efficient means of the accomplishment of the social order, especially in Russia with its highly educated population. As it is well-known, law was the main form of power in Europe in the 17th and 18th century. The new form of power is not repressive, it is positive since it implies a rational form of activity making life better.

The assumption that the power in Russia is exclusively ideological in its nature is the cause of persistent search for a universal idea which is capable of mobilising the masses. On the contrary, in highly developed countries the power does not advertise itself, but in its anonymity it manages people

LAW AND ECONOMIC ORDER IN RUSSIAN EVERYDAY LIFE

through the system of mass media. Of course, a sufficiently high level of development is needed for the population to follow commercials, medical recommendations, etc. But even taking into account the present poor situation of Russia one cannot help seeing that the more power tries to be everywhere and to control by its regulations different spheres of life, the more it seems to be weak to the people.

The power technology in the modern society has been very much modified. Institutes of experts and counsellors, therapists and psychologists, specialists in housing planning, relaxation organisation and various kinds of insurancies which take into account professional risks and street dangers, all this composes a dense network excluding freedom. That is why the protest takes strange forms: people from time to time start protesting against doctors imposing expensive methods of treatment, against fees for teachers and supervisors, against all kinds of specialists in fitness, compelling people to get involved into the perpetual fight against themselves in the form of dieting and training. And what can one do when, on the one hand, all these specialists are trying to guarantee the fundamental vital values: health, law, education, work, housing etc., and on the other hand, all this knowledge eventually deprives people of an opportunity of making decisions and choosing one's own destiny. The everyday life more and more resembles a conveyor of a huge plant which is operated by many specialists. One cannot efficiently organize one's own life and gets under the power of advertising and of all sorts of agencies serving people.

The history of civilization is the history of restrictions and prohibitions. Throughout the history man struggled against his passions and desires, argued against weakness of the flesh and against selfishness. The domination over oneself is the first and main requirement of the humanistic philosophy. It is difficult for us to understand the ancient with their restrictions and efforts designed to preserve the society. Threats and prohibitions, external compulsion and violence were gradually transformed into self-control and self-discipline. But this system of moral duty and internal censure is rapidly disappearing now. This resulted not from some hidden nihilism or corruption, but from the changes in the order of everyday life. Asceticism, self-denial, solidarity, altruism, saving and restriction on consumption are now obsolete virtues, since the modern order is built not upon saving but upon expenditure.

The modern society does not restrict the needs, but it manages them. Calculation, prudence and foresight are not cultivated anymore at the individual level and do not form the basis of human ethos. Advertising, counselling, different kinds of recommendations for keeping fit, the whole system of life-support, mildly and unobtrusively, but quite firmly get people into their web. Man is not supposed to restrict himself and to fight his desires. He is supposed to satisfy them. But these desires themselves are created artificially and therefore their realisation does not destroy the system of order, it even reinforces it.

Among the basic human rights there is the right to protest. Exercising this right does not lead to the revolutionary changes of the social order, on the contrary, it is designed to protect this order. But in the modern society, it has been subjected to substantial restrictions since different branches of modern power fit each other more than for example in the epoch of the division of the royal, public and clerical powers. The modern state is legitimized as an expression of the people's will. At the same time, it guarantees personal rights and those of different social minorities. The latter can exercise their right only in the form of protesting. Therefore, there is an intensification of the negative experience which in the modern society appears in the form of defending the civil rights and freedoms.

Intellectuals, being dependent on the power and in fact serving it, consider themselves enemies of the power and protest by means of ideological critique. By that they pay tribute to the obsolete concepts according to which the power is an external, compelling and repressive force. But in the modern society, they represent the power and therefore they are morally obliged not to be with the radical left. Thus, new forms of liberation are sought for. The general direction of the search is characterized by the gradual understanding that the power, hostages of which are the people and intellectuals, politicians and the public, is rooted not in the subjects demonstrating against it but in the impersonal structures of everyday life. It is on the reorganisation and liberalization of this order that the intellectuals should focus their attention.

But today the Russian intelligentsia is inclined to politization and ideological forms of protest: taking the side of the repressed, organizing a protest action or unveiling the power of ideology. Both these positions are quite naive. On the one hand the masses do not need enlightenment since they know the reality better than the intellectuals. On the other hand, not being anymore deceived, the masses want the authorities to exist even if they are of a repressive character. Thus, both the protest and the critique should not be considered to be universal means of struggle against the power which cannot be knocked down by one stroke because it includes the knowledge which is produced by the intellectuals themselves. If they usurp the right to think and to make decisions, they will start repressions themselves. Since the power is not autocratic, and everybody simultaneously is the repressing and the repressed, it would be naive to think that one can get rid of it by a coup. In the epoch of the "Great Terror" there was just a quantitative difference between a clerk and the dictator, and the power did not change with the personnel shifts. Social liberalisation takes place only there and only when there is a change not in the subjects but in the structures of power, in those disciplinary spaces from school to the barrack, from home to the enterprise, where people do not only study, work or serve, but are created, get ideas and norms, desires and needs, necessary for the surviving in these structures.

Which power and which compulsion are meant today and how can one feel their pressure? Nowadays, when the authorities do not drag innocent citizens out of their houses at nights and do not torture them to frighten others, it seems that the power has become shallow. The forms of expenditures and protest became shallow too. Today you will find yourself in a moral blockade for violating the public norms but this is not so bad as the isolation in concentration camps and prisons. That is why speaking of the shallowness of the power and forms of protests, one should not forget that they have moved inside man, and his behaviour is now regulated by an artificial system of concepts, values, needs and desires. Man has to rebel against himself which is much more difficult than to point to an external enemy and to call for an uncompromising struggle against him.

Instead of political revolutions in which large social groups and classes clashed, now there emerge other forms of protest which are performed by individuals, small groups and national minorities. This is a real protest against the domination of the general against the homogeneity, erasing differences and diversity, this is the situation of postmodernity. It is based on a different image of the human being. Today the individual does not identify himself with an abstract subject of law and ethics. He is cautious about rationality and does not identify himself with the European or national culture. He is a multicultural, multinational but not cosmopolite being. Living in one of the cultural ghettos of the modern big city, he easily walks in other territories and is tolerant to the representatives of other cultural worlds. He does not think that he is a superman or a representative of absolute moral norms. He is a pioneer of particularity who dreams not of a lofty ideal but of the possibility of various forms of life.

Chapter 13

A Symbiosis with Reserve: Social Market Economy and Legal Order in Germany

KNUT WOLFGANG NÖRR

I.	Müller-Armack and the Concept of Social Market Economy
II.	On the Impact of Ordoliberalism. The Era of Ludwig Erhard
III.	An Ambiguity in the Concept of Market Economy
IV.	Three Meanings of "Social" in Social Market Economy
V.	Social Market Economy and Keynesianism: the Era of Karl Schiller
VI.	Social Market Economy: A Concept Still Alive?
VII.	Irrelevance of the Term 'Social Market Economy' to the Legal System
VIII.	Two Performances of a Play: Germany's Binary Economic Order
IX.	Social Market Economy and the Federal Constitutional Court
X.	A Harmony Conducted by the Interpreters of the Constitution

From the viewpoint of economy and economics, it is possible to characterize one or another country by certain economic models or visions or concepts. In the case of the Federal Republic of Germany, nobody will question the fact that the term 'Social Market Economy' would play the part of such a characteristic concept. We can also speak of a trade mark, as it were, of a quality label under which German history in the second half of our century could be studied and analyzed. Of course, no conception may escape criticism and disapproval, and therefore Social Market Economy has also been rejected for various reasons again and again. However, the majority among politicians and economists, and the majority of the population, to judge from the results of parliamentary elections, approve and support Social Market

Economy, considering it even as an essential contribution to the legitimacy of their political system. It is therefore worthwhile to have a look at the concept of Social Market Economy and to review a few phases of its history.

I. Müller-Armack and the Concept of Social Market Economy

We just referred to Social Market Economy as an economic concept but this was not entirely correct. Rather, we are dealing with a concept that belongs to economic thinking but at the same time extends beyond and transcends its boundaries. To explain this remark, we have to turn to the origins of the concept "Social Market Economy" or rather to the person who had coined the term and developed it, and to his intellectual background. In 1946, a year after the end of World War II, in an environment of destroyed cities and millions of expellees, with periods of hunger and lack of coal and fuel, there appeared, printed on paper of poor quality, a book with the title *Wirtschaftslenkung und Marktwirtschaft* (Government Control and Market Economy)[1]. The book, birth certificate, as it were, of Social Market Economy, was written by Alfred Müller-Armack, then professor of Economics and later on under-secretary in the Ministry of Economics in Bonn[2]. During the war and in the years after, in all European countries the economy was rigorously controlled by government and bureaucratic agencies, and there was a strong political tendency to continue this system also under regular conditions. Only a few voices were to be heard that pleaded for transforming the system into market economy.

When Müller-Armack wrote the book, he was 45 years old. In this age the shaping of the mental and intellectual background of a person is more or less brought to completion. In the case of Müller-Armack the decisive years

---

1 A. MUELLER-ARMACK: *Wirtschaftslenkung und Marktwirtschaft*, Hamburg 1947.
2 For information about Müller-Armack's life and work, cf. J. STARBATTY: "Alfred Müller-Armacks Beitrag zu Theorie und Politik der Sozialen Marktwirtschaft", in: *Soziale Marktwirtschaft im vierten Jahrzehnt ihrer Bewährung*, Stuttgart/New York 1982; CH. WATRIN: "Alfred Müller-Armack (1901-1978)", in: F.-W. HENNING (Ed.): *Kölner Volkswirte und Sozialwissenschaftler*, Cologne/Vienna 1988, p. 39.

of his intellectual history coincided with the last years of the Weimar Republic, before Hitler and the Nazis had taken over. In regard to the economic theory, several currents of thought can be distinguished, one of them being the theoretical approach to the concept of capitalism. Müller-Armack participated in the dispute on capitalism and wrote a book which appeared in 1932[3]. In this book he rejected the Marxian idea of a law of evolution or law of history i.e. the deterministic conception of a necessary and inevitable process and progress in history. As a result of this conception, the category of time has changed its meaning, so to speak; what had been chronology turned into a kind of nomology, and under the sign of an evolutionist linearism causality and finality merged into one another again. Müller-Armack refused to accept the deterministic dogma which exposes mankind to the danger of passivity and fatalism, and in the last analysis incapacitates the human being.

In other words, evolutionism and determinism imply a wrong perception of man, a mistaken anthropology, and for this reason Müller-Armack began to look for another and more convincing anthropology. He turned not to the classical texts but to philosophers of his time, namely Max Scheler and Helmut Plessner. What seemed attractive to him in their teaching was the reactivation, so to speak, of the human being. It is commonly held that a distinction has to be drawn in man between body and mind, between his affiliation to nature and his cultural disposition which would at the same time relieve him from the chains of nature. This distinction, however, is entirely wrong because man's nature indispensably and inescapably demands cultural completion and satisfaction, or conversely, his culture is indissolubly connected with his nature[4]. This oneness of nature and culture, of course, is not fixed in advance and once for ever but changes and varies in time and space, it

---

3   A. MUELLER-ARMACK: *Entwicklungsgesetze des Kapitalismus: ökonomische, geschichts theoretische und soziologische Studien zur modernen Wirtschaftsverfassung,* Berlin 1932. Cf. also his 1973 retrospect: *Der humane Gehalt der sozialen Marktwirtschaft,* reprinted in: A. MUELLER-ARMACK: *Genealogie der sozialen Marktwirtschaft,* Bern/Stuttgart 1981, p. 167.

4   Plessner's "natural artificiality", see H. PLESSNER: *Die Stufen des Organischen und der Mensch,* Berlin/Leipzig 1928, p. 309. - In the winter semester of 1930/31, Müller- Armack and Plessner (and Erwin von Beckerath) jointly gave a seminar on Marxism; Hans Mayer reports on it in his memoirs (HANS MAYER: *Ein Deutscher auf Widerruf,* 1982, p. 129).

moves and develops, and in this way anthropological interpretation ends up in the conception of the historicity of man, not an abstract but a concrete historicity which and only which allows him to find out himself and his destination. The historicity of which we are talking here, contrasts sharply with the historicity in the sense of the law of history of which we were talking above, because for the law of history the future is set in advance, already closed as it were; historicity in the anthropological sense, however, reiterates itself in every moment, its crystallization cannot be anticipated, the future is open. This historicity - and that is important for our subject - yields the possibility of free and responsible action, more: it evokes the human duty to act. This applies to all areas of human action, with economics as an area of creative action as well. In this way economics obtained an anthropological legitimation.

But the idea of historicity had still another dimension for Müller-Armack. In 1941, he published a book on economic styles[5]. The concept of style was to serve a comprehensive, synthetic view on history; our author referred here to Max Weber and, again, Sombart. Dealing with a synthetic approach of this kind, an inquiry into economic styles had to answer questions of cultural history as well. To Müller-Armack, an inquiry into the style of an epoch meant an inquiry into the unifying expression, the formative physiognomy of this epoch. Therefore, when explaining the development of economic styles, one should investigate the structural conditions[6] of the epoch in question, its

---

5   A. MUELLER-ARMACK: *Genealogie der Wirtschaftsstile: die geistesgeschichtlichen Ursprünge der Staats- und Wirtschaftsformen bis zum Ausgang des 18. Jahrhunderts*, Stuttgart 1941. On the concept of the economic style in general, cf. B. SCHEFOLD: "Zur Entwicklung von Nationalökonomie, Rechtswissenschaft und Sozialwissenschaft im 20. Jahrhundert", in: K. W. NOERR, B. SCHEFOLD, F. TENBRUCK (Eds.): *Geisteswissenschaften zwischen Kaiserreich und Republik*, Stuttgart 1994, p. 215.

6   Avoiding ontological interpretations, since they cannot do justice to the historicity of the styles: This dismissal of ontological interpretations included also the rejection of the National Socialist ideology; cf. A. MUELLER-ARMACK: *Genealogie der Wirtschaftsstile* (cf. above, footnote 5), p. 18 and p. 216ff. Müller-Armack was among the numerous intellectuals who had initially been dazzled by the aims and slogans of the Nazi party but soon discovered the real nature of the new system. Thus, the deliberately historical approach of this study implied also a dissociation from his 1933 publication "Staatsidee und Wirtschaftsordnung im neuen Reich".

perceptions and values, as well as the actions and creations of the people of the time. Generally speaking, our author sought access to the epochs of economic history in terms of the history of ideas and of humanity. Thus he did not hesitate to bring out religion and religious world-view as the main reason for the rise and historical change of economic styles.

Now, Müller-Armack's significant move is that, after the war, he went beyond the historical investigation and applied the concept of style also to the Social Market Economy. His aim was twofold and had an inward and outward direction, so to speak: inward - since the economic order as a whole was to be governed by consistent principles, and outward - since the idea of style could not be limited merely to the economic order but was to comprise all parts of the overall order, including state, society, law, intellectual and cultural life, so that common principles, values and objectives would be in force everywhere. Note that for both directions the idea of style was dynamic and open to the future; style does not come by itself but has to be created: a historical task to which we should devote ourselves. In some respect, this idea of style is akin to the theorem of the interdependence of orders as Walter Eucken, the great economist, had emphasized it. However, Eucken's theorem was narrower in scope and for the most part geared to the needs and tasks of the state.

II. On the Impact of Ordoliberalism. The Era of Ludwig Erhard

In this way Müller-Armack considered economy not an automatic course of events but a matter of human action and human responsibility. This philosophy, however, did not imply an answer to the question which economic system should be preferred, and in case a model of polito-economic thinking was to be followed, which of these models should be chosen. Müller-Armack's anthropology had been open towards the future, but open as well towards economic ideas and economic policies. The open space, of course, had to be filled as soon as political decisions on the future economic system were approaching which was the case two or three years after 1945. A struggle began between socialist, conservative and liberal conceptions, all of them on their part divided in several schools and directions; but in the end the tenets of the so-called Ordoliberals prevailed. The protagonists of this school of thought were on the side of the economists, Walter Eucken and, on the side of the jurists, Franz Böhm[7].

Again we have to refer to the Weimar period if we want to find out the roots of their thinking. The economy in the Weimar Republic was marked by heavy cartelization and trustification. There was much criticism of this but little theory developed to combat the organisational trends of thought on which arrangements and conspiracies were founded. The critical catchword was private economic power, and victim of the power of organized economy was not only the weaker party on the market but government or the state as well. The organized economy began to attain political power and to control the machine of government. "The state falling prey to the crowds of interested groups" was an often quoted phrase in this respect. In this situation the idea of free competition was rediscovered as a means to prevent monopolization and cartelization and to confine economic power. Free competition, however, cannot be preserved without setting rules which are appropriate to forestall restraints of trade. To lay down rules for this purpose is the task of legislation, and to implement the rules laid down is the task of administrative bodies and of the courts. Thus, the state through its agents is responsible for seeing that a legal and institutional framework, and "order" is established and maintained within which competition can proceed and the market will operate undisturbed. In this way the concept of economic order in the sense of market economy under governmental guardianship was invented and developed. In the wake of this concept Eucken coined a new term, namely *Ordnungspolitik* which may be translated as policy towards setting the framework and devising the rules for the maintenance of the market. A strong state for the sake of free market: this is one of the labels which try to epitomize the Ordoliberal teaching as briefly as possible.

Now, it is not difficult to see how Müller-Armack's anthropology was able to adopt the Ordoliberal idea of order. For, this order was not a product of nature or of a self-regulating evolutionary process but required human decisions and human actions in producing institutions and rules. This conception of order corresponds exactly with the conception of man as seen above, the conception of his historicity from which the duty to act derived, the duty to consciously create an economic order.

---

7   Cf. K. W. NOERR: *Die Leider: des Privatrechts*, Tübingen 1994 (chapter 5).

Thus the ideas of anthropology and of economics met each other. This occurred first on the theoretical level. The practical or political implementation was connected with another well-known name, Ludwig Erhard. After the unconditional surrender in 1945, Germany was divided in several occupation zones. But in 1947 the American and the British zones were merged into the so-called *Vereinigtes Wirtschaftgebiet* (Combined Economic Area) which was to be the predecessor of the Federal Republic of Germany. The main government-like authority for this structure was the Economic Department, and Erhard was appointed chief official of this body. In the famous statement in April 1948 Erhard announced the abolition of the war-time and post-war-time system of planned and controlled economy and the introduction of competition and market economy. He did so against fierce opposition from different quarters but in the end he succeeded in getting the majority among politicians to accept his objective. In 1949 Federal Chancellor Adenauer made him the first Minister of Economics of the Federal Republic, and three years later Erhard on his part offered Müller-Armack a key position in his ministry.

III. An Ambiguity in the Concept of Market Economy

Much has been written about the story of success of Social Market Economy, about the reasons thereof, and also about some shortcomings in the practical conversion of the concept[8]. But let us return to some more theoretical considerations. When we give the concept of Social Market Economy a second look, we can distinguish, as it were, between a solid core and a soft skin. The core is constituted by competition and free market, and it is only this core that is theoretically shaped in the strict sense: this is the domain of economics. Around this core, there is a porous skin, a zone with rather indeterminate boundaries. Saying that Social Market Economy is more of a big

---

8   For the abundant literature on Social Market Economy see J. STARBATTY: "Soziale Marktwirtschaft als Forschungsgegenstand: ein Literaturbericht", in: *Soziale Marktwirtschaft als historische Weichenstellung: Bewertungen und Ausblicke (Festschrift zum hundertsten Geburtstag von Ludwig Erhard)*, 1997, p. 63.

piece of reality than a theory refers to this zone which has been given the attribute "social". We shall come back to the social component of Social Market Economy in a minute. At this point we should make a short comment on the concept of the market.

For, we are faced with an ambiguity of the concept of market economy which has been noticeable from its beginnings but which has only rarely been expressed. We are concerned with the role and significance of the market. On the one hand, market has only one purpose: to maintain and increase the national product. In order to do this, the agents on the market coordinate. They must have freedom of action since this is the only way in which the proverbial cake (which is then to be distributed) gains Maximum size. This is a fact taught by experience, and in this way one was able to "discover" a law of nature. (Anthropologically speaking, market is a piece of "nature".) Theory succeeded in analyzing the freedom of market participants in all respects, spelt it out, modelled it, optimized it, and thus the famous *homo oeconomicus* came into being, our *homunculus* of economic theory whose services also Social Market Economy cannot dispense with. On the other hand, market is not an isolated phenomenon; its designers and constructors themselves "do not live on the market alone". If market economy (not yet with the social attribute) is confronted with its big alternative, the bureaucratically controlled economy, then it guarantees, with all its instrumentality and functionality, at least a piece of freedom and human dignity, as Müller-Armack put it. In that case, however, the picture of the *homo oeconomicus* is abandoned, and the concept of freedom in the market economy has changed its meaning: Freedom is no more merely an instrument or method, but implies a message of the philosophical or moral or political kind (anthropologically, market now belongs to the sphere of "culture"). It can be noticed again and again that the advocates as well as critics of the market economy continually shift the concepts of market and freedom and also of individualism back and forth from one meaning to the other, thus obscuring them, sometimes perhaps on purpose.

IV. Three Meanings of "Social" in Social Market Economy

We shall not pursue this ambiguity further but direct our attention to the epithet "social" in Social Market Economy. The political significance of the attribute was clear enough. After 1945, the state-controlled war- and post-war-economy was to be converted into regular economic conditions. However, the political circles were for the most part unable to imagine economic forms other than those of, again, controlled economy. Therefore, the small minority who wanted to introduce the system of market economy had to provide concepts, programmes, points of view which could take the sting out of the traditional accusations against the market economy. These points of view were then subsumed under the umbrella term of the "social". If we take a closer look, we can distinguish three aspects or groups of questions hidden behind this concept of the social.

Firstly, there are economic sectors where, for whatever reason, the rules of the market economy are only partially or not at all in force. Among these sectors are labour relations, agriculture, housing and building, and the money and credit system, to give a few examples. The sectors, of course, are not fixed once and for all but open to changes and modifications; in other words, the borderline between market and non-market depends on decisions of economic policy[9]. The same is true, incidentally, for the public enterprise or public corporation, whether controlled by the state or by municipalities. Public enterprises do not have a common past but each of them looks back on a particular history; they emerged piecemeal and not from enforcement of an overall political programme. Market economy of course, favours privatisation; Social Market Economy again would not on principle oppose the existence of a moderate number of public enterprises as long as they are not exempted from the rules to which private enterprises are subject.

Secondly, the word "social" refers to public care and help for those groups of the population that are not or only partially able to participate in the market, for reasons of age, health, lacking source of income, etc. Thus, social is used here above all in the sense of social security. Germany had

---

9 Cf. K. W. NOERR: "Das Unternehmen in der Wirtschafts- und Rechtsordnung 1880 bis 1930: ein Beitrag zur Morphologie der organisierten Wirtschaft", in: H. COING et al. (Eds.): *Staat und Unternehmen aus der Sicht des Rechts*, Tübingen 1994, p. 15.

been the first country to enact social insurance legislation on a large scale, it started in the 1880s. A landmark of a more recent date was the so-called dynamization of pension in 1957, i.e. the introduction of the wage-linked retirement pension where pensions increase synchronously with the rise of gross wages and salaries. The social insurance system is based partly on the contributions from employees and employers, partly on the subsidies given by the government, thus by the community of the taxpayers. Today a reform of the system is overdue since the possibility of financing it in the future has become extremely doubtful.

To understand the third meaning of "social" in Social Market Economy, we should remember the anthropological approach which had shaped Müller-Armack's thinking. Anthropology, of course, cannot confine itself to the field of economics, or to the field of social policy, or to any other field or segment of the social system but will envisage society at large. Thus, attention was drawn to man's position within his or her environment and to the necessity of giving a meaningful form to this environment. In this context "environment" was taken not from ecological but from anthropological terminology and therefore referred to the phenomena of civilization in general or to specific situations within society. In terms of politics, the aspect of governmental activity in the socio-political system (*Gesellschaftspolitik*) came into play. Müller-Armack as well as Ludwig Erhard spoke, since 1960, of the second phase of Social Market Economy[10]. Socio-politics is meant to take a position of its own next to economic policy without, of course, coming into conflict with it (the idea of style would prohibit conflicts). For Müller-Armack, a socio-political equilibrium was just as necessary as the economic one. He made a list of socio-political problems and objectives, we quote a few of them: the education system which is to be extended in order to facilitate access to qualified employment; furthering independence in the sense of self-employment, e.g. through assistance to infant enterprises and companies; improvement of the internal structures and processes of the enterprise through decentralization of decision making on the one hand, and humanization of the working conditions on the other hand; stimulating wide-

---

10 MUELLER-ARMACK: *Die Soziale Marktwirtschaft nach einem Jahrzehnt ihrer Erprobung*, Vortrag 1959; Id.: *Die zweite Phase der Sozialen Marktwirtschaft: ihre Ergänzung durch das Leitbild einer neuen Gesellschaftspolitik*, 1960; Id.: *Das gesellschaftspolitische Leitbild der Sozialen Marktwirtschaft*, 1962; reprinted in: *Wirtschaftsordnung und Wirtschaftspolitik*, 1966, 2nd ed., 1976.

spread wealth formation by means of distributive income and property policy; environmental reforms in the (narrower) sense of regional and city planning, traffic policy, nature conservation, etc. The socio-political list also included activities of structure policy in regard to temporary adjustment aid for hard-pressed industries such as coal-mining, as well as in regard to the promotion of small and medium-sized enterprises. Most important, however, was the inclusion of trade cycle policy in the socio-political programme (we shall come back to it in a moment).

The reasons, why the protagonists of Social Market Economy began in those years to emphasize socio-politics, were twofold. Firstly, the Social-Democratic Party (SPD), which had been in opposition since 1948 politically as well as economically, finally came to terms, in principle at least, with the market economy; the shift took place in the Godesberg platform of 1959 after long preparations which were stimulated not least by Karl Schiller, an economist who was to become Minister of Economics in the period following Erhard. After a decade of mutual unintelligibility, as it were, a common economic language was discovered between Social Market Economy and democratic socialism; and this new and not unwelcome situation could be even been strengthened by expansion of the concept of Social Market Economy into the domain of socio-politics. Secondly, the European aspect had a part to play. In 1958 the European Economic Community (EEC) began to exist. The Community embraced nations with quite different economic orders; above all, German Social Market Economy was not compatible with the French idea of planification. Müller-Armack represented the German position in many European negotiations, and thus became acquainted with the French conceptions[11]. Also at home, political and academic circles began to flirt with the idea of planning in many directions. In this situation, extending Social Market Economy into the socio-political sphere could serve as a kind of antidote against planification; the field was to be occupied before the rival will be prepared to enter.

---

11 See his memoirs: *Auf dem Weg nach Europa*, 1971.

V. Social Market Economy and Keynesianism: the Era of Karl Schiller

In this way the term "social" in Social Market Economy was enriched with a socio-political connotation. As mentioned above, the trade cycle policy was one of the objectives that Müller-Armack had in mind when he began to speak of the second phase of Social Market Economy. Now, the trade cycle or stabilization policy was anything but alien to Müller-Armack since as a young scholar he was one of the first to deal with this topic. The same is true, by the way, in respect of another economist, Wilhelm Röpke, who had stood by Müller-Armack's side. Thus the cycle policy was a part of the thinking of Social Market economists from the very beginning. The cycle policy, however, has quite different meanings. Müller-Armack and Röpke began their research before the Great Depression of the early 1930s; thereafter, of course, the technics of anticyclical policy were developed by Keynes and his school which were to gain enormous influence upon economics and economic policy in the Western world. In Germany the Ordoliberal school strongly opposed Keynesianism but in the 1960s the political situation changed with the result that the general theory entered the politico-economical stage also in Germany. In 1963 Erhard followed Adenauer as head of the federal government, and in 1966 the so-called grand coalition was formed between the Christian Democrats and the Social Democrats who for the first time in the history of the Federal Republic got into power. They succeeded in appointing Karl Schiller as Minister of Economics who was to embody, as it were, the Keynesian period of German political and economic history (Schiller resigned in 1972)[12].

It is controversial whether the direction that Schiller took still can be ascribed to the concept of Social Market Economy or not. Schiller himself would have given an affirmative answer. The macroeconomic approach of Keynesian provenance was not meant to destroy but to complement the microeconomics of the market. The demand management policy or *Globalsteuerung*, as it was spelled in German, should prevail over the supply-side

---

12 Among the publications of KARL SCHILLER we quote: *Sozialismus und Wettbewerb*, 1955; "Wirtschaftspolitik", in: *Handwörterbuch der Sozialwissenschaft*, 12 (1965) 210; *Preisstabilität durch globale Steuerung der Marktwirtschaft*, 1966.

economy but not absolutely replace it. The same applied to the fiscal policy in relation to the monetary policy. Turning to the objectives that were to be achieved by the New Economic Policy or the Enlightened Market economy (as the wording ran) we can discover the so-called magic triangle or quadrangle which means a combination of different macroeconomic targets, namely price stability, high level of employment, equilibrium of external payments, and adequate growth. Polygones like that were not an invention of Schiller but familiar for a long time, at the latest since the International Monetary Fund Agreement (Bretton Woods) of 1944 which had included a catalogue of purposes and, being the "primary objectives of economic policy", emphasized the promotion and maintenance of high levels of employment and real income as well as the development of the productive resources (art. I, par. II). The Treaty of Rome which in 1957 created the EEC, obliged the member-states to "pursue the economic policy needed to ensure the equilibrium of its overall balance of payments and to maintain confidence in its currency, while taking care to ensure a high level of employment and a stable level of prices" (art. 104, first version).

As a matter of logic, if different objectives are pursued, none of them can be completely achieved without neglecting somehow the others; in other words, tensions between the objectives emerge and compromises have to be made. Furthermore, the tensions are perceived in different ways. In all Western nations, the Great Depression had made people and politicians extremely sensitive about unemployment, and they were therefore prepared to emphasize the objective of full employment. In Germany, however, in addition to this, there had been two cases of abnormal currency depreciation, in 1923 and 1948, which have deeply engraved themselves on the memory of the nation. For this reason, each government tries to avoid a policy (or at least the impression of a policy) that pushes employment at the cost of monetary stability.

In this respect, therefore, *Globalsteuerung* could have come to terms with the market economists; by no means, however, in other respects. What irritated most was the planning element in the toolbox of the anticyclical policy[13]. For, there was quantification of the future required by using forecasts

---

13 See e.g. E. TUCHTFELDT: "Soziale Marktwirtschaft und Globalsteuerung - Zwei Wirtschaftspolitische Experimente", *Wirtschaftspolitische Chronik,* Heft 1 (1973); E. HOPPMANN: "Soziale Marktwirtschaft oder Konstruktivistischer Interventionismus?", in: E. TUCHTFELDT (Ed.): *Soziale Marktwirtschaft im*

and target projections; to this end figures were created that obliged the public sector in one or another way, but influenced as well, willingly or not, the conduct and expectations of the players on the market. To be sure, it was a kind of soft planning, so to speak, but establishing collective ends and targets contradicts the essence of the market economy. In other words, economic growth rates, all the rates of the magic polygon, should be the outcome of the market process but not its signpost or steering wheel. For this and other reasons many economists denied the compatibility of *Globalsteuerung* with the conception of Social Market Economy.

VI. Social Market Economy: A Concept Still Alive?

But, as it turned out, *Globalsteuerung* enjoyed only a short life. When it was introduced, in 1967, it succeeded in balancing the economy after a recession had occurred, but then it was unable to cope with the mounting inflationary turbulences. This and other circumstances resulted in a reversal of the opinion among economists, politicians, and the public at large. We can observe the changes best through reading the reports that were delivered by the Council of Economic Experts *(Sachverständigenrat)* which is a politically independent board of five economists created in 1963 (thus, in the pre-demand management era); the Council was entrusted with the evaluation of the cyclical development in the light of the polygon mentioned above. Now, this Council, which had built up a high reputation, began to resist the spell of Keynesianism; in 1974 it expressed preference of the quantitative monetary policy over the anticyclical fiscal policy, and in 1976 it advocated shifting the emphasis from the demand-side to the supply-side policy[14]. On the political stage, the Social Democrats were excluded from government in 1982, and the era of Helmut Kohl has begun - for fifteen years so far.

But has Social Market Economy, to ask our last question, since then positively recovered old or even attained new ground? The answer is rather

---

Wandel, 1973, p. 27; J. STARBATTY: *Stabilitätspolitik in der freiheitlich-sozialstaatlichen Demokratie*, 1977 ("jede konjunkturpolitische Konzeption muß die Begrenztheit menschlichen Wissens ins Kalkül ziehen").

14 Cf. e.g. N. KLOTEN: *Der Staat in der Sozialen Marktwirtschaft*, 1986.

ambivalent. On the one hand, the monetary policy as it has been implemented by the *Bundesbank* (German Federal Bank) resulted in low inflation rates and thus guaranteed one of the main prerequisites of a smooth functioning market system; also, the politicians excel themselves in professing the creed of supply-side policy. On the other hand, words and facts do not necessarily harmonize. Thus, point by point interventions persisted when continuous and calculable policies had been desirable; a strong sectoral protectionism including all kinds of subsidies petrified ailing and non-competitive industries and thus impeded appropriate structural changes; and as far as the public sector is concerned, the ratio of public spending to GNP remained (before reunification) almost unchanged on a high level somewhere between 45 and 50 per cent (as compared to 30 per cent or so in the 1950s). In short, policy mix has been the slogan of the day, and at present nobody would be able to define the borderline between Social Market Economy on the one side and the economy of a welfare or redistributory state on the other. It is true, the concept of Social Market Economy was never narrowly defined, as we have seen from the very beginning, but today quite a few economists consider the concept to be fissured and hollowed out in a way that the founding fathers would have had some difficulty to recognise the child they had brought into the world. The situation has not been influenced by the German reunification, which took place in 1990; of course, the former socialist economic system of the acceding GDR was transformed into the economic system of the Federal Republic, but the uncertainty about the conceptual state of Social Market Economy of which we were talking, has continued to be the same.

VII. Irrelevance of the Term "Social Market Economy" to the Legal System

We have seen above that Social Market Economy was developed as a conception after the end of World War II. However, our legal system, in so far as it comes into contact with the elements and structures of Social Market Economy, is for the most part older and dates back to the last third of the 19th century. If we look at the relations between the market participants, i.e. at the element "market" in Social Market Economy, then we are mainly con-

SOCIAL MARKET ECONOMY AND LEGAL ORDER IN GERMANY

cerned with the two great codifications of private law, namely the *Bürgerliches Gesetzbuch* (Civil Code) of 1896 and the *Handelsgesetzbuch* (Commercial Code) of 1897 (with the latter based on an even older code, the *Allgemeines Deutsches Handelsgesetzbuch* of 1861). To a large extent, these Codes are characterized by a liberal understanding of economy. This statement, however, has to be qualified in two directions. Firstly, the liberalism of the Codes was of a microeconomic and not a macroeconomic kind. That is to say that economy was viewed in terms of individual households and individual enterprises but not conceived of as a whole, as a coherent unity; in other words the Codes were not based on a specific concept of national or political economy. The reason for this lay in the historical background of German private law. There are, of course, always several roots that produce a legal system but in the German case it was Roman law which dominated when the terminology and structure of private law was being shaped. (The same is true, by the way, for French, Italian, or Spanish law.) If we consider the law-professors who in the 19th century taught Roman law and advanced it, we can easily see that they were denied the possibility of incorporating economic aspects in the sense of political economy into their dogmatics, since any manner of looking at things in terms of political economics was, of course, completely alien to Roman antiquity and thus also to Roman law, the subject the 19th-century jurists were occupied with. Secondly, one has to bear in mind that the majority of the regulations in these Codes are purely technical and devoid of all philosophical, political or otherwise metajuristic content. This technical quality explains why the Codes or parts of them could be transplanted into entirely different cultures. Thus, in China they were among the models for the codification of 1929/31[15]. Further, technicality accounts for why they were in use even in socialist-communist states, e.g. the Civil Code in the GDR until 1975. However, the German legal tradition dates from the 19th century not only in regard to the market, but also in regard to the social component. We mention only the famous social insurance legislation introduced by Bismarck in the 1880s.

Moreover, looking at history in terms of economic typology, it was also in this period that organized economy started to grow which came to take up

---

15 K. W. NOERR: "The Problem of Legal Transplant and the Reception of Continental Law in China before 1930", in: H. G. LESER/T. ISOMURA (Eds.): *Wege zum japanischen Recht, Festschrift für Zentaro Kitagawa*, Berlin 1992, p. 231.

more and more room at the expense of the market economy. What did the contemporaries mean when they talked of organisation, organized economy in this context?[16] There are three aspects which can be pointed out. Firstly, organisation could refer to the internal structure of the company, the framework of authorities and controls, coordinations and subordinations, which are primarily based on the institution of property but have increasingly been enriched by measures of social policy in order to work toward the political idea of the company as a product of property as well as of labour. (Of course, the bigger the company, the more significant became the internal structures in terms of the national economy and the social policy.) Second, organisation concerns the external relations that the company maintains with other companies, as soon as they do not face each other as market subjects but establish connections among themselves that construct a new comprehensive or partial unity, which then acts in loose or closely knit forms, depending on its goal. Organisations in this sense are mainly combines or affiliations on the one hand and cartels on the other; if one wished to emphasize the negative aspects of the large economic bodies they were called trusts. However, companies could also collaborate in order to pursue common interests either in relation to politics and governmental activities - in this case commercial associations were formed -, or in relation to the trade unions - the case, then, of employers' associations. This kind of organisation takes us to our third aspect, namely to the interaction between the economic units on the one hand and various types of public or semi-public authorities on the other, such as the state, the municipalities or communities, the trade unions, and so on. The idea of "national" economy, that is to say the political element in the political economy, was aimed mainly at the state's thirst for action in the economic field, whether in the form of public enterprise or in the many forms of control over the private enterprise by means of legislation and administration.

Of course, the clocks of legislation never stand still, and after 1945, parts of the old body of laws were renewed or entirely new laws created. An example from the sphere of the market is the Joint-Stock Company Act of 1965; an example of legal precautions pertaining to the market as well as to organized economy is the Act Against Restraint of Competition of 1957; and the latest example from the social sphere is the nursing insurance introduced in 1994, caused by the changes in age structure. This is only a small selec-

---

16 Above, footnote 9.

SOCIAL MARKET ECONOMY AND LEGAL ORDER IN GERMANY

tion of examples. Generally, in contrast to certain current and past trends within economic liberalism, Social Market Economy does not object on principle against state activism, at least not if it takes place within the framework of parliamentary legislation.

Thus, in our legal system, old and new ideas meet. But the jurists and the courts have by and large succeeded in pouring oil on the troubled historical waters: they have ensured and developed the unity of the legal order, i.e. the systematic correspondence of norms and norm interpretations. This unity or, rather, the urge to unity presupposed, the question might be raised whether the concept of Social Market Economy has contributed to the systematic-uniform structure of our legal order. There can be no doubt that human life, in so far as it consists of legal relations, takes place mostly in sectors that we would assign to Social Market Economy (in whatever way it may have developed over the generations): does this not suggest the idea that Social Market Economy has had a crucial influence on the legal system? However, nobody has arrived at such a conclusion. In terms of conception, Social Market Economy has never been relevant to the legal system. There is no accepted theory which, for the economic-social sphere, made Social Market Economy the model of the legal system. Social Market Economy does not even serve as a commonly used *topos* in the argumentation of jurists and courts.

It would be interesting to look into the reasons for this negative result. Here, we can only give a few hints. Firstly, like the economist, the jurist usually looks for some philosophical or subphilosophical support; but legal studies or court decisions have hardly been impressed with philosophical anthropology or the idea of style in the manner of Müller-Armack who had created the concept of Social Market Economy. Secondly, in our legal system, the dichotomy between public law and private law is essential despite all overlaps which are to be found; the dichotomy, however, is hardly to apply when Social Market Economy as well as its large subdivisions are considered as a whole. In the third place, when we turn to the market-economic core of Social Market Economy, we are confronted with fundamental differences as well: Think, on the one hand, of the *homo oeconomicus* who is a hypothetical figure necessary for explaining and theorising about the infinite number of market relations. The jurist, on the other hand, in his decision of the individual case, always faces a real human being, also with regard to market relations and in spite of all the categories and typologies he has to devise from legal points of view. Or, put it another way: the economist models *ceteris paribus*, whereas the task of the jurist begins where the *cetera* cease to be alike.

VIII. Two Performances of a Play: Germany's Binary Economic Order

There is yet another reason, and we want to take a closer look at it. Despite all broadness and flexibility of definition one cannot fail to notice that the concept of Social Market Economy implies the idea of an overall structure, of a virtual order which, of course, can never reach completion but which will constantly inspire thoughts and actions of the persons who take part in it. As soon as such an economic-social order implies rules and institutions, a state conceiving of itself as a liberal democracy, has to answer the question about the relation of this order to the political constitution, be it unwritten or codified in a charter as is the case in Germany. We may call this the constitutional question to the economic-social order. The question has hardly been raised in the 19th century, whereas in the *Weimar* Constitution of 1919 it was given fullest attention (for the first time in Europe by the way). But is the same true for the German constitution in force, the Basic Law *(Grundgesetz)* which was enacted after World War II, in 1949, to be exact?

Here, we are approaching one of the fundamental phenomena in the history of the Federal Republic of Germany. As we have mentioned above, World War II had entailed a system of state-controlled economy directed toward the requirements of the war; when the war was over, this system was maintained temporarily. Soon, however, programmes and proposals were made for the normal economic conditions to come. They ranged from a planned economy in the socialist manner over a re-establishment, more or less, of the old-style organized economy, to a market and competition economy propagated by the Ordoliberal school. Before long, the model of planned economy was fighting a losing battle, but on the part of the other two positions - organized economy and free-market economy - there were no clear victories or defeats. Far from it: the years 1948 and 1949 set the points for the economic order that was to give form to the new republic, and an analysis of the situation at this time shows that we have to speak of a double

SOCIAL MARKET ECONOMY AND LEGAL ORDER IN GERMANY

staging, of two performances of the same play, which took practically no notice of each other.

This needs further explanation[17]. Let us first look at free market economy. In the crucial year of 1948 (after the American and British zones had been merged into the *Vereinigtes Wirtschaftsgebiet*, Combined Economic Area), free-market economy had enemies and allies who balanced each other more or less. What tipped the scales - if we wish to credit an individual person with a historical development - was the election of a market economist, Professor Ludwig Erhard, as head of the Economy Department of the Combined Economic Area. In June 1948, in the days of the currency reform, the first and decisive step to introduce market economy was taken when the so-called *Leitsätzegesetz* (Guiding Principles Law) set the course. This law had several articles. The article on government control, or rationing, of staple commodities started with the following sentence: "Lifting of government control is to be preferred to retaining it". The corresponding formulation on the prices was "Lifting of controls on prices is to be preferred to price maintenance by authorities". Additionally, there were plans to prepare a law on competition and against monopolies.

This *Leitsätzegesetz* is among the foundation documents of the Federal Republic. In a broader context, when we look at recent German history with regard to the economic order and keep in mind that the protective tariff laws in the late 19th century had opened the door to organized economy, which dominated the field since then, in a broader context, I say, we are presented with a paradigm change - a process that divides our history into two clearly distinguishable halves. In the language of politics as well as in everyday economic vernacular, the new paradigm became a success, as we have seen, by the name of Social Market Economy; the political economists contributed the term *Ordnungspolitik* (policy towards setting the framework and devising the rules for the maintenance of the market), and when the jurists wanted to interpret market economy as a normative whole including the Basic Law as the document of the political constitution, they applied the concept of *Wirtschaftsverfassung* (economic constitution).

We promised to show the second staging of our play. A few months after Erhard and his comrades-in-arms had set the points for the market economic policy, preparations began for drawing up a constitution for the western

---

17 K. W. NOERR: *Im Wechselbad der Interpretationen: der Begriff der Wirtschaftsverfassung im ersten Jahrzwölft der Bonner Republik* (forthcoming).

German republic to come. (This constitution was then called Basic Law in order to emphasize its provisional character.) The debates about the charter were dominated by the view that unlike the Weimar constitution no chapter on the economic-social order was to be included in the Basic Law. Rather, this question was to be decided by the future, i.e. by the parliament as the all-competent law-maker to come. As far as I can see, none of the discussions contains any hint that the decision might already have been made a year before. Generally, almost no voices supporting market economy were heard among the representatives who debated the new constitution.

Thus, the economic order of the new republic was deliberately not included in the constitution. An entirely different matter, however, is the question of whether the representatives might have had some specific picture of this order in mind, that is whether the texts can be read in terms of economic typology. Now, there is indeed a find to be made here. This typological content of the Basic Law has fallen into oblivion; as far as jurists are concerned, this has to do with the methods used to interpret wordings of laws (in our case constitutional texts). There are several moves to interpret a law; one of them is the so-called subjective or historical interpretation. This kind of interpretation focuses on the intention of the legislator. But the jurist has to apply the law and take a decision; so, when he is interpreting historically, such a reading is oriented toward application and decision as are all the other ways of interpretation. With respect to questions of the economic order, then, historical interpretation would mean that the intention of the maker of the constitution is interpreted in the direction of that economic order that the interpreter takes to be the right one. In this way, historical interpretation as well is motivated by economic and constitutional policy. If it is impossible, despite all efforts, to make the historical argument serve the decision, then the historical method is quietly abandoned or it is subordinated to the other methods of interpretation.

The historian, of course, is not allowed to do any of this. Therefore, the historical method of the jurist has to be sharply distinguished from the historiographic method of the historian. Historigraphy, however, cannot overlook the fact that the picture of economy that became entangled in the texts of the Basic Law was just the above-sketched organized economy. We do not even have to go into the debates (which sometimes give one the impression of being in a Weimar museum); rather, it is sufficient to quote three texts of the Basic Law. Like the earlier constitutions, it contains regulations that distribute the legislative competence among the Federation and the individual states

(*Laender*). According to Article 74, No. 16, the so-called concurrent legislation includes "prevention of abuse of economic power positions". This formulation repeats literally the title of the 1923 Cartel Ordinance, which was a show piece of organized economy. In the same catalogue (No. 15) and in a similar formulation in Article 15 of the Basic Law, the legislator is authorized to convert land, natural resources, and means of production "into public property or into other forms of publicly controlled economy". Forms of this kind of a collectively organized economy had been introduced in 1919 in the coal and the potassium industries, and our Article 15 opened the way to transform other industrial branches into this species of organized economy as well. Finally, Article 9 of the Basic Law guarantees the right to form associations to safeguard and improve working and economic conditions; in this way the trade unions and the employers' associations, therefore two essential elements of organized economy, were constitutionally recognized and stabilized.

Thus, the Basic Law, as it emerged from the discussions, did not take any notice of the model of market and competition economy that had been legally established one year before. It did not acknowledge it but did not dismiss it either. The double staging, as we called it, is a basic phenomenon in the history of the origins of the Federal Republic. It marks a dual-track policy that became manifest with the ordinary legislator on the one hand choosing the way to a liberal order of economy and walking it determinedly (or so he tried), and with constitution makers on the other hand closing their eyes to this and not responding to the current developments. Rather, they were sympathetic to an organized economy, although they did not explicitly formulate it as a project for the future.

IX. Social Market Economy and the Federal Constitutional Court

In this way market economy or Social Market Economy, to take up the term again, was thoroughly ignored by the Basic Law. Of course, that does not say too much, since, apart from the text of the constitution, an extensive, almost rampant interpretation industry has established itself which could have easily made up for what the text itself had neglected. However, the interpreters, too, were reluctant to put the constitutional question to the economic-social order as a whole, and to affirm the concept of Social Market Economy. According to them, Social Market Economy could not be anchored in the constitution; the constitution was not committed to it. This is the crucial point for our topic: we said above that Social Market Economy did not become conceptually relevant to the legal system, and this statement must be particularly emphasized now with respect to the constitution and the constitution's interpretation.

This reserve and distance has been expressed by the Federal Constitutional Court (which we can apostrophize the institutionalized form of constitutional interpretation) from early on. In the first years of its existence, and in the more than forty years since then, it has not deviated from this line. In the leading decision of the Court[18], the point at issue was the constitutionality of a federal act of 1952 (Investment Aid Act) which obliged industry and commerce to contribute a billion Deutschmarks (by way of buying securities from the ailing industries) in order to satisfy the investment needs of coalmining and certain other ailing branches of industry. Against this act, several of the enterprises obliged to contribute filed a complaint on account of infringement of the constitution, which the court dismissed. The enterprises asserted that the investment aid did not accord with the established economic and social order, i.e. with Social Market Economy. Furthermore, they argued that the legislator was allowed to intervene in the market; that the instruments of interference, however, would have to be "*marktkonform*" (conforming to or consistent with the market principle), and that this was not the case with the investment aid. The judges dismissed both lines of argument. They stated that, according to the constitution, Social Market Economy was a possible economic order, but by no means the only one possible; the legislator could certainly decide otherwise "as long as he would follow the provisions of the Basic Law". The consequence is that the legislator was not committed to instruments either which would conform to the market. The term *marktkonform* had been coined by Röpke and other advocates of Social Market Economy; within the large scope they had left to the legislator, the term was meant to mark out a limit, that would safeguard the hard core, as we have called it, of the market- economical structures. To give an example: in case people of low income were not able to pay the market price for rent-

---

18 *Entscheidungen des Bundesverfassungsgerichts (BVerfGE)* (Decisions of the Federal Constitutional Court), Volume 4 (1954), p. 7.

ing, a price-ceiling would be non-market-conformable, directly subsidizing the tenant, however, market-conformable. Of course, if market-conformable interventions will exceed certain dimensions, qualitatively as well as quantitatively, the market economy could be hollowed out, could erode and lose its meaning, but no economist so far has been able to define the point where the tide would be turning. At any rate, the jurist somehow understands why the Constitutional Court did not subscribe to the maxim "conformity with the market" since this is a term from economics and therefore subject to all the hazards that come with the difference and dynamics of opinions in this discipline.

It is another problem, however, to find out the reasons why the Court dissociated itself almost apodictically from Social Market Economy. There were methodical deficits in the way some jurists had developed the thesis that the Basic Law had opted for an economic constitution which was represented by Social Market Economy. This may have been the - rather outward - reason why the Court did not have to feel obliged to come to terms with this thesis. The deeper reason, however, might have to do with the personal experience of the judges who made the decision. All of them had grown up in an economic system which had been structured by the characteristics of organized economy and not by those of a market and competition economy. The renaissance of the market economy as it was launched in 1948 was alien to them, and as little were they familiar with the "social" variant of the market idea. Incidentally, a piece of evidence for the judges' deep rootedness in the thought patterns of organized economy was their emphasis on the communal idea. They explained that the Basic Law's conception of the human being was not that of an isolated and sovereign individual; rather, with regard to the tension between the individual and the community, the Basic Law opted for the community-relatedness of the person without thereby encroaching on his or her intrinsic value: these were their actual words. But this reference to the individual as being embedded in the community - which the Constitutional Court has repeated in its judgements ever since - belongs to the *topoi* used again and again since the end of the 19th century to justify organized economy.

We have not yet finished our attempt to explain the reserve of the interpreters of the constitution against Social Market Economy. As we have seen, Social Market Economy had been linked by the jurists with the concept of economic constitution, which we can define as the aggregation of basic legal norms, applied to the economic system. The reason for this terminology (as it was put forward by Franz Böhm) was the idea that the sovereign, i.e. the people, would have to decide on the economic constitution just like it decides on the political constitution. Now, the political constitution, of course, is the battleground for experts of constitutional law, whereas the economic constitution would be dependent upon the theories and explanations of economists[19] or, at best, upon experts of private law. However, the interpreters of the constitution are unwilling to share their domain and their power with anybody else; they keep a watchful eye on every attempt that would break up their monopoly of constitutional interpretation.

This distrust of the alien gods has prevailed until today, although in the meantime economics has made its entrance into the Basic Law itself. As we have seen above, the fiscal policy gained approval in the later 1960s. In Germany, however, when speaking of fiscal policy, we have to count with three political levels, among which budgetary autonomy was distributed, namely first the Federation itself, secondly the individual *Laender* or federal states, and thirdly a countless number of communities or local authorities. Therefore to make fiscal policy effective, at least the states had to be in line among themselves and with the Federation in their budgetary policy. Thus Article 109 of the Basic Law says that the Federation and the states shall be autonomous and independent of each other in their budget management but in 1967 a paragraph was added which read as follows: "The Federation and the *Laender* shall have due regard in their budget management to the requirements of overall economic equilibrium." In addition to the constitutional amendment a new law was enacted, the Law on the Furtherance of Economic Stability and Growth, which can be called the highlight of Keynesianism in German legislative history. But what an "overall economic equilibrium" in these texts should stand for, the legislator deliberately did not define more precisely in order to keep it open for new discoveries in the field of economics. Thus, economics was called the competent discipline, as the Constitutional Court once put it[20], to concretise what the "overall economic equilibrium"-formula would mean in a given situation. In this respect we can speak of a kind of macroeconomic constitutionalism, which was recognized by the legislator and the judges. But this intrusion of economics into the constitutional text has remained an isolated phenomenon, and apart from it

---

19 Cf. BVerfGE 7.377,400 (1958).
20 BVerfGE 79.311,338 (1989).

economics has remained to be excluded from the court of the crowned masters who interpret the constitution.

Thus, taking it all in all, we come to the conclusion that there has been no conceptual connection between Social Market Economy on the one hand and the political constitution on the other. In this sense, economic order and constitutional order face each other at a certain distance, consider each other with some reserve. However, we should not forget that the Constitutional Court conceded the legislator free play in economics only "as long as he would follow the provisions of the Basic Law". These provisions, of course, would preclude a system of centrally administered or controlled or planned economy or whatever form a command economy would choose. But otherwise the provisions are open to any kind of economic order and economic policy if we take the interpretation of the Basic Law by the Constitutional Court into account. By way of example: Article 2 of the Basic Law says that "everyone shall have the right to the free development of his personality in so far as he does not violate the rights of others or offend against the constitutional order or the moral code." There is no doubt that the right of the free development of personality includes the general right of free action and therefore also the economic freedom of contract; but the Constitutional Court, on the other hand, has given the term "constitutional order" in this article a broad meaning by stating that it would include every legislative act as long as this act for its part conforms with the constitution[21]. In this way Article 2 as such is not able to prevent the legislator from restricting freedom of contract for reasons of economic policy. Or take Article 12 of the Basic Law which guarantees the right to freely choose trade, occupation, or profession. But like almost all other basic rights this occupational freedom, too, can be limited by statute, provided that the common good or public interest requires such a limitation. What the public interest requires in a given case is for the most time left to the legislator and will not be scrutinized by the Constitutional Court. Thus e.g. the Court upheld a statute which restricted the overall number of trucks for the long distance freight traffic in order to protect the state-controlled railroad system[22]. Another important provision is Article 14 which says that property and right of inheritance are guaranteed. Without doubt the provision covers private ownership of the means of production and the free disposal of it as well as of the products, thus securing

---

21 BVerfGE 6.32 (1957).
22 BVerfGE 40.196 (1975).

fundamental conditions of market economy. On the other hand, the content of property and its limitation shall be determined by statute, and property should also serve the public weal. From these restrictions the Constitutional Court deduced a twofold conception of property, namely an immediate-personal type of property, and a mediate-indirect-social one, the latter needing less protection against legislative limitations. The main example for this reduced conception of property has been the shareholder's position in the joint-stock company. As a result, workers co-determination, which has been introduced in 1976 in regard to corporations of a certain size, was upheld by the Constitutional Court[23]; from the standpoint of pure market economy a doubtful decision, to be sure, from the standpoint of Social Market Economy, however, the result of the decision can be justified or at least tolerated.

X. A Harmony Conducted by the Interpreters of the Constitution

From all that we can draw two conclusions. Firstly, economic policy certainly has to pay attention to the basic rights as well as to other principles of the constitution (I only mention the rule of law). Now, constitutional lawyers have developed several theories in order to break away from an isolated interpretation of the different basic rights and basic principles, and to create instead a coherent and integrated understanding of the texts in question. But nowhere was the economic aspect deemed good enough to serve as a yardstick or criterion for the systematic comprehension of the rights and institutions laid down in the Basic Law. Consequently, the constitution would not be able to draw a line which organized economy may not transgress to the detriment of market economy, nor in principle to set limits to government intervention, nor to define a borderline for public spending in relation to the GNP. Secondly, even if we confine ourselves to an isolated appreciation of the basic rights: there are without doubt harmonies between the market economy and the constitution, since most of the basic rights are rooted in the great theories of natural law and freedom, thus in theories which have fostered the idea of the market economy as well. But we should not forget that

---

23 BVerfGE 50.290 (1979).

SOCIAL MARKET ECONOMY AND LEGAL ORDER IN GERMANY

the inclusion of natural rights into a constitutional charter most of the time ends up in changing their character: like all other articles of the constitution, they become subject to the jurists' *ars interpretandi*, are caught in the whirl of constitutional construction, and modified in such a way that the historical fathers of the ideas would find it difficult to recognize them; freedom of property was such a case as we have seen. And Social Market Economy has little to offset such politically and institutionally legalized fruits of interpretation; it cannot support itself on an adequate legal theory which by its own efforts would have been able to elaborate, using the above example, an independent legal concept of freedom of property. In other words, the harmonies which we would discover are produced by interpreters of the constitution, and since Social Market Economy is denied access to the constitution, the sound comes from everywhere but not from instruments supplied by Social Market Economy. Thus, heteronomous harmony from the point of view of Social Market Economy - this would be our pointed summary of the result.

Further References for Publications in English

CURRIE, DAVID P.: *The Constitution of the Federal Republic of Germany*, Chicago and London (The University of Chicago Press) 1994.

GIERSCH, HERBERT: "Liberal Reform in West Germany", *Ordo,* 39 (1988).

GIERSCH, HERBERT / PAQUE, K.-H. / SCHMIEDING, H.: *The Fading Miracle: Four Decades of Market Economy in Germany,* Cambridge (Cambridge University Press) 1992.

HALLETT, GRAHAM: *The Social Economy of West Germany,* New York (St. Martin's Press) 1973.

PEACOCK, ALAN and WILLGERODT, HANS (Eds.): *Germany's Social Market Economy: Origins and Evolution,* London (Macmillan) 1989. (Published for the Trade Policy Research Centre)

VANBERG, VIKTOR: "'Ordnungstheorie' as Constitutional Economics: the German Conception of a 'Social Market Economy'", *Ordo,* 39 (1988).

WUENSCHE, HORST FRIEDRICH (Ed.): *Standard Texts on the Social Market Economy* (Ludwig Erhard Stiftung), Stuttgart/New York (Gustav Fischer) 1982.

Discussion Summary
NORBERT F. TOFALL

Paper discussed:
KNUT WOLFGANG NÖRR: A Symbiosis with Reserve: Social Market
Economy and Legal Order in Germany

The discussion was opened by the question about the historical development of the Social Market Economy and the legal order in the Federal Republic of Germany since the end of the fifties (SOLOVIOV).

Since the end of the fifties, Müller-Armack and Erhard planned the so-called second step of the Social Market Economy. By calling attention to the rank of human beings in society, they pointed out the necessity of arranging the social world in a wise way. This idea formed the basis for Erhard's concept of a "formierte Gesellschaft" (formed society) during his years as chancellor (1963 - 1966). With this concept the policy of forming society was treated as being independent of the economic policy. The rise of Keynesianism during the time of Karl Schiller (1966 - 1972), who advocated the "Globalsteuerung" (global controlling of the economy) and who tried to act politically on the base of this concept, was followed by a change of the legal order. With an amendment of the "Grundgesetz" (constitution of the Federal Republic of Germany) the "Globalsteuerung" was founded constitutionally. In the seventies after the oil-crisis and a parallel increase of the inflation-rate, Willy Brandt and his successor Helmut Schmidt untied themselves from this concept step by step, although Schmidt tried to induce entrepreneurs, trade unions and the state to act together in economic policy under the lead of the government (so-called "konzertierte Aktion"). After the change of government from the Social-Liberal to the Christian-democrat-liberal coalition, Chancellor Helmut Kohl revived the original concept of the Social Market Economy (NÖRR).

The relation between the Social Market Economy and the legal order follows in Germany - and this is very important - from the German constitution. Although the concept of the Social Market Economy is not codified in

DISCUSSION SUMMARY

the "Grundgesetz" by the term "Social Market Economy", there are specific elements, which constitute the great vicinity of the economic and legal order: especially, on the one hand, the right of private property also in the means of production for securing economic liberty, on the other hand, the "Sozialstaatsprinzip" (principle of the social or welfare state). One can literally read in the German constitution, that the Federal Republic of Germany is a "sozialer Rechtsstaat" (social constitutional state) (NÖRR).

It was inquired, whether the term "Wirtschaftsstil" (style of economy) means, that justice and the economy are different domains, which nevertheless are producing the same results in society (SOLOVIOV).

Exactly this was the reason, why Müller-Armack wanted to harmonise the legal order and the economic order. The framework for this harmonising was the theory of "Wirtschaftsstil" (style of the economy). By transferring the theory of style to the Social Market Economy, Müller-Armack aimed at two goals: Firstly, the whole economic order should be constituted on the same principles, values and aims. Secondly, the uniform style should not only form the economic order, but also all other areas of society. In the speaker's opinion, only the Social Market Economy corresponds with the liberal democratic order of the Federal Republic of Germany. But this is not the opinion of the majority of the law-professors in Germany (NÖRR).

The term "Wirtschaftsstil" is interpreted in a way of integrating the concept of the Social Market Economy into cultural philosophy. Therefore there might be the danger of forgetting the importance of education in addition to the juridical foundation (MAKARYCHEVA).

It is a great problem that the Social Market Economy is not a theme in German schools. The school subject "Social Sciences" teaches not enough of and mostly nothing about the basis of the Social Market Economy. Ethical aspects of human life are discussed in the subject "Religion". But the subject "Religion" and the subject "Social Sciences" are not harmonised, so there is no relation between them (NÖRR).

Another problem: In the Social Market Economy large interventions of the state are made. Is there not the danger that overregulations and interventions might endanger the efficiency of the market? How can one know where the boundary or the limit between useful and detrimental interventions lies? Which criteria are important for a judgement? (LIAKIN).

The limits are changing during the economic development. They depend on the state of the technical progress and on the state of the development of the market. Today the postal monopoly is privatized in Germany. Also in the energy sector monopolies are given up. But it is not clarified yet if this institutions could have developed in a welfare-increasing way without suspension of competition at the time when they were built. Nobody can exactly say, where the limit between useful and detrimental interventions and regulations lies. This is a never ending process of discussion. But from this process of discussion, one can become aware of the necessity of a liberal democratic order, in which the political parties have the right to fight peacefully for their concept of this limit and in which people have the right to choose one concept over another (NÖRR).

It is only a nonrealistic theory that the Social Market Economy is an order of liberty. Material shortages and necessities could produce situations at every time in which one cannot respect liberty. Therefore one needs a powerful government. Liberty is not possible before the abolition of shortage and necessities (PIGROV).

But liberty or freedom is not a sheet of paper, is not a theory. Liberty is a necessity that everybody needs. Without liberty nobody can live with dignity. Liberty is part of the human nature. Liberty is the original nature of the human being in contrast to animals (NÖRR). WATRIN completes that nevertheless it is a rule that the economic development precedes the political development. An analysis of this fact can give hints for the relation of the legal order and the economic order (WATRIN).

KOSLOWSKI adds that the right of private property is a right of liberty, that is more important than the market itself. The market is an instrument which is only efficient with property-rights also in the means of production. In China one wants to introduce a Socialistic Market Economy without private property rights. On the other hand, the theory of "Wirtschaftsstil" (style of the economy) points out that the social subsystems must follow one principle, in our context the principle of the value of liberty. This does not mean that the whole society should act in the same way. Liberty means that everybody can act according to his personal aims. And the free competition of the market makes it possible that everybody can pursue his own aims. The competition of the market is a kind of institutional and peaceful civil war. Where competition is extinguished, a kind of "Rentnertum" (pensioner-hood) and ethos of living on public benefits is threatening, while the competition between the different countries persists. The terror enters in this lack of competition. The terror of the special social aim of one special social group is the alternative to competition (KOSLOWSKI).

DISCUSSION SUMMARY

In Western Europe the liberal societies come from the dualism of church and state. The development of a liberal and free social order is not possible without this dualism (KOSLOWSKI).

BIBIKHIN opposes this concept of competition. If the state makes rules and if the society makes the economy, then we need a general consensus. Without a general consensus no functioning society is possible (BIBIKHIN).

Part B

Social Market Economy
Four Basic Texts

Section I

The Theory of Economic Order

Chapter 14

The Principles of the Social Market Economy (1965)

ALFRED MÜLLER-ARMACK

I

To many people, the Social Market Economy has appeared to be only a compromise - a practical formula for getting through a phase of reconstruction. Under the demands of the time, those who devoted themselves to this system succeeded only rarely in defining exactly its ideological basis. Misunderstandings were the result, and what had been achieved satisfied an easy conformism, while the intellectual efforts on behalf of the Social Market Economy system as a whole receded too far into the background. However, active and constructive organisations are needed for an idea, a style of social policy - which is how I would like to regard the Social Market Economy - if it is to hold its own in the changing circumstances of the times. The idea was taken as a convenient formula also by those parties which adopted the Social Market Economy as their slogan, and they made little effort themselves to understand, or to explain to others, the scope of the Social Market Economy concept. Their task will probably be to occupy themselves more profoundly, more systematically, more actively and more comprehensively with this concept of an order, applying their political will and the facilities available to them in collaboration with science. A social and economic order will only be able to hold its own in the changing circumstances of history, if it takes into account the changes in our overall situation. The achievements of the Social Market Economy in the first few years of the reconstruction of industry, in overcoming shortages, in the growth of income and in full employment, will in the present phase seem a matter of course, to which must now be added fresh objectives following different standards. Over the last few years, I have frequently pointed out that, now that this initial stage is ended, the goals for our order must also be set by problems of social policy. Further economic growth alone is not enough, and it will be relatively unattractive as compared with other kinds of problems that need to be overcome. The following arguments are to be understood in this sense of a comprehensive definition of the essential nature of the Social Market Economy, and an explanation of its future tasks.

II

The Social Market Economy is a social and economic order. It does not affect the great political decisions; but since a substantial part of our life is involved in economic and social relationships, it also has political significance. The whole world is in a state of tension between East and West, and within this framework fixed by the nuclear deterrent of either side, the possibilities for action by the free West are limited. So much more important, therefore, is the deliberate assertion of its inherent form of freedom. The Social Market Economy certainly cannot, and should not, be used as a counter-ideology; yet it is a formula by which the self-knowledge of the West can be organized in a form appropriate to it. If we make a conscious attempt to safeguard our way of life against the East, it is not enough to take this or that pragmatical step; the deliberate organisation of our life under a guiding principle is required much more.

As far as I can see, only two such principles exist at present, which can demonstrate this power of the West to assume new forms as compared with the East: these are European integration and the Social Market Economy. The free West needs to have ideas for integration, as an answer to the challenge of the East that it offers a better solution to social problems. Anyone in

THE PRINCIPLES OF THE SOCIAL MARKET ECONOMY

the West who fails to make the guiding principle absolutely clear, and pursues only day-to-day policy instead, will be no match for the East. Nothing will hit the ideology-bound thinking of the East harder than the clear ability of the West here to find better, more humane, freer and more socially acceptable solutions to life's problems in the modern world. The reaction of the East to the progress made by the European Economic Community - which is gradually being recognized as a new, established fact - shows what possibilities exist if we make clearer also to our own selves the ideas behind our way of life.

III

My attempt to explain the idea behind the Social Market Economy begins with the question as to what the Social Market Economy is. This question may seem to enquire too far; but it is necessary for any understanding of this system. Little is gained by taking as one's starting point the actual words that define a free market economy with social goals and opportunities. This association of words came as a surprise at the time of the naming in 1946, when economic controls and regimentation were asserting their monopoly of social security, and when it seemed paradoxical to see, in a market economy that had deliberately been dismantled for social reasons for a decade, a better order also for the broad masses of the people. It has long been recognized, however, that a deliberately organized free market economy, safeguarded by means of a system regulating competition, gives a surer guarantee of social progress - especially because social progress can be organized all the more effectively on the basis of a free system, through the deliberate elaboration of measures in accord with free market principles and through the redistribution of incomes in the public budgets, when competitive progress forms the economic basis for social measures. Thus, the Social Market Economy does not mean abandoning social measures or measures of social policy. It has been possible to elaborate a perfectly valid system of economic policy, with full co-ordination preserved, to a free market economy whose essential needs are to be given attention.

Confusion has arisen as a result of the similarity to neo-Liberalism. Thus, it is not incomprehensible, but it is wrong, to regard the Social Market Economy merely as a variety of neo-Liberalism. The similarity to neo-Liberalism need not be denied; we have it to thank for many decisive ideas; but whereas neo-Liberalism regards the machinery of competition as the sole principle of organisation, the concept of the Social Market Economy has grown from different roots. These lie in dynamic theory and in philosophical anthropology, both of which were evolved in the '20s, under a different view of the State and a development of the concept of a way of life that was largely rejected by neo-Liberalism. The co-ordinated functions of the Social Market Economy do not conform exclusively to the mechanical rules of competition. Its principles of organisation relate to the State and to society, both of which impress their notions of value and responsibilities on the whole system of the Social Market Economy.

The Social Market Economy is not an exclusive competitive theory; it may best be described as an ideological concept, in the sense that a co-ordination of form is striven after, in the Social Market Economy, between the spheres of life represented by the market, the State and the social groups. Its basis is therefore as much sociological as economic, as much static as dynamic. It is a dialectical concept, in which social goals are equally important as economic goals, and thus combines economic and social policy.

The Social Market Economy is in some cases criticized with the argument that its philosophical background is the nominalistic belief in the mechanism of the free market. I see in this a failure to appreciate the essential nature of the Social Market Economy whose advocates have been particularly concerned, in their researches, to take into account the social system of values - that which exists "beyond supply and demand" - and the religious roots of our political and social convictions[1]. But I do not wish now to make

---

1   Thus, for example, WILHELM ROEPKE, in his books: *Die Gesellschaftskrise der Gegenwart,* Erlenbach-Zürich 1942, 5th ed. 1948, English edition: *The Social Crisis of our Time,* 1950; *Civitas Humana,* Erlenbach-Zürich 1944, 3rd ed. 1949, Engl. ed. 1948; *Mass und Mitte,* (Measure and Mean) Erlenbach-Zürich 1950; *Jenseits von Angebot und Nachfrage*, Erlenbach-Zürich 1958; Engl. ed. *A Humane Economy*, Chicago (Regnery) 1960. - ALEXANDER RUESTOW in the following works: "Zwischen Kapitalismus und Kommunismus" (Between Capitalism and Communism) in: *Ordo,* vol. 2 (1949); "Wirtschaftsethische Probleme der Sozialen Marktwirtschaft" (Problems of Economic Ethics in the Social Market Economy) in: *Der Christ und die Soziale Marktwirtschaft* (The Christian and the Social Market Economy), Stuttgart 1955; *Ortsbestimmung der Gegenwart. Eine universalgeschichtliche Kulturkritik* (Determining the Position

THE PRINCIPLES OF THE SOCIAL MARKET ECONOMY

the opposite mistake and refer to the Social Market Economy as a system derived from specific theological and philosophical convictions. This raises the question of the position of the Social Market Economy particularly in relation to Christian economic doctrine, which attempts to provide from theology a basis for prescriptive economic policy. The last decade has brought a great number of attempts to evolve standards for our social life, by both Protestants and the Catholic Church. I should like to mention here the memorandum "Eigentumsfrage in sozialer Verantwortung" (Questions of Property and Social Responsibility), published by the "Rat der Evangelischen Kirche in Deutschland" (Evangelical Church Council in Germany), and the social encyclicals by the Pope, "Mater et Magistra". In the evolution of Europe, the physical expression of social responsibility has always unmistakably acquired its real depth from the basis of religious faith. No social order can exist without being based upon a sense of values, which is the pre-condition also for one's responsibility for one's fellow men. The mechanism of the free market tends rather to feed on the value-basis than to be able

---

of the Present. A cultural critique against the background of world history), Stuttgart 1950-55. - Of my own works, I shall mention only: A. MUELLER-ARMACK: "Die Wirtschaftsordnungen sozial gesehen" (Economic Systems from the Social Aspect) in: *Ordo*, vol. 1 (1948); *Wirtschaftslenkung und Marktwirtschaft* (Economic Controls and the Free Market Economy), 2nd ed. Hamburg 1948; "Stil und Ordnung der Sozialen Marktwirtschaft" (The Form and System of the Social Market Economy) in: Lagler-Messner (Eds.): *Wirtschaftliche Entwicklung und soziale Ordnung* (Economic Development and the Social Order), Vienna 1952; "Soziale Marktwirtschaft" (The Social Market Economy) in: *Handwörterbuch der Sozialwissenschaften* (Compendious Dictionary of the Social Sciences), vol. 9, Stuttgart, Tübingen, Göttingen 1953; "Wirtschaftspolitik in der Sozialen Marktsvirtschaft" (Economic Policy in the Social Market Economy) in: *Der Christ und die Soziale Marktwirtschaft* (The Christian and the Social Market Economy), Stuttgart 1955; *Religion und Wirtschaft. Geistesgeschichtliche Hintergründe unserer europäischen Lebensform* (Religion and the Economy. Backgrounds in the history of ideas to our European way of life), Stuttgart 1959; "Soziale Marktwirtschaft nach einem Jahrzehnt ihrer Erprobung" (The Social Market Economy after a Decade on Trial) in: *Wirtschaftspolitische Chronik* (Chronicle on Economic Policy), Nos. 2-3 (1959) and in: *Studien zur Sozialen Marktwirtschaft, Untersuchungen des Instituts fur Wirtschaftspolitik an der Universitat zu Köln*, Nr. 12 (Studies by the Institute for Economic Policy at the University of Cologne, No. 12), Cologne 1960.

to enrich it, or even replace it. However irreplaceable the function of Christian awareness of our problems in society may be, it seems to me to be equally necessary, on the other hand, to stress the relative independence of the system through which this function is exercised. The society in which we live is a pluralistic society with Catholics, Protestants, Jews and the secular living together. These different groups can provide ideas on the question of their general order of society; but the organisational problem of a free order of society lies in the fact that different value systems must exist side by side under it, without it being possible for any one group to be granted a total claim to represent all. The Christian social orders, too, relate to a society that embraces different groups and notions of value. For example, the Christian social doctrines include concepts of a universal order, concerning the whole of society, in addition to their religious basis. But an order derived from the substance of a specific faith can hardly answer the needs of this pluralistic society. Thus, although the social orders must satisfy the essential requirements of Christians - i.e. they must be so constituted that Christians can bear their responsibility under them - it will not be possible, within the sphere of our social policy, to accept or reject specific systems according to their particular theological basis.

What, then, is the Social Market Economy as a guiding basis for economic and social policy? It is an order that absorbs values, but does not itself fix them, and to this extent it has no theological basis. It is thus a mode of behaviour in our world, striving towards a specific way of solving social problems.

Let us consider this problem rather more closely. Our society is a whole in which some groups strive more after their freedom, and the others more after social security; in which all are interested in growth, but only to the extent that their private "milieu" is not disturbed too much. We may speak simply of a "magic triangle" - as frequently happens in monetary and foreign trade theory - whose corners represent the objectives of personal freedom, economic and social security and growth. In the past, these conflicting objectives have created a situation of social conflict, through one attempting in each case to succeed at the expense of the others. This led to extreme forms of radical liberal or radical interventionistic social objectives, but also to the expedient of rigid adherence to the traditional, or to the chaotic combination of all principles, as has occurred in State intervention in economic affairs.

The Social Market Economy is not a philosophy of the value-basis of our society; it leaves this to the system of standards by which judgements are made on a religious or philosophical basis. It is, rather, the concept of an irenical order - a strategic idea within the conflict of different objective-situations. It is a formula for a way of life, by which an attempt is made to bring the essential aims of our society into a new, practical harmony, never before achieved.

Experience has shown that this goal, which seems almost obvious, requires a very finely-drawn concept of an order. The Social Market Economy is an integration formula by which an attempt is made to lead the crucial forces of our modern society into genuine co-operation. This situation of tension in society cannot be regarded as a static tension that could be met by a once-for-all combination of free enterprise and social security. The situation of conflict and tension in our society is, of course, subject to the changing circumstances of history, and requires continual renewal of the strategic formulae for this harmonisation in each particular case, in order that they may be adequate for their task. The Social Market Economy is thus a strategy in the social sphere; whether it is successful and achieves its aim can never be exactly determined - it will be confirmed only in the continuing process of the solution of those internal conflicts in our society that we must accept as a fact. In an initial phase of its existence, the Social Market Economy has, I believe, solved this problem of easing tension in Central Europe and has radiated its political effects outwards.

The essence of the Social Market Economy lies in producing - beyond the solution of a restorative policy which preserves the past, or economic controls which stunt free initiative in society, or an uncontrolled, unregulated market mechanism- a social solution in which all objectives are brought into a workable, realistic harmony. It is an irenical formula, not a Utopian approach which sets about the social problems from any aspect by using power, interventions, economic controls, conservatism or faith in a harmony to be automatically achieved.

The integration formula of the Social Market Economy is applicable generally as such; but it stands and acquires its fruitfulness in the situation of our modern society. Its position is due to the unparalleled speeding-up of production development in all fields by technology, and to a mass society, mobilized and threatened by this development, striving for harmony within the framework of a free world. The value of this formula is confirmed by our experience that such a course - stabilizing the modern mass society on the paths of a free system - is possible in principle. This does not mean fixing a basis that sets the path for all time, but one pointing a road that must be taken now. It is the task not only of making the upheaval of modern development tolerable for the mass society, but also of enabling all of it at the same time to share in the achievements of this development.

IV

As an irenical formula, as a comprehensive conception the Social Market Economy not only embraces an economic order co-ordinated by the market; the adjective "social" also indicates that this system also pursues social objectives. The precise significance of this social policy aspect has not yet become very clear in the initial phase of the creation of the Social Market Economy. The social effects of the operation of a competitive system were observed with surprise; but people otherwise rested content with a narrower interpretation of the word "social", in the sense of older social policy - assisting certain economically handicapped classes. However, it seems to me now to be time to give greater prominence to the social goals of the Social Market Economy. With the rise in the standard of living of the mass of the people, the picture changes, and the very needy classes become concentrated in specific groups. To the extent that the problem of income distribution has been satisfactorily solved and, with the almost generalized consumption of many modern luxuries and semiluxuries, the consumption dividing-lines in society are disappearing, the social problem is shifting at the same time. Full employment has been achieved, and the European countries are approaching self-sufficiency, but in this very process of the objective solution of shortageproblems through the existing economic system, an uneasiness, a "malaise", can be felt. However foolish its manifestations may be at times, this is a factor and points to a deeper problem of our social life, which has achieved much with full employment, but is nevertheless still a long way from a state of social harmony. The upheaval of our technical development, and the structural changes in our productive system, do more than is needed to destroy past social forms, and remind us of the need to find a new social harmony.

THE PRINCIPLES OF THE SOCIAL MARKET ECONOMY

V

What, then, is the guiding principle for social policy of the Social Market Economy? The view attributed to Liberalism - that a free market economy is, as it were, itself a substitute for a social policy in the sense of the formation of social positions and human relationships is certainly misleading. The machinery of competition must indeed be considered an indispensable means of co-ordinating the plans of individuals and of firms, and of allowing them to become mutually adjusted; Franz Böhm has pointed this out very effectively[2]. Co-ordination can have a remedial social effect, in the sense of establishing human relationships and mitigating social conflicts. Competition can diminish positions of monopoly and power, and bring about a rise in the incomes of the mass of the people; but it is still a mechanical process, indifferent to values and goals. Although we must already support the working of the free market, in accordance with modern thinking, by means of an active cyclical and growth policy in its mechanical functions, this is even more true of the guiding principle for social policy, which we can evolve only from the highest objectives and values. What the idea of the Social Market Economy has contributed to this principle is the technique of creating a particular social policy, and the answer to the question as to how disparate social objectives can be reduced to a workable common denominator.

In the discussions among our own circles, and among the wider German public, we must start from the fact that, following a phase of economic reconstruction and an advance, beyond all expectations, towards a higher standard of living and improved social conditions, the Social Market Economy is now entering a second phase in which, while all that has been begun is being continued, everything must take on a new accent. It is my belief that we should try, with careful intellectual preparation, to embark upon a second phase of the Social Market Economy in which the problem of social policy must be given prominence, in so far as the economic problems appear to be solved, or soluble in the growth of the next few years.

What can be said, at this stage, about such a policy of the Social Market Economy? It has been said already: its objective is to establish the triangle of

---

[2] FRANZ BOEHM: *Die Ordnung der Wirtschaft als geschichtliche Aufgabe und rechtsschöpferische Leistung* (Organization of the Economy as a Historical Problem and Legislative Achievement), Stuttgart 1937.

tension between growth, personal freedom and initiative and social equilibrium, embracing the whole complex of social security, from full employment to individual assistance.

VI

When I speak here of a guiding principle of social policy for the Social Market Economy, this does not mean planning any rational, religious, socialistic or liberal ideal order. We have been amply supplied during the last few centuries with ideals of this kind, which, unlike the real situation, did not lose their intellectual brilliance or their attraction, it is true; but they did forfeit their effectiveness. We meet with social reality which is a network of relationships in a society that is free, but impressed with the stamp of numerous groups and special attitudes, disputes and agreements. The task of social policy must be to provide, for this view of our society, an integration formula which - although neither precluding departures, differences or disputes, nor promising their final solution - nevertheless intervenes constructively, in order to constrain as much tension as possible and produce a realistic basis for joint action. The Social Market Economy - if we take this idea seriously - seems to me to be synonymous with the conviction that it is possible to attempt to overcome the antithesis of social progress and free enterprise - as we have done in the last decade - also in the wider context of society as a whole.

The social guiding principle of the Social Market Economy is aimed at the whole of society, and so we must endeavour to supplement the problems that are forced to the forefront in day-to-day policy with future objectives evolved on the basis of this society. Special structural problems of the "middle classes"[3], the farmers and the workers, do indeed exist; but we must not lose sight of the questions that embrace all groups. At the same time, I would point out that the improvement in the sphere of public tasks in the widest sense - of what I would like to call the "environmental conditions" of society, is also perfectly compatible with full operation of the free market

---

3 "Mittelschichten" - i. e., owners of small and medium-sized enterprises, and craftsmen. (Translator's Note.)

THE PRINCIPLES OF THE SOCIAL MARKET ECONOMY

economy. In the field of financial policy, these conditions are expressed in the public services and capital projects (one speaks of "infrastructure" in a sense that is usually very closely related to the economic field). The destruction of the matured environment of our towns and cities, villages and rural districts by traffic, and the chaotic development of our towns and rural settlements, makes an effort necessary, supported by the power of all public bodies and of society, to bring this environment into harmony with the people once more - also under modern conditions. The sphere of intellectual investments in its widest sense needs the strongest possible support. To the extent that social aid becomes dispensable among the rising classes, our policy should meet the unavoidable obligation to improve our social environment, side by side with the impressive increase in our production and supply of goods.

If this goal is not taken as paying mere lip-service, but as a serious proposition, then a general social policy that is not to ignore the fact of the stratification of our society also needs to be supplemented by efforts on behalf of particular classes, in so far as no special rights for certain groups are thereby created. The idea that the middle classes or the farmers, too, could reach their economic and social positions on the basis of competition, as it were, seems to me to be just as wrong as the other view, that social policy could evolve under the protection of such groups. I consider the theory of the Social Market Economy to be perfectly compatible with the granting of adjustment subsidies to secure for those sectors of the economy that are particularly exposed to the pressure of economic forces, or under pressure from competing products or larger markets - such as agriculture, mining, the textiles industry - the transition to a new, acceptable position. In the Social Market Economy, we must accept economic and technical progress, but also the possibility of any necessary adjustments - by means of subsidies and tax relief, say - in order to facilitate constructively the transition to the new competitive situation. Although it would be wrong to go against the broad market trends, a wide field nevertheless still exists here, for those concerned with economic policy who have ideas, to reduce social tensions in the transition period, without abandoning the concept of a general order for society which we must take as our basis. Thus, the social policy must not be based only upon a guiding principle as to the form of social life we are to strive for in the long term; it must at the same time investigate the continuing process of transformation of our society, and find in reasonable control of the processes which we can predict, and whose course we can shape with less tension

- the workable solution between simply allowing the transformation to take place, and resisting development in favour of particular classes. At the same time, it must direct its attention not only to maintaining an independent middle-class as large as possible, but also devote special attention to the process of becoming independent and of individual social advancement within the group of workers and salaried employees. The emergence of the large-scale organisation has greatly diminished the opportunity to become self-supporting and advance oneself. Offering initial aid in these cases, facilitating advancement to skilled workman status, providing workers with an opportunity to become salaried employees, must be the objective of a social policy that rests on the notion of keeping ours a free society as far as possible. In the day-to-day work of economic and financial policy, a great many goals of social policy are already being achieved today. No one will object to such efforts, if they are founded upon an overall concept of society. Even though the realization of the basic principles about which we are writing here may be only a remote goal, it would be wrong to leave this work to the future. It must begin immediately, side by side with the day-to-day work, in order to give the latter work shape and direction, and prevent the ultimate social goal from fading into mere ideology.

VII

In the discussions on social policy of the last few years, wealth formation has been prominent as the means towards a new social policy. During the last few years, the growth of income of the mass of the people has gone so far that the increase in wages and salaries has made remuneration in Germany the highest of all the EEC countries, even allowing for the rise in prices. If the boom can be safeguarded against set-backs, then what has not yet been achieved in this field today can be accomplished within a few years. This would be so, if people became interested in wealth accumulation, which is undoubtedly an excellent means of giving the individual in our mass society, through saving, a more secure position with home-ownership and savings. It is not questionable to concentrate the forms of saving on smaller units of shares and debentures, to give the individual saver easier access to actual capital assets. It does not seem open to question, either, to offer those

THE PRINCIPLES OF THE SOCIAL MARKET ECONOMY

who are first to be induced to save, initial aid - in the form of bonuses or tax relief - corresponding to the many forms of relief for wealth formation by the self-supporting that have been made available by fiscal policy in the last few years. What is questionable is to permit wealth formation through uncontrolled and unregulated tax privileges.

The growth in income affects monetary policy. Continually rising prices - particularly in the field of house-building, which is the primary object of saving - mean a gradual reduction of wealth barely offset by relatively high interest rates. Thus, over wide areas, a pre-condition for successful wealth formation is a relatively strict policy of financial stability. It is certainly a Utopian ideal to wish to combine the advantages of permanent prosperity with those of absolute stability in the value of money. The upward movement of our wages, salaries and pensions is offset by the unavoidable rise in prices in the sphere of income growth.

One thing seems to me to emerge from what has already been said, and this is that income policy is only *one* objective of a social policy under free enterprise. It would be taking too narrow a view to regard material wealth formation of this sort as the key to social policy. Shaping the social environment, safeguarding the actual group to which the individual belongs, safeguarding his independence, his opportunities for advancement and the improvement of human relations in industry, are objectives of equal - if not far greater - importance. The uneasiness experienced by people in spite of all the economic achievements in our society cannot be banished by property alone. A special problem in this connection is the question whether what is known to the general public as the "Investivlohn" will secure for the worker a share in wealth formation in industry. Like the profit-sharing by the workers in industry that was also frequently discussed earlier, this notion arose from a special cyclical situation. In a period of relatively low competitive pressure, profit-sharing was intended to secure for the worker a share in the rich profits of business. There was no fear at that time that this would influence the level of prices. The idea of the "Investivlohn" emerged in a situation of much greater competitive pressure, in which it was feared that a further rise in prices would be induced through wages outstripping productivity. The aim behind the idea is one of distribution policy - viz., to secure a larger share in aggregate wealth formation. At the same time, the intention is to prevent price-rises, by splitting wages into a wage-increase kept within the bounds of the increased productivity, and an investment portion.

There is thus every reason to urge caution over this questionable approach to a new wage policy. I believe that the present system of our wage policy can by all means continue to function, with the autonomy of employers and employed within the framework of the Social Market Economy - provided, however, that the concept of a restrictive financial policy can be effectively enforced, and a damping-down achieved in house-building, which is systematically financed beyond its capacity from public funds and through tax privileges. It seems to me to be wrong to change the system of our wage policy (and the change would apply to only some of the employees), because of uneasiness over the period of a few years, in which prices have risen for very clear reasons. It should be remembered that we have succeeded, within a few years, in raising German wages among the highest in Europe. I see in this an achievement for the Social Market Economy. No new system should be introduced, especially as the free market forces at work internally and from outside have long been worsening the profit situation of firms and, in addition, stabilizing the price and wage situation. It would probably be dangerous to introduce a further element here.

A restrictive financial policy, and the limitation of housebuilding to the necessary level of its capacity should, in conjunction with reasonable agreements between trade unions and employers, suffice to check a danger which would probably not fail to react on our market, with its international ties. This would help no-one, neither unions nor employers. The "Investivlohn" system seems to me to conflict with the idea of the Social Market Economy, in that its technique involves it in direct intervention in market operations, and it could have consequences not yet foreseeable today. At the same time, I wholeheartedly approve of the aims of those who would like to bring wealth to the mass of the people; but this seems to me to be more lastingly assured by the steady increase in real wages, which I believe to be without parallel in economic history. Any necessary correction should be made, according to the principle of the Social Market Economy, clearly, deliberately and under control, through national redistribution of incomes - i.e., by taxing those whose increase in income is considered too large, and favouring those whose wealth accumulation is desired to promote. I would therefore strongly advocate the extension of Government measures to encourage saving. But to introduce an incommensurable factor into the clear distinction between costs, prices and profits would spoil considerably the clarity which the calculation of market prospects must have. I can see little sense in attempting to solve problems of monetary policy by re-arranging income policy. The problems of monetary policy today must be clearly attacked where they arise - in financial policy and in building construction.

VIII

If we analyze the factors of our current position properly, it seems to me inevitable that we should take a more comprehensive view, in the sense of social policy, of the problems of the second phase of the Social Market Economy, now beginning. This is not a matter of a personal liking for innovation; it is in accord with the observation that past reasons - especially those of overcoming shortages and of pure growth - are losing their importance. The very fact of success makes much of what has been achieved be taken for granted. Under prosperity, the centrifugal forces of our society are perceptibly increasing and make extra effort necessary, to integrate our social order. The democratization of consumption and the consistence, with general growth, of all the basic interests of nearly all groups - proved by experience - offer a basis upon which such a policy can be pursued. I have pointed out the practical problems of such a policy elsewhere, in my publication, "Soziale Marktwirtschaft II. Teil" (The Second Part of the Social Market Economy)[4]. However, I believe that it is sound policy not to allow the idea of a fundamental new system for our Social Market Economy to be lost in details at the very beginning. Details are important; but in the beginning, the basic ideological decision must be taken as to whether we wish to act with a view to establishing a harmonious structure for our society, or whether economic policy is to seek its cure in supplementary laws and day-to-day policy. I do not ask that the emphasis should be shifted to general measures of social policy, attaching less importance to economic policy measures. An economic policy pursued under the economic-order concept will invariably also be social policy, anyway. I shall mention monetary policy here. Monetary stability is an excellent means of establishing stability in our society. Creeping inflation will cast doubts once more on any effort towards wealth formation

---

4 In: *Studien zur Sozialen Marktwirtschaft* (Studies on the Social Market Economy), loc. cit., p. 23.

if, owing to depreciation of the currency, it is counteracted by a reduction of wealth not generally visible, but undeniable.

Today, the notion of currency stability is inextricably bound up with cyclical policy. Much is said about it; but in my opinion, too little action is taken. It is not so much a question here of statistics, with which we are adequately supplied. To the extent that, with the full development of productive resources, the upward adjustment of business activity seems no longer to be so assured as hitherto, more institutionalization of cyclical policy, and expansion of the means to implement it, are needed. A committee of experts can do useful work, it is true; in addition, however, the institutional co-operation within the Government must be organized on a permanent basis, and intellectual and practical preparation is needed - especially in the field of financial and credit policy - in order to achieve that progress which seems to me to be indicated, in view of the clear experience of the past. Here, too, the cyclical policy of the Social Market Economy is faced with the task of achieving the "magic triangle" formed by the objectives of currency stability, growth and full employment and also equilibrium in the balance of payments. The experience of economists over the last four decades seems to me to provide sufficient bases for an acceptable compromise between these objectives - which conflict with one another to some extent, but can be brought into harmony in a carefully thought-out scheme. Some years ago, I formulated for international cyclical policy a code of proper cyclical behaviour, which was approved by all the European countries in the OECD. The intellectual preparatory work should be carried much further, also for national cyclical policy, by the appropriate committees. This is not only a question of economic policy; it is at the same time a genuine objective of social policy, since without any development of economic policy in this direction, we shall not be able to allay the uncertainty of the individual - continually aroused by the rapid market changes and by the inevitable changes in the market situation - who belongs to a large-scale concern with a structure that he only imperfectly comprehends.

A discussion has arisen as to whether a greater degree of economic planning is not indicated here. I do not think so. Admittedly, it has become fashionable to cite "Le Plan", and the view that essential elements of the free market economy must be sacrificed to the conception of a national budget is often associated with the demands for improvement of our econometric data. This discussion seems to me to go astray. A free market economy rests upon the plans of individuals, who may plan for the short term, as income-recipients do; but even the building of a house requires planning some time ahead here, as well. Large firms - in petroleum and coal or the motor industry, for example - must make fairly long-term plans for their capital projects, and in my opinion, there is nothing against the Government, too, formulating its short-term budgetary policy at longer term with regard to certain fields such as transport and building. A review of market prospects exists for the next year and the year following. We have always done this in the reports to the OECD, achieving very exact results on the basis of the German statistical material - which is certainly as good as that of the planning-minded countries, is not better. The clear distinction that must be observed, however - because of the concept of the Social Market Economy system - lies in the fact that forecasts, especially those relating to individual fields, are not bound to be fulfilled, so that in the event of the anticipated figures not being reached, any measures taken do not paralyse the market. It seems necessary here that supporters of the Social Market Economy should not allow themselves to be forced on the defensive. The progress made in the last few years - also in France, where "Le Plan" has been applied for more than a decade - is so clearly connected with free market procedure (with the Rueff reform, in France), that there is no reason here for holding back the free market concept.

Economic stability cannot be sought in the stability of individual factors, prices and wages. It aims at a dynamic stability, a harmony in growth, which makes more complex demands than a mere requirement of stability.

IX

If a conception of social policy of this kind is seriously to be sought, it requires the other fields of our modern policy to be studied again very carefully on this basis. In social policy, it is a question, on the one hand, of drawing the conclusions from a social policy aimed at all strata of society and, on the other hand, of attempting in certain fields to give the individual - in part, at least - greater self-responsibility, so as to enable social aid to be concentrated more on the really needy cases. The mere extension of social security, overlooking or ignoring the changes that have occurred in the meantime, is not an up-to-date solution.

ALFRED MÜLLER-ARMACK

The distinct development of our competitive policy - which is also to be placed on the Common Market basis, anyway - must be continued. Here again, in the planning of a statically conceived competitive order, such as that all which the concept of neo-Liberalism was based, it should be understood that, in an economy already undergoing dynamic re-organisation through the Common Market, the mere principle of persisting with a system competitive in form is not sufficient. The changes of location and shifts of emphasis that await important sectors of our production in the expanding EEC markets and the Atlantic co-operation now under way, cannot be brought about without some degree of adaptive intervention by the Government. It is a matter here of maintaining the principle of the free, competitive economy, but at the same time, of providing the temporary initial aid and aid for adaptation, with which the conscience of the entrepreneur does not need to be burdened for any longer than is needed for him to move to the ultimate objective of the free market. We have provided aid of this kind in the Federal Republic, in the capital assistance given during the years 1952-59. The aid was successful, because it was deliberately developed from the very beginning as a means of achieving free market status.

X

In the initial stage of its elaboration, we regarded the Social Market Economy as a specifically German form of overcoming the problems of reconstruction. The emergence of the common market in the economic community of the Six, and also the anticipated entry and association of other countries in Europe, will henceforth pose for us the question whether we can retain this conception of an order, or what the general system of the European Market is to be. The reticence shown so far, in seeing no export product in the Social Market Economy, has a limit, in view of this widening of our horizon brought about by the market. It is not a question of the name here; but as I interpret the meaning of the Social Market Economy, the real problem in Europe is as follows: A market kept free internally by tariffs, quotas and Government intervention is sheltered externally, it is true, by a certain measure of protectionism, which will be reduced by internal extension of the area of the Market and increasing negotiating pressure from the world out-

THE PRINCIPLES OF THE SOCIAL MARKET ECONOMY

side. Thus, elements of a free market economy will be in conflict to some extent with the forces of an internal expansion that can already be observed, and also with a social protectionism directed both inwards and outwards.

It is the same case of conflicting aims as I have already described as the starting position of the Social Market Economy. It will not be possible to decide this initial situation from one or the other extreme. For Europe as a whole, therefore, it will be necessary to seek the irenical formula which, I am convinced, really constitutes the essence of the Social Market Economy. Europe can no more be surrendered to "laissez-faire" competition than to social planning. Generally speaking, it is faced with the dialectical problem of directing its economic policy towards the objective of social security and to that of free initiative. A dialectical problem of this kind is in itself too complex to be dealt with through day-to-day policy; it requires preparatory work on principles, which must precede any practical work, in so far as it has not already been done in the Treaty of Rome. In the efforts of the Commission on regional policy, social welfare co-ordination, competitive policy and the formulation of a constructive cyclical policy, I see important starting-points in this direction, to which support must be given. The integration of Europe is, in the last analysis, not only a political integration; it postulates integration of the economic systems. Extreme solutions leaving everything to the automatics of a free competition, have no more chance than the attempts of a liberal socialism at cautious planning. The Social Market Economy formula does not mean choosing the pragmatic course of allowing all elements of the prevailing situation to mix together and determine themselves. It points rather to a constructively planned third way to overcome as far as possible the situation, full of conflict, within a common system.

Thus, we in Europe, too, must make an intellectual effort to grasp more deeply the basis of our economic order, and seek the formula for integration of the European society.

This assumes, of course, that we shall begin "in our own house" and get out of the habit of regarding the Social Market Economy as an agreeable, easy formula that is adequately covered by its undisputed success. This formula contains more; it is intended to be an answer to the challenge of our time to put forward, under a free system and in a period of unprecedented development in industry and technology, the full import of its social and structural problems. It should not be a facile, pragmatic formula. A general order of society can only last, in practical politics and in the consciousness of the people to whom it appeals, if it sets standards and evolves up-to-date methods. The hope that we shall fulfil contemporary tasks properly and to the full measure of our powers can grow only from faith in the ideological basis of our society and in its future.

***

First published in: *The German Economic Review: An English Language Quartely on German Economic Research and Current Developments*, 3 (Stuttgart 1965), Nr. 2, pp. 89-104.

Section II

The Ethics of the Economic Order

Chapter 15

The Ethical Content of the Social Market Economy (1988)

OTTO SCHLECHT

I.	An Economic Order for Politically Mature Citizens
II.	Socio-Ethical Safeguards I: General Framework, Competition in Efficiency, Social Equality
III.	Socio-Ethical Safeguards II: Macropolitics, State Contribution to Infrastructure, Ecology
IV.	Social Market Economy and Democracy
V.	A Humane Economic Order

For some time now there has been vocal criticism of the market economic order from both clerical and theological circles. As well as doubts as to the moral dignity of such an order, there has also been talk of structural evil and of idolatry. The tendency to exaggerate in this respect can, to a certain extent, be dismissed as nothing more than overstated demagogy but, nevertheless, if reputable sources are questioning the ethical legitimacy of our economic order it is something that we should take seriously. This is why I hold it to be one of the most important aspects of economic policy that, in addition to dealing with the purely economic problems of efficiency, it deals in a visible manner with the socio-critical questions that are asked in relation to our economic order.

Before I go on to explain in more detail in the form of ten theses why I believe in the social market economy, allow me, as a former Freiburg student, and a former colleague of Ludwig Erhard and Alfred Müller-Armack, to remind you of something that is all too easily forgotten outside the Ludwig Erhard Foundation.

The concept of the Social Market Economy was developed and realised out of, amongst other things, humanist and socio-Christian principles with the intention that it should provide, not only a liberal and humane alternative to the centrally planned state-controlled command economy but also, to the same degree, an alternative to laissez-faire capitalism in its pure form. Forty years ago, I was fascinated by the central regulatory policy question posed by my lecturer Walter Eucken: "How can the modern industrialised society be given a structure that is both capable of functioning and at the same time humane?". Ludwig Erhard's guiding principle was "not the free market economy of the liberalist exploitation of a bygone age nor was it the 'free play of market forces' and such phrases that are frequently to be heard, but, instead, the socially committed market economy within which each individual could once again find their place, where the value of the individual was placed above all else and in which achievement received its just reward". Alfred Müller-Armack postulated that "the new economic order that has to be created .... requires a deeper foundation provided by moral ideals .... We feel bound to two great moral goals, liberty and social justice".

I. An Economic Order for Politically Mature Citizens

Thesis 1. The superiority of the market economy, as opposed to all the other known forms of economic co-ordination, as a means of increasing general affluence lies in the very fact that it places the emphasis on the co-ordination of decentralised decisions on the future of the market taken by individuals who do not require superhuman moral standards. The market economy is based upon sovereign individuals whose free decisions are, first and foremost, restricted by their own sense of responsibility.

What does this mean?

THE ETHICAL CONTENT OF THE SOCIAL MARKET ECONOMY

One of the most commonly held misconceptions against which economists have to fight is the perception of the market economy as a chaotic order that is based on egotistical motives and that apparently lacks any planned control of the allocation of resources, the result being that it is virtually impossible to achieve desirable and, above all, humane objectives. Like everything that functions in an exemplary fashion, the control that is exercised by the mechanism of market prices is virtually imperceptible. However, as if governed by an invisible hand, the market ensures that investment is targeted at those areas that need it most and that markets are cleared, wasteful practices punished and that, for example, goods produced in a European factory using American primary products can be sold to an Australian buyer at a price that no competitor anywhere in the world can better.

The aim of managing a society's economy is to guarantee that the material needs of the members of that society are met and poverty combated. In addition, particularly in an ethical analysis, the system must also provide the necessary basis and leave the necessary scope for the personality of the individual to develop and for human dignity to be upheld. If the material tasks of the market economy are achieved in such an outstanding manner that the results of market economic efficiency are regarded with unconcealed respect, even from within competing economic systems, then this certainly also has an extremely important moral dimension.

The success of the market economy, something which it is entirely possible to judge from an ethical point of view, is based to a large extent on the fact that, in order to function, it relies only on individuals with average moral standards; people of the kind that have inhabited the planet since the Fall of Man, whose main concerns are their own well-being, that of their family, and perhaps their small group in society. It would, however, be a fundamental mistake to confuse a natural level of self-interest with selfishness or pure egoism. A general concern for the needs of distant groups in society is not of vital importance to the functioning of market mechanisms. Indeed, to expect such concern would be a little unrealistic since altruism thrives most on intimate, individual relationships of the kind that are quite simply unimaginable in today's world with its mass societies and economies based on the division of labour.

One could, of course, object that individuals cannot avoid making mistakes altogether and that they are inadequately informed, if not deliberately misinformed, or hindered from exercising their sovereignty by the might of others. This is why it is up to the body public to protect individuals, to protect them from being exploited by others and, if necessary, to protect them from themselves. However, the desire to protect individual civil rights and liberties by encroaching upon these very rights through collective constraints cannot be justified in terms of fundamental Christian principles, nor does it correspond with our concept of democracy. Indeed, if we take it for granted that people have the right to vote and express their views as mature citizens on complex political issues, can we not also expect these same people to take on responsibility for their own economic decisions, in their working lives or when making comparatively simply purchasing decisions?

Thesis 2: Even if the high level of economic efficiency of the market economy stems not least from the fact that it does not place any excessive demands on the morals of individual economic players, the market economic system neither creates a moral vacuum nor can it survive without individual morality.

What does this mean?

In addition, the system still requires sovereign individuals who are willing to take on moral as well as economic responsibility. The ground rules in the market economy will, as Müller-Armack said, "function more effectively the more people there are who seek to develop not only their economic and technical knowledge, but also other qualities required of them in life beyond the market, which they then apply to the economic sphere".

Relations within the market could function a lot more smoothly if nobody sought unfair advantage - if contracts were founded on the mutual provision of frank and honest information or if consumers took account of the consequences on health and the environment of their purchasing decisions, instead of trying to shift ultimate responsibility onto the producers or onto the state.

Yet it is above all in those areas where market mechanisms must be supplemented by forms of collective support, where social morals are particularly important as a means of regulatory control, that this morality is in short supply. The many cases of abuse of the social system, for example, show how quickly collective provisions that reward immoral behaviour can lead to a situation where ethical standards are no longer granted sufficient respect. This slide in human behaviour towards a general "borderline morality", where society ultimately condones everything from minor infringements of the law to corruption, is at its most visible in nations in which coercion and the state's limitation of personal responsibility curb personal freedom but in which the economy is unable to provide for people's basic needs.

One can argue whether this most-posited erosion of values and fall in moral standards exists and, if so, what is at its root. However, I believe we would be mistaken to blame this trend on the fact that the market, more than any other economic order, accords greater scope to individual conscience in its role as the ultimate control mechanism. It is more true to say that, within a liberal economic order based on decentralised decision-making according to individual preferences, there is room for philanthropists and misers, hard workers and dodgers, pioneering entrepreneurs and social drop-outs.

It is not the market but other institutions such as the family, the church and political parties that are charged with making people aware of their own individual responsibility and, at the same time, engaging in dialogue to provide the necessary guidance to enable people to take a responsible approach to their individual freedom. Yet the economic role of the churches and other socio-cultural institutions is in no way restricted to the level of individual ethics. In my opinion, the socio-ethical task facing these institutions is to influence the decisions taken by those participating in the market by creating an economic and regulatory framework with a Christian and humanitarian outlook. The following theses are related to this task of channelling market economic development along a socio-ethical path.

II. Socio-Ethical Safeguards I: General Framework, Competition in Efficiency, Social Equality

Thesis 3. A market economy in its purest form that is left to its own devices neglects essential social tasks. A market economy requires organisation by society.

What does this mean?

In order to ensure that the advantages of individual economic action do not come into conflict with social aims, the common good or the freedom of others, the market process must be channelled into a legal and institutional regulatory framework. This is the only way - whilst avoiding piecemeal state intervention, which can throw the economic order off balance - to achieve a synthesis between liberty and solidarity. And here finally one can begin to see the ethical content of the social market economy.

OTTO SCHLECHT

Far from having a weak role, the state does in fact play an extremely strong role in any social market economy. And this in two respects; firstly, in order to provide the market economic order with its inner legitimacy, a state must be a determined guarantor of the conditions required for a market economy to function, must create a stable currency as a means of exchange, unit of account and a store of value, create genuine competition based on performance, and stabilise the economic process in such a way that the fruits of immense economic efforts and the revenue amassed over several lifetimes cannot be wiped out by a few years of economic crisis, hence stripping the young of any prospects for the future. And, secondly, for a state to claim moral legitimacy, it must face up to its responsibility by solving those social tasks that can not be solved by the market and competition in a socially acceptable manner, such as, for example, protecting the weaker members of society or conserving our natural environment.

And although it is necessary for a pure market economy to be regulated by an active state, if it is to be called a Social Market Economy, in practice it is extremely difficult to implement this task without, at the same time, overloading the market mechanism to the extent that is incapable of functioning to its full advantage. It is probably the "fascination with the immediate" inherent in ad-hoc intervention by the state tailored to the needs of specific one-off problems that makes it difficult to recognise that the state can do more for the achievement of social goals by establishing, shaping and securing the regulatory framework than it can by permanently intervening on the markets and in the private spheres of responsibility of entrepreneurs, employees and consumers.

However a closer look at many instances of intervention reveals that although each intervention considered in isolation may well appear to be an appropriate reaction from the state in line with conventional values, the state's activity is in fact often nothing more than a sign of its weakness, a retreat in the face of pressure from some particularist economic interest. On the other hand, recognising privatisation, deregulation, reduction in state ownership, abolition of subsidies, guaranteeing free international trade of goods and services as active measures on the part of the state to support the market economic order is obviously much more difficult.

Thesis 4. The market economy only remains an ethical and socially justifiable order on which freedom can flourish if it is based on competition in efficiency.

What does this mean?

THE ETHICAL CONTENT OF THE SOCIAL MARKET ECONOMY

This thesis was one that, out of all the intellectual founders of the Social Market Economy, Franz Böhm particularly emphasised. In addition, the late Cardinal Höffner (also awarded a PhD in political sciences from Freiburg University), speaking during a remarkable presentation in Innsbruck, stated that freedom of competition and competition in efficiency had ethical legitimacy provided they were facilitated and secured by the existence of a regulatory framework.

In other words, for competition to be a regulatory factor it must operate within an efficient legal framework. Competition can only truly exist when certain basic liberties are guaranteed: freedom to choose a profession, freedom to trade, freedom of consumption, freedom of contract including the right to set prices freely. Ludwig Erhard's great achievement in terms of regulatory policy was his success in reactivating the price mechanism on the market. It is only if the prices of both products and factors of production are set freely that competition can be truly effective, ensuring an economy is dynamic and able to adjust to changing situations and - vitally important to the issue at hand - ensuring that achievement receives its just reward and that effective curbs are imposed on economic might.

The power to enforce unjustified prices in the name of self-interest or to enter into unreasonable business contracts is automatically excluded in a system where economic freedom and competition constitute the norm. Competition, described so pithily by Franz Böhm as the "most inspired tool in history for stripping away power" therefore becomes a constituent element of our economic order. Nevertheless, competition also becomes the Achilles' heel of the market economic order since the market lacks the perfect device for precluding automatism capable of excluding any concentration of power that could destroy the market. There is no built-in immune system.

That said, the market does in fact regularly succeed in frustrating attempts to achieve a concentration of power. This presupposes the existence of markets that are open both inwardly and outwardly. The history of OPEC illustrates this point particularly well. Nevertheless, it would be a direct contradiction of our values, not to say politically unwise, if we were to simply wait and see whether the market will, of its own accord, smash any emerging or existing concentration of power. Even if, in the longer term, this should be the case, the damage that could be done in the meantime through a paralysis of the market would be of unacceptable proportions. This is why the economic order must be equipped with effective tools to guarantee that profits and scarcity-induced income retain their function of promoting performance and raising efficiency, instead of escalating out of all proportion simply because, for example, shortages have been artificially engineered due to monopolies and cartels capturing and abusing market power.

The law to combat limitations on competition, introduced over thirty years ago now, strengthened our economic order's immune system, injecting it with a shot of ethics, so to speak. In view of subsequent economic and structural change, checks must still be carried out regularly to verify whether, true to the spirit of the original fundamental ideas, the existing body of legislation is still capable of guaranteeing effective competition and preventing concentrations that could hamper this in any way. It would, however, be a considerable error if, in the years to come, the trend towards the reformulation of what Ludwig Erhard correctly described as the "basic law of the Social Market Economy" into a law providing protection from competition and enabling individual sectors to promote particularistic interests were to increase and eventually win the day.

Thesis 5. Social equality is far more than a fundamentally alien appendage to the system. Rather, it is an essential integral component of the Social Market Economy.

What does this mean?

"The concept of the Social Market Economy constitutes an attempt to create a synthesis between an awareness of the indispensability of the phenomenon of the market and the wish to reconcile this market economic organisational structure with social progress" (A. Müller-Armack). Market economic efficiency and social equality are therefore very closely interrelated in what is a basically harmonious relationship, but not one that is completely free of friction. Without efficient economic management it is impossible to raise the enormous level of funding required to provide a dignified and socially acceptable livelihood for those who, under market conditions, are not in a position to earn their own living, be it on a temporary basis or in the longer term.

Within the concept of the Social Market Economy, the principle of subsidiarity governs the provision of social security, which certainly does not contradict our traditional fundamental ethical beliefs, especially as the ability of individuals to look after their own needs rises in line with the general level of prosperity. Market economic efficiency, on the other hand, is founded on the acceptance of an economic order that has as its prerequisites social security, the abolition of social barriers, and a fair distribution of wealth, just as much as social co-responsibility. This is why it is justifiable to talk about social consensus as the fourth factor of production.

The symbiotic relationship outlined above between social equality and market economic efficiency is not without certain limits. These limits are reached whenever the social framework and the redistribution of wealth jeopardise the production potential of the economy as a whole, since the economic system of incentives ceases to operate and the individual responsibility of the citizens is worn down. John Stuart Mill raised this problem in very clear terms some time ago when he said that the problem that has to be solved is both a very delicate and a very important one - how to give the greatest amount of required help whilst creating the least possible incentive to become dependent on this assistance. In both the 1970s and the 1980s the system began to come up against these limits.

The task of pulling the market economic order into a "social straitjacket" is one that arises time and time again as the prevailing social conditions change. Social security and security in terms of labour law not to mention our system of industrial co-determination have now become well-established components of our "social labour-based economy". The "social capital-based economy" on the other hand, could be expanded further. The more intensive participation of the workforce in production capital and the revenue it brings, the importance of which is even greater in a regulatory policy context than it is in the social context, still leaves a lot to be desired, despite the effect affluence has had on people's ability to save and state policies to promote investment and savings. However, this development is necessary if the opposing interests in our society are to be reconciled, if equal opportunities are to be placed on a better footing, and if the consensus for an incomes policy that is in line with employment and that takes account of the need for sufficient income from venture capital is to be strengthened.

III. Socio-Ethical Safeguards II: Macropolitics, State Contribution to Infrastructure, Ecology

Thesis 6. Given that there is no way of guaranteeing pre-stabilised harmony, market control of prices, volumes etc. - in other words micro-relations

– needs to be complemented by a macropolicy oriented towards the economy as a whole in the interests of stability and employment.

What does this mean?

Although the persistently high levels of unemployment, which have not yet been tackled radically enough despite a continual increase in actual employment levels since 1983, could perhaps be regarded as the greatest challenge facing the market economy, I will resist the temptation to try and tackle this subject in a comprehensive manner and in concrete terms. Instead, I want to limit myself to more general comments on stabilisation policy.

Dynamic economic development has, so far, always occurred in waves, albeit waves of varying intensity. However, fluctuations in supply and demand do not always occur with sufficient speed for the payment of social security benefits (in this case unemployment benefit) to be a sufficient expression of society's solidarity with those affected. The main task of macroeconomic policy is to create favourable conditions for investment and innovation within the framework of a growth strategy geared towards the medium term. Nevertheless, the economic timing of such a measure cannot be ignored.

Above all, whenever a cyclical recession threatens to degenerate into a cumulative downturn or when there is dramatic malfunctioning in the economy as a whole, it falls to the state to adopt macroeconomic measures. Indeed, the current government coalition met this demand on taking power in autumn 1982 with the introduction of its emergency programme. By bringing forward sections of its planned overhaul of the tax system to 1988 it was able to meet both its responsibility to take control of the current economic situation and to comply with the need to improve the overall economic conditions for growth and jobs.

But in pursuing an anticyclical policy it is also a matter of maintaining a balance and acting to ensure that any necessary corrections made to the market economic process do not themselves generate serious disruption or have a negative impact on the basic fibre of the economic order. We are still suffering today from the fact that, in the euphoria over demand management, the maintenance of the supply side was neglected and the technical policy used degenerated, to a certain extent, into nothing more than fiscal interventionism. This is not to say that we should throw the baby out with the bath water and do away with demand management altogether. Instead, what we must do is display a willingness to learn from our mistakes. For example, we ought to have learnt by now that, in the end, the state cannot relieve employers and trade unions of their responsibility when misguided income policies have consequences on the economy as a whole.

Thesis 7. The provision of financing for infrastructural development ranks among the complementary functions to be fulfilled by the state in a Social Market Economy.

What does this mean?

Ever since the emergence of the theory of external effects, if not before, we have known why market exchange driven by self-interest is not capable of generating infrastructural projects - educational facilities or transport routes for example - in either sufficient quantity, of high enough quality or with the necessary measure of concern for vital environmental aspects. The fact that the market economic order also requires complementary state activities in these areas is something that has been virtually undisputed since the days of Adam Smith. However, what has been steeped in major controversy has been the issue of the scale on which state activities of this kind should take place.

The state of public services supply is lamented as being insufficient and of excessively poor quality, usually by contrasting it starkly with the alleged surplus of private goods. And it is not unusual for the neat thesis of public poverty and private profligacy, as put by Galbraith, to be used to draw the conclusion that the market economic order has failed, hence casting doubts on a further central element of its ethical content. However, I do not believe that this conclusion is correct - on the contrary, the contrast between public and private achievement highlights the superiority and efficiency of free market decentralised co-ordination as opposed to bureaucratic management and spoon-feeding. As a result, not only should the extent of public services be examined in detail over and over again in terms of regulatory policy but the efficiency of market economic mechanisms should also be exploited as far as possible wherever the supply of public goods and services is concerned (competitive tendering for example). It is not market failure but state failure that is the problem here.

Thesis 8. Protecting God's own creation by securing our natural environment is one of the central ethical postulates, if not the greatest challenge facing the responsible individual and society in the industrial age.

What does this mean?

The ethical content of the market economic order would indeed be in an extremely bad way were ecology and economy really as irreconcilable as is so often claimed. Of course, many viewpoints and the comparison with the functioning of socialist economic systems in practice clearly appear to prove that, given the prevailing conditions in terms of technology and civilisation, there is no form of economic system better suited to solving environmental problems than a socially tempered market economy. Wasteful production and consumption, as I have already pointed out, are kept in check by competition, unless no price is placed on environmental goods, which are in fact in scarce supply, and these are wrongly regarded as free goods. Yet such was the attitude adopted towards air and water for far too long.

Provided the market and competition are functioning correctly - and provided there is an appropriate framework - producers and consumers can adapt in a rapid and comprehensive manner to new ecological constraints and demands. This does not mean the emphasis can be placed on the subsequent clearing up of environmental damage, but rather that production processes and consumer decisions are altered so that environmental damage is in fact avoided in the first place. Private initiative in an atmosphere of competition promotes technological development and innovation, in the environmental sector as elsewhere. In the end, it is the level of affluence that technical progress made possible in the first place that is an essential prerequisite for the effective protection of our natural environment. Ultimately, environmental awareness will not flourish where there is economic and social need.

It is true that environmental protection comes at a price. Correspondingly, it becomes a problem for the economy if its costs are not taken into account. It is up to the state to take account of the scarcity of environmental goods through the imposition of high prices, usually in the form of orders and prohibitions, or by imposing conditions. It must be ensured, however, that these prices are paid. In practice this could mean, for example, that if expensive environmental conditions imposed on production practices are not to jeopardise the international competitiveness of the industrial sector concerned, then the rise in costs prompted by scarcity-induced prices must be compensated by a corresponding lowering of income demands.

This relatively simple economic principle also explains the reservations expressed not only by entrepreneurs but also, on frequent occasions, by individual trade unions when presented with new environmental demands. Provided that the willingness is there to tackle the problem with appropriate means, the apparent conflict between ecology and economy can be resolved in a comparatively positive way, since it is within the market economy that environmental policy aims can be at their most ambitious and their most forward-looking. And this will happen all the sooner if, through the use of market economic instruments, the costs of environmental protection are kept to an absolute minimum.

IV. Social Market Economy and Democracy

Thesis 9: In view of the interdependence of the economic, state and social orders, the social market economy is the counterpart to a democracy based on the rule of law.

What does this mean?

At the beginning of this article I emphasised the difficulties involved in imagining a system in which politically responsible and mature citizens are deprived of the empowerment to make decisions for themselves on economic matters by the controls of a centralised state. All interventionist models require a state that exercises central control and, by definition, is vested with overall power. It was Lenin who put this most clearly - all power to the soviets! Nothing is allowed to exist alongside the state - neither free entrepreneurs, nor free employees be it on an individual basis or organised into free trade unions. Just as a centrally managed economy is the appropriate economic instrument for the dictatorship, conversely, a centrally controlled economy can only be run on an authoritarian basis.

Freedom is indivisible. To this extent our liberal, democratic basic order is also irreconcilable with a liberalist laissez-faire approach and the uncontrollable balance of power that emanate from it. The interdependence of the regulatory systems in place in the state most certainly leaves plenty of scope in the definition of the framework within which they operate. Nevertheless, private ownership, competition, freedom of contract and the freedom of production and consumption as well as the provisions of the social state represent the key cornerstones guaranteed by constitutional law.

Thesis 10: The Social Market Economy is not something that should be idolised. It is a concept for organisation and co-ordination that offers more than affluence and economic liberties.

What does this mean?

If one draws a comparison between the questions that are today directed at industry and policymakers with an undertone of social criticism and the problems that occupied the early advocates and founders of the Social Market Economy, an entire range of parallels very quickly emerges. Anyone who goes to the trouble of leafing through the comprehensive works of Alexander Rüstow will very quickly be able to identify major parallels between his values and the central values upheld by "Greens", in the true sense of the word. As far as Rüstow was concerned, however, and here he differs from the vast majority of present-day "Greens", there was no doubt that a socially tempered market economy was the economic order that best corresponded with these values.

We cannot, however, leave it there and simply refer the younger generation with their critical questions to old texts or, as happens very often nowadays, simply evade their questions altogether. And when I say "we" I mean the politicians concerned with regulatory policy, I am thinking about committed economists as well as moral and social scientists with an open mind on economic theory - we must try and provide modern answers to these questions. This is the only way in which, in the long term, our economic order can survive the critical investigation to which it will be subjected by generations to come, just as Ludwig Erhard's work has stood the test of time.

For instance, we must place greater emphasis than in the past on the element of "grass roots democracy" inherent in the market economy. Franz Böhm drew our attention to the fact that the market economy "when seen in the light of day is nothing more than a form of democracy that has been tuned to perfection and that is subjected to daily and hourly plebiscites - a referendum that goes on all year long, morning, noon and night".

Nor does the market economy require the prior consensus of all those involved, be it on political, moral or even religious issues. This creates an atmosphere in which tolerance and non-discrimination can thrive. Minorities, and even sub-cultures, gain the opportunity to make their voices heard and to satisfy their needs. And whilst it may appear attractive for a small number of social drop-outs to do this at the cost of others, this is hardly an approach that can be reconciled with our moral code.

And finally, the Social Market Economy is also a system with the minimum of personal and state arbitrariness. Many of the hundreds of thousands of conflicts of interest which arise on a daily basis can be solved in a peaceful and dignified manner, more so than would ever be possible under a bureaucratic system of collective control. In this way, the market economic order contributes to the easing of social tension. As far as international relations are concerned, it contributes through its character as a world-wide in-

THE ETHICAL CONTENT OF THE SOCIAL MARKET ECONOMY

strument of co-ordination to an economic "peace order", and to the untroubled, peaceful exchange of goods and services.

V. A Humane Economic Order

Having gone through these ten theses, I hope that I have been able to demonstrate in clear terms that the "social market economy is primarily aimed at socio-ethical objectives" (Bishop Lohse). However, it must also be said that a just economic order cannot be achieved solely on the basis of legal regulatory principles, but that this socio-ethical commitment is required from each and every entrepreneur, employee, trade union official and politician (Professor Manfred Spieker).

Whether the Social Market Economy blueprint will, in the long term, meet the requirements posed by the Christian and ethical standards of the West, will depend, first and foremost, on whether the scope provided by the system is put to full use in the service of socio-ethical goals and whether this is ever successfully implemented in practice. At the same time, the ethical demands must not lose touch with reality. Morality is only a good master if, like the King visited by the Little Prince, it issues only those orders that its subjects can obey. As far as both factors are concerned, the practical success and realistic formulation of requirements, a high degree of expertise in the matter in hand is an essential condition. We should however, at the same time, take to heart the advice of the Swiss expert on social ethics Professor Arthur Rich, who said that whilst concentrating as objectively as possible on the matter in hand we should be insistent in seeking out the human concerns at the heart of the matter.

Critical questioning of the economic order - inherent criticism from within the system - is from a socio-ethic perspective, both necessary and welcome in the Social Market Economy. It permanently pinpoints structural flaws and excludes the possibility of operating errors. However, it is all too easy for criticism to lead us up the wrong path if it rejects expert knowledge and condemns the system as such rather than dedicating itself with enthusiasm and commitment to dealing with the continual emergence of new organisational tasks, linked, for example, to the dramatic ageing of the population awaiting us in the years and decades to come.

OTTO SCHLECHT

"Morality", said Cardinal Ratzinger, "that believes it can side-step the intelligence of economic laws is not morality but moralism, in other words the opposite of morality".

Translated from German by the author

***

First published under the title "Der ethische Gehalt der Sozialen Marktwirtschaft", in: *Die Ethik der Sozialen Marktwirtschaft. Thesen und Anfragen,* Symposion der Ludwig-Erhard-Stiftung Bonn am 21. Oktober 1987 (The Ethics of the Social Market Economy. Theses and Questions, Symposium of the Ludwig-Erhard-Foundation), Redaktion von Volkhard Laitenberger, Stuttgart, New York (Fischer) 1988, pp. 5-23.

Section III

Attempts to Form a Broader Basis for the Ownership of the Means of Production in the Social Market Economy

Chapter 16

The Formation of Private Property in the Hands of Workers (1956)

OSWALD VON NELL-BREUNING S. J.

I.   The Formation of Private Property in the Hands of Workers (1956)
        1. Distribution of Property and Willingness to Become a Proprietor
        2. The Ownership of the Means of Production
        3. The Purpose of Social Structure Policy
        4. Forming the Public Will

II.   The Formation of Property of the Working Class by its Sharing in the Production Funds of Our Economy
        1. The Old Concern...
        2. ....and the Old Objection
        3. The Will to Save
        4. Compensatory Reductions of Consumption
        5. Avoiding Expenditures for Tax Evasion
        6. The Hazard of Curtailing Production?
        7. Getting Ready to Overcome the Employer-Employee Relationship
        8. The Efforts of Individual Entrepreneurs
        9. The Macro-Economic Approach
        10. The Quantitative Scales
        11. The Position of the Trade Unions

12. The Ratio Between the Rate of Investment and the Rate of Consumption in the Long Run
13. Property and the Participation in Decision-Making
14. The Risk of Losses?
15. The Impact on the Capital Market
16. Chances and Risks
17. Time Pressure

III. The Formation of Private Property in the Hands of Workers. A Sequence of Theses

I. The Formation of Private Property in the Hands of Workers

We stand for the institution of property as for the natural right institution necessary to attain order and prosperity of human society. However, we have to admit, that nowadays the institution of property is in danger, as well as two pillars supporting any social order - the family and the state. The attitude of many people to property is hostile, while too many others are indifferent and not interested in it. What has caused such a phenomenon, both strange and dangerous and worrisome? And what should be done to bring things in order again?

1. Distribution of Property and Willingness to Become a Proprietor

The reason why so many people do not trust in property lies, without any doubt, in the degeneration it underwent. By no means has this degeneration come by itself. Most obviously it is demonstrated in the way property *is distributed*, which is beyond any criticism. The scheme of distribution of property during the last two centuries, passing through the two world wars with their ways and means of demolition that people considered right and proper, has been developing, displaying its features more and more distinctly to take, at last, grotesque and bizarre shapes. At present the distribution of property has nothing to do with the owner's merits (or the absence of such), with his ancestors' being frugal or prodigal; it is based on chance or, even

THE FORMATION OF PROPERTY IN THE HANDS OF WORKERS

worse, on arbitrariness. Too much of the property acquired in an honest way fell victim to demolition.

The expropriation process going on for the two hundred of years of the Capitalist Era has led to the concentration of property in the hands of the social minority, while the increasing majority is still deprived of property - at least, of the property of the means of production - and, to earn the living, has to sell labour and to use means of production owned by other people, or has to rely on the state to be taken care of. The existing order has taken roots in people's mentality so deeply, that many of them - not proprietors only but non proprietors as well, - take it for granted and even cannot imagine any other situation. Though the latter are not satisfied with their conditions, they have never thought of improving the situation by means of the wide-spread dispersion of property. On the contrary, many are eager to aggravate the situation by turning the means of production into common property shared by everyone, hoping that the almighty and wise state will provide their subsistence: they will be able to exercise their "right to work", as the full-employment policy will create jobs for those who are able to work, while those who are not able to will be supported by the state through the government programmes. Our Catholic workers refuse to take this idea as a *basic element of the programme*, because it is 'socialist' and 'collectivist', but in practice, putting forward concrete claims, they go in the direction leading to this very outcome.

The fact that the overwhelming majority of people have no property is, by itself, a grave violation of the social order, moreover, it threatens its very existence. But even more dangerous, if not fatal, is the people's obedience: they do not rebel against the injustice, they do not do all they can to change these conditions but are likely to accede to them - their reflections on improving the society are based on the existing scheme. Thus, it has become the social policy of the state and of the political parties, if we put aside some programme slogans that have but the slightest effect on the political practice. It is easy to understand why *trade unions* are inactive: these are the conditions in which they were established and developed as the workers' organisations designed for assisting their members, and so they are not too eager to fight against "the law under which they were set up" and, on the other hand, they do not want to leave the ground *on* which, for decades, they have been successful in fulfilling their mission and to enter an unexplored area. There is only one worthy exception from the general rule of the total obedience, only one venture to introduce the order into the entangled, distorted, perverted scheme of the distribution of property. This is the movement for having a dwelling and one's own home.

2. The Ownership of the Means of Production

To establish healthy social relations, to liquidate the dependence of a great number of people on finding a job and working for other people, on being paid by other people and on using means of production belonging to other people, or on state welfare or social programmes, to put again this vast majority of people on their feet, and to bring them back into society and economy and to provide them with the social and economic status they lost - to achieve it all under our present relations, it is *not sufficient* to provide them with dwelling and own home *only*. *Participation in decision-making*, now regarded as the issue of a paramount importance in the political struggle, also cannot solve this problem; on the contrary, the way the participation in decision-making is interpreted and declared at present would rather mean recognition and confirmation of the fact that the majority is deprived of the property of the means of production. Our nation cannot be supported only by agriculture - the Morgenthau-Plan: potato fields from Flensburg to Konstanz! - it needs a highly developed industry, at least to supply the agriculture with the manufactured tools necessary to cultivate soil and to produce food that people need for living; it is not enough for an industrial nation to provide individuals or families with houses and/or with a plot of land of their own, if the nation strives for a just and fair distribution of property. A sound distribution of the titles of land property is of great importance, with some necessary reservations, one can claim: they are of vital importance. But that is not all. Land is not the only means of production. Besides land we have an enormous variety of *manufactured means of production* made by craftsmen and, for the most part, by engineering enterprises. There are many of them, but we still need more. While the acreage of land, as a rule, remains the same (except for the development of virgin lands), the amount of industrial production increases incredibly rapidly, *in direct* proportion with the population engaged in production, while the number of people *directly* engaged in agriculture falls steadily, not always absolutely, but relatively, according to the circumstances. We should not ignore the struggle for having a dwelling and one's own home, on the contrary, we must do much more than we have done before to support it. But we should not confine our efforts to the struggle for

THE FORMATION OF PROPERTY IN THE HANDS OF WORKERS

this. Striving to attain a fairer distribution of property, we must attack all over the front.

Concentration of the property of the means of production in the hands of the social minority creates instability. Granting property to 'everyone' on a universal principle, whether this "everyone" belongs to something called a society, or a state, or a commune means the same as replacing one evil with another. Hence, there is only one other way: distributing property as widely as possible among those who have the *natural right to be a proprietor*. Of course, it is not enough to give property to people, especially when they are not quite convinced in the advantages of the absolute necessity of property; we must take appropriate measures to make people, - both the actual proprietors and the prospective ones - feel happy because they *enjoy* their property. This is the second great shortcoming of the contemporary property relations, but there is no need to dwell upon this issue, as it is the *distribution* of property that is the subject of our discussion.

It might be useful to mention the following related issues that often remain unnoticed. When the majority of people is deprived of property of the means of production, these people have to support themselves by applying their labour to the means of production belonging to somebody else. But this is not all. Such deprivation calls into existence the so called 'class monopoly', or 'class rent' (the rate of return for the class of capital owners) which is a part of capital gain. If everyone had his own plot of land and cultivated it, thus earning his living, the agricultural ground rent would disappear (the differential rent still existing); furthermore, the so called 'absolute ground rent' would start gradually decreasing and eventually disappear. In a similar way, if everyone had his own (manufactured) means of production, the class monopoly would disappear. As to capital gain, it will not disappear completely, there will disappear only that part of it that is derived from the class monopoly and for this reason called 'the class rent'. The farther from property of the means of production the workers are kept, the more the class monopoly is, and the higher the capital gain is. Or, to put it in another way, the more advantageous is the share of the rent in the co-operation of the capital and the labour, the less advantageous is the labour (the less are the workers' shares, the more is the capital rent for one class). And vice versa, the more people share in the means of production, the less is the class rent appropriated by the capital, because the share of the jointly produced income that falls to the workers, in the form of labour income, grows. The explanation is quite simple: as workers are those who offer labour, they feel the pressure of demand, and the more pronounced the concentration of the means of production in the hands of a social group or a class, the greater the pressure of demand is. And the other way round, the wider the dispersion of property of the means of production, the less the pressure; the atmosphere gets less oppressive and the worker may wait until the better conditions are offered.

Therefore, it is not absolutely right to say: by distributing property on the means of production of our economy, we intend to add a part of 'property income', of capital gain to the labour income of working people. Of course, we would like it to be this way; but in fact it will happen so that, in general, we shall decrease the actual capital gain and increase the actual labour income. The worker will receive *more*. But this 'more' will not be derived from his sharing in the property income (the actual capital gain), it consists of other *two* parts: the increased labour income and a part of the *decreased* capital gain.

3. The Purpose of Social Structure Policy

Opinions concerning the goal do not differ: it is necessary to help the people now deprived of property of the means of production ("proletarised") by making property, including the property of the means of production, available to them. Now, the question arises: *where is it possible to get it, without stealing*? In fact, at first it looks as if the property could be redistributed only by taking it from one person and giving to another. Of course, it is understandable that the present proprietors would resist this, referring to the property *right*.

That this right is not perfect is made clear by something that is not quite imaginable, that this unjust and unfair way of distribution of property could in a faultless way comply with the law. Nevertheless, many of the present-day proprietors can put forward the argument that neither they nor their legal predecessors became rich in an unlawful way (by stealing, extorting, swindling, usurping etc.), but that their wealth has multiplied as a result of the *social dynamics* of the Capitalistic Era. Therefore, it is not their personal actions, but the very social dynamics that has turned unjust; as to the proprietors themselves, they have never done anything wrong, and so, are not liable for having them redressed.

THE FORMATION OF PROPERTY IN THE HANDS OF WORKERS

This argument, however, is inadequate, for it does not answer the question: is it for the sake of social justice (and hence, to the benefit of each person) that we propose to redistribute the property? The mission is beyond the powers of a single man, it can be carried out only by introducing some legal measures, by passing some acts compulsory for everyone. This question is the matter of principle only in case of *land* that does not grow in acreage. History teaches us that there have been many chances given to improve the unfair system of land property and to redistribute land to the benefit of the whole society; but history also calls for caution, as it gives us terrifying examples of the ways land property relations were subverted - they were the ways of violence and injustice, unacceptable from the point of view of law and human morality. Concerning the goods *which can produce more* there are two possible options: either to redistribute the property that already exists or to distribute the property that has just appeared. The example of the former approach is *"the equitable distribution of the burden"*; its provisions, based on the principle of equity, stipulated the compulsory redistribution of the property that had remained untouched in spite of the war and post-war damages. Hardly is there anyone who finds this aim and the necessity to intervene into the established relations of property unjust. Another example of the conscious and intentional regulation of the established distribution of property is the *inheritance tax* at the rate it is levied in Britain. In this case, however, the property that has been already created is taken, but it is not given to other owners and is used to relieve the burden of other people paying taxes into the state budget, so, in fact, it is 'siphoning off the profit', not the actual redistribution of property.

The old argument, held also in the Catholic circles, took into consideration only the first way. Wilhelm Emmanuel Freiherr von Ketteler took interest in Ferdinand Lasalle's ideas of the production co-operatives. While Lasalle, however, intended to raise the funds necessary to found the production co-operatives by *imposing taxes* on the propertied classes, Ketteler considered that way unlawful and, instead, offered to appeal to the generosity of the rich - they should give as a gift the poor workers the money necessary to bring the production co-operatives into being. As the appeal for the generosity was unsuccessful, things remained as they had used to be, and nothing happened.

Nowadays, we witness the way that is different in principle from that mentioned above. It was Pius XI who described it under the heading 'Overcoming Proletarianism by Forming Property'. He said the following:

OSWALD VON NELL-BREUNING S. J.

"We must work hard and strenuously on providing the conditions under which the propertied classes will accumulate only the slightest portion of the newly created property, while the bulk of it will flow to the wage workers" (Q.a.n.61). The income from national economy, the net social product must be distributed between Capital and Labour in the way different from the one it had been done in the past; it should be sufficient to enable the wage workers deprived of the property of the means of production to save money and gradually to become able to acquire property. As we have stated above, the *social dynamics* of the recent decades has lead to the unjust and ugly system of distribution of property and to the stratification of the society - capital is still being concentrated only in the hands of the capitalists. Therefore, everything will depend on whether this social dynamics is altered or whether a different social dynamics starts. As all the honest and fair people have always regarded the existing social dynamics as *unjust*, it would not be unjust to replace it with a more just or, at least, with a less unjust one. One can but ask, "*In what way* is it possible to do so?"

An economist, first of all, would think of transfers or switches in the economic process. Therefore, he does not care much whether there are any political forces or authorities eager to undertake the changes and, if there are such, whether they are strong enough to implement their intentions. He would ask about the consequences, his first question being, "And what if the development of the events would bring us to the state we have started from, the state we wanted to get rid of, as this was the inevitable result of so many attempts to improve it?" This problem is considered in the paper delivered to the members of the circle of the Association of Catholic Institutions of Adult Education in Socio-Economic Matters on April 28, 1953. It was published in the form presented below. By no way does the paper treat this subject profoundly and comprehensively. Nonetheless, I hope that, on the one hand, I was able to demonstrate the conditions under which the sphere of influence of the former social dynamics could be broken, and, on the other hand, to prove that these conditions are not so unreal as one might think. First of all, it should be understood, that things end well *if* they are properly started, and that there are no economic regularities that doom our cause to failure, as was the case of many other worthy deeds, well begun but never done. However, the paper does not give the answer to the questions: *whether and how* this should be started.

THE FORMATION OF PROPERTY IN THE HANDS OF WORKERS

4. Forming the Public Will

Once the possibility of this has been proven in principle, the question *whether* it would be possible becomes merely the question of social and political forces, of their will and might. The proprietors are the minority group, while those having no property make the overwhelming majority. So, the democratically oriented society should not have any doubts that the people having no property - if they know what they want and if their leaders are aware of their mission - are strong enough to accomplish their fair demands in a democratic and quite legal way. There is only one thing that may be doubtful: Do they really have the will? Do they really know what they want? Do their leaders understand clearly enough their goal and the way how to accomplish this will?

At present it is doubtless that this will has not been formed yet, although the wage workers, with an increasing interest, follow the discussion on the issue of the wide-spread dispersion of property in general and in particular, of the workers' sharing in the means of production in the economy. In the *minority* of them this interest has already grown into the desire and even into the demand. But their desire and demand are still weak, too weak - perhaps mainly because the idea seems "too good to be true". One is afraid that this is an illusion, and one does not want to pursue an illusion. Thus, one cherishes this desire as a spark in the ashes and does not let it flare up in a blazing flame of a political claim. As a result, nothing around is set on fire. The claim for a 8-hour working day, however utopian it might have seemed in its time, turned out to be flammable - one would say: it conformed with the capitalistic system. As well as the recent claim for a 40-hour working week. The idea of the formation of property of the production funds of the economy fails to set anyone on fire, - one would say: it transcends the customary capitalistic scheme and leads to unknown virgin lands. It is, therefore, hard to overcome the fear of its just being a *fata morgana*.

The *majority* of the employees and their trade-union leaders reject the idea completely. Partly, because it is presented in a really vulnerable form, and as the idea is known only in this form, the content is rejected along with the form. The other reason of rejection is the distrust involved. The idea originated in the Christian social doctrine; is not it a good reason for those who are used to regard the church as the stronghold of reaction to distrust the idea absolutely? Besides, this idea - or rather, its versions and fragments - is advocated even by the entrepreneurs themselves; is it not a good reason for doubling the vigilance and distrust? After all, one should not forget that such a basic change in the workers' position would influence the goals of the trade-unions. At first sight, some trade-union leaders might think that under the new conditions there would be no need in trade unions at all; they observe - or they think that they observe - the decline of the trade-unions' efficiency, and are afraid of the impact on the trade-union influence; they are not able to realise yet which new trade unions goals will appear. It worries them that the trade unions will be damaged; and as they praise the extraordinary importance of the trade unions for the employees, it seems to them that their own damage will damage the employees.

At the moment we have to regard trade unions as the opponents of what the Christian social doctrine considers to be an important, perhaps, the most important contribution to the cause of overcoming the present-day social shortcomings. But we believe that trade unions that have learned much during their history will change their opinion on this issue in the near future; we hope that they will prove to be progressive and responsive. Nonetheless, at present, it is quite out of the question, that trade unions will use all their might to fight for the redistribution of incomes with the *goal of providing the responsible participation* of the widest social circles in the capital formation necessary for the economy.

In my lecture of April 28, 1953, it is stated that the free democratic socialism (der freiheitlich-demokratische Sozialismus) was on the point of taking the idea. The published later "Handbook of the Social-Democratic Policy" ("Handbuch sozialdemokratischer Politik"), a sort of an encyclopaedia with the comments on the Dortmund programme of activities of the SPD, and a great number of entries (all of them seemingly written by Professor Gerhard Weisser), demonstrated this quite clearly. There may be no strict conformity of the programme slogans with the everyday practice of the SPD: sometimes, in the Catholic countries it takes a little longer for the parties that call themselves 'Catholic' to implement in their political practice the ideas of the Pope's social encyclicals. In any case, the position of the spiritual leaders of the free socialism not only deserves attention, but should be welcome as well; it must stimulate us not to stop on our way, until what we have fought for theoretically for over decades is step by step put into practice.

II. The Formation of Property of the Working Class by its Sharing in the Production Funds of Our Economy*

1. The Old Concern ...

Forming property of the broad masses of people, especially of the working class, has been the old concern of the Christian social doctrine (*Rerum novarum* n. 4 and 35, *Quadragesimo Anno* n. 61/62). But many times it was rejected as being a 'pious', that is, an unrealistic, an unfeasible dream; this was based on the assumption that an increase in the earnings of the broad masses of people would result in an increase in consumption, as these circles were not able and were not willing to save money. That the wage is a consumption fund and nothing more is an old thesis. This thesis had been doubtless as long as the wage provided but the meagre minimum required to sustain life, and in some cases even less than that. Under those conditions it was justified to compare the broad masses objectively incapable of saving owing to the lack of sufficient income with the "saving classes", i.e., those social groups whose income exceeded the amount necessary to support themselves and those who would use the increased income only to a limited extent for supporting their lives, while the goal of having increased incomes would be "to accumulate".

2. ... and the Old Objection

Referring to this even today there will be a strong objection to the thesis that it should be strictly forbidden to hold at the minimum level the incomes of the broad masses that do not belong to the saving classes as it is the only way to provide capital investments required by the national economy; while the increase of the share of the broad masses in the social product would inevitably result in the decrease in the share of investments, which retards the economic progress and further growth of the social product, so that even

---

* Paper delivered to the members of the Association of Catholic Inastitutions of Adult Education in Socio-Economic Matters at Ketteler House, Cologne, on April 4, 1953.

the groups that are supposed to get the greater share would receive less in monetary equivalent.

3. The Will to Save

First, we have to examine whether this thesis is right. To do so, we should clarify the following. It is not questionable that our social product is made up of two parts that stand in a certain ratio: the first part includes the goods of consumption and the second - the goods of investment, the capital means of production. One part of our labour must serve the goal of producing the means required to meet the basic necessities of the whole nation, while the other one must serve for the acceleration of the process of supplying our economy with fixed assets, namely, both with the means of production and with durable consumer goods, in particular, for providing housing. We cannot change this ratio arbitrarily, though some changes, within the certain limits, are possible. Then, there arises a question: are we able to *distribute* the social product among different social groups, in favour of those who hitherto had been content with the earnings which were too small to make any savings or to accumulate, without destroying the *structure* of the social product in the way that would cause stagnation of the economy? Stagnation results in nothing but regress. The answer to this question is very plain in its essence: If any alternative way of distributing the social product caused the situation when those who had become richer were spending their extra income on consumption, which would result in the decrease in the share of investments, no economy could cope with it, especially the economy that needs to maintain the share of investments at the highest possible level, as it is in the case of our economy. That is why we can increase the share of these circles of the population in the social product - at first I shall express the idea very roughly - only in case that these social groups are ready *not* to spend the increased income given to them on consumption but to do with it exactly what 'the capitalists' used to do, namely, to put money aside, that is, to *accumulate*. Now, the question arises: is it realistic to expect that it will happen this way? If this is not to be expected, the whole plan is doomed to fail. Then there is nothing else to do but to say what the liberal economists take for granted: the economicly necessary function of forming capital can be performed only by the capitalists, and that is why it is necessary that all the share to be accumulated should be given to them, thus depriving all other

THE FORMATION OF PROPERTY IN THE HANDS OF WORKERS

social groups of it. The early Marxist socialism was of the same opinion, Marxists saw only one way: to transfer the function of forming capital, the function of accumulating the surplus value which is now performed by 'the capitalists' to the universal capitalist, no matter what his name were - 'State' or 'Society'. Marxist socialism thought as little as liberal economics did of the possibility to entrust this function to the broad masses of the members of the society, to the workers. It is the convergence in the opinions that is usually overlooked, while it is one of the many principles that Marxist economic system borrowed from the liberal economics, thus developing its traditions. So, we must answer the question: are there real chances to accomplish something that for a long time had been openly ignored by liberal economists and silently ignored by Karl Marx?

First, let us ask ourselves: is the implementation of the idea determined absolutely (or to a great extent) by the will of the income recipients? In this connection one should say: the income recipients' will is a decisive factor, it goes without saying. But it is not the will only that is important in making this decision, and, sure enough, their will is not so almighty as one might think. Imagine that the income recipients have received their income nominally, that is, in cash and, encouraged by its increase and amount, rush to get consumer goods; meanwhile, the production of these goods has not grown adequately, so the prices are getting inflated; as a result, the increased prices of consumer goods will absorb the nominal income increase and, in fact, will eliminate it; thus, the things would be no better than before. In this case nothing is to be done but to restructure the production in the way of manufacturing more consumer goods and, correspondingly, less means of production. However, as the process of restructuring takes long, by the time it is accomplished, the nominal income will be fully exhausted, and not so much will happen in this respect.

If we consider the problem in terms of goods, we must but admit that only a part of them is suitable for consumption, while the other part of the goods produced and integrated into the social product is not consumable. "The capitalists", if we choose to use the familiar term, are not able to "eat up" this part of the social product for two reasons: first, as we have stated above, these goods are objectively "inedible" - one cannot eat mines, furnaces, rolling-mills and so on, and second, "the capitalists" are not gluttons, their stomachs would not digest more than they can. So, this is the point at which the objective and subjective constraints meet. If the income is shifted to the broad masses, the subjective limitation to consumption will be removed, to a great extent: millions and millions of the broad masses subjectively will be able to consume much more; objectively, it will, however, remain impossible, as the (capital) goods are inedible. If, in spite of this, an attempt is made to consume more, it will inevitably result in the nominal incomes being exhausted, and in their loosing their purchasing power. Thus, there are only two options to make a choice of: either to spend this increased income on investment, or to waste it, to deprive yourself of property once again by turning the purchasing power of the increased income on the liked plenty of consumer goods (this "plenty" is limited, it is not more than the amount of goods normally produced); one does not get more than this limited plenty of goods for the increased income.

Of course, we cannot expect that the common sense will prevent the masses from behaving unwisely. One should seriously take into account the danger that the efforts might be made to increase the production of consumer goods and to raise the living standard to the highest level not permitted by the production capacities of the economy, which also would exhaust the nominally increased income. Here, no doubt, proper steps must be taken to make people turn their thought and will to what is wise from the point of view of the economy and, if possible, give up the striving for consumption - the excessive consumption results in nothing but in the retardation and even elimination of social progress. So, everything depends on whether we know the ways and means (of economic or educational character) of affecting people's behaviour, whether we are able to persuade people to act in a way which will inevitably create the prerequisites for progress, the conditions required to perform the mission of forming property in the hands of the broadest layers of the population.

4. Compensatory Reductions of Consumption

One thing makes us feel comfortable: everything is far from being so hard and bloody as it seems at first sight. For achieving the goal, it is not necessary that both, consumption and investment, should remain absolutely unchanged. One might even think: to maintain the investment rate we should not increase consumption at all. At first sight, the following situation might be possible: nothing has been done and changed in the field of the production and the consumption of goods; it is only in the area of law, the area of legal distribution where something is happening, namely: the social groups

THE FORMATION OF PROPERTY IN THE HANDS OF WORKERS

that hitherto did not have their share in the newly created capital investments, now are receiving their due share of the property produced. Actually, things happen a little bit different, and namely, better. We must not be contented and we also cannot be contented with the fact that a part of those who have increased their nominal income will really raise their living standard and increase consumption. With a big number of family members, this is unavoidable and not undesirable, on the contrary: it is positively desirable. As a result, it is doubtless that some changes in consumption will occur. It is quite possible that when certain circles begin to increase the consumption of certain goods, this will be opposed by compensatory restrictions on consumption. If we succeed in reviving the idea of saving in the broad masses of the population and provide them with the earnings allowing saving, then it will be possible to expect that the new income (together with a certain part of the former income that hitherto has been spent on consumption) onward will be turned to investments; this will happen the moment when it has become clear that the accumulation is not just a drop in the ocean, but a very efficient way of managing one's money, of making progress. Therefore, the compensatory restrictions on consumption should be taken into account, if we manage, by proper means of economic incentives and by means of economic and social education, to revive and to flame up the idea in the minds of the broad masses.

5. Avoiding Expenditures for Tax Evasion

There is one more reduction of consumption, and, perhaps, the most important one, that can be expected and induced by an appropriate policy. It is well known that the existing system of the income and the corporation taxation causes great expenditures for tax evasion, that is, expenses, one part of which goes directly into consumption, and the other part - into investments. These investments are useless and unnecessary and lay a heavy burden on the investments that are useful and necessary from the point of view of the economy. Therefore, these untaxed investments are, in fact, consumption, and must be regarded as such. The adequate alterations of the income and corporation tax laws might considerably decrease the incentive to produce costs for the mere purpose of tax evasion. It is impossible to forecast the amount of this reserve, as well as the extent to which we shall be able to use it, but there is one thing we know for sure: people will profit considerably from the reduction of tax evasion expenditures. It will be possible to increase consumption and to raise the living standard in proportion to the amount to be saved in this way, without doing any harm to the rate of return on investment necessary for the economy.

6. The Hazard of Curtailing Production?

All the shifts in the distribution of incomes and in the way the incomes are used will cause changes in the production area and, therefore, in the area of capital investments. At present, we need not worry about it, especially as it is possible that these changes will manifest themselves in the most attractive way. However, there is another problem to be worried about. We face another crucial problem. We should ask ourselves: In what way might entrepreneurs react, if such a scheme of redistribution of incomes were adopted and the corresponding drastic changes in the distribution of the social product took place? Would the entrepreneurs respond to it by striving to increase the social product through enforcing efforts to maintain the absolute value of their share in spite of the fact that its relative value has been decreased? Or would they respond to it by curtailing the production, saying: under the new conditions it is not profitable for us to employ workers and to produce as many goods as possible? In this case the decrease in the social product would follow, which, in its turn, would demonstrate the groundlessness of our ambitions. We cannot say for sure in what way the entrepreneurs may respond, for one simple reason: they are people endowed with free will, and so the way they would respond depends on their free exercising of that will. We can influence only the conditions under which the entrepreneurs will make the decisions concerning this issue.

Let us assume that the increase in the income of the broad masses is achieved under the familiar system of the employer-employee relations, that is, as the increase in wages. In this case the danger that the entrepreneurs will respond to it by curtailing the production is not far from being realistic, at least in the respect to the psychological attitudes of the greater part of German or, in general, of the continental entrepreneurs. As to the American entrepreneurs, this danger is not so real for the reason not of material, but rather of psychological nature. The material reason cannot be excluded at all, but, let us take it for granted, the potential of the USA for a progressive dynamics is greater and more favourable than ours. Perhaps, the decisive factor

THE FORMATION OF PROPERTY IN THE HANDS OF WORKERS

is that of psychological stability, and in this connection we have no reason to regard the anxiety we have just expressed as ungrounded.

7. Getting Ready to Overcome the Employer-Employee Relationship

The danger of such an erroneous response of the entrepreneurs can be avoided, if we choose another way of expanding the participation of workers in sharing the social product - not the way of increasing wages, but the way of participation in performing the functions of the entrepreneurs and, by means of this, in getting profits. Quite recently we have discussed this issue, though privately, among economists, and came to the conclusion that under certain conditions it is risky to increase wages. The growth of wages beyond the limits of the marginal productivity of labour may result in the fall of the demand for labour, in other words, in redundancy and unemployment. But this mechanism will not work in case labour is treated not as an ingredient of cost, but takes the form of an integral part of income and profit. For a long time we have been thinking on the problem of altering the production relations, so that the workers of an enterprise could enter the relations different from the paid employee-employer ones. Unfortunately, the economists seem to be the only supporters of the idea. Concerning the opinion that is also popular with certain Catholic circles, that the relations established in the area of production are unworthy and unlawful, the popes Leo XIII and Pius XI stated that it is not so and pointed out: the relationships between Labour and Capital in themselves are irreproachable, one cannot condemn them as unjust. So convincing are these prominent people's voices in support for the existing production relations, that it is no wonder we have got used to thinking only in terms of the employer-employee relationship, exaggerating and over-estimating it. The possibilities to change the established labour relations to something else - to change them not because they are imperfect and worth condemning but because they can be replaced with some other relations that are even more perfect - moved to the background to vanish almost completely. The advocacy of the principle that the labour relations are basicly lawful prevented us from directing our thoughts in another direction.

Meanwhile, a great many issues have been discussed in this area; moreover, a great many things have happened. So, we should try to solve this problem. Let us ask ourselves: are we able to clear the way to the growth of the real income of the working class of our nation by means of overcoming the employer-employee relations as we overcame the servile relations of the days of old? In their time those relations were regarded as just, they were approved of and respected by everyone, while being far from perfect; but later they were replaced with a more progressive form of the labour relations, those based on agreement between an employer and a free employee. Perhaps, we are on the eve of a new change of this kind.

8. The Efforts of Individual Entrepreneurs

Various attempts to improve labour relations have been made recently by many entrepreneurs; taking into account the circumstances mentioned above, their efforts are very important to us. Their schemes are open to criticism, it is very easy to find their vulnerable points, none of them will survive through the long run of years. But these attempts are very important, as they form the experimental concept. Examining the multiple unsuccessful experiments, we shall learn what is not to be done, thus gaining skills and knowledge; only then we shall come to know what is to be done to succeed. I should like to add: all the experiments under way are made within individual enterprises, for example, in the Duisburg copper works, Spindler or Negele. They are based on the micro-economic approach, the only possible approach from the point of view of the entrepreneur. But going this way will never take them to the destination, they will never reach the goal as we see it. All these efforts (and, sure enough, trade unions are right when they criticise them) will, in fact, result in the redistribution of incomes within a single enterprise only. Sure enough, the enterprise will make the best of its position on the market pressing the monopolistic or nearly monopolistic situation. Letting the workers share in the monopoly profits or in the differential rents, can, in fact, cause unfriendly enterprise egoism among the employees. But what is still more dangerous is that taking the micro-economic approach, one can miss the chance to succeed in various undertakings aimed at the common good, for one will strive for the benefit of one's own business, for increasing the monopoly and the differential rent, instead of trying to reduce them, by means of competition, to zero, for the benefit of the consumer.

THE FORMATION OF PROPERTY IN THE HANDS OF WORKERS

9. The Macro-Economic Approach

From the macro-point of view of the economy, the enterprises whose profit rate is above the average, are supposed to help not their workers only but the consumer as well - under the pressure of severe competition they have to cut the prices, thus providing the latter with his share of profit. That is why the whole problem needs consideration not in the micro- but in the macro-economic aspect. This is not the point of sharing the success, the result, the profit of a single enterprise, this is rather the point of the participation of various social groups in sharing the *social product in general*. Of course, distribution takes place in individual enterprises. But it makes a difference whether I start from the individual enterprise and convince myself: if the workers of each company get more, the workers as a whole will also get more (which is true), or whether I say: the matter can be settled only on the national economy scale, when we gain the proper shares in the social product, or, which means the same, when we gain the proper structure of the costs of each factor of production, the structure that will necessarily be made effective in each enterprise. There are two possible ways to approach this problem. Till now, the only path taken seriously has been the one I called the "micro-economic". I should like to say once again: zealous experimenting should be applauded and is worth gratitude; but an experiment is an experiment, and nothing more. The experiments will give no solution to the problem; in general, the only way to verify an experiment in vitro is practice in vivo; we must test the proposed schemes under the conditions when the system of competition existing in our economy is cleared, and see whether the conditions of the broad masses have become better or worse.

10. The Quantitative Scales

Now let us consider the figures and try to express quantitavely the discussed issues. The 10 to 15 per cent increase in the workers' share in the social product is quite possible. Of course, we do not mean the wage increase, as it will maintain the worker' share in the product of labour at the same level, even in case the product has grown. We mean something more than different: the share of the factor of production labour in the social product might be increased at the expense of the shares of the two other factors of production. The increase by 10 to 15 per cent is economicly grounded, it can be introduced as *uno-acto* measure valid for a long period.

If we approach the problem from the point of view of the *investment rate* in our economy, we should take into account the net investment rate only. Let us assume that our economy is expanding at the annual rate of 5 per cent for one decade and that we can secure the accumulation of no less than a half of it in the hands of workers. This would mean that in 10 years almost one fifth of the assets our economy possesses would become, in a direct or indirect form, the property of workers; of course, we do not mean a fifth of the existing property, it is a fifth of the property created due to the expansion rate. One may object that the 5 per cent expansion rate has been achieved and even exceeded during the first post-war years of the reconstruction but it cannot be maintained at this level in the decade to come. Another objection can arise: transferring a half of all the net investments to workers is a figure too high and optimistic. One could, however, also ask the question: why only a half but not more? Be it as it may, the stated figures can be replaced with more grounded ones. Anyway, it is clear: we do not mean homeopathic doses, this is not the case when something worth mentioning is only achieved by the time the people living now die. The figures we deal with are very *large*, and the changes we discuss will be considerable, provided, of course, some day we decide to make a sharp turn, which, surely, means to commit a political act, the political act in the finest sense of the word 'policy,' an act of social *structure* policy.

We have to make our choice: either to pluck up our spirits and to commit this act or to shrink in the face of the danger as nothing can be gained. My conviction is that to commit this act is *possible*, and not because of our good intentions. I think there is the absolute necessity involved. I believe that we, the Catholic Christian part of the nation, are under the pressure of this absolute *necessity* and it is absolutely necessary for us to make the choice: either to fight for and to realise this decision or to be excluded from solving social problems for a long time. I hold the opinion that we should fight, one of my reasons being as follows. We are not the only ones who have been discussing this problem; this old idea of the Christian social doctrine has become firmly established in the leading minds of the circles of free socialism. For all I know, they are so serious in considering the idea, so vigorous in tackling it, so great is the importance they are attaching to it, that we must hurry up not to be late to take the rightful place in the fight for *our* cause, otherwise it

THE FORMATION OF PROPERTY IN THE HANDS OF WORKERS

would be somebody else who fulfils the dream that the Christians have cherished for such a long time.

11. The Position of the Trade Unions

We might object that the solution to this problem lies beyond our competence, beyond the competence of entrepreneurs, beyond the competence of political parties; it is within the competence of the trade unions. I agree. Whether the masses of working people are able to clear the way to forming property, to growing into the co-ownership of the capital wealth of our economy - it would depend on the position of trade unions, on their accepting or rejecting the idea. It was as late as in 1950 when trade unions came to realise that it was up to them to make the decision. Till now they have been able - for better or worse, it depends - to put it off. Perhaps, very shortly the situation will change: it might become absolutely necessary for the trade unions to make up their mind, for they will be entitled to making the decision; the right will be granted to them not by the Christians and not by the government intending to alter the market economy to the benefit of the whole society by implementing the corresponding social and economic policy, for which the trade unions have been hoping for some time; the urge for a decision will be imposed on them by the socialists, however strange it might be. We cannot say for sure what the final decision of the trade unions will be, we can only hope that they will have to consider the problem in the nearest future. Under such circumstances, in order to arm ourselves with knowledge, especially in order to store the knowledge of economics, we should better avoid the discussion. When we repeat over and over again that the issue in question is the old demand put forward by the Christian social doctrine, we impress only our adherents. Dealing with other audiences is a special case - the less we repeat that this idea is our mental property and the more reasonable arguments we set forth, the more we can achieve.

12. The Ratio Between the Rates of Investment and the Rates of Consumption in the Long Run

At the very beginning of our discussion, the anxiety seized us that the strive for raising the living standard will frustrate our plans, the consumption will make everything null and void and all our efforts will be fruitless. This danger needs further consideration. Is it true that the only way to succeed in this undertaking is to put insurmountable barriers in the path of raising the living standard beyond the level permitted by the productivity increase? Erecting such an insurmountable obstacle would be risky. Fortunately, it is not necessary - such is the unanimous diagnosis made by economists all over the world, especially when they consider the case of the German economy. Almost all economists agree that the present-day investment rate cannot and must not be maintained at so high a level for a long time, that it will be necessary to increase the consumption rate in the social product and to decrease the investment rate. Now the investment rate is rather overstretched, and as a result, the expansion rate of our economy has stepped over the 5 per cent level and will go further. Under such conditions, the continuous gradual decrease of the investment rate and, as a result, the corresponding increase of the consumption rate is not only possible but necessary. Thanks to these favourable conditions, we are not facing the fatal choice: either to erect the insurmountable obstacles or to have our plans doomed to failure. If we do not want to miss the chance, if we are going to make the best of the existing situation, we must be patient, which is necessary to approach this far-reaching undertaking with fortitude and, I should say, with responsibility.

Those are the macro-economic considerations.

13. Property and the Participation in Decision-Making

The *choice between the two ways*: either to increase wages in line of the traditional labour relationships or to share in profits and capital, is important in one more respect. We shall deal with this aspect right now. It is closely connected with the problem of the right to participate in decisions, especially of the right to participate in economic decision-making. We know from experience that the so called individual or social right to participate in decision-making, at least in principle, will not bring about any problems, and that there cannot be raised objections against it. As for the right to economic co-determination, it seems to be somehow blocked. An only *reactive* right to participate in decision-making can be easily introduced into the relations of hired labour, as it was in the case of Hessian law on factory councils, while the *active* right to participate in decision-making, in the sense of the French word '*co-gestion economique*', 'corporate co-management', cannot be introduced into the relations of hired labour at all. The way the trade unions are

THE FORMATION OF PROPERTY IN THE HANDS OF WORKERS

doing it, is but a mere attempt to solve the problem of squaring the circle. Companies and factories can be constructed *on* the basis of the *existing* property or in the direction *to* new property. The company employing labour is grounded on the existing property rights and constructed from the principle of property. That is why the right to co-determination and the rights of property are here in collision. This problem is avoided in the company or in the factory that is constructed on the principle of creating new property.

To demonstrate what we mean, let us consider a special private company (oHG - *offene Handelsgesellschaft*) as a simple illustrative example. There are two partners in the company, a senior one and a junior one. At the moment, we ignore the staff of employees, we are interested in the two partners, the two partners of the oHG. The first one is the entrepreneur who hitherto owned an independent company and now is associated with a junior partner. What happens then? The parties conclude a contract, and under this contract send their workers to the new company. The junior partner may have nothing but manpower, so he invests *only* the manpower. The senior partner has not only workers, but also business experience and business connections, so he invests them. Moreover, the senior partner, as a rule, is a rich man, and he is able to invest his *property* as well. Whether he really does it, is another question. Most of the oHG type companies are built on another principle: capital assets are *not* invested into the company but are lent to it. As a rule, only necessary current assets are invested, along with uncertain, that is, unaccomplished and unaccounted for transactions and operations; capital assets are not invested. What we are interested in, from the point of view of forming property, is the way the result of business is distributed. To make it, the partners negotiate the key principle. If the company rents the capital assets, their owner cannot claim the profit, he is to content himself to the rent. Both partners can claim the profit derived from the business, but in case one of the partners has invested current assets, he can also claim the profit from them. After a year of co-operation, the partners set the amount of profit. Under the articles of the agreement, during a year the junior partner could make withdrawals from the company's income to the amount necessary to sustain his living; what has remained from his share of profit after this amount is deducted is put on his account. In accordance with another article of the agreement, this sum will remain on his account, no matter whether he associates the company as a financial partner or withdraws the money from his account and spends it as he likes. One more issue must be negotiated in such agreements, namely, the agreement that the junior partner's unlimited liability to the creditors of the oHG that cannot be provided in external relations, shall be secured by the senior partner's commitment to protect the junior partner from being misused in any way by the creditors of the company. The junior partner has neither the possibility nor the desire to go into details of the risk of such a liability. The senior partner relieves him from it. The risk premium to be paid is taken into account in distributing profit.

Now, the question is: is it possible to apply the relationship between senior and junior partners that we have just described on a larger scale, so that those who have a share in an enterprise - shareholders or other owners - will take the part of the senior partner, while the staff, or those of the staff who are interested in *partnership* - will appear in the role of, so to say, the junior partner. Here, at first, we shall discuss the development of the model, and only then try to evaluate it.

A new form of a firm would be created allowing two groups of shareholders: those who have shares in assets and those who have shares in labour, or the third group - the ones who have shares both in assets and labour. The way this association is structured is a matter of expediency but not of principle - it might be a one-level structure, or those who have shares in assets and those who have shares in labour, or those who have shares *both* in assets and labour might form independent groups of their own (the latter share-holders doing so only under certain conditions), a sort of sub-associations, later to join the superior association responsible for managing the enterprise. The crucial issue is securing the rights of labour share-holders, that is, workers, if they do not prefer staying within the limits of the relationship of hired labour. These labour share-holders will be entitled, as the company's junior partners, to make withdrawals of money from the firm within reasonable limits. These withdrawals would perform the same function of sustaining life as wages do for wage-earners and salary for employees; so, their amount would be approximately equal to the present-day wages or salaries. Besides, at first the workers having no property would need the guarantee that the company's creditors cannot put their claims for credits on them. Of course, this guarantee must be compensated with the appropriate risk premium; but the cover for this risk premium must be provided not at the expense of the minimum withdrawals made to sustain life, but at the expense of the individual's share in profits. Each member of the staff is free either to leave his share in the company and thus to put the sum into his account or to withdraw it, so that the money withdrawn be invested in some other way, for example, in building his own house, in buying mortgages, shares or investment-trust certificates, or simply to deposit it with a saving bank*.

Considering the model from the point of view of law, we must confess: in principle, it is possible, but its implementation will be complicated and retarded, because we are to use the forms of associations allowed by the articles of business and civil law in their present wording; under the legal red-tape, the efforts to put this idea into practice might fail. In this respect it would be interesting to develop new forms of associations, as was the case of business law that has been developing the concepts of the private trading company, the other forms of personalised business firms and joint-stock firms; the new forms appeared one after another, as the economic need for them developed. The German Congress of the Legal Professions (*Der deutsche Juristentag*) dealt with this problem in 1951, but yet there are no practical results. The problem, however, has been set and affirmed, though no technical solution has been found yet. Therefore, it does not cause serious difficulties to the law-maker.

14. The Risk of Losses?

Naturally, economists will raise an objection at once: As long as the profit is secured, everything is all right, but as soon as losses appear, everything goes wrong. It is known, that in *economic* activities one can never rely on profit only, one should not forget about losses. Thus, their objection has two aspects: 1. *Economic* activities are not always profitable. 2. *In* economic activities both profits and losses should be taken into consideration. The second argument is evidently more convincing than the first one. The economy, as a whole, will produce more than is required to satisfy the current vital needs of the people. This always happens in the economy, except for the period when a war is also the people's vital need, and in such periods of war, the economic substance produced in the previous decades is consumed. Disregarding the instances of wars, we could say: The economy, and especially the highly efficient economy, such as ours, produces more than is consumed by the population, there is always a surplus that can be distributed.

---

* At first the model was developed to make up for the difficulties; it was *not* intended for the realisation of '*joint ownership*' or, '*co-determination property*' as it was misinterpreted, but for the *entirely free ownership*.

As to an individual enterprise, each one can experience failures and incur losses, even go bankrupt. Therefore, it should be taken into account: in general, there will always be something available to secure the working population a share in the profit. That a total loss of the entire economy is put on the working class, on the broad masses of working people, can hardly be of any practical importance, except for one instance of involving these groups into loss-sharing: the excessive consumption of the substance of the economy caused by wars has been put as a heavy burden on the broadest masses even hitherto.

There is also another problem, that of the ways and means to be used to restrict the risk of loss-sharing in each individual enterprise. The limits of this risk should be determined by the extent to which the masses that still have no property will and can take this risk. I have not any particular prescriptions for this case, but I am sure the problem is solvable. Roughly speaking, it could be settled in a very simple way: the minimum withdrawals substituting the wages shall be secured against bankruptcy, as wages are now, thus decreasing the risk of sharing in the losses of the firm.

15. The Impact on the Capital Market

There will be another objection, now on the part of the firm: We are not able to develop the profit-sharing scheme under which each member of the staff is free either to leave his share of profit with the company or to withdraw it. Why are we not able to do it? Because, as long as the capital market does not function properly, financing the firm by capital from outside will not be viable and we are doomed to self-financing. This self-financing, however, is doubtful when each person is free to take his share of profit. Might it be the case of confusion between cause and effect? It goes without saying: As long as the capital market is not functioning properly, the enterprises have to follow the path of self-financing, and the projects that cannot be financed from surpluses - now, first and foremost, it is housing construction - must be financed by public subsidies; in case both capital market and self-financing fail to provide funds, the only escape is to raise the capital *by* the public sector, and, unfortunately, the capital formation is done mostly *within* the public sector. But what is the cause, and what is the effect? The clear diagnosis of cause and effect in such cases is impossible, as a cat bites its tail and does it in a circle. A vicious circle arises here. But I am sure, if the enterprises became no more capable of self financing, either due to the severe competition having deprived them of profits, or because of the profits having been withdrawn in a liquid form and invested into capital or investment markets through saving banks, investment trusts and so on, the capital market would again be able to perform its function. Therefore, the enterprises can take the risk without any fear. It must be understood rightly that no single individual enterprise can take the risk and let its workers withdraw their share of the profit. This will not result in capital market's being liquid; it would happen only if the practice of withdrawing the profit shares became universal amongst the workers. Let us give a similar example: No single bank can make the forerunner in the creation of credit and exceed the others as a single institution; the bank that would do so would run the risk of becoming insolvent. But, on the contrary, if all the banks did it simultaneously, they could, without any fear for their liquidity, provoke inflation; the brake of minimum reserves would not hurt them and would not be able to hinder their operation. The same thing, as far as we know, would happen in our case; that is why the individual entrepreneur realising social progress in his firm cannot do this without fixing the use of the workers' shares of profit. But here we are considering the problem not from the point of view of an individual entrepreneur, but as a comprehensive reorganisation of the whole social structure. Therefore, we do not discuss what would happen, if this or that pioneer entrepreneur launched the reform not supported by others, but how a general reform is supposed to function if structural changes take place. These two questions are similar to the micro- and macro-economic considerations we have given above when the issue was examined in the respect of the social product on the one hand, and from the point of view of an individual entrepreneur's policy, on the other.

16. Chances and Risks

It is out of the question that starting such an undertaking without being ready to run a certain risk is impossible. But this, by no means, can be an obstruction to any great project; there are no projects that involve no risk. As we are Christians, both options are not open to us: We can neither accept the programme 'to live dangerously' in the spirit of Nietzsche or Mussolini; nor can we content ourselves with acting only when we are 100 per cent sure in success, without running any risks. Not only can we start, we also *must* get down to work, otherwise we shall miss the chance - not the very last one, though such a very last chance exists in world history very seldom, but the last chance in the nearest future. For decades we have been calling for redistribution of incomes and property; as a result, people hope that something will happen. It is beyond our powers to enforce the realisation of this call, as we do not live by ourselves; we are not the whole nation, neither are we the people representing the state bodies and making political decisions, nor are we those people who, living in the economic society, regulate the economy and use the results of their economic activities. We make only a part, and thus bear not the full but partial responsibility. But as I have mentioned before, our ideas, all of a sudden, flared up in the camp of others, and that is why we are running the risk to lag behind from these others, if we do not rush to take the position. That is why I am talking about the last chance for the nearest future that we must take; so we must hurry up.

Under this time pressure, I think this is the right word for it, we cannot exclude certain risks and cannot take the precautions to avoid danger, as it could be done, if we had time. We shall have courageously to take some risky steps and say to ourselves: As we proceed we shall see hope to do the next step. If this or that feature of our reform actions does not justify our hopes, it should be corrected or improved in time. The human fallibility and the propensity to moral weakness and the resulting wrong attitudes make it impossible to exclude risks. If we, scared of risk, abstain from putting something great and important to work, nothing will be attained.

17. Time Pressure

In the conclusion I should like to remind you of the two reasons that put us under time pressure. The first reason is that other circles, especially the leading intellectual circles of the free socialism, the circles that now seem to be gaining influence in the social-economic area (I am not commenting on their influence in other areas, especially in those of culture and cultural politics), are going to take over our idea and project, and under certain conditions can surpass us. The second reason is the difficult situation in which we have found ourselves fighting for co-determination. There was a time when we were the leaders in this question, but later we fell back behind others. The question of co-determination, as time has shown, has cost us, in my opinion, a considerable credit of trust in wide circles of the workers. The solution of the problems that have not yet been solved in the field of co-determination and that still remain partly unsolved and even characterised as insolvable is to be found in the following: The firm must be founded not *upon* property but *to* property, in the direction of property, as I have stated above. This will ensure a clear relationship of rights and responsibilities. Under this scheme, the employees of the enterprise and other people involved are entirely free to decide whether to choose lasting joint ownership of the enterprise they work in, or to withdraw their share of profit and use it to form other sorts of property; many workers of the enterprises, both public and private, may choose the latter way, and this should be taken into consideration.

These two reasons, our hesitation and being in delay in the area of co-determination, and the competition of other circles that already entered it (and there are even wider circles that might be involved in it in the future), compel us to stop discussions and to start doing something. We must consider the steps to be taken thoroughly, as thoroughly as the time pressure allows. We have no time to lose.

III. The Formation of Private Property in the Hands of Workers
A Sequence of Theses*

1. The present-day scheme of the distribution of property under which the property of a great part, or even the majority of people is limited to the property of (mainly nondurable) consumer goods and when most of people are deprived of the property of durable goods and items (for example, of houses of their own) and, even to the greater extent, of the property of means of production, is a grave structural defect of our society, which seriously threatens the *continuance of a liberal order* (*freiheitliche Ordnung*).

2. The existing scheme of the distribution of property especially threatens the *very institution of property*. He who possesses property will generally

---

* First published in *Der Arbeitgeber* (The Employer), issue No 15/16 of August 15th, 1955.

know the importance of property and will be ready to stand for the preservation of the institution of property, while he who sees only the property belonging to "somebody else" will be little interested in the institution of property; he will see in the property belonging to somebody else, especially in the property of the means of production, only a hostile and exploiting power, and therefore, he will be inclined to destroy this power.

3. To preserve our free social order based on the principles of property, the wide dispersion of property is necessary, which would allow the workers who still do not have property of the means of production to participate in the property of the means of production; "co-ownership" not of the *enterprise*, but of the *means of production* in general.

4. To attain the wide dispersion of property, two different ways are possible:

- the revolutionary way of redistribution of the existing and already owned assets;
- the evolutionary way of measures that would put all the newly created wealth (net investments) or a greater part of it to those who hitherto have no property, especially to the wage workers.

5. The *new redistribution* of the existing property, which can be justified by emergency only and can be made on a *very limited scale* and which is accompanied by inadequate losses due to the controversies it will stir up, will *not*, therefore, yield the proper result, as the wealth *thrown* to the poor in such a way, taking into account moral, cultural, social and political factors, will not mean for them the same thing that property *ought to* mean to the owner. The property given as a "gift" in such a way is not property.

6. The *new redistribution* of property as a one-time and single measure - the scheme that some neo-liberals suggest as an argument for the necessity of providing *equal starting conditions* necessary from the point of view of neo-liberals, or ordo-liberals, for the competition system, will not do what we need, as, in case the scheme begins operating and is not supported by other measures at once, there will appear and develop the tendency to restore the former state of things.

7. That is why the only way to be taken seriously is that of the organic, *evolutionary* process, that will bring a greater part of the newly created wealth to those who did not have property.

8. The newly created wealth that has not been used at once, is deposited as net *investments*. It should be made possible that the net investments either in their *natural form*, or their *equivalent* in all other possible forms (the material property being only one of them) become the property of the social

THE FORMATION OF PROPERTY IN THE HANDS OF WORKERS

groups that hitherto do not have property or, to be more precise, the net investment should become *wealth of the hitherto wealthless groups*.

9. How long and at which rate the process will develop and whether the appreciable results of redistribution of wealth or property will be achieved, if we take this way, depends much on the *growth rate of the economy*, that is, on the amount of net investments expressed in the material means of production the economy possesses, and on the amount of the share that falls to the social groups that do not have property.

If, in a certain period of time, the total capital wealth of the economy increases twice as much, and half of the increase falls to the social groups having no property so far, their share in the common wealth will become one fourth;

if all the total capital wealth of the economy trebles and half of it falls to the social groups having been deprived of property, their share will become one third, and in absolute figures this one third is equal to *all the capital wealth we have now*.

The higher the expansion rate, the less the time necessary to achieve the doubling and trebling.

During the years of *reconstruction of the economy in 1948-55*, if we do not consider the land property, the productive capital wealth doubled in comparison with the wealth that had survived the devastation. Of course, one cannot account for so high an expansion rate in the nearest future, in spite of the swift growth in the social product. Nonetheless, there are so many possibilities to form property for the non-owners, that the new redistribution of the existing property is *unnecessary*, and without it the appreciable results may be achieved in a rather short time.

10. In principle, no one is exempted from the process of forming property. Hardly anything more can be done to the benefit of those who do not work (old people, disabled), except for providing them with means of subsistence that are in an adequate ratio to the living standard of the rest of the population. The scheme aims mainly at forming property in the hands of *working people*. Property or wealth creation must, however, be given to them without restrictions; the limitations concerning those who are engaged in the *sphere of hired labour*, such as depriving of this right civil servants, some groups of wage workers, for example, the workers of certain joint-stock companies or of particularly profitable firms, are inadmissible, and do not meet the social-political (social-structural) requirements.

The constraints imposed by the title of this paper ("The Formation of Property in the Hands of Workers") and the specific character of the journal *Der Arbeitgeber* (The Employer), in which these theses are supposed to be published, do not allow us to consider the problem comprehensively, so the following theses will be strictly confined to the subject of forming property of the people engaged in the *sphere of hired labour* and, first of all, of the workers.

11. The fact that workers are employed by factories, or legally speaking by firms, might suggest the idea that the problem of the formation of property should be solved at the *"enterprise level"*. This *micro-economic solution* is not, however, feasible, or, it has too many limitations to yield the desired result. The objections to this scheme made by *trade unions* seem to be *grounded*.

12. The solution of the problem as *a whole* can be found only at the *national level,* that is, it can be solved only at the macro-economic scale; but this does not mean that the process will not take place in the end in the *factories and companies*, on the one hand, and in the *households*, on the other. What I mean to say is, that the *labour factor's* share in the social product will be increased, but this increment should not be spent on *increasing the consumption*. In our case it does not matter much what legal term we choose to denote the labour factor's earnings - wages, profit-sharing, or some transitional forms, or, as some propose, the sharing in the increase-in-substance. The term *"wages"* used below must be interpreted as the general term for all forms of the *labour factor's earnings*, whatever their economic manifestations and legal formulations might be.

13. The increase in the *share of wages in the social product* means the *proportional decrease of all other shares*. Those, who hope that this increment will be covered by the *entrepreneur's profit*, are not only short-sighted, but entirely wrong; they erroneously apply the solution to the problem possible at the *national economy level* to an individual enterprise. The considerable increment of the labour's share in the social product can only be covered at the expense of the *incomes of the other two factors;* it is, however, possible that the residual income, *"the entrepreneur's profit"* may also have to make sacrifices. However, this residual income must not be withdrawn nor, and even less, be conserved for future withdrawals; as to this income, the economic policy has the permanent task to redress the firms' profits by competition to the *authentic pioneer profits*. It should *not* be looked upon as the source of the desired property formation.

When in the course of public discussions the question of "profit" is touched, the word "profit" is usually used in the sense as the *balance* sheet or the *tax form* use it, subsuming indistinguishingly the *capital gain*, the *entrepreneur's wage* and the *entrepreneur's profit* under the notion of profit.

THE FORMATION OF PROPERTY IN THE HANDS OF WORKERS

14. Increasing the share of wages in industry at the expense of the *capital gain* will result in the (relative) *rise* of prices for the commodities produced in labour-intensive industries, and in the (relative) fall of prices for those produced in *capital-intensive* ones. The price structure will change. Under certain conditions it might have a negative effect on the *external* economic relations. But there is no ground for the German economy to be afraid of it, on the contrary, the German economy would receive a strong weapon to refute the accusation in the "*wage dumping*" brought against it on the world market.

15. The *growth in real labour income* is possible in principle, either in a way of increasing nominal wages or in a way of a total decrease of prices. But the accomplishment of the latter possibility would be obstructed by the fears so grave and by the difficulties so great, that the only practicable way would be that of increasing *nominal* labour income.

16. No matter which way is chosen, one thing is clear: it is not the question of trying to share *something unavailable*, nor that of *redistribution,* but the question of the *uno-acto distribution of the real net investments created in a time period*. Here, there is only one thing to be afraid of: what if the attempts to give the assets that *have been or are being produced* to those who do not have any property will result in the fact that this property will not be produced at all any longer, or will be produced in far less amounts than before. Whether this will happen or not depends on the way the entrepreneurs will respond to the new situation, that is, if they will respond in the *expansive or restrictive* way. The kind of the response of the entrepreneurs is *partly* a matter of *mentality*, or *psychology*, and partly (and for the most part) the response of the entrepreneurs will be determined by the actual economic situation and the economic necessities.

17. Realising the reform by way of a considerable increase of the *wages negotiated centrally by the trade unions* and of the *effective wages* that are based on them might result in the wage cost exceeding the *marginal productivity of labour*; hence many workers will be dismissed, unemployment will grow and production will fall. This way is viable only in as far as it curtails the number of enterprises at the margin and concentrates the production in the most efficient firms. For this reason, it will be necessary to secure the increase in labour earnings not in the form of the *negotiated income,* the exact figure of which is stated in the contract, but - at least, in the beginning - to relate it to the *results of work.*

18. There are enterprises that need *net investments* to stay in business. They will not be able to stand the increase in labour income, as this leaves them nothing or very little for *self-financing*; shortly, they go bankrupt due to their insolvency. To prevent them from bankruptcy, the workers must *bring* rather a large part of the money which they have received for forming property to the *capital market*, and use it not as a loan capital but as a *responsible investment capital*, to avoid in future the establishment of *unbearable ratios* between the company's *own assets and the loan capital*. There is one more group of enterprises - public enterprises on the one hand, and one-owner and family businesses on the other - that habitually attract the *third party capital* only as *loan capital*. To give them chances for growth and development on the peer with joint-stock companies that do not experience any difficulties on this path, it is necessary to develop the suitable forms of attracting *external capital* as equity capital.

19. Assuming the (nominal) increase in labour income has become reality, the further course of events will depend on the way workers will *use* the increased income.

20. As long as the size and the structure of the social product remain unchanged, especially in respect to the *ratio between consumer goods and capital investments*, it will be impossible to buy consumer goods for the increment in income; the attempts to do so will result in the rise of prices for consumer goods, thus actually *obliterating the nominal increase in wages in real terms* (the wages - price spiral will be set in motion not by wages as a cost component, but by the wages as a purchasing power!). This is of no importance, when the goods *have been stored in the amount large enough* to repel the attack of purchasing power. To escape the situation, we might increase the production of consumer goods; if the production capacities are not used to the full extent, this would result in the absolute increase of the social product without doing any harm to capital investments; otherwise, it might be done at *the expense of the investment rate*.

21. *There is no guarantee that the recipients of the increased income recipients would spend their money properly*; this guarantee could only be reached *by using force*. Compulsion, however, will eliminate the sense of the undertaken measures. As property given as a "gift" is inferior and not real (see thesis 5 above), so is, even to a greater extent, the "imposed" property, the property that the proprietor can not use bearing his *own responsibility*. *Forced saving* in any form being unacceptable, we can take another way: the worker is *free* to take this *liability* when entering into the contract, either as

an *individual* or as a member of a *collective*. The article of the contract of employment *states* the wage rate and provides the *wage increase* which is possible from the point of view of the company's income, but cannot be paid in cash for the reasons of liquidity under the conditions of the capital market functioning not efficiently enough; or the wage-rate contract can secure the repeated use of this money in a different way, for example, to allocate it, through investment companies, to the same enterprise or to the same industry (*"Häussler Plan"*).

22. *From the macro-economic point of view*, everything will depend on the (net) investment rate - whether it will remain at a sufficient level. If it were necessary to maintain it at the level of the period of reconstruction, we ought not to dare pass the right to use such a great share of the social product into the hands of social groups of the population that hitherto did not belong to the *"saving classes"*[1] - though only for the lack of anything to be saved.

We can venture to take this step provided there is no ground for the fear of too great a decrease in the investment rate, on the one hand, and, on the other hand, that some decrease in the investment rate is not harmful or can be borne by the economy.

23. As to the latter, no one doubts that the *steady gradual decrease in the investment rate* is inevitable; the majority of economists are prone to think that maintaining the high employment rate and the further growth of social product can be achieved only by increasing consumption and correspondingly, by *decreasing the investment rate*. As the investment rate is supposed to decrease *not too much*, the game is worth the candle.

24. Whether too *great a decrease of the investment rate* is risky or not, is a matter of supposition, and nobody can tell it for sure. No doubt, some *precautions* are to be taken. First of all, it will be necessary to offer workers a *wide variety of ways of investing capital*, explaining these ways clearly, so that a worker could find them reasonable; then he would be free to make his choice based not only on his conditions and needs, but on his inclinations and tastes as well. The incentives of all kinds might be added, for example, *tax benefits to facilitate saving*, as it was during the reconstruction period,

---

1   It is a well known and acknowledged fact that workers, in spite of their little income sufficient mainly for affording basic consumption needs, have, nevertheless, always been saving money, and still are saving.

when the entrepreneurs' capital investments were exempted from taxation, to provide them the means for self-financing.

25. The role of *social education* is very important. It is not an exaggeration to say: the idea of forming property in the hands of workers will work only if the *trade unions* are persuaded that it is in *workers' interests* to have it implemented; as soon as the trade unions have realized this they will use all the means they have at their disposal to direct their members' energies first of all to *forming property* and only then to raising the *living standard*, which means increasing consumption and nothing more. If such changes in the mentality and the aspirations had occurred, we might suppose that many workers realizing that the increased income has cleared the way to making *effective savings* and understanding that such savings make sense, would save even parts of their income they have hitherto been spending on consumption.

26. Wage workers can increase consumption not only at the expense of the investment rate. The tax reform would release funds for efficient investments: capital investments that were only made for the sake of tax evasion would vanish with the result that considerable funds would be freed for efficient investments. To this extent an increase in the consumption of the wage-earners would be possible without reducing the net rate of investment.

27. Making the conclusion from research in the economic nature of the problem, it can be stated that the amount of income (by which we mean the *share in the social product* that might fall to a social group) is determined by the way the recipient of an income is found to *spend* his income. The group of the population that principally decides to spend it on *consumption* deprives itself of *receiving higher income*. The quota of the social product that is allocated - if we treat it as assets - in capital investments *can*, by the virtue of its nature, yield profit only to those recipients who *are eager to receive their income - directly or indirectly - in the form of capital investments* and, all in all, to keep it in this form. From the monetary point of view, the *rate of the social product* to be invested *can* also become an income of those recipients who are willing to invest this part of their income, no matter whether directly or indirectly, in business as an ownership or loan capital.

28. The personnel of a firm *must not claim* all the surplus value as a *"fruit"* of their labour, nor must an entrepreneur claim all the creation of net surplus or all increment of the company's substance as the "fruit" of his efficiency, intelligence, energy, and entrepreneurship. It is logically impossible to trace exactly and in detail the success or the results of an economic

period among the factors of production by their *cause-and-effect contribution*. The share in the success or in the result can be measured by what an individual needs for taking his place in society or for performing his *economic functions*. If people think that forming capital, which is necessary for the economy should be the privilege of a certain social group, all the net investments must fall to them as an income and add to their property. If we consider it, however, necessary from the point of view of the *common good* that *the entirety of the population being active in the economy* shares in the formation of capital, their income must also include a share in that part of the social product that consists in capital investments.

29. The wider are the circles participating in *forming capital* necessary for the economy, the more stable, that is, the less subjected to crisis, is not only the economy, but also the whole *social structure*.

30. As long as a great part of the population remains *dispossessed of property*, the functional distribution of income will also determine the distribution of personal incomes of those belonging to this group. As soon as the widest circles - in our case, workers - *share the ownership of capital*, that is, of the material assets, especially of the material means *producing profit* (means of production), their total income will be made up of *more than one kind of functional income*. This helps immediately to alleviate the acute problems that originate in the functional creation and distribution of income.

31. The wider the groups are that receive *various forms* of functional income and that are thus not *confined only to labour income*, the less pressing is the pressure on the workers to sell their labour. And hence, the higher, ceteris paribus, the market conform wages will be (without there being *any need for the use of trade union power*). And, as a result, also ceteris paribus, the smaller, proportionally, will be the market conform rate of capital gain or of capital interest.

32. Forming capital in the social groups having hitherto had no property, especially in the group of the workers, and as a prerequisite to it, the necessary redirection of incomes, in our case the *factor income of labour* will not come about by itself but must be set into motion. The choice to be made and the means to be used are either using the power and compulsion of governmental regulation by means of *legal acts* or the *agreement between the social partners*, between the employers' association and the workers' trade unions. Only the latter way conforms with the constitutional autonomy of the social partners. *Legal* acts will become necessary in as far as the existing legal prescriptions that create unnecessary, and mainly, unintended difficulties

must be abolished; besides, *new legal forms* of ownership can be created (see 18) and can be set by the legislator at the disposal of those interested. All the rest the *social partners* ought to take *themselves* into their hands.

Translated from German by Victoria Pogosian

***

First published as a monograph: OSWALD VON NELL-BREUNING: *Eigentumsbildung in Arbeiterhand*, 2., um eine Thesenfolge vermehrte Auflage, Paderborn (Verlag Bonifacius-Druckerei) 1956.

Section IV

The Theory of Competition

Chapter 17

The Role of Competition in a Liberal Society (1979)

ERNST JOACHIM MESTMÄCKER

I. Anarchy or Despotism
II. Rules of Freedom
III. Rules Against Restriction on Competition
IV. Conflicts in the Policy of Competition

A liberal polity, or - as Kant put it - the civil state, should be based on the *liberty of* individuals as human beings, on their equality as subjects and on their independence as Citizens[1]. Concern for liberty does not signify, however, state care for happiness; equality before the law does not mean equality of estate and wealth; independence does not mean rising above dependent labour. There exist these economic differences, which arise from the guarantee of civil rights and from the equality of opportunity ensured by them, on which the debate about the theoretical and political legitimacy of liberal principles was kindled. The social processes which generate the distinctions of wealth, of property and of influence are characterised by competition, rivalry and conflicts. It is not a matter here of unforeseen side-effects, of

---

1   I. KANT: *Ueber den Gemeinspruch*; (On the saying: That may be correct in theory, but does not answer in practice), Akademieausgabe, Vol. VIII. p. 290.

abuses or of degeneration; it is much more the competition for prestige and honour, influence and power, prosperity and riches that are regarded as necessary consequences arising from the natural inclinations of human beings. The love of self[2], the amour-propre that draws parallels and the antisocial gregariousness of mankind[3], Man's constant and insatiable striving for power, ending only with death[4], are viewed as the anthropological causes of the universal antagonism in society, of the struggle of all against all, ergo: the *competition*. Therefore the debates about the feasibility and the boundaries of liberal societies can be reduced to being debates about competition. This applies to the evaluation of modes of behaviour, which are rewarded by competition, and to the effects, which it produces. These questions are relevant not just to economic *competition,* even though it is here that they have found the most comprehensive scientific and political attention. The bases of the fundamental critique of liberal principles are, rather, only to be deduced, if one views the criticism of competition in its overall political associations. At present, these associations have acquired decisive importance for the critique of market orientated economic systems.

I. Anarchy or Despotism

The possibility of bringing about uniform liberty under universal laws was comprehensively challenged by Thomas Hobbes. His theory has up to now formed one of the most important bases for the critique of liberal principles and especially for the thesis that individual liberty is not compatible with the public interest in a well-ordered society.

> "But when private men or subjects demand liberty, under the name of liberty they ask not for liberty, but *dominion;* which yet for want of understanding they little consider. For if every man would grant the

---

2   ADAM SMITH: *Theory of Moral Sentiments,* edited by Raphael and A. L. Macfie, 1976, p. 304.
3   KANT: *Idee zu einer allgemeinen Geschichte in weltbürgerlicher Absicht,* Akademieausgabe, Vol. VIII, p. 20.
4   HOBBES: *Leviathan, or the Matter, Form and Power of a Commonwealth Ecclesiastical and Civil,* Molesworth Edition, Vol. III, pp. 85-86.

same liberty to another, which he desires for himself, as is commanded by the law of nature, that same natural state would return again, in which all men may by right do all things, which if they knew, they would abhor, as being worse than all kinds of civil subjection whatsoever."[5]

With the matter regarded in this way, competition is not the price of liberty but the cause of its destruction in anarchy. The liberties of individuals and the competition resulting from them are conceived of as a manifestation of the war of all against all and thereby as the decisive challenge to the function of the state to maintain the peace.

The thesis of competition as another state of nature has become the most important component of the critique of the civil society under the rule of law. The most influential interpretation was the one, which Hegel assigned to labour and the division of labour in civil society. In full cognisance of the rationality of the economic system based on competition, founded on classical English political economy, he maintained firmly that labour and the satisfaction of needs brokered by it remained part and parcel of mankind's "nature". Indeed the mediation of the particular with the general interests effects the metamorphosis of systematic selfishness into a contribution towards the satisfaction of the needs of all; the inequalities that arise from these contributions to the common weal are not to be equalised, but they should not be perceived as inevitable:

> "This sphere of the particular, which imagines that it is the universal, retains, in this regard only, relative identity with the same, the natural just as much as the arbitrary particularity, i.e. with the rest of the natural state."[6]

To keep the rest of the natural state under control, to tame the self-centredness and thus make it at least of service to, if not at the disposal of, the purposes of the state, was for a long time, on this basis, an uncontroversial assumption in the German theory of the State.

From that, right-wing Hegelians inferred a substantially unlimited legitimation of the realisation of state aims in the economic sphere. In theory this

---

5   HOBBES: *Philosophical Rudiments Concerning Government and Society*, Molesworth Edition, Vol. II, p. 135.
6   HEGEL: *Grundlinien der Philosophie des Rechts*, published by Johannes Hofmeister, 4. Aufl., p. 200.

conception opened the path to the state-regulated economy. In practice, however, the other approach inherent in this theory became the more important, that is, as a justification for the co-operation between the state and the economy, leading to a special form of a corporate state. The theory of the state could, by this perception, confine itself to assigning the economy in general - and competition in particular - to the new discipline of economics and politically to that social material, which the state has to give form to in the public interest, according to changing circumstances. Looking at matters in this way, there is no more to be said about the content of the public interest than of the nature of the state in general. The consequences of this conception become most clear in those theories, which have further developed the doctrine of the state into a theory of *political conflicts*. The potential of all social conflicts to develop political dimensions opens the door to the politicisation of even privately owned enterprises. As a rule, the insight into the political potential of the economic system is combined with a strict refusal even to diagnose the causes of this development in economic terms and to develop remedial measures on this basis. Readiness to act only becomes decisive in the case of political emergency and then to do this independently of the rules in force for everyday civil and economic life in general.

In the tradition of the Hegelian left, *Karl Marx* not only disputed the neutrality of the state and the law under capitalism but explained it as mere form, in which the members of a ruling class assert their common interests.[7] He described the system of "natural liberty", as it had been conceived by Adam Smith and his successors as a system of natural *lack of freedom*. All the reasons, from which classical political economy deduces the compatibility of freely taken economic decisions of households and enterprises with the public interest were turned around by Karl Marx into being the causes of repression, in that he equated capitalism developed by competition with the natural state.[8]

---

7 KARL MARX, FRIEDRICH ENGELS: *Die deutsche Ideologie. Kritik der neuesten deutschen Philosophie in ihren Repräsentanten Feuerbach, B. Bauer u.a. und des deutschen Sozialismus in seinen verschiedenen Propheten*, MEW Vol. III, p. 62.

8 *Das Kapital, Kritik der politischen Oekonomie*, MEW Vol. XXV, p. 377. MARX repeatedly highlighted the links between his theory and that of HOBBES in *Die Deutsche Ideologie*: "If power be accepted as the basis of the jurisprudence, as Hobbes etc. do, then jurisprudence, law and so forth only a sympton, an expression of *other* situations, upon which the power of the state rests" (MEW Vol. III, p. 311). Cf. also Marx's approving reference to

THE ROLE OF COMPETITION IN A LIBERAL SOCIETY

His theory differs from that of Hobbes in that the latter perceived the determinant social area, where competition becomes radicalised into anarchy, not in the economic field but in religious liberty and freedom of opinion. Hobbes regarded free economic activity and the competition that flowed from it as "harmless liberties", which the sovereign tacitly allows. Analogous to this class of liberty are the liberty to buy and sell, to conclude contracts, to choose one's residence and profession and to provide for one's children as one thinks fit.[9]

Hobbes does not, however, conclude from this that the sovereign has given up or limited his control over these liberties. It is solely a refutable experience, that striving to satisfy economic needs, to achieve prosperity and affluence is conducive to peace in society. For even to strive for power in economic competition leads to attacks on others out of greed for gain and is a constant source of discord and struggle in society:

> "This striving for power inspires man's fantasy, it determines his thirst for knowledge and leads his thoughts. These thoughts are scouts and spies for the desires, which look for ways and means to achieve the goal that is striven for."[10]

Accordingly, it is merely a question of prudence, whether and to what extent the sovereign follows the insight that the simplest peasant is far more shrewd in his own affairs than a privy councillor in the affairs of another person.[11]

Marx has radicalised the political assessment, established by Hobbes, of competition and rivalry in society to the extent that he includes even the state

---

the evidence for the "*bellum omnium contra omnes*" based on the very nature of Man, *ibid.*, p. 460. MARX: Letter to Engels of 18.6.1872 (*MEW*, Briefe Bd. XXX. p. 249) remarks on DARWIN's theory: "it is noteworthy how Darwin recognised among the flora and fauna his English society with its division of labour, competition, elimination of new markets, "inventions" and a Malthusian "struggle for existence". It is Hobbes' 'bellum omnium contra omnes' and is reminiscent of Hegel in the phenomology, where civil society figures as an"animal world", while for Darwin the animal world figures as civil society".

9 HOBBES: *Leviathan, or the Matter, Form and Power of a Commonwealth Ecclesiastical and Civil*, as referred to above, p. 199.
10 *Ibid.*, p. 61.
11 *Leviathan*, loc. cit., p. 60.

and law, especially civil law, in the arsenal of the ruling class. With Marx too, however, it is competition that is the mechanism that stimulates and drives the struggle for power, which in origin is always supposed to be economic power. From this emerges the self-accelerating process of capital accumulation and centralisation, in which economic power becomes political power. "The nature of power", as is said by Hobbes, "is like fame, becoming greater as it proceeds, or like the movement of heavy objects, which fall all the faster the longer they move".[12]

The parallels between Hobbes' theory and that of Marx appear even more clearly, when one considers them as corrective measures required against anarchy. As, with Hobbes, the sovereign, so, with Marx, "the society" is supposed to maintain full competence over all those means with which power in society is acquired. Since private ownership of the means of production establishes the dominance of capital, the means of production ought to be transferred to "society". Since the economic system develops spontaneously under the pressure of competition, it ought to be guided by an overall plan for society. Since the social consciousness is a mirror image of the society, society should also take over responsibility for the shaping of public opinion, in order to put it at the service of socialism's function of maintaining the peace at home and abroad.

The rights of individuals in the Marxist tradition belong to the harmless freedoms as long as they remain private, that is socially irrelevant. This conception is somewhat reflected in the constitution of the GDR, when it ordains in Article 9, Paragraph 1, that the economy is based on the socialist ownership of the means of production, while Article 11 guarantees the personal property of the citizen and the right of inheritance.

II. Rules of Freedom

In liberal society the conflicts and antinomies which arise from competition are not denied. They are, however, taken into account, because they are part of the process, in which the individual liberties reciprocally *restrict* themselves. The law's mission does not consist only in respecting the private

---

12 *Leviathan*, loc. cit., p. 74.

autonomy of individuals and apportioning them their rights; much more is it the *social process* too, requiring regulation, in which these rights are attuned and made compatible with one another. The thesis that this process of self-limitation as such is responsive to regulation by law is denied not only by those who regard competition as being by its nature antagonistic to the rule of law. Rather in the 19th century it has been argued in the name of liberalism, that a free society depends upon the absence of state intervention and unfettered competition. This notion has probably contributed more to the political discrediting of liberalism than antiliberal ideas would have had the power to do of themselves.

When Adam Smith speaks of the simple system of natural freedom, he does not have in mind a system of conflict-free harmony, but rather a system, which exhibits significant elements of *self-regulation,* without it being, however, a perfect divine or natural order admitting of no improvement.[13] Insight into the autonomy of the system is rather a prerequisite for a solution of those conflicts with the help of the law or of politics, where self-regulation is unworkable. The contradictions do not permit of their being reduced to conflict and harmony-theories of civil society, such as often occur in current public debates. Rather anarchy-theories and harmony-theories must be distinguished from a conception, which relies on the resolution of social conflicts with the help of competition, legislation and politics.

The historical event of classical English political economy consists in the discovery that it is possible to combine the resolution of social conflicts through rules with the preservation of the underlying economic freedoms. In opposition to Hobbes, freedom of opinion for Adam Smith is not the cause of discord in society but the *prerequisite for free communication.* The contemporaneous founding of the *"Neue Züricher Zeitung",* to which this paper is dedicated, illustrates the historical association between the ideas of the Enlightenment and the social reality. In the competition of ideas, those rules should emerge which are suitable for reducing self-love to that measure which even an impartial observer would allow himself to approve. The capability of the individual to manage his own affairs and his insight into the effects of his actions upon others should become the basis of a social process in which it would be decided which moral or legal norms are to be recognised. For Kant,

---

13 Cf. E. J. MESTMAECKER in detail regarding this: *Die sichtbare Hand des Rechts. Ueber das Verhältnis von Rechtsordnung und Wirtschaftssystem bei Adam Smith.* See above p. 104 ff.

too, there arises out of the inalienable rights of man no right to oppose the power of the state, but indeed there does arise the authority to make publicly known "his opinion on what seems to him to be unjust in the sovereign's decrees against the community's life";

> "So, - within the limits of respect and love for the Constitution, under which one lives, maintained by the liberal manner of thinking of the subjects, which itself inspires them, (and the pens themselves restricting one another so that they do not lose their freedom) - *the freedom of the pen* is the sole bastion of the people's rights."

With a phrase directed explicitly against Hobbes, Kant adds that otherwise every right is denied to the citizen against the holder[14] of the highest authority and all knowledge of affairs is withheld from him, which, if he knew of them, he himself would rectify.

On the other hand, a society that wishes to organise itself in accordance with the rule of law cannot renounce power and organisation: only where power is combined with liberty and law, could one speak of a true civil constitution.[15]

Constantly under threat of dissension, Mankind, as Kant concludes in his *Anthropologie, is* only in a position to strive for a cosmopolitan society through mutual pressure under rules emanating from peaceful conflicts. Even in their cosmopolitan association, men would not live without conflict, for no law and no organisation would have the power to overcome the differences, which would be associated with the private leanings of the citizens, with their contradictory perceptions of happiness and well-being. If one looks at the role of the law in civil society in this connection, then it is evident that the antinomies of individual freedom persist in the legal and societal order. The law is supposed to be an *order to maintain the peace*, without it being able to establish the peace wholly or permanently; it is supposed to be an *order to preserve freedom,* without it being able to renounce force in order to secure it; it is supposed to maintain equal liberty with constant rivalry in order to facilitate the full development of the skills of mankind.[16] Kant recognises the antinomies that are linked with liberty and the resulting competi-

---

14 *Ueber den Gemeinspruch,* loc. cit., p. 304, in spaced type in the original.
15 *Anthropologie in pragmatischer Hinsicht*, Akademieausgabe, Vol. VII, p. 331.
16 *Idee zu einer allgemeinen Geschichte in weltbürgerlicher Absicht*, Akademieausgabe, Vol. VIII, p. 22.

tion as inevitable: the expectation of a universal peace existing in the midst of the liveliest action and counteraction by men is according to him an unachievable idea. He nevertheless insists upon the regulative idea that mankind has no choice but to pursue diligently the idea of peace and equal liberty under the law.[17]

It is evident that Hobbes's question and that of Marx as to how it might be possible to limit economic or social power in such a system mean for Kant the possibility of liberty under universal laws. The precept to enter into a society, governed by the rule of law, is directed against the constant danger of reverting to the state of nature, where the right of the stronger prevails, since everybody believes he has the right to do what he fancies is right and good.[18] To overcome these natural dangers, without destroying freedom, is at one and the same time the boundary and the justification of liberal society.

The force, which is necessary, to guarantee freedom under universal laws legitimises *the supremacy of the state,* which for its part endangers freedom. Therefore liberal societies have devoted greater attention to the control and limitation of the state monopoly of power and coercion than to the dangers of social antagonism. The goal of the balance of power ought to be arrived at through the democratic organisation of government, through the principle of the *division of powers* and through the guarantee of human and basic rights. This goal is not to be reached, however, without consideration of the relation between state and society. The demand for the separation of state and society, considered frequently as a liberalistic axiom, means properly understood, the principle of the division of powers as a constitutional task. For the economy, as the politically most important element of society, this relationship was assumed by Adam Smith to be self-evident. He did not consider the political legitimacy of a free system, but rather its economic feasibility. The thesis that the state should stand aloof from everyday economic life and give up its monopolies over domestic and foreign trade was accordingly based not on the division of powers aspect but on *the division of labour.* Freedom to move about between town and country, freedom to choose one's profession and free access to markets at home and abroad are analysed as elements of competitive processes, not postulated as human rights. Nevertheless, the accomplishment

---

17 *Anthropologie,* loc. cit., p. 331.
18 *Die Metaphysik der Sitten,* Akademieausgabe, Bd. VI, 312. Cf. also: Die Religion innerhalb der Grenzen der bloßen Vernunft, Akademieausgabe, Vol. VI, p. 97.

of political rights and liberties in bourgeois revolutions and the theory of the civil society in German idealism are not to be separated from the examination of the economic viability of a free society. The resultant tension between political principles and economic expediency is also characteristic of the economically relevant liberties in modern industrial societies. Large scale entrepreneurial and trade union organisations emerge from the exercise of individual rights. They intensify the questions regarding their compatibility with the public interest and the division of powers in society. This problem lies at the basis of the legal rules, applied against restrictions on competition and against the acquisition of economic power.

III. Rules Against Restriction on Competition

Experience has given the lie to the expectation that competition, which arises from the decisions of consumers, enterprises and owners of economically usable goods, would be sustainable of itself if only the participants were to be guaranteed by law the necessary freedoms for their economic planning. By restricting competition, competitors are in a position to upset or put out of action the signals on which their own economic planning or that of a third party is oriented. Enterprises can *restrict* competition by making use of the instruments of the civil law, legitimised by individual autonomy, or by applying economic pressure. Governments restrict competition in order to obtain results in the market which differ significantly from those which would have prevailed under free competition. National legislation in regard to competition restrictions is, as a rule, directed only against measures by private undertakings; European competition law, that stands to serve the integration of hitherto separate national markets ensures the freedom of interstate trade in the same way against state measures. Rules against privately imposed restrictions on competition must give consideration to the potential conflict with the basic economic freedoms, the safeguarding of which they serve. Rules against state restrictions on competition must, moreover, reckon on conflict with the policy monopoly of governments. Much overlapping arises from the fact that private restrictions on competition are used or sanctioned, in order to realise political aims set by the state and state measures are laid down in the service of private restrictions on competition. It is not only in foreign trade

THE ROLE OF COMPETITION IN A LIBERAL SOCIETY

that overlapping of this kind is met, within the domestic field too market indicators are corrected, as they are held to be incorrect or it is desired to correct them in the "public interest". Accordingly, the debate about the policy of competition, which stands here at the focal point, covers only a section of the questions which are connected to the deliberate intervention into the competition process.

The content of the rules against restrictions on competition, their interpretation and their application are determined over the long term by the basic constitutional and political policy aims, which they are supposed to serve.

American competition policy, as it is standardised in its anti-trust laws, has influenced legislation, initially in the Federal Republic, and then in the European Community. Corwin Edwards has summarised the American tradition of competition policy thus:

> "We appreciate competition for its own sake, as the political analogy to political democracy and as a necessary aid to the maintenance of this democracy by avoidance of dangers, which stem from the extension of the power of private organisations and of the government. The political roots of the policy on competition lie deeper and are older than their economic roots. The basic ideas on the dangers of concentrations of power were developed before the economic theory of competition became generally known ... . To be sure, the economic implications of the policy regarding competition have to be carefully considered, but our interest in a profusion of goods and services, in a full exploitation of resources, stability, technical progress and similar economic aims does not justify disregarding the political foundations of our free society."[19]

This interpretation of the Sherman Act as the *"basic law of economic freedom"* has found expression often in the rulings of the Supreme Court.[20] Thus, measures against the concentration of economic power can be legitimate, independently of whether they lead to conflicts with the requirements of economic efficiency:

> "The whole history of these laws (anti-trust laws) lies in the basic acceptance of their having the purpose of maintaining an industrial organisation with small units, which can compete with each other effec-

---

19 *Big Business and the Policy of Competition*, 1956, p. 5.
20 Northern Pacific Railway vs. U.S. 356 U.S. 1,4 (1958).

"The whole history of these laws (anti-trust laws) lies in the basic acceptance of their having the purpose of maintaining an industrial organisation with small units, which can compete with each other effectively; this purpose should be realised for its own sake and in spite of possible economic costs."[21]

The consideration of competition as an instrument for the neutralisation of private power[22] leads to standards other than a policy on competition, which on the basis of good or bad market results is intended to decide, which "imperfections" in competition should be accepted or fostered. This difference explains a major part of the discussion as to which competition is still "workable" in the face of general market imperfections in spite of or on account of private restrictions on competition. In the teachings on *workable competition* the attempt is made to turn into a policy of competition the theory of monopolistic competition, as it was put forward by Chamberlin and Robinson at about the same time[23].

The model of perfect competition and the accompanying analyses of equilibrium in price theory retain, however, their categorical significance in so far as deviations from this model are supposed to justify the theories of monopolistic competition and workable competition. The theory of competition remains under the influence of the theory of prices, while competition policy and law seem to be only coincidentally related to the guarantee of economic liberties. All the more attention deserves the theory of competition, which deals with free competition and consistent rules of conduct.

Erich Hoppmann defines competition as that complex system of market processes, that develops on a basis of freedom to participate in market processes and, within which individuals are able to act in accordance with their own plans[24]. The rules of the game which are supposed to maintain freedom of competition should not be prescriptive but would have to be prohibitive: further, they would have to be universal and abstract and generally applica-

---

[21] "Learned Hand", United States vs. Aluminum Co. of America, 148 Fed. 2d 427, 429 (1945).

[22] FRANZ BOEHM: "Demokratie und wirtschaftliche Macht", in: *Kartelle und Monopole in modernem Recht*, 1961, pp. 9, 22.

[23] CHAMBERLIN and ROBINSON: *The Theory of Monopolistic Competition*, Cambridge 1933; *The Economics of Imperfect Competition*, London 1933.

[24] E. HOPPMANN: "Fusionskontrolle", *Walter Eucken-Institut. Vorträge und Aufsätze*, Vol. 38, p. 11.

ble. Using the example of merger control, Hoppmann concludes that a *per se* prohibition of all mergers would be compatible with these standards. Additionally, he relies on the development of the *per se-rules* in American jurisprudence. The criteria of the "substantial restriction" of competition and of "market-dominance" according to Hoppmann are contradictory and methodically off the mark:

> "However, if only those manifestations of the market processes, which are attuned to the game-rules that assure competition, are to be understood as being competitive, then the development of the model, which is desired in a specific case, is to be constructed only if the results of the process are determined by the model. In this way, the function of the game-rules is changed around to its opposite: The game-rules determine directly the permissive activities for participants in the market and thus determine the individual competitive processes as well."[25]

In ascertaining a dominant position it is the forecast outcome of the game that determines the application of the rules.

Irrespective of whether one ascertains the desired course of the market process with the help of market structure, market conduct or market performance, the forecast of concrete results of the game becomes the basis for deciding whether in a particular case the rule should be applied or not. Then it is no longer a case of rules of the game but of a warrant being given to the authorities to intervene in individual cases where the results of the game appear to be undesirable.

Similar objections are raised against the policy of judging mergers according to their restrictive effects on competition. The relevant market or the area of the market that is relevant for an enterprise in terms of products, time and distance are not objectively given but are co-determined by the enterprises concerned. Consequently in determining the relevant market, knowledge of competitive relationships is being assumed which that determination is to produce.[26]

Should these considerations be correct, the consequences for competition rules would be far-reaching. All rules attaching legal consequences to a certain degree of competition restriction, particularly rules applicable to market dominating enterprises would be warrants to make interventions, self-

---

25 *Ibid.,* p. 33.
26 *Ibid.,* p. 51.

contradictory by nature and incompatible with the rule of law. The doubts whether this concept is amendable becomes stronger if one defines competition not on the basis of market structures but by reference to all economic positions that are liable to be improved through exchange as entrepreneurial and all processes resulting from exchange procedures as competitive.[27] The most important kind of this competition is potential competition, which presupposes free access to markets by sellers and buyers. Even a monopolist participates in competition by his market transactions and, he imparts knowledge to third parties on the conditions of market access. This understanding of the market as a *learning process,* in which knowledge is being generated is superior to the traditional equilibrium analyses, presupposing complete market transparency.[28] Confirmed is the finding that market structures and the restrictions of competition discovered with the aid of the relevant market are, in their turn, an outcome of market processes. In spite of this, these criteria are not as flawed as those that propose to evaluate restrictions of competition on the basis of market results (performance test). To be sure, the difficulties connected with the delimitation of positions of market dominance or of substantial restriction on competition are considerable. These difficulties, however, do not necessarily lead to the alternative of *per se* prohibitions and legislative inaction. For we are not dealing with opposing types of perception but with knowledge drawn from experience. The more substantial the restrictions of competition and the resultant market power actually are, the less convincing is a theory that excludes corrective measures on the ground that legislators, judges or administrative authorities do not have the necessary knowledge that must be a product only of competition. All the other participants, not least the enterprises themselves, have on the basis of their experience knowledge that can be used in judging the restrictions on competition. One would greatly overestimate the dynamics of "competition" on monopolised markets, if one were to assume that forecasts for the future on the basis of past developments are impossible.

These considerations do not argue against the thesis that *per se* bans of restrictions of the freedom to compete are most likely to be compatible with

---

27 Above all, I. M. KIRZNER: *Wettbewerb und Unternehmertum,* 1978, especially pp. 20ff and 56ff.
28 Primarily and fundamentally F. A. von HAYEK: "Economics and Knowledge", *Economica,* 1937, p.33ff. See for the reference to von HAYEK in detail I. M. KIRZNER: *Wettbewerb und Unternehmertum,* 1978, p. 176ff.

the competitive system and the rule of law. However it does not follow that a *per se* ban would be appropriate for mergers of enterprises. The market on which businesses are bought and sold, is part and parcel of the markets for those production factors, which are parts of the enterprise. The buyer of a going business expects to be able to use these resources more profitable than the seller. If this expectation is based on an economically more effective combination of production factors, then the transaction is in accordance with the proper function of competition. Insofar though as the expectation is based on a restriction of competition brought about by the merger, a prohibition may be appropriate. Since mergers of businesses can be rational even if competition is not affected, a *per se* prohibition, as it may be applied to price fixing cartels, cannot be justified.

The differentia specifica freedom of competition consequently is insufficient to deduce therefrom a general system of rules against restrictions on competition. This finding is to be attributed primarily to the fact that restrictions of competition and monopolisations can in reality rarely be isolated from the processes of exchange, from which competition flows. On this account, it is elementary that rules against restrictions on competition should be developed on the basis of the requirements of and in harmony with the competitive process. The restriction of competition and the domination of markets as a particularly high degree of competition restriction, however, are standards, which a policy should not abandon, that aims at the protection of freedom of competition. Here too starting from the principle of equal liberty we must pay heed at the same time (in subsidium) to the nature of things which obliges one to move where one does not wish to go.[29] It is the nature of economic power that makes standards inevitable, which do not correspond in full to the idea of the rules of the game for freedom of competition.

---

29 KANT: *Ueber den Gemeinspruch*, loc. cit., p. 313.

IV. Conflicts in the Policy of Competition

In no legal system are the rules against restriction on competition orientated exclusively towards the objective of guaranteeing freedom of competition. Even where the legislator as a rule takes for granted the compatibility of these rules with the optimal allocation of resources, this assumption does not apply in certain areas of the economy or, is declared to be refutable in individual cases. Examples are special regulations for the generation and distribution of energy, for transportation, for banking and insurance and for agriculture. Individual exemptions from general prohibitions are frequently provided for cartels and mergers.

In the majority of European states, the current law dealing with restriction of competition goes back to price control legislation as an instrument of economic policy. Within this tradition, the use of competition policy as an instrument of governmental economic policy appears to be a matter of course. An example of this approach was the English Price Commission Act of 1.08.1977 (no longer in force). In its first report of its activities the Price Commission characterised its task as one of bringing the public interest to bear upon the pricing policies of enterprises. Between the two extremes of markets with free competition and state controlled monopoly markets there would be numerous situations in which the pricing mechanism is distorted by imperfections in the market. The emphasis for interventions by the Commission would have to be laid on these markets not fully controlled by competition.[30] Thus the task of the Monopolies and Mergers Commission and the Office of Fair Trading were to be supplemented.

With similar arguments, the prohibition on abuse of positions of market dominance can be used as an instrument of price control, as the German experience teaches. If the ability of individual companies to raise their prices are seen as an indication of market power, then the prohibition on misuse of market dominating positions can be turned into general price controls. On the other hand, an interpretation of the prohibition of misuse orientated to-

---

30 PRICE COMMISSION REPORT for the period 1st August to 31st October 1977.

wards securing free competition leads to prohibition on the further monopolisation of markets.[31]

The most important conflicts inherent in the competition policy itself are due to political pressures to safeguard equal conditions of competition in domestic markets and international competitiveness in foreign markets. As a rule competitive equality is to protect small and medium-sized businesses from competition, whereas the international competitiveness is to justify the further growth of national large-scale undertakings.

a) It is particularly a competition policy that is aimed at guaranteeing the freedom to compete and of restricting power for political reasons that is exposed to the risk of becoming an instrument of *mere protection for the middle classes*. The potential conflict is expressed in the well-known ruling in the Alcoa case by Judge Learned Hand, already cited, according to which the prohibition on monopolies is to protect independent enterprises even if such a policy should be associated with economic disadvantages.

The prohibition of cartels and other co-operative restrictions on competition is frequently attacked as being contradictory in itself, since it prevents small and medium-size businesses obtaining through co-operation those advantages, which are accessible to large undertakings through integration. Only American law has resisted this argument and stuck to the *per se* illegality of cartels controlling prices, production and market shares. On the other hand, in the Federal Republic the policy regarding cartels and co-operation stands under the banner of "promoting the efficiency of small or medium-sized business". This policy is implemented by legal exemptions from the ban on cartels, by promotion of cartelfree co-operation and by administrative practices of the cartel authorities.

The Commission of the European Community accepted this policy with hesitation. This was indicated by the Commission's announcement of 27.05.70 concerning agreements, resolutions and concerted practices of minor significance, which do not fall under Article 85, Section I of the Treaty of Rome. The same rationale has the public announcement of 29.07.68 concerning agreements, resolutions and concerted practices which facilitate co-operation between firms. These announcements do not, how-

---

31 On this, see MONOPOLKOMMISSION: *Sondergutachten 1, Anwendung und Möglichkeiten der Mißbrauchsaufsicht über marktbeherrschende Unternehmen*, 1977.

ever, have the character of legal norms; they cannot prejudge the interpretation of Article 85 by the European Court and have, at most, the power to influence the Commission's administrative practices.

Whether cartels actually protect small and medium-sized enterprises is highly doubtful. Defensive cartels can protect their members against strong competitors, only when the latter join the cartel. Cartels, moreover, bear the risk of depriving their members of the very capacity they need in order to compete successfully with large rivals. In addition the weight of giant enterprises within a cartel organisation is not less but rather greater than in the market. The frequently proposed test as to whether a cartel influences competition or market affairs only insubstantially leads to the examination of a question, which the participating enterprises have already answered for themselves in a positive way. Since cartels can never exclude competition completely, every cartel, which one compares with a higher degree of competition restriction, may be portrayed as a petty "bagatelle" cartel. Such a standard tends therefore to justify and accelerate the process of further restriction of competition. From the possibilities thus opened up to eliminate competition, it is not primarily small and medium-scale business that profit, but oligopolitic giant undertakings, in whose markets interest in the co-operative elimination of competition risks is particularly great.

The conflicts between freedom of competition and equal conditions for competition come to the fore, when one considers the legislation which is supposed to prevent behaviour by individual enterprises inimical to competition without regard to their market power. The most important example of such legislation is the prohibition of price discrimination enacted initially in the Clayton Act of 1914 and strengthened in the Robinson Palman Act of 1936. In the United States the political weight of middle-class retail trade was great enough to push through legislation that was intended to protect wholesale and retail traders from competition by chain-stores. Currently, similar measures are under consideration in Switzerland and the Federal Republic to fight against abuses of the buying power and to ensure effective competition on the merits.[32]

---

32 SCHWEIZERISCHE KARTELLKOMMISSION: *Die Nachfragemacht und deren Mißbrauch.* Veröffentlichungen der Schweizerischen Kartellkommission, Heft 1, 1976, 11. Jahrgang. MONOPOLKOMMISSION: *Sondergutachten, Mißbräuche der Nachfragemacht und Möglichkeiten zu ihrer Kontrolle im Rahmen des Gesetzes gegen Wettbewerbsbeschränkungen,* 1977.

THE ROLE OF COMPETITION IN A LIBERAL SOCIETY

It is still scarcely possible to review all instruments that have been under consideration for this purpose in the Federal Republic. Examples are proposals to make the cartels' conditions or agreed rules of competition enforceable against outsiders; the prohibition of certain competitive conduct as unfair; an extended or general prohibition of discriminatory practices over and above the currently applied law (§ 26, Section 2, GWB). Such a policy is favoured also by the proprietary goods industry, apart from the medium scale retail trade. This new harmony of interests is fostered by the growth of chain stores and consumer markets, by the prohibition of resale price maintenance, and by increased crossborder competition in the European Community and by low consumer demand in recent years.

It is of course quite legitimate to counter the formation of market-dominating positions or further concentration by taking precautionary measures. The American experience, however, indicates, that the attempt to catch restrictions of competition right from their beginnings is likely to encourage private restrictions of competition. A universal prohibition of discrimination without its legislative purpose being made specific does empower courts, cartel authorities and trade associations to decide over the conditions under which suppliers or buyers are to be equally treated. Competitive strategies and consequently competition, are constrained if circumstances of consequence for competition (such as offers made by competitors) are to be disregarded and circumstances that are inherent in competition (such as, delivery costs or the customary nature of discounts and rebates) may justify discrimination.

In the European Community, the Commission and the European Court have not interpreted the system of undistorted competition, guaranteed by the Treaty of Rome, as being a guarantor of equal conditions for competition. On the contrary, administrative practice and the jurisprudence of the court are directed towards opening up access to the national markets and thereby to facilitate price competition favoured by different price levels in these markets. This principle lies at the bottom of the policy of competition as defined in the Articles 85, 86 of the EC Treaty and of the interpretation of the prohibition of measures with equivalent effect as quantitative restrictions in Article 30. This development is an encouraging illustration of how it is possible to guarantee competition and access to the market at international level and, in this way, to arrive at a division of labour independent from national boundaries and policies.

In cases where efforts are made, at the national level, to enforce through law equal conditions for competition, crossborder competition is the most likely remedy. If one takes the judgements of the European Court on industrial and intellectual property and on national marketing regulations as a yardstick, then it is questionable whether member states are still in a position to apply such national rules to intercommunity trade.

b) International Competitiveness

Capability to compete internationally is frequently identified with the size of national companies. The maxim of Thomas Hobbes, which he recommended for the trading companies of his time, holds sway up to today in international competition: for corporations, which possess monopolies for buying and selling in both domestic and foreign markets, to maintain the monopoly for the market abroad and abolish it for the home market. In this manner the profit can be increased to the disadvantage of the foreign market and the price be lowered by competition on the domestic market.[33] On such considerations rests the privileged position, at times tacit at times explicit, of export cartels common to all industrial states.

German legislation has adopted a similar principle in the regulations governing the control of mergers. A merger, which the Federal Cartel Office has forbidden on account of it creating or reinforcing a market dominating position, may be permitted by the Federal Minister for the Economy "if, in the individual case, the restriction on competition is overbalanced by the economic advantages of the combination or the combination is justified by the general public interest. In this the capability of the undertakings to compete in markets outside the jurisdictional area of this law is to be allowed for." The competitiveness in foreign markets has played a considerable role in all the cases, in which the Federal Minister for the Economy has granted an exemption.[34]

---

33 HOBBES: *Leviathan*, loc. cit., p. 219.
34 The VEBA/Gelsenberg amalgamation. Erlaubnisentscheidung vom 1. Februar 1974 (Decision on the Permission for the Merger); see MONOPOLKOMMISSION: "Gutachten 2", *Wettbewerbliche und strukturelle Aspekte einer Zusammenfassung von Unternehmen im Energiebereich,* 1975. Zusammenschluß Deutsche Babcock mit der Artos-Gruppe. Erlaubnisentscheidung vom 17. Oktober 1976; see MONOPOLKOMMISSION:

THE ROLE OF COMPETITION IN A LIBERAL SOCIETY

In Europe, contradictions have come to the fore between the competition policy and an industrial policy, which is to promote the concentration of enterprises at Community level in order to improve the competitiveness of "transnational European enterprises."[35] The concept, for which there is no legal basis in the Treaty of Rome, is in conformity with the French policy of promoting the international competitive capability of national enterprises by systematic furtherance of concentration of enterprises. On 20 July 1973, the Commission submitted the draft of an ordinance for merger control to the Council of the European Community. The draft was approved by the European Parliament and by the Economic and Social Committee. The prospect of the Council passing the ordinance seems to be slim. In the 8th Report on competition policy for the year of 1978, regarding this it reads:

> "The Council's Economic Matters Group has continued its deliberations on the proposed ordinance for the control of mergers of enterprises. In dealing with the underlying problems of the proposal, however, during the year of 1978, again, no progress worth mentioning was achieved. Like the European Parliament, the Commission can only express its concern over the present situation."[36]

In conclusion, it should be pointed out that the possibilities and the limits of competition policy at national and international level are not to be separated from the development of economic policy as a whole and from the role which competition is allotted within it. It is an open question whether it is possible to develop rules for competition internationally without a minimum of harmony between the economic orders of the participant states. Leaving agricultural policy to one side, then the great advances which the European Economic Community has secured on the way to an internal market rest on the fact that the Treaty of Rome guarantees cross-border competition as a means of integration without compensating its obvious imperfections through comprehensive planning at Community level and without reserving to the member states the right to make corrective interventions. A compara-

---

Sondergutachten 4, 1977. Zusammenschluß VEBA/BP, Erlaubnisentscheidung vom 5.3.1979; see MONOPOLKOMMISSION: *Sondergutachten 8*, 1979.

35 *The Industrial Policy of the Community. Memorandum of the Commission to the Council*, 1970.

36 *8th Report on Competition Policy*, Brussels/Luxemburg, April 1979. Fig. 1. (Merger Control was finally introduced by the ordonance 4064/89 of 21.12.1989 effective as of 21.9.1990).

ble arrangement is hardly to be expected within the framework of the "New Economic Order". For the opposing viewpoints of western industrial states, developing countries and planned socialist economies relate directly to the role which ought to be allocated to the market and to competition in this order. The discussion is often reminiscent of the historic arguments about competition as a state of nature or part of the freedom under the rule of law. The western industrial countries have made this choice, firstly for themselves and then in their relationship to one another. Whether a world economic order, which is worthy of the name, will emerge from international rivalries will depend on comparable political decisions establishing a system of undistorted competition.

Translated from German by Philip Scully

***

First published under the title "Die Rolle des Wettbewerbs im liberalen Gemeinwesen", in: *Liberalismus - nach wie vor. Grundgedanken und Zukunftsfragen. Aus Anlass des zweihundertjärigen Bestehens der Neuen Zürcher Zeitung. Im Auftrag der Redaktion der Neuen Zürcher Zeitung,* hrsg. von Willy Lindner, Hanno Helbling, Hugo Bütler, Zürich (Buchverlag der Neuen Zürcher Zeitung) 1979, pp. 103-121. The text has been translated from the German language and taken from E. J. MESTMAECKER: *Recht und ökonomisches Gesetz. Über die Grenzen von Staat, Gesellschaft und Privatautonomie* (Jurisprudence and Economic Law. On the Boundaries of the State, Society and Individual Autonomy), Baden-Baden (Nomos) 2nd edition 1984, pp. 136-157 (= Wirtschaftsrecht und Wirtschaftspolitik, vol. 50).

A Message of Greeting from the Mayor of the City of Saint Petersburg

I am greeting the participants of the Russian-German Conference "Social Market Economy. Theory and Ethics of the Economic Order in Russia and Germany".

In this period difficult for the Russian economy, your discussions can make a great impact on establishing the economic order in Russia. The Russian philosophy in its historical tradition has always been a moral philosophy. Thus, it seems quite justified that it is in Russia that the moral aspects of the emerging market relations are being discussed.

I am sure that the practical and theoretical experience of German scholars will turn to be useful for working out universal foundations of humanistic moral and legal practice in our countries.

I wish the conference to have successful and fruitful discussions.

Anatoly A. Sobchak, Mayor

List of Authors and Discussants

VLADIMIR S. AVTONOMOV is Professor of Economics at the Institute of World Economy and International Relations, Russian Academy of Sciences, Moscow, Russia.

VLADIMIR V. BIBIKHIN is Professor of Philosophy at the Institute of Philosophy, Russian Academy of Sciences, Moscow, Russia.

ALEXEY A. ELIASHEVICH is Director of the Department of Science and Higher Education of the Government of St. Petersburg, St. Petersburg, Russia.

LARISA A. GROMOVA is Professor of Business Ethics at the Department of Ethics, Herzen State Pedagogical University of Russia, St. Petersburg, Russia.

MICHAEL A. IVANOV is President of the Institute and Publishing House Ekonomicheskaya Shkola, St. Petersburg, Russia.

PETER KOSLOWSKI is Director of the Centre for Ethical Economy and Business Culture, The Hannover Institute of Philosophical Research, Hannover, Professor of Philosophy and Political Economy at the University of Witten/Herdecke, and Director of the Project EAST | WEST | PHILOSOPHY of the Hannover Institute of Philosophical Research, Germany.

ALEXEY L. KUDRIN is First Deputy Mayor of the City of St. Petersburg and Chairman of the Committee for Economics and Finance of the City of St. Petersburg, Russia.

ALEXANDER I. LIAKIN is Professor of Economics at the Department of Economics and Law, University of St. Petersburg, St. Petersburg, Russia.

ELENA B. MAKARYCHEVA is Director and Coordinator of Economics Programmes, St. Petersburg Broadcasting Company, St. Petersburg, Russia.

BORIS V. MARKOV is Professor and Head of the Department of Philosophical Anthropology, St. Petersburg State University, Russia.

LIST OF AUTHORS AND DISCUSSANTS

ERNST JOACHIM MESTMÄCKER is Former Director of the Max-Planck-Institut für ausländisches und internationales Privatrecht - Max-Planck-Institute for Foreign and International Private Law, Hamburg, Germany.

The Late ALFRED MÜLLER-ARMACK (1901-1978) was Professor of Economic Policy at the University of Cologne, and Secretary of State to the Federal Ministry of Economic Affairs, Germany.

The Late OSWALD VON NELL-BREUNING (1890-1992) was Professor of Ethics and Christian Social Teaching at the Philosophical-Theological Academy, Frankfurt am Main, Germany.

SERGEY A. NIKOLSKY is Professor and Head of the Department of the Philosophy of Economy, Institute of Philosophy, Russian Academy of Sciences, Moscow, Russia.

KNUT WOLFGANG NÖRR is Professor of Private Law and History of Private Law at the University of Tübingen, Germany.

WOLF-DIETER PLESSING is Expert for Privatization in the Leitungsstab Deutschland, Bundesministerium für Wirtschaft - Federal Ministry of Economic Affairs, Bonn, Germany.

WILLY A. PETRITSKI is Professor and Head of the Department of Political Sciences, Academic Council of the House of Scholars, St. Petersburg, Russia.

KONSTANTIN S. PIGROV is Professor and Head of the Department of Social Philosophy, St. Petersburg State University, St. Petersburg, Russia.

VICTORIA A. POGOSIAN is Professor and Head of the Department of English, Herzen State Pedagogical University, St. Petersburg, Russia.

OTTO SCHLECHT is President of the Ludwig-Erhard-Stiftung, Bonn, and Former Secretary of State to the Federal Ministry of Economic Affairs, Germany.

EVGENI F. SHEPELEV is Head of the Department of Land Privatization, Property Fund, St. Petersburg City Hall, St. Petersburg, Russia.

SVETLANA V. SIMONOVA is Professor of Philosophy at the Department of Philosophy, University of Economics and Finance, St. Petersburg, Russia.

ANATOLY A. SOBCHAK was Mayor of the City of St. Petersburg, Russia, in the years 1991-1996.

SILKE STAHL is research assistant, Max-Planck-Institute for Research into Economic Systems, Department for Evolutionary Economics, Jena, Germany.

LIST OF AUTHORS AND DISCUSSANTS

MANFRED E. STREIT is Director of the Max-Planck-Institut zur Erforschung von Wirtschaftssystemen - Max-Planck-Institute for Research into Economic Systems, Jena, Germany.

NORBERT F. TOFALL is Research Assistant, Centre for Ethical Economy and Business Culture, Forschungsinstitut für Philosophie Hannover, Hannover, Germany.

ALISA P. VALITSKAYA is Professor and Head of the Department of Ethics, Herzen State Pedagogical University of Russia, St. Petersburg, Russia.

CHRISTIAN WATRIN is Professor of Economic Policy at the University of Köln, Germany.

ANDREY YE. ZIMBULI, Department of Ethics, Herzen State Pedagogical University of Russia, St. Petersburg, Russia.

Index of Names

Page numbers in italics refer to quotations in footnotes or references

Adenauer, K. 24, 226, 231
Aksakov, K. S. 214
Albert, M. 2, 4, 7
Alekseyev, N. 115, *116, 120*
Alexander I 213
Alexander II 213
Altukhov, V. *32*
Andreeva, G. *34*
Aquinas, Th. 9
Aristoteles *116*, 117
Atkinson, D. 160, *181*
Augustine 9

Bacon, F. 38
Baikina, A. *112*
Balandin, R. K. *47*
Barlaam 100
Barry, N. P. *25*
Beckerath, E. von 222
Behrens, W. W. *47*
Benda, E. 55
Berger, P. *201*
Bernholz, P. 19f., 23, *25*
Besters, H. 53
Beveridge 6
Bibikhin, V. V. *122, 127*
Bismarck, O. von 6, 29-31, 237
Blackwell, W. 178, *181*
Blanchard, O. 160, *182*
Boarmann, P. M. *1*

Böhm, F. 16-18, *25f*, 55, *62*, 225, 244, 263, 281, 290, *340*
Bovillon, H. 63
Brandt, W. 251
Bresciani-Turroni 14
Briggs, H. L. 164, 166, *181*
Brockhaus 33
Browns *182*
Bugrov, N. A. 112
Bulgakov, S. N. 42, *44*
Bunich, I. 141

Castro Ruz, F. *47*
Chaadayev 99
Chamberlin 340
Chicherin, B. N. 215
Chirot 15
Chubais, A. 140, 152,
Coing, H. *228*
Cournot, A. 171
Curry, D. P. *247*

Dahl, V. 41, 44, 64, *104*, 106, *107*
Danilevski, N. Y. *207*
Darwin, Ch. 335
Demin, A. S. 102, *103*, 108, 109, *112*
Demsetz, H. 161, *181*
Denzau, A. T. 178, 182
Descartes, R. 38

INDEX OF NAMES

Diakonov, M. *103*
Dietze, von 16
Dilthey, W. 87, 99
Dodonova, I. *112*
Dostoyevsky, F. M. 103, 106, 213

Edwards, C. 339
Ekonomtsev, I. *100*
Elias, N. 212
Eltsin, B. N. *140*
Engels, F. 35, 76, *108, 332*
Engels, W. 52, *62*
Erhard, L. 13, 16, 23f., *26*, 226, 228, 230-232, 239f., 248, 276, 281f., 290
Ern, V. F. *106*
Euken, W. 14, 17-19, *26*, 55, 224f., 276

Fabian 23
Fischer, A. G. B. *26*
Fitzgerald, F. 121
Föllesdal, A. *6*
Frank, S. L. 34, *35, 45, 127*
Freud, S. 201, 211
Friedman *26*

Galbraith 285
Gandhi, M. 42, *43*
Gaydar, Ye. 70
Gerchenkron, A. 178, *181*
Giersch, H. *26, 247*
Gorbachev, M. 65f.
Grek, M. 105
Grigoriev, G. S. *40*
Guchkov, A. I. 112
Guilferding 44
Gutnik, V. *150*

Habermas, J. 8
Hagerdorn, K. 165f., 179, *182*
Hallet, G. *247*
Hardwiger *182*
Haver, P. *93*
Hayek, F. A. von 14f., 21, *26*, 50f., *63*, 161, *182*, 342
Hegel, G. W. F. 91, 123-126, 214, 331
Heidegger, M. 121
Hennig, F.-W. *221*
Hensel 16
Heraclitus 116
Hirschleifer, J. 163, 167, *182*
Hirschman, A. O. 15, 60
Hitler, A. 18, 222
Hobbes, T. 330-337, 348
Hoffmann, D. 160, *182*
Höffner, C. 281
Hoppmann, E. 53, *232,* 340f.
Humboldt, W. von 14
Husserl, E. 211
Hutchison, T. *26*

Isomura, T. *235*
Isupov, K. *116, 127*
Ivan the Terrible 101

Jones, E. L. *14*
Joseph, Sir K. *26*
Jouvenal de 14
Jünger, E. 89

Kant, I. 14, 97, 329, *330, 330, 336f., 343*
Kareev, N. I. *35*
Kathrine 213f.
Kavelin, K. D. 215

INDEX OF NAMES

Ketteler, W. E. F. von 297
Keynes, J. M. 23, 231
Khomyakov, A. S. 215
Khoruzhii, S. S. 101
Khrushchev, N. S. *46*
Kirzner, I. M. *342*
Kislev, Y. 163, *182*
Klein, H. *80, 93*
Kloten, N. 53, *62, 233*
Kocheryguin, V. V. 48
Kohl, H. 233, 248
Kolesov, V. V. 102
Konstantin Monomakh 215
Koslovsky, P. B. 41
Koslowski, P. *4f., 8, 75, 80, 90, 93*
Kosolapov, R. I. *40*
Krings, H. *81, 94*
Kuske, B. 76

Lampecht, K. 75
Lampert, H. *67*
Lasalle, F. 297
Lenel, H.-O. 22, *26*
Lenin, V. I. 287
Leo XIII 307
Leser, H. G. *235*
Levada, Yu. *34*
Lipton, D. 160, *182*
Lith, U. van *26*
Lohse 289
Luckmann, T. *201*
Lutz, F. A. 16, 20, *26*
Lyashchenko, P. 160, *182*

Macfie, A. L. *330*
Maier 16
Maistre, J. de *41*, 45
Malgginov, G. *150*

Mandeville 202
Marx, K. *35*, 75f., 107f., 123-125, 201, 303, 332-334, 337
Mayakovsky, V. 119
Mayer, H. *222*
Meadows, D. H. *47*
Meadows, D. L. *47*
Mestmäcker, E. J. *26, 335*
Meyer, F. W. 16
Mikhailovski, N. K. *214*
Miliukov, P. N. *207*, 212
Mill, J. S. 14f., 283
Miller, W. F. *48*
Mironov, B. 178, *182*
Mises, L. von *27*, 50, 76
Mitchell, G. 159
Montesquieu 214
Möschel, W. 18, 24, *27*
Müller-Armack, A. 16f., 23, *27*, 29-30, 55, *62*, 73-88, *94f.,* 97, 221-231, 237, 248f., *259*, 278, 280, 282
Mussolini 317
Myhrman, J. 160, *182*

Napoleon 213
Nell-Breuning, O. von 1f.
Netopilik, J. 39
Nietzsche, F. 317
Nikolas II 213
Nikolsky, S. A. *65*, 177, *183*
Nörr, K. W. *225, 228, 235, 239, 247*
North, D. C. 178, 182
Novgorodtsev, P. I. 215
Novikov, V. *68*

Oliver, H. M. *27*

INDEX OF NAMES

Olson, M. 23, 164-167, *182*

Pacque, K.-H. *26, 247*
Palamas, G. 100
Pavlov-Silvanski *207*
Peacock, A. T. *25-28, 247*
Peter the Great 41, 101, 110, 213
Peterson, W. 163, *182*
Petrov, Avvakum 102
Pius XI 297, 307
Plessner, H. 87, 222
Popper, K. R. 14, *27*
Prosterman, R. L. 159, 180, *182*
Proudon 127
Pugachev 212

Radiggin, A. *150*
Radnitzky, G. *63*
Randers, J. *47*
Raphael *330*
Ratzinger 290
Reichhard, M. 160, *182*
Renard, V. 180, *182*
Ricardo 87
Rich, A. 289
Richter, R. *27*
Robbins *21, 27*
Robinson, Ch. 340
Rolfes, L. J. 159, *182*
Röpke, W. 14-16, 23, *27f., * 55, *62,* 231, 242, *258*
Rosanov, V. V. *41*, 44-45, 105, 121
Roskamp, K. W. *28*
Rousseau 214
Rowley, C. K. *28*
Runge, C. F. 159, *182*

Rüstow, A. 15f., *28,* 55, 59, *62, 258,* 288
Ruvinsky, I. *46*
Ryabushinsky, M. 112

Sachs, J. 141, 160, *183*
Sapir, E. *123*
Sarovsky, S. 102
Savkin, I. *116, 127*
Say, J. B. 14
Schefold, B. *223*
Scheler, M. 87, 200f., 222
Schelsky, H. 51
Schiller, K. 22f., *28,* 53, 230-233, 248
Schmidt, H. 248
Schmidtchen, D. *3, 28*
Schmieding, H. *26, 247*
Schmitt 16
Schmoller, G. 31, 75
Schumpeter, J. 55, 76
Schütz, A. 200
Shafarevich, I. *47*
Shakespeare, W. 203
Shatalin 39
Shevardnadze, E. 66
Shiller, F. 14
Shtammler, R. *37*
Silajev, I. 159
Smith, A. 2, 8f., 14, 18, 35, *37*, 54, 87, 203, 285, *330*, 335, 337
Sohmen, E. *28*
Sombart, W. 75f., 223
Sorsky, N. 105
Speransky 213
Spidlik, T. 100
Spieker, M. 289
Stahl, S. 176, *183*

INDEX OF NAMES

Staikov, Z. 48
Stalin 15
Starbatty, J. *95, 221, 226, 233*
Stegmaier, W. *204*
Stolper, W. *28*
Stolypin 160, 213
Streissler, E. *28*
Streit, M. E. *62f.*
Strieder, J. 75
Studit, F. 104

Taylor, V. *47*
Tenbruck, F. *223*
Tinbergen, J. *33*
Tocqueville, A. de 51
Tolstoi, L. 43
Toporov, V. 103
Troeltsch 87
Trubetskoi, E. N. *44, 45*
Tuchtfeldt, E. 53, *232*
Turgot 172

Van Atta, D. 159, *183*
Vanberg, V. *247*
Vaubel, R. *63*
Vladinir II Monomakh 214-215

Waldenfels, B. 211
Wallich, H. C. *28*
Watrin, Ch. *28, 221*
Weber, M. *39,* 75f., 87, 105, 107, 199, 205, 223
Wegren, S. K. 159, 180, *183*
Weisser, G. 300
Wetenek (Vostokov) 44
Wigel 41, 44
Wilhelm I 30
Wilhelm II 30

Willgerodt, H. 20, *25-27*, 247
Wiseman, J. *28*
Wittgenstein, L. 202
Wortman, R. 177, *183*
Wuensche, H. F. *247*

Yakovlev, A. 66
Yavlinsky 39
Yeliseyev, S. M. *215*

Zaitseva, M. I. *40*
Zakharova, L. 177, *183*
Zhukov, K. *156*
Ziuganov, G. 45
Zlatoust, I. 106, 108
Zweig, K. *28*